Stability and change in Australian politics

Don Aitkin
Stability and change in Australian politics

St. Martin's Press
New York

Preface

Survey research is a mighty consumer of energy, money and time, and he who embarks on it must hope that the results warrant the effort. More than 200 people have helped to produce and to analyse the survey materials used in this book, and the whole project was never free of financial crises. I set down my first thoughts about the project early in November 1965; these words are written more than nine years later.

The need to thank is correspondingly great:

my former colleagues in the Department of Political Science, Research School of Social Sciences, Australian National University, especially Robert Parker, Don Rawson, Peter Loveday, and Harry Rigby — for all manner of help;

my friends in the Institute for Social Research, University of Michigan, Ann Arbor, especially Don Stokes and Warren Miller;

David Butler, an enthusiast for this project and a good friend to Australian political science;

Michael Kahan, who worked with me from 1966 to 1970 as co-director of the project, and whose skills and sensitivity as a political scientist are responsible for the excellence of the samples and the questionnaires;

those who worked on the project full-time at one period or another: Sue Fraser, Patricia Hall, Geraldine Foley, Ann Norrie, Sue Wrightson, Kim Morgan, Anne Smurthwaite, Natalie Staples, Sam Mueller and Eleanor Langley;

the interviewers and their supervisors, who worked enthusiastically and diligently, and developed a keen interest in a project they felt to be quite out of the ordinary;

the coders, slave and free, who did a difficult job well;

the legion of typists who battled their way through questionnaire and codebook drafts, scribbled notes and chaotic tables, especially Bridget Coles, Mary Carter and Allie Buckby;

the Australian National University, which housed the project from the beginning, and assumed responsibility for its cost; especially its former Vice-Chancellor, Sir John Crawford, and the former Director of the Research School of Social Sciences, Professor W. D. Borrie;

those who helped with money or services at times when the whole project seemed in jeopardy, especially the Australian Research Grants Committee, the Ford Foundation (through the University of Michigan), the Australian Broadcasting Commission, John Fairfax and Sons Pty Ltd, and News Limited;

and finally, the Australian citizens, nearly 2500 of them, who consented to be interviewed and by doing so provided scholars with a precious store of data about Australian politics.

My thanks to them all.

Two explanations are needed in advance. Firstly, the reader will find in the Appendix the two questionnaires that provided much of the material on which the book is based, together with the frequencies of response to the alternatives in each question, where that is practicable and sensible; these frequencies will provide an indication of the size of sub-samples where this is not given in the text. Secondly, I ask for the indulgence of readers who find numbers and tables difficult to grapple with. Statistics, simple and not-so-simple, are an integral part of this book, but they are vexatious subjects for any writer: to spell out the message of each table would be both tedious and redundant, yet the reader unfamiliar with the material is entitled to some guidance. Compromise is therefore essential; I hope that on balance I have erred in the right direction.

Sydney, December 1974   D. A. A.

Contents

TABLES

Figures

1 Stability and Change

This is a study of political stability and political change in Australia. Begun in the second half of the 1960s, it has a primary concern with Australian politics at that time, especially with respect to the nature of short-term change. But stability implies a long time perspective, and a characteristic state of the political order throughout. In this book I argue that the shape of Australian politics has been largely unchanged since 1910, and that the causes of this stability are to be found in the adoption, by millions of Australians then and since, of relatively unchanging feelings of loyalty to one or other of the Australian parties. These party loyalties, and what goes with them, are the centre of attention throughout the book. But this does not mean that I think politics can be reduced simply to voting, that policy struggles are irrelevant, or even, since much of our interest will be directed to national politics, that state politics are unimportant.

If there must be a defence for concentrating so heavily on elections and voting, it is this. Australians take national elections seriously, and accept their outcome as binding. So too do their politicians. There have been no *coups d'état* since the deposition of Governor Bligh in 1808 and even in the depths of the Great Depression the abandonment of parliamentary democracy was only faintly probable. The result of the 1975 election, which followed the unprecedented dismissal of a Prime Minister by the Governor-General and a period of turbulence unequalled in national politics, was accepted at once. Election results are the milestones of the nation's political history, and their direction has determined not only the coming and going of governments, but also the constraints under which successive governments have felt able to govern. On the whole, Australian governments have been reluctant to undo the work of their predecessors, whatever noises they may have made before and during election campaigns. The relatively even division of the Australian electorate at any time, the ever-present possibility that the next election will see the replacement of the party in power by its rival, have fostered on both sides of politics a cautious, incremental approach to government.

Of course, Australians have been fortunate in having inhabited a country rich by world standards, and one in which contrasts in standards of living have not been pronounced. The urge to rebel, to overthrow the established order, has been weak. Yet I am not arguing that political stability is simply a function of an underlying social and economic calm. For there have been major changes in Australian society in the present century: a many-fold increase in its population and affluence, the dilution of its Anglo-Saxon ethnic character, a drift to the cities, and a shift from an agricultural-pastoral to an industrial-service economy. These changes, it will be seen, have not greatly disturbed Australian politics. One purpose of the book is to explain why this should have been so.

The Stability of the Party System

The most important dynamic element in Australian politics since Federation has been the growth in the power and reach of the central government. The growth can be measured in terms of current expenditure from consolidated revenue: in 1906/07 the six state governments spent more than six times the sum spent by the Commonwealth government; in 1936/37 they spent nearly twice as much; in 1965/66 they spent only two-thirds as much as the Commonwealth.[1] There are other sign-posts. National politics are now the principal source of political news,[2] and the Australian electorate is now 'nationalised': national forces (parties, leaders and issues) are much the most important influences on federal election outcomes.[3] The nationalisation of Australia in the twentieth century is easy for the student to overlook, if only because its pace has not been dramatic. It has occurred nevertheless; the nation in prospect at the

---

1 Don Aitkin, 'Political Review', *The Australian Quarterly*, **40**(4), December 1968, p. 106.
2 No comprehensive study of the relative coverage of federal and state politics has been carried out, although an article by C.A. Hughes and J.S. Western ('The Geographical Sources of Domestic News in Australian Newspapers', *Politics*, **9**(2), November 1974) shows the way. An impressionistic exercise done for the purposes of this chapter, comparing the *Sydney Morning Herald*'s front-page treatment of day-by-day news in 1905, 1933 and 1970 (ignoring elections and referenda as being special events), suggested that Federation was followed by the submergence of state political news (there were two federal news items for every one state news item in 1905). By 1933 (three federal news items to two state items) state politics had regained some of its former importance, perhaps because of the state government's role in the depression. But World War II and its aftermath attracted more attention to the federal sphere: the 1970 ratio was three federal news items to one state news item. These proportions are probably more favourable to my argument than would have been the case had, for example, the Hobart *Mercury* or the *West Australian* been chosen for analysis. See below, Chapter 11.
3 In an earlier paper based on an analysis of the components of variance in federal election results since 1913, I showed that national factors had become most important by the late 1920s. The emergence in 1955 of the DLP, whose electoral support varies markedly between divisions and between states, had the effect of reducing the importance of the national component in the period 1955-66, but by then the dominance of national politics in Australia was unchallenged (Don Aitkin, 'Electoral Forces in Federal Politics', a paper read to the 10th Annual APSA Conference, Hobart, Tasmania, August 1968).

turn of the century has become a nation in fact. Australia is constitutionally a federation, but its federal structure is a skeleton that represents the anxieties of colonial days better than it does the realities or needs of industrial Australia in the late twentieth century.

The growth of Commonwealth power has been a persistent theme in Australian politics, and occasionally a strident one — as it was at the end of the 1960s. But it has only occasionally been an issue that has caught the attention of the mass electorate, and it has not affected the shape of party politics. The party system has taken in its stride the changing balance in federal-state relations, and the dislocations caused by two world wars and a major economic depression. We shall see in Chapter 4 that the images of the parties and the rhetoric of party conflict have been very stable for more than two generations. Stability is characteristic of the whole party system.

Table 1.1 displays the rise and fall in party support at elections for the House of Representatives from the first election after Federation to that of May 1974, the election precipitated by the third double dissolution since the establishment of the Commonwealth.[4] The first federal elections returned three roughly equal groups, a Labor Party and two non-Labor parties; the latter were divided on the tariff issue, a legacy of the 1880s. Within eight years of the founding of the Commonwealth these two had coalesced in an 'anti-socialist' formation that was to be called the Liberal Party, and the election of 1910 can be said to mark the establishment of the modern Australian party system. Since 1910 the Liberal Party has undergone three changes of name and twice incorporated Labor parliamentarians and supporters (to its great electoral advantage), yet in 1976 it was recognisably the descendant of the Liberal Party of 1910. The Australian Labor Party's claims to a continuous existence in federal politics cannot be denied; its origins lie even further back, in the industrial turbulence of the early 1890s. Since 1910 the party system has admitted only two minor players to join the big two: the Country Party, which was in essence a regrouping from within the Liberal Party, in 1919, and the Democratic Labor Party, which was in the beginning a dissident faction of the ALP, in 1955. Neither minor party was able to do more than establish

---

4 Australia's federal legislature is bicameral, and there is a case for regarding Senate voting figures as the better test of party allegiance since each state votes as a unit, all electors vote as there are no 'uncontested seats', the influence of personalities is much reduced, and voters can choose among all the parties. But these advantages are more than offset by the clear indications that voters care less about Senate elections and their outcomes. Informal voting is much higher (a sign also of the difficulty of the ballot procedure) and 'donkey voting' (numbering candidates from the top of the ballot paper to the bottom, regardless of party affiliations) much more frequent. Survey data provide further evidence. In 1969 respondents were asked how they had voted at the Senate elections in 1967: 13 per cent claimed not to have voted, and 24 per cent could not remember. Asked how they had voted at the House of Representatives elections in 1966 — one year earlier still — only 3 per cent claimed not to have voted, and only 6 per cent had forgotten. Voting is compulsory at both elections.

a beachhead, and the electoral support for each is now set in a downward trend, a situation that led to the amalgamation of the two parties in Western Australia and discussions about mergers in Queensland and in other states. Independent MPs, owing allegiance to no party, have always been rare in federal politics, and support for independent candidates was notable only during the Depression and the early 1940s, when the party

Table 1.1   Party shares of the formal first preference vote in elections for the House of Representatives, 1910 to 1975

Election Year	Labor %	Free Trade %	Share of vote won by Protection %	Country Party %	DLP %	Others %
1901	19	34	45	—	—	2
1903	31	34	30	—	—	5
1906	37	40	21	—	—	2
			Liberal	—	—	
1910	50		40	—	—	5
1913	48		49	—	—	3
1914	51		47	—	—	2
1917	44		54 (Nat.)	—	—	2
1919	42		47	7	—	4
1922	42		40	13	—	5
1925	45		42	11	—	2
1928	45		39	12	—	4
1929	49		34	11	—	6
1931	38 (two groups)		42 (UAP)	12	—	8
1934	41		37	13	—	9
1937	43		34	16	—	7
1940	48 (three groups)		30	13	—	9
1943	50		21 (various groups)	11	—	18
1946	50		33 (Liberal)	11	—	6
1949	46		39	11	—	4
1951	48		40	10	—	2
1954	50		39	8	—	3
1955	45		40	8	5	2
1958	43		37	9	9	2
1961	48		34	8	9	1
1963	45		37	9	7	2
1966	40		40	10	7	3
1969	47		35	8	6	4
1972	50		32	9	5	4
1974	49		35	11	1	4
1975	43		42	11	1	3

Note: From 1910 to 1917 simple majority counting was in force; thereafter, preferential voting. Voting was compulsory in 1925 and subsequently.
Source: Colin A. Hughes and B.D. Graham, *A Handbook of Australian Government and Politics, 1890-1964,* Canberra, 1968, and the corrigenda published in their *Voting for the Australian House of Representatives 1901-1964,* Canberra, 1974; unofficial reports published by the Chief Electoral Officer, Commonwealth of Australia. Note that, especially for the early period, the party labels of some candidates are matters of debate.

system itself was under some attack.[5] Even in 1943, when 136 in-dependent candidates won more than 12 per cent of the total vote, only one of them was elected.

From 1910 to the present the ebb and flow of party support in federal elections have been most subdued. In virtually every election the Labor Party has won between 40 per cent and 50 per cent of the vote. Since the Country Party and the National Party first joined forces in a composite government in 1923 the same has been true of the non-Labor group. As Figure 1.1 demonstrates, the even competition between Labor and non-Labor has taken place while the electorate has trebled its size. So accustomed have Australians become to this electoral stasis that terms like

Figure 1.1   Electorate size and votes won by parties, 1910 to 1969

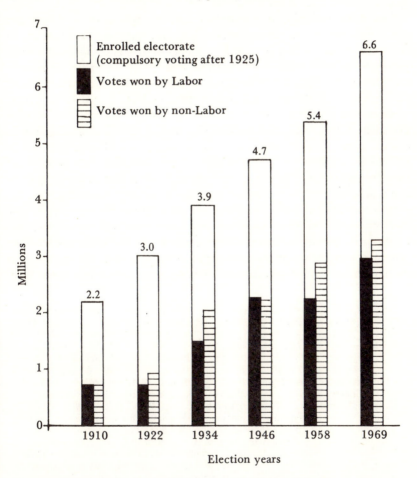

5 For some of the flavour of the rejection of parties during this period, see Don Aitkin, *The Colonel: a Political Biography of Sir Michael Bruxner*, Canberra, 1969, pp. 128-33, and Robert Cooksey (ed.), *The Great Depression in Australia*, Canberra, 1970.

'landslide' or 'crushing defeat' are used to describe quite small movements in support; the coalition government's 'landslide' victory in November 1966, for example, gave it 50 per cent of the vote, and represented a 4 per cent increase in its 1963 share of the vote. The minor parties have been no less stable. The change from one election to the next in the Country Party's share of the vote has been greater than 2 per cent only twice since 1919, and until 1974 that of the DLP has also been slight, although its life-span has of course been much shorter. The only changes in the shape of the party system that are in prospect are the continuing decline and eventual disappearance of the Country Party and the DLP;[6] amalgamation can only postpone their departure. It is entirely possible that during the 1980s Australia could return to the same pure two-party situation in federal politics that it knew between 1910 and 1919.

The massive stability of the system does not appear to have been the result of chance. At first glance Table 1.1 portrays a situation of equilibrium, in which powerful forces operate to keep support for each party within well defined boundaries. But we do not have to rely on intuition alone. Stokes and Iversen, confronted with American electoral data of like stability, employed an ingenious model of the electoral process to demonstrate that the probability of the party shares of the vote for President having remained within their actual historical boundaries by chance alone was less than four in a hundred.[7] Although the same operation has not been performed using Australian data, there is no doubt that the results would be of the same order. There is then, something to be explained.

It is not difficult to show that electoral stability is connected to the stability of the larger political system. Australia's political parties (the Communist parties excepted) do not challenge the legitimacy of the general constitutional or socio-economic arrangements in the society. The parliamentary form of government offers rewards to the losers as well as to

6 For the Country Party's prospects, see Don Aitkin, 'Country Party — Fortunes and Options', *Current Affairs Bulletin*, **42**(8), September 1968) for those of the DLP, D.W. Rawson, 'The D.L.P. — "Get On", "Get Out" or Neither', in H. Mayer (ed.), *Australian Politics — A Second Reader*, Melbourne, 1969, Paul Duffy, 'The D.L.P. in the Seventies', in H. Mayer and H. Nelson (eds.), *Australian Politics — A Third Reader*, Melbourne, 1973, Henry Mayer (ed.), *Labor to Power: Australia's, 1972 Election*, Sydney, 1973, and P.L. Reynolds, *The Democratic Labor Party*, Brisbane, 1974. For a counter-view, which sees the Country Party alive and well at the end of the century, see J.M. Barbalet, 'Tripartism in Australia: the Role of the Australian Country Party', *Politics*, **10**(1), May 1975.
7 The model (termed a generalised 'random walk') is a simple one. If there are no 'restoring forces' operating on a party's share of the vote, and the average movement of the party's share of the vote at any election is x per cent, then that share is as likely to move in one direction as the other, that is, the party is no more likely to improve its position than to worsen it. Over a long series of elections the probability is high that the share of the vote of a party, considered as a particle engaged in a 'random walk', will wander widely between 0 and 100. But in fact this has not been the case in the USA or Australia (Donald E. Stokes and Gudmund R. Iversen, 'On the Existence of Forces Restoring Party Competition', in Angus Campbell *et al.*, *Elections and the Political Order*, New York, 1966).

the winners, and the three-tiered system of federal, state and local government provides a variety of arenas in which the party battle can take place, making it likely that positions of power will be shared. Between 1910 and May 1969, for example, when a Liberal-Centre (Country Party) coalition took office in Tasmania, the Labor Party was in power in at least one state or in the Commonwealth. Labor's only period of total exclusion from office (1970-1) lasted a mere thirteen months. By the end of 1971 it was the government in Western Australia and South Australia, and a year later in the Commonwealth and Tasmania as well. And the Liberal Party, alone or in coalition, has been in power somewhere in every year since 1910.[8] The parties themselves have become career structures for many of the politically ambitious, who have a keen interest in preserving the power and efficiency of the existing parties. The mortar that binds together the interlocked bricks of this edifice is of course the attitudes and loyalties of the electorate, for the most immediate reason that parties survive is that people keep on voting for them.

Yet this catalogue of circumstances does not provide an explanation of political stability in Australia. To begin with, much of it could be repeated for the Weimar republic of inter-war Germany, which was easily and legally demolished by Adolf Hitler. And many of these items are consequences or illustrations of stability as well as causes. We still do not have in this account an explanation either of the tiny movement in electoral support over sixty years or of the crystallisation of the party system in the first few years of the new century. Why did the rise and fall of parliamentary and electoral groupings that had been characteristic of colonial politics come to an end at the beginning of the twentieth century? Why has the party system frozen in the position it took up in 1910?

These are not questions that apply only to Australia. Lipset and Rokkan have emphasised that, across the world, '*the party systems of the 1960s reflect, with few but significant exceptions, the cleavage structures of the 1920s*'; the 'freezing of the major party alternatives' is a 'crucial characteristic of Western competitive politics ... *the party alternatives, and in remarkably many cases the party organizations, are older than the majorities of the national electorates.*'[9] In western Europe party systems have often survived the experience of wartime invasion and occupation by a foreign power. Lipset and Rokkan have a tentative explanation:

---

8 Don Aitkin, Patricia Hall and Kim Morgan, 'Some Facts and Figures', in Mayer and Nelson, *Australian Politics*; for more detail, see Colin A. Hughes and B.D. Graham, *A Handbook of Australian Government and Politics, 1890-1964*, Canberra, 1968.

9 S.M. Lipset and Stein Rokkan, 'Cleavage Structures, Party Systems and Voter Alignments: An Introduction', in their (eds.), *Party Systems and Voter Alignments: Cross-national Perspectives*, New York, 1967, p. 50. Emphasis in the original. See also two papers by Richard Rose and Derek Urwin: 'Persistence and Change in Western Party Systems since 1945: a Study in Aggregate Analysis', a paper prepared for the Conference on Comparative Social Science, University of Cologne, May 1969; and 'Social Cohesion, Political Parties and Strains in Regimes', *Comparative Political Studies*, 2(1), April 1969.

party politics in the period before the freezing was the politics of a restricted electorate. The extension of the suffrage to all adult males shook the political and electoral structures of the day. As in the tale of the three little pigs, those parties that were solidly constructed, with foundations deep in social reality, endured the blast; the others were blown away. The surviving party organisations divided the mass electorate among themselves, and the web of loyalties that binds citizens to their parties soon acted to make impossible the successful intrusion of any new political formations; they would always lack a base from which to make a challenge.

This is a plausible account, but in one crucial respect it will not work for Australia at all: manhood suffrage in the Australian colonies was as old as responsible government, and preceded the modern party system by a good half century. Indeed *adult* suffrage preceded the modern party system in Australia by a decade, since women were enfranchised early.[10] Why did a party system not come into being with adult male suffrage and responsible government?

The Growth of Party Politics

The most convincing answer has been advanced by Loveday and Martin, in writing about factional politics in New South Wales.[11] Manhood suffrage was granted in 1858 before there was any strong demand for it, principally because it seemed a sound political move to the liberal politicians dominant at that time: they saw the lower classes as natural allies against the conservatives. The lack of a struggle for the franchise removed one important stimulus to party organisation, and no others appeared in its place. Responsible government had begun in 1856 without the presence of any organisational base for political parties, even though relevant political outlooks — liberal and conservative — were present among the political élite. Liberals greatly outnumbered conservatives, however, and thus were decisive in determining the shape of the colony's

10   In federal elections, by the Commonwealth Franchise Act 1902, but women had had the vote in South Australia since 1894, and in Western Australia since 1899; see Coral Lansbury, 'The Feminine Frontier: Women's Suffrage and Economic Reality', *Meanjin Quarterly*, **31**(3), September 1972. The Lipset-Rokkan explanation will not do for France, either, where manhood suffrage dates from 1848 but the party system is still, on some accounts, in process of formation. See Sidney Tarrow, 'The Urban-Rural Cleavage in Political Involvement: the Case of France', *American Political Science Review*, **65**(2), June 1971.

11   *Parliament Factions and Parties: the First Thirty Years of Responsible Government in New South Wales, 1856-1889*, Melbourne, 1966. A comparable account of the growth of party politics in South Australia, which supports the arguments of Loveday and Martin, is Dean Jaensch, 'Political Representation in Colonial South Australia 1857-1901', unpublished PhD thesis, University of Adelaide, 1973. The course of events in Victoria was rather different, though not so much as to destroy the generality of the case being put forward here. See G. Serle, *The Golden Age: a History of the Colony of Victoria, 1851-1861*, Melbourne, 1961, and *The Rush to be Rich*, Melbourne, 1971.

new Constitution. That achieved, liberalism became a victorious orthodoxy, which thereafter lacked an opponent. Many members of the new
Legislative Assembly had more than one occupation and more than one
outlook. Neither the first government nor its loyal opposition was homogeneous in social or economic composition, and neither exclusively
represented any important grouping within the small community of New
South Wales.

The consequence was factional politics, in which a shifting pattern of
alliances and personal loyalties determined the rise and fall of governments. Political issues were wholly personal or practical, ideological
disputes hardly existed, and there was no stimulus to the development of
electoral organisation. Members of parliament and faction leaders worked
through personal committees, resident agents and individual partisans,
and the organisations that did spring up, like the Protestant Political
Association or the ubiquitous Railway Leagues, had restricted goals.

The key to factional politics was almost certainly poor communications
and a preoccupation with 'development'. Many local communities were
very recent creations, born of the gold rushes and subsequent agricultural
expansion. Cut off from one another by distance and lack of efficient
transport, they saw their interests in parochial and material terms: they
wanted improved public services, especially roads, the railway and the
telegraph. Since the period from 1856 to 1888 was one of almost
continuous growth and prosperity, these communities were self-absorbed,
jealous of rivals, and intent on pressing onwards to their glorious
future.[12] The MP was judged very largely in terms of his ability to secure
social capital for his constituency. Factional politics and nineteenth
century prosperity came to an end almost at the same time. By the late
1880s most of the colony's citizens were connected by the railway, and had
already experienced the economic changes brought about by it, principally
the extinction of much small industry in the country towns, and the
competition of goods from other colonies, especially Victoria.

Already free trade and protectionist organisations had developed in the
electorate, and their influence grew because of their ability to link people
in what had once been isolated communities. When economic depression
began to visit the colony New South Wales had its first taste of party
politics, for free trade and protection were matters of principle as well as
of economic interest. The election of 1887 was the first in which parties
competed for power, and Parkes's free trade ministry was the first party
government. The crucial test came when Parkes resigned from office in
1889: his followers tried to stay put and replace their leader. By doing so
they served notice that factional politics was near its end. Principle, or
ideology, was the new fuel of politics, and the party was its expression.

---

12 I have discussed this phenomenon in the first chapter of *The Country Party in New South
Wales. A Study of Organisation and Survival*, Canberra, 1972.

Two years later, after industrial action to secure unionists' goals had proved fruitless, Labor Electoral Leagues helped to elect thirty-five Labor candidates to the Legislative Assembly; the parliamentary Labor Party thus formed was only slightly smaller than free trade and protection. Party politics had arrived.[13]

But its shape was not final. Free trade and protection were rival economic doctrines, which had become important as the six colonies developed more complex industrial structures. They served very well as theories of government, each catering to the interests of one broad group of producers.[14] With the federation of the colonies in 1901 the *raison d'être* of the free trade versus protection division greatly altered. The new federal Constitution required free trade across the borders of the states, and thus knocked away one of protection's chief props. The debate now shifted to the new federal parliament: was Australia, with respect to the rest of the world, to be a free-trade nation, or would she defend her infant secondary industries against overseas competition by erecting protective tariff walls?

There was scarcely any doubt as to the direction to be taken, especially as the protectionists governed the Commonwealth for most of its first ten years. By the election of 1906, the free traders had virtually abandoned their goal of completely free trade, and were prepared to accept current levels of tariff protection. Their leader, G.H. Reid, his goal an anti-Labor fusion, was directing all his energies to 'stalking the socialist tiger'. The Labor Party allowed its members a free vote on the tariff issue until 1908 but it generally supported the protectionists, especially where (as in Deakin's 'new protection') the protection of industries was linked with provisions for safeguarding the economic interests of the employee. The tariff ceased to be an issue in federal politics by 1908, and in state politics it had been irrelevant since 1901. Deakin's fusion of the three non-Labor groups early in 1909 (during a period of Labor government) represented the recognition that nothing much now separated the former free traders

13 Three years later again, in 1894, came the first Country Party, a faction of the Protectionist Party which collaborated with the Farmers and Settlers' Association during the campaign. It did not survive; there were other later attempts to create a farmers' party, culminating in the successful breakthrough of the Progressives (as they were then called) in 1920. See B. D. Graham, *The Formation of the Australian Country Parties,* Canberra, 1966. The beginnings of party politics have been the subject of considerable and continuing debate among Australian historians, stemming from the work of Martin and Loveday. For a useful bibliography see Brian Dickey, *Politics in New South Wales 1856-1900,* Melbourne, 1969, pp. 191-3.

14 It is worth noting that as Sawer has pointed out, the connection of interest to ideology was very different from colony to colony. In New South Wales the protectionists were rural, defending local farmers against the products of their counterparts in Victoria and South Australia. In Victoria, South Australia and Tasmania, on the other hand, the protectionists came from the city, and the free traders from the country. Western Australia was a free trade bastion, and in Queensland protection was an alliance of the city and the tropical north against the free trade pastoralists of the inland. (*Australian Federal Politics and Law, 1901-1929,* Melbourne, 1956, p. 14).

and protectionists. At the same time, the success of the Labor Party in increasing its share of the vote had forced the free trade and protection parties to place greater emphasis on ideology — to find a language, a point of view, that could compete on equal terms with Labor's class creed. The Liberal Party that resulted from this fusion possessed a radical wing and a conservative wing, an urban group and a rural group, and a splendid variety of personal outlooks. But its members were united in the feeling that on the whole they preferred Labor to be in opposition. This general description fits the Liberal Party of today no less than its predecessor.

In four states non-Labor parties already wore, rather uneasily, Liberal and Conservative labels. By 1910 the Labor versus Liberal division existed everywhere. In retrospect Federation can be credited with the generation of the modern party system; that is to say, one major political event set in train another. Yet had Federation not occurred, or been postponed for a further generation, it seems likely that the six colonies would sooner or later have seen the tariff issue fade in importance, probably because of the gradual success of protection. A regrouping of the non-Labor forces into a single party was a logical consequence, partly because of the challenge posted by Labor. The Labor Party proposed to use the power of government to alter some of the economic and social relationships hitherto characteristic of the community. From the point of view of those outside the party this was distasteful heterodoxy on one or both of two counts: the changes proposed were not wanted, and the use of state power to achieve them was itself objectionable. In short, Labor was seen as a major threat to the existing political order, and the Liberal Party a defensive coalition against it. There was no other possible alignment of comparable importance; nor has one emerged since.

The suggested solution for Australia of the Lipset-Rokkan puzzle, then, is as follows. A firm party system did not immediately follow the introduction of manhood suffrage, because communication within the colonies was slow and difficult, ideological differences among politicians were subdued, and local communities were absorbed in rapid economic growth; these conditions allowed factional politics to flourish. When party politics emerged, in the late 1800s, the alignment of parties turned on the political economy of the colonies, an issue which allowed a rich interplay of interest and principle. But the tariff issue had a currency of only twenty years: the decision of the colonists to federate reduced the relevance of the existing party alignment. The developing confrontation of Labor versus non-Labor took its place; it has not been successfully challenged since. Indeed, a successful challenge is not likely, since the political community has become nationalised and the parties have learned to adapt to changing circumstances. The free trade versus protection alignment (with Labor an observer in the neutral corner) was too much tied to a single issue to survive indefinitely; the modern party system is hardly defined in terms of issues at all. [15]

This chain of circumstances may serve to explain the crystallisation of the modern party system in Australia, but it offers no clues to the explanation of the slight variation in the levels of party support since. The question is not why is there continuity, but what is responsible for such massive stability — and for the change that does occur? Continuity is easy to explain in quite general terms. Berelson and his colleagues argued in one of the early voting studies that political stability was based on social stability: a web of personal associations with like-minded people, and the maturation of children within them, encouraged the persistence both of individual loyalties and attitudes and wider political traditions; these social conditions did not change sharply, nor did their political consequences. [16] But they do change: people die, others come of age, still others immigrate, the economy grows, cities expand, employment opportunities alter. Even if no allowance were made for political conversions, for voters becoming angry with a government or an MP, we might still expect trends of some kind to develop. Yet the major parties still possess much the same share of the vote that they enjoyed in 1910, and they win their votes in much the same places.

A few writers have posited an equilibrium theory in which elections form a cyclical pattern: a party's share of the vote increases to a peak and is then progressively eroded to a trough from which, once again, it begins to rise. [17] The proposed sources of this equilibrium are various, but nearly all have to do with the consequences of being in power: [18] for example, a large parliamentary majority (a sign of electoral success) encourages divisiveness, factional disputes and splits, which operate to lower public confidence in the party and reduce its share of the vote, while defeat stimulates unity; or the widespread belief in some kind of rotation in office helps to convert shortcomings in a government's performance into proof that it is time for a change. However plausible these conjectures are in general, they do not help to explain why support for the Labor and Liberal parties has stayed within such narrow bounds; and they throw no light on

15 This argument suggests that too much emphasis may have been given to the effects of extension of suffrage in other polities. A more plausible account seems to be that the freezing of party systems occurred because of the joint effects of economic and technological progress (facilitating a national electorate or at least some regional electorates) and wide suffrage (ending further opportunities for mobilising new, unfranchised, sections of the community). The later enfranchisement of women seems to have made no special impact in those polities where it ocurred after party lines had hardened — though there are other explanations for that, of course.

16 Bernard R. Berelson, Paul F. Lazarsfeld and William N. McPhee, *Voting*, 2nd edition, Chicago, 1966, pp. 315-17. See also Barrie Stacey, 'Inter-Generation Mobility and Voting', *Public Opinion Quarterly*, **30**(1), 1966.

17 Charles Sellers, 'The Equilibrium Cycle in Two-Party Politics', *Public Opinion Quarterly*, **29**(1), 1965; Neal Blewett, 'A Classification of Australian Elections: Preliminary Notes', *Politics*, **6**(1), May 1971. Blewett's article contains other references.

18 A list of hypotheses is given by Stokes and Iversen, 'Forces Restoring Party Competition', pp. 180-1.

the stability of the electoral performance of minor parties.

Part of the explanation is intuitively clear. To govern, a party or party bloc must win more than half the seats in the House, and that goal can generally be secured by winning half of the votes cast in the election. To gain the magic 50 per cent parties try to secure the support of as many as possible of the important interests in society, and they adapt their policies and ideologies to this end.[19] At times, therefore, they will be competing for the support of the same people. Once a party has gained power, its ability to satisfy these interests is to some extent a function of their number: the more supporters, the greater the number of rewards expected, and the greater the likelihood of disappointment. In such a situation, the weaker interests are liable to suffer most, to end their support of the party in power, and to be attracted to the camp of the opposition. This process continues when the other party gains office, for expectations will always exceed the capacity of a government to satisfy. In short, in a party system where 50 per cent plus one is the point at which seats are won and governments defeated, it is reasonable to expect 50 per cent to be the fulcrum on either side of which the parties are balanced. But why are the balancing movements from one election to another so gentle?

In a persuasive attempt to deal with this problem Gösta Carlsson has compared two alternative hypotheses, which he labels 'stimulus' and 'response'.[20] In the first, voters occupy a social situation that changes slowly (Berelson's point), and changes that affect voters tend to make up a smooth series in time. There is something in this argument, as governments do better when economic conditions improve; but, as Carlsson notes, there is considerable electoral stability even in the midst of depressions. Governments may be slaughtered in depression elections, but such results follow from movements in electoral support that are only slightly greater than usual. (In Australia one consequence of the Depression was to divide the ALP into warring groups, but these groups still polled 38 per cent in 1931, Labor's blackest year). According to the response hypothesis, on the other hand, voters react to a wide range of circumstances, but with varying degrees of speed. There is accordingly a time lag, which acts to smooth out electoral responses to important political events. Indeed, since many of these circumstances have contrary implications (some voters will be attracted to a party because of its foreign policy, while others are repelled by its leader), the net movement of partisan loyalties within the electorate may be very slight.

Carlsson has tested the response hypothesis successfully against randomly generated data, and it seems to fit the realities of American and

19 This argument is explored thoroughly by Anthony Downs, *An Economic Theory of Democracy*, New York, 1957.
20 'Time and Continuity in Mass Attitude Change: the Case of Voting', *Public Opinion Quarterly*, **29**(1), 1965.

Swedish electoral experience. Yet if it provides a basis for a convincing explanation of why electoral change is slow, the response hypothesis tells us nothing about why change does not continue in the one direction.

The missing link in the chain of explanation is the development of widespread, stable, partisan loyalty within the mass electorate. In the colonial era citizens voted for a local man, or a colonial notable, whose talisman was his ability to get things done for his constituency. Free trade, protection and Labor extended the notion of politics as the regulation of economic interest to groups that spanned communities. Modern parties have added a thick ideological coating to the bases of economic self-interest on which the party system rests. It is ideology, not organisation, that most distinguishes the parties of the twentieth century from their predecessors of the nineteenth century, and it is ideology which encourages the citizen to cleave to his party rather than to chop and change. These ideologies are not fully elaborated; they do not need to be. But they contain an account of the good society and how to arrive at it, an explanation of the present situation of the community, and a delineation of its notable champions and villains. Above all, these party ideologies obtain their power because they are related to the social experience of the major groups on which the various parties depend for support. For this reason, the ideologies slowly change to accommodate changes in that experience; while the group survives, therefore, the ideology remains relevant.[21]

The voter's loyalty to his party is so important in this argument that the first third of the book is explicitly devoted to it, and it is a principal object for study in the remainder. But it should not be thought that the modern, ideological, party system came to Australia overnight. Party alignments appeared first in parliament, and it was some time before they were matched by robust party organisation in the constituencies. And the work of party branches and councils was a necessary preliminary to the replacement of loyalty to individual MPs by loyalty to the party, the replacement of a local perspective by a wider one. Party organisation developed unevenly from place to place, and from one party to another, and the development of party loyalty was similarly erratic; indeed, it is fair to say that there are parts of Australia, notably the north coast farming districts of New South Wales, where the idea of party has still not fully supplanted traditional preoccupations with local issues and personalities.[22]

---

21 Some may find the use of 'ideology' in this context vexatious, on the ground that the term should properly be reserved for well fashioned, elaborated schemes such as Marxism-Leninism. But few party ideologies in Western democracies have much of this quality, and the term is too useful to confine it to such restricted use. Besides, there is no obvious alternative. I have argued the case for paying attention to party ideologies more fully in *The Country Party in New South Wales*, Chapter 1, which contains also a discussion of the ideology of the Country Party.

22 Ibid., generally; for an English example see R.W. Johnson: 'The Nationalisation of

The ideological flavour of party politics also increased gradually, and ideology was probably more characteristic of national politics than of state politics, at least in the beginning, because of the greater opportunities for general discussion and national planning provided in the federal arena. Nor were colonial politics entirely without ideology. A Working Men's Defence Association, a forerunner of the ALP, campaigned in the 1877 elections in New South Wales with an explicitly class appeal, which drew an almost immediate response from established politicians.[23] Labor's style was ideological from the start, and although most non-Labor politicians found it distasteful they could not ignore it. The Country Party, like the ALP, combined ideology with self-interest from the beginning, but the development of a positive Liberal ideology was very slow, since its first systematic expression is *The Forgotten People*, by R.G. Menzies which was published in 1943.[24]

To fix on 1910 as the beginning of the modern party system, then, is to concentrate on the parliamentary arena as the real focus of party politics: in the electorate the victory of party was rather slower. At the end of Chapter 6 an attempt is made to measure the penetration of party politics into the outlook of the electorate. It is sufficient to say here that this penetration was already substantial by 1910, and it reached a point of stability in the 1940s. The change that has occurred since has been very slight.

But changes still occur, and governments still alternate, even if the *rate* of change has slowed appreciably.[25] If it is the case that most citizens do not alter their party preference from one election to another, then the

English Rural Politics: Norfolk South West, 1945-1970', *Parliamentary Affairs,* **26**(1), Winter 1972/73; for Norway, Stein Rokkan, *Citizens, Elections, Parties,* Oslo, 1962, p. 227. Rokkan terms the process 'politicization', but 'nationalisation' seems more appropriate for Australia.

23 See in particular, *Sydney Morning Herald,* 16 October 1877, and Sir Henry Parkes's remarks (19 October 1877): 'All honour to labour, but the men ill-served the cause who did not respect it as part of a great community of interest as a means to raise themselves and their children but not as a banding together which would end only in suicide.' (I am indebted to Ann Norrie for much patient research in this area.) An early worker's association in South Australia was criticised because it avowed 'Socialist and Communist doctrines', *Thursday Review,* 23 February 1860, quoted in Jaensch, 'Political Representation', p. 458.

24 Alfred Deakin (Prime Minister at various times between 1903 and 1910) was the first great liberal ideologue, but his liberalism was not congenial to those who followed him as Leader of the Liberal Party, even though modern Liberals like to picture themselves as Deakin's ideological descendants. See J.A. La Nauze, *Alfred Deakin, a Biography,* Melbourne, 1965, and P.G. Tiver, 'Political Ideas in the Liberal Party of Australia', Ph. D. thesis, Australian National University, 1973. Dr Peter Loveday has pointed out to me that Bruce Smith's *Liberty and Liberalism,* published in Melbourne in 1887, contains a broad ideology which has proved its survival power in the Liberal Party in the twentieth century. Yet its progenitor remains unhonoured: Smith, though a prominent politician in his day, is virtually forgotten in this one.

25 See Colin A. Hughes, G.M. O'Connell and G. Evans, 'The Decline of Inter-party Competition in Australia', *Australian Quarterly,* **40**(3), September 1968, and D.E. Butler, 'The Advantage of Incumbency', in Mayer, *Australian Politics.*

small minority who do are of very great interest, both to the politician and to the analyst. For in an evenly divided party system the behaviour of these citizens not only determines which party is to govern, but also illuminates some crucial components of democratic theory. In considering stability we shall range from the 1850s to the 1970s. In considering change our attention will focus closely on the years between 1966 and 1969, when the survey materials on which this book rests were collected.

But that latter strategy is required because of the problem of evidence. In general what was true of the period 1966 to 1969 was, we may assume, true of other comparable periods of time, and will continue to be true while Australian politics holds its present shape. We shall spend more time on stability than on change, but that too is chiefly a function of the evidence at our disposal. Change is not less important than stability, nor — if some such affirmation must be made — less desirable in principle. Change and stability are two sides of the one coin: to recognise the currency we must know them both.

The bulk of the evidence on which the many arguments of the book depend has been provided by two national surveys of Australian citizens undertaken in 1967 and 1969; these surveys are described in detail in the Appendix. But the survey evidence would have had little meaning without the prior work of many historians, political scientists and sociologists whose contributions to the study of Australian society are acknowledged in the footnotes. The interweaving of contemporary and historical evidence, an essential task given the subject matter, has not always proceeded gracefully or surely, if only because of all-too-human errors of memory on the part of the respondents. Yet the attempt, I hope it will be clear, was worth the risks.

PART I The Nature of Party Choice

2 Politics and the Voter

I've always been a staunch Labor Party man, but I've never actually followed politics much. (*skinclasser, thirty-two, Tasmania*)

It may be true that man is a political animal, but in parliamentary democracies he is called on to exercise that aspect of his nature only rarely, and then on prescribed occasions. There are no legal bars to a citizen's engaging in politics, but few care to do so. In Australia, as in other western industrial polities, the development of democratic institutions has led to 'a political division of labour that reserves most governmental decisions to a relatively small elite';[1] indeed, 'governmental' may be extended to 'political' without affecting the accuracy of the statement. To understand why the modern party system works as it does, we must begin with an examination of the place of the citizen in the political world.

Political Participation in Australia

There exist two fanciful portraits of the Australian electorate, which may be labelled the Happy and the Gloomy. The first corresponds to the vision of participatory democracy usually attributed to Rousseau and J.S. Mill: all citizens are responsible, rational and concerned; they are alive to problems and issues, and play their part in debating and formulating policies. In turn, governments are quickly responsive to the popular will, and give effect to its decisions. Politics is thus an ongoing dialogue in which every citizen has his say and of which the point is the shaping of a better Australian society.

No-one suggests that the Australian electorate is in every respect like this, but it is assumed to be a state of affairs worth aiming for; certainly the nation ought not to settle for less. In consequence, political leaders

1 David Butler and Donald Stokes, *Political Change in Britain. Forces Shaping Electoral Choice,* London, 1969, p. 24.

and other opinion-makers tend to address the polity at large, citizens accept readily that they ought to vote, newspaper proprietors and other media controllers provide large quantities of political news and information to their publics, and election campaigns continue to be portrayed as occasions on which 'the nation takes stock', on which each of seven million electors reviews the events of the past parliament and the relative performances of government, opposition and other parties, considers the likely problems of the near future, and decides for whom he will vote.

The Gloomy portrait is an antipodean example of what one writer has described as 'the contemporary theory of democracy'.[2] Australia's politics is characterised by apathy; its citizens for the most part take no interest in political issues, and leave the business of policy-making to the political machines, which carry out this function to suit themselves and the vested interests they represent. In consequence, Australians are poorly governed by mediocre men, who are in turn derided by the electorate; and politics ceases to be an activity that can engage the interest or the participation of those best fitted for it. The causes of this malaise are variously located: the absence of deep cleavages in the society, its protective isolation from the rest of the world, a continuing preoccupation with 'growth' and 'development', the lack of a traditional élite that sees in politics an opportunity for disinterested public service, and even the frequency of elections.[3] Indications of a pervasive lack of interest in politics are easy to find, and the phenomenon itself is frequently criticised by those who see external threats menacing Australia, by preachers from pulpits, and by politicians themselves, especially on having been defeated.

Survey data certainly support the view that politics is of small moment to most of the electorate. Nearly half of the 1967 sample declared that they had no interest in politics, or 'not much'; more than half did not follow news about politics in the press; two-thirds had no idea of the name of their federal member of parliament, although it was only a few months since they had last voted in a federal election. Barely half thought that what the federal government did made any difference to how well off they were. The helpless and often embarrassed comment 'I really don't know much about this sort of thing' recurred throughout the interviews, even though the questions asked for personal opinions rather than for information. Indifference was almost as widely distributed as ignorance: two in five professed not to care very much which party won an election, and much the same proportion saw little difference between the parties.

2 Carole Pateman, *Participation and Democratic Theory*, Cambridge, 1970, p. 13.
3 The bemoaning of 'apathy' has been a recurrent theme in Australian politics since the beginnings of representative government in the mid-nineteenth century. For a contemporary discussion of Australia's 'disenchantment with politics' see John Hallows, *The Dreamtime Society*, Sydney, 1970, and Donald Horne, *The Lucky Country*, Melbourne, 1964.

Activity in politics attracted only a tiny handful — a mere 4 per cent were paid-up members of a political party, and of those only one in three considered themselves to be active party workers. Even if 'activity' is defined to include simply talking about politics to other people, the politically active would include only one in three of the electorate.

We can obtain a summary of the extent to which politics is an interest of electors by combining some of the measures of interest into one index. Since the essentials of a general interest in politics include access to political information, and less certainly, a preparedness to talk about it, we may usefully combine (a) following politics in the newspapers, (b) following politics on television, (c) following politics on the radio, and (d) talking about politics with other people. The result is set out in Table 2.1.

Table 2.1   Interest in politics, 1967

Group	Description	Percentage of Sample
I	Talk politics with others, and follow politics *via* at least one medium	27
II	Don't talk politics, but follow it *via* at least two media	12
III	Follow politics *via* at least one medium, or talk politics but do not follow it otherwise	26
IV	Do not talk politics, or follow it	35
Total		100 (N = 1832)

Voters in Group I have the best claim to be entitled politically active, but they include only one in every four of the sample. Those in Groups II and III have little political output apart from voting but, together with Group I, they provide the audience for Australian parliamentary and electoral politics. Group IV — one-third of the electorate — are hardly in the polity at all. In broad terms, then, we can consider the electorate as consisting of three roughly equal groups: the active, the audience, and the uninterested.[4]

The kind of political awareness characteristic of those who fall into the last group is well revealed in one of the interview records. The respondent is a married woman, sixty-two, from Tasmania, whose formal education lasted only until the end of primary school; she belongs to no clubs or societies, and has no opinions on most political issues. A

4 For a thorough analysis of political participation based on other data, but with essentially the same findings, see J.S. Western and P.R. Wilson, 'Politics: Participation and Attitudes', in Mayer and Nelson, *Australian Politics*. See also A.F. Davies, 'Suburban Political Styles', in his *Essays in Political Sociology*, Melbourne, 1972.

reference to America in one of the questions prompts her to say 'America — that's where we get our money from now, isn't it?'; Vietnam she categorises as a 'lower-crust Japan'. Early in the interview she is asked to say what she likes and dislikes about the parties and leaders. Her answers are remarkably evocative (the questions of the gifted interviewer are abbreviated after the first two). [5]

> *Is there anything in particular you like about the Liberal Party?* I don't know much about them. Oh, I follow them. Mr Holt speaks very nice... I was listening last night — I can't remember his name... I don't follow them that much to listen to their arguments, but I do listen to them debating and that.
>
> *Is there anything in particular you don't like about the Liberal Party?* No.
>
> *Like about Labor?* No — they're both, you know, much of a muchness to me.
>
> *Don't like about Labor?* Oh, there's a lot but I wouldn't put it down [i.e. want it recorded]... I don't like the looks of the other fellow [Mr Whitlam] — he may be very nice. I can't think of his name. Mr Reece is all right. You see a lot on television — English Labour Party and all that; of course my father come from England when he was twelve years old.
>
> *Like about the Country Party?* No — I don't know them.
>
> *Don't like about the Country Party?* No — I really don't know. I don't know what he is... I've heard him speaking and that. [He's] one I've heard talk but I just can't think of their names. They're nearly all much of a muchness when they're talking aren't they?
>
> *Like about the DLP?* Oh — they're all the same to me really. I listen to them, but I don't know anything much about any of them...we'll soon be having an election here — the Senate — I don't know who's coming up.
>
> *Don't like about the DLP?* No. I really don't know anything about them to tell you the honest truth. I just hear them talking...but you really can't say can you?
>
> *Like about Mr Holt?* That's hard to answer. I've heard him speak and seen him a good bit when Mr Johnson was over. I've got nothing to say about him — he's a good speaker. I've never heard him personally — only over the air.
>
> *Don't like about Mr Holt?* No.
>
> *Like about Mr Whitlam?* Oh, I don't like him!... I don't like the way he speaks — he's all right [I suppose]. I heard him debate on 'Four Corners' last Saturday night. I don't take much notice of what they're talking about. I only go by looks.
>
> *Don't like about Mr Whitlam?* No...No.

5 The questions are those from 6(a) to 9(b), and from 12(a) to 14(b), in the 1967 question-naire.

Like about Mr McEwen?   Oh, I don't know whether I've seen him or not...

Such citizens are the despair of politician and propagandist.

Yet the degree of apparent political nonchalance in Australia requires some careful inspection. In the first place, participation in politics is not a constant thing. People can take up politics as an interest and later abandon it for other activities. This is especially the case when there emerge political issues that the party system cannot quickly accommodate. In the last ten years, for example, issues such as state aid to church schools, fluoridation, conservation, immigration, the war in Vietnam, and the agricultural crisis have drawn into active politics many people who had previously been relatively uninterested. As such issues arise and decline in importance so do the ranks of the politically active swell and thin. It is likely, therefore, that the proportion of those who *have* at some time been interested in politics is rather larger than the proportion presently interested;[6] the latent capacity for the electorate to become actively political may be considerable.

In the second place, there is nothing distinctively Australian about political apathy. The extensive literature of political participation makes clear that the pattern of political involvement sketched in Table 2.1 is characteristic of all Western democracies: in none of them does consistent participation attract more than a minority.[7] Nor are Australians notably indifferent to politics in comparison with the citizens of other countries. Almond and Verba's comparative study of participation in the United States of America, Great Britain, Germany, Italy and Mexico[8] placed Great Britain close to the USA and well ahead of the other three nations; a more recent comparison of Great Britain and Australia over an array of measures of political involvement suggests that these two polities are remarkably similar. The British data are drawn from the 1963 national survey conducted by Butler and Stokes, the Australian data from the 1967 survey;[9] both surveys were carried out in periods of relative political quiet.

What is immediately apparent is the striking similarity between the responses of the two samples; it is as though the two were drawn from the

---

6 Firm evidence to support this argument is hard to come by. But Western and Wilson ('Politics', p. 321) discovered that 11 per cent of their sample were *or had been* financial members of a political party, compared with the 4 per cent of the 1967 sample who were currently members of a party. And my study of Country Party members in 1962 suggested that, although only 10 per cent held and office in that year, another 20 per cent had been office-bearers or active in other ways in the past (*The Country Party in New South Wales*, pp. 141-2).

7 The best summary is Lester W. Milbrath, *Political Participation. How and Why do People get Involved in Politics?*, Chicago, 1965.

8 *The Civic Culture*, Princeton, 1963.

9 Butler and Stokes, *Political Change in Britain*, pp. 464ff. The equivalent questions in the 1967 questionnaire are 49(a), 49(d), 1(b), 2, 3, 5(a), 30, 10, 48, 35(a), 35(c).

same population. The largest difference is that between the proportions reporting following politics on television, a difference that may require little more explanation than the fact that British television carried much more politics in 1963 than Australian television did in 1967.[10] Compulsory voting in Australia may have reduced the incidence both of party membership and of party activity; yet the British figures, though larger, are of the same order.[11] On some of the indices the Australian score is in

Table 2.2   Political participation in Australia and Great Britain

Proportion who...	Australia, 1967 %	Great Britain, 1963 %
are active in party work	1	2
are financial members of a party	4	12
follow politics on the radio	17	19
talk much about politics with others	31	27
think of themselves as 'very strong' partisans for a party	34	36
follow politics on television	34	55
follow politics in the newspapers [a]	41	38
see at least 'some' difference between the parties	51	56
care 'a good deal' which party wins elections	60	65
think of themselves in party terms	87	90
(N)[b]	(2054)	(2009)

[a]In Australia, first newspaper mentioned; in Great Britain, first morning newspaper.

[b]Total sample size; the base of the percentage is the proportion of each sample replying to the question.

10 The disparity has probably now disappeared, because of the much greater attention of Australian television to politics since 1967, a change associated with the very successful ABC current affairs program 'This Day Tonight'. There was a sharp increase in the proportion following the 1969 *election campaign* on television compared with that following *politics* on television in 1967, from 34 per cent to 63 per cent. The comparable jump in the British figures (an election in 1964) was 55 per cent to 75 per cent.

11 Australian citizens are required by law to register and to vote, and the electoral roll is kept continuously up to date. The difference between 4 per cent and 12 per cent in party membership may not seem large in absolute terms, but its effects can seem substantial to those, such as British emigrants to Australia, who have experienced both political cultures. More than one such migrant in the sample criticised the poverty of Australian political life and the apparent apathy of Australians. The remarks of a fifty-six year-old Sydney hairdresser are typical: '[in Australia] it's not politics in the true sense: it is all haphazard — you've got your ALPs and DLPs. The people are not demonstrative enough. Back home, if a politician did something they didn't like the people'd soon let them know about it. The very essence of democracy is for the man in the street to demonstrate and do something about it. You never see it here; people grumble but do nothing.' Other students of migrant political behaviour have encountered comparable attitudes (see June M. Hearn, 'Migrant Political Attitudes', unpublished MA (Hons.) thesis, University of Melbourne, 1971, p. 28). But it is clear that greater Australian apathy is more apparent than real, and is probably the consequence in large part of compulsory voting, which removes the need for the parties to get out the vote.

fact the higher one. There may be other ways in which the two polities are distinct — the style of politicians and the nature of political debate are two that come to mind — but it is clear that, in terms of the participation and involvement of the mass of its citizens in national politics, Australia is much like Great Britain.

Three Views of the Political Order

To describe the citizen's condition as 'apathetic' is to some extent to judge the real world by misconceived standards, to assume that unless all citizens are participants there is but a sham democracy, and, more specifically, that unless citizens take a constant interest in politics they do not care about it at all. The first of these assumptions has become a central point in the modern debate on democratic theory,[12] and the second touches on the citizen's perception of his own relationship to the state; both require further consideration. Sartori has argued persuasively that political apathy is a non-problem. We ought not to expect widespread political interest, he suggests, because much of politics is about abstract matters and much of the rest of it is out of the experience of the common man (or for that matter of the learned man), who therefore cannot understand it. We cannot take a deep interest in what we do not understand and we therefore leave politics to others. Accordingly, politics is 'the output of the politically active', and a democracy is a political system 'in which the power resides in the active *demos*' — that is, the politically active themselves — the only stipulation being that entry into the ranks of the politically active must be open to anyone who wants it. [13] In reality, of course, the every-day participants, the politicians, advisers, party workers, trade union leaders and others in similar positions who really understand politics directly are only a tiny handful of the citizens. Why do the politically inactive leave politics so completely to the active?

Three general answers suggest themselves. The first is that lack of participation is based on a general trust in the benevolence of the political order. Such an answer is encased in an account of Australian politics which might go something like this. From childhood on each citizen is socialised into an acceptance that he lives in a democratic polity, where rulers govern in the public interest, are chosen by the citizens and are subject to their verdict at periodic elections; where governmental decisions, important and trivial alike, are reached honestly; where in short, the system is intended to work for him. His principal obligation is to vote, and to vote deliberately; but he is not required to participate more actively unless he feels strongly about an issue. It is true that the reality is not wholly like this. Rulers patently do some things in their own interest; it is, in any case, of the stuff of day-to-day politics to argue about the nature

12 This debate is usefully summarised in Pateman, *Participation*, and in Giovanni Sartori, *Democratic Theory*, Detroit, 1962, especially Chapter V.
13 Sartori, ibid., p. 90.

of the public interest on any matter; graft and corruption in public life are not unknown; elections do not always place in power the party or parties that won a majority of the votes; and so on. Nevertheless, the resemblance appears close enough, and it is reinforced by public behaviour that conforms to the ideal, and by the endless repetition of democratic rhetoric from many parts of the polity. The notion that we have democratic 'standards', for example, implies both prescription and description: we know in what fashion the polity *ought* to behave, and even if behaviour on a given occasion is described as falling short of democratic standards the implication is clear that behaviour commonly does adhere to the standard. In consequence, the citizen who is not for personal or situational reasons especially interested in politics can exercise his vote, and then let the government get on with the job, secure in the feeling firstly that he has done his own duty and secondly that the government by and large may be trusted.

The second answer, the reverse of the first, pictures the mass of the people as thoroughly alienated from politics: the ordinary citizen does not trust the system, he takes care to avoid it, and endeavours to put politics from his mind. Whatever 'They' decide, he reasons, there is not much that can be done about it, and he abandons politics, mutely or mutinously according to temperament, for money-making, gardening or beer. Although surveys have never found alienation of this kind on a large scale, the hostile citizen is a familiar enough object in real life and in the rhetoric of the far left; the argument cannot be dismissed out of hand.

The third possible answer is that ignorance of political matters is so widespread and deep-seated that the ordinary citizen is not equipped to play any part in politics. He knows nothing, and therefore he does nothing, allowing himself to be manipulated by those in public life who can stir him to action through his emotions and prejudices. Circumstantial evidence rather undermines this argument, at least in its extreme form. In an urban, literate and affluent society like Australia where politics is open and respectable, it is very difficult for any citizen to avoid learning something about the basic shape of the political system, the players, the rules of the game, the questions at issue. In almost every year he will observe the flurry of political activity that surrounds an election; in New South Wales, for example, there has been either a state or a federal poll in all save three years since 1949. Politics is constant fare in news broadcasts and newspapers; even if he is not interested in detail of events he will pick up, perhaps subconsciously, something of the flow. Old, fading posters and the hard-wearing political *graffiti* to be found on bridges, rocks and railway cuttings — OUST MENZIES, BAN THE BOMB, VOTE NO, END CONSCRIPTION — serve as reminders of past political crises and the continuity of politics. In short, unless he is a recluse, the ordinary citizen will have a stock of political information.[14] Much of it may be

14 There *are* recluses, like the eighty-two year-old pensioner in Brisbane who reflected, 'It's a

sketchy, and some will be inaccurate, but for most voters it is available for use when necessary — in voting, in casual conversation, in making sense of new circumstances. The picture of a polity half of whose citizens are almost completely ignorant of politics, and indifferent to it for that reason, is an implausible one.

The study of Australian political culture has hardly begun, and how firmly the concept of Australia as a democratic society is held within the community is not known.[15] What can be gleaned from the survey interviews, in both 1967 and 1969, is material to support all three arguments, with the great weight of evidence behind the thesis that Australians accept their political system matter-of-factly, without either enthusiasm or hostility. In 1969 7 per cent of the respondents expressed themselves 'very satisfied' with the state of government and politics in Australia, and a further 70 per cent were 'fairly satisfied'; fewer than one in four, then, were not satisfied. These proportions were much the same among Labor supporters and Liberals. Asked in 1969 what things about government and politics in Australia they most approved of, the respondents were very often caught short for an answer: 'I never think about it like that' was a common — and indeed proper — remark. But this stimulus eventually produced items and instances from some 45 per cent of the respondents. Their replies were frequently set in a comparative context, implied or explicit, in which Australians were seen as more fortunate than others. The wife of a timber-mill supervisor in northern Tasmania answered: 'The democratic way: we have freedom and a good life, not like some other countries.' And an engine-driver's wife in Western Australia, a supporter of the Australia Party, said fervently: 'I approve of all of it — the way it's run generally...I think that we have a very good system of government.' A shop assistant in Toowoomba (Qld) believed that 'they [the people in government] all have Australia at their hearts'. Most of the comments centred on the structure of government and politics (a few interpreted the question in much wider terms) and approximately one in five mentioned specifically democracy, elections or political liberty. A companion question seeking examples of things *disapproved* of elicited fewer responses.

These data present a generally comfortable picture of the Australian's perception of the political order, but they must be set against the answers to a triad of questions that explored attitudes to 'the people running the government in Canberra', a group that the interviewer had already explained meant not 'Liberals or Labor in particular, but just the

---

long time since I took any notice of the outside world', and there are others, like elderly Italian or Greek immigrants, or Jehovah's Witnesses, who are effectively outside the polity through force of circumstances or volition. But their number is not large.

15 See Colin A. Hughes, 'Political Culture', in Mayer and Nelson, *Australian Politics*, and H.W. Emy, 'The Roots of Australian Politics: a Critique of a Culture', *Politics*, 7(1), May 1972.

government in general'.[16] The first question sought opinions about whether those in government 'give *everyone* a fair go, whether they are important or just ordinary people', or 'pay more attention to what the big interests want'. Only one in five gave an approving reply. When asked whether 'the people in government are too often interested in looking after themselves' or 'they can be trusted to do the right thing nearly all the time' the respondents divided almost evenly. It was only when they were asked whether the people running the government were usually pretty intelligent people who knew what they were doing, or whether there were too many who didn't seem to know what they were doing, that a majority could be found in support of 'the government' — and then the majority was only two-thirds. In sum, Australians seem to see their government as efficient, rather self-interested, and under the thumb of the big interests in society. If the answers to these three questions are treated as a rough index of support for 'the government' (a somewhat unfair test, as these questions cannot help tapping party loyalties as well) then the result is rather equivocal (Table 2.3). The respondents can be divided into two approximately equal groups, one for and the other against the government; but the more important grouping is probably the three-fold one of 'supporters' (15 per cent), 'acceptors' (67 per cent) and 'critics' (18 per cent). These data by no means give us a full understanding of the place of politics in the lives of the voters, but they suggest at least that positive enthusiasm for and downright dislike of the political system are both less common than a cool acceptance: 'I just take it for granted', as more than one of the respondents said.

A close examination of the interview schedules, especially of the incidental comments, provides a further clue to the motives underlying the tendency towards disengagement from politics. Very many voters appear to dislike politics because it emphasises disagreement, conflict and disunity. This attitude is expressed in a number of overlapping themes.[17]

Table 2.3   Support for 'the people in government', 1969

	Percentage
3 supporting answers	15
2 supporting answers	32
1 supporting answer	35
0 supporting answer	18
Total	100
	(N = 1709)

Note: Includes only those respondents who had opinions on all three questions.

16 Questions 60, 61 and 62 in the 1969 questionnaire.
17 It must be emphasised that this material is essentially impressionistic. The comments reported here were offered in reply to questions on other subjects, or as explanation for answers, and it is not possible to measure accurately how widespread these attitudes were; they were, nevertheless, very common indeed.

(i) *'Everyone does the best he can'*. Many respondents refused to be critical of parties and party leaders, even when their own loyalties were openly acknowledged. 'We've all got our faults — he [Holt]'s got his ... I suppose he's got a job to do and he does it to the best of his ability' (Hobart housewife) — the final phrase recurs again and again. A longer, edited extract from another interview suggests how passionless such an outlook on politics can be. The respondent is a sixty-five year-old mixed farmer from Victoria, who describes himself as 'very strong Liberal' — but who says of politics, 'it's a safe topic to leave alone'. The interviewer's questions are again abbreviated after the first two.[18]

> *Is there anything particular you like about the Liberal Party?* I like their policies. They try to get things done.
> *Is there anything particular you like about the Labor Party?* No, but I guess they're all right in their place. I suppose they have some good in them.
> *Like about the Country Party?* They are doing their best for the man on the land.
> *Like about the DLP?* I don't follow them much.
> *Like about Mr Gorton?* I think he's going a good job.
> *Dislike about Mr Gorton?* No...he's the leader and he's doing all right.
> *Like about Mr Whitlam?* I suppose he is doing his best, even if I don't agree with him.
> *Dislike about Mr Whitlam?* I don't go much for the Labor Party — nothing personal.
> *Like about Mr McEwen?* Good old bloke.
> *Dislike about Mr McEwen?* No...I reckon he's pretty honest. Must be getting on in years, though.

It is a short step from the belief that each party will try to do its best (and, implicitly, that each party's best is in everyone's interest) to

(ii) *'there's not much difference between them'*. This sentiment comes in two colours, rosy and dark: 'There's some very good men in both parties' and 'Whitlam's the same as Holt — they're all tarred with the same brush'. There are also the emotionally neutral: 'they're much of a muchness' (a very popular phrase), 'one's the same as the other to me', and 'they each have their points'. If there is indeed little difference between the parties then it is probably true that

(iii) *'they should be working together'*. There were some respondents who saw no need for parties at all. 'If the top two [parties] pulled together we could get a lot done.' During the Depression the party system came in for much similar criticism, and such a comment, or this one — 'I'd like to

18 Questions 8(a) to 11(b), and 14(a) to 16(b) in the 1969 questionnaire. The claim that all parties and leaders are working for the common good, or have good in them, was frequently expressed as a logical deduction from the fact of their existence: 'They must be all right, or people wouldn't keep voting for them', or 'He must be pretty good to hold his position'.

see everyone working together instead of actually a party' — is most evocative of the 1930s. Others were upset by the separate existences of the Country and Liberal Parties. 'Why can't the Country Party and the Liberal Party agree? There should just be the one party.' Unity of the parties, allied with or consequent upon unity of purpose and goodwill, would remove the most unpleasant aspect of Australian public life, which is that

(iv) *'there's too much bickering'*. While the first three themes were voiced equally in 1967 and 1969, this last was most common in 1969, when respondents were interviewed immediately after the federal elections in October: it stood out in the responses of those 30 per cent who disliked the TV coverage of the campaign. The considerable volume of this plaint (perhaps one voter in eight or nine made such a comment) is testimony not to the fury of the 1969 election campaign so much as to the distress that strong disagreement in public life can evoke within the electorate. Sometimes the judgment was aesthetic, 'I was against the way each leader ran the other down', sometimes moral, 'snide names do not do any good to those saying it' and sometimes frankly contemptuous: 'I can't stand the candidates picking on each other — they are like a lot of big kids.' But often the tone was anxious, as in the case of the engine-driver's wife in Western Australia, who declared 'There was too much criticism against one another; it's not good for the children.' We shall see in another chapter that the ALP was frequently criticised for its lack of unity; we may note this phenomenon here as a special case of the more general desire to see Australia as a harmonious society marked by agreement upon goals and means. There is no mistaking the tone: 'I think they should all grow up and stop their silly squabbling', '[I disapprove of] the backbiting and fuss that goes on in the parties themselves', 'I hate the sense of discord'.

These four themes imply a rejection of the necessity for disagreement, for competition over scarce resources, for conflict — a rejection of politics itself. In the main, those who voiced these opinions also possessed tepid party loyalties (the few who claimed to be 'very strongly' partisan were all Labor voters) and had either a slight interest in politics or none at all. Moreover, they tended to think of themselves as middle-class rather than working-class. It is perhaps too early to offer a theory to account for the frequency of such sentiments, but any such theory would include in its explanation the homogeneity and affluence of Australian society, its historic freedom from civil disturbance, and the relative lack of extremes of rich and poor: these circumstances have helped to produce an outlook on the world in which conflict is otiose and government is essentially the administration of the nation along understood lines towards widely shared goals. In this context politics is a wordy and windy irrelevance, and objectionable when it divides people. Again, there need be nothing uniquely Australian about this point of view, which can be encountered readily enough in other polities. Yet Australian conditions may have been especially favourable to its germination and spread.

In a society where there is a cool matter-of-fact acceptance of the political order, plus a widespread lack of interest in politics, what is to safeguard the people against tyranny? The answer, according to our respondents, is elections — a conventional answer indeed. In 1967 interviewers asked one question that sought to explore that linkage in the democratic structure: 'How much do you think that having elections makes the government pay attention to what the people think? Would you say a good deal, some, or not much at all?' And then, for those who had some opinion, 'Why is that?' The respondents' answers demonstrated a widespread belief that elections were important. Nearly one half of the whole sample thought that elections made the government pay a good deal of attention to what the people thought, and another quarter were less positive. Those who thought that there was little popular influence on governments through elections were altogether in a minority.[19]

R.W. Connell has argued cogently that knowledge of voting in elections is one of the few aspects of politics that Australian children acquire (mainly through participation in class elections and group decisions) at school:

> The children learn early and learn well how decisions and appointments may be made by voting...some of them develop general criteria for casting a vote. The reason they learn this well is of course that voting is a form of action which the children themselves participate in. Learning takes place through actual experience.[20]

The likelihood that such early learning internalises a belief in the importance of the ballot is supported not only by survey data but also by the very small numbers of deliberately spoiled votes cast in general elections (usually much less than 1 per cent). Voters may not always be voting for instrumental reasons when they enter the polling booth, but

---

19 It is worth nothing that in this matter also the Australian polity is much like the British, as the following comparison suggests (British data from Butler and Stokes, *Political Change in Britain*, p. 32):

Effect of elections on government

	Good deal %	Some %	Not much %	Don't know %
Australia (1967)	49	25	19	7
Great Britain (1963)	46	26	9	19

One might have expected that the much greater frequency of elections in Australia would have enhanced (or perhaps devalued!) their role in the democratic process. The similarity of these figures suggests, however, that what is important is the *concept* of the election, and that its importance is widely perceived in both polities.

20 R.W. Connell, 'Propaganda and Education: Political Training in the Schools', *Australian Journal of Education*, **14**(2), June 1970, p. 162.

they unquestionably believe that voting in elections is important enough to warrant casting a valid vote. Something of the perceived importance of the vote comes through in this almost anguished comment of a forty-year-old receptionist in Brisbane: 'I did the wrong thing once and it was informal; there was only one informal vote at Indooroopilly — and I knew it was mine. I'd been sick and I didn't remember.' And a common (if muddled) criticism of Mr Gorton in 1969 was a reference to the circumstances of his selection as leader of the Liberal Party in January 1968 — he had not had to face the people at elections first.

The great majority of respondents could support their opinions about the value of elections with reason and argument, and the models of the political system summed up in these reasons put beyond doubt that the Australian electorate has a firm sense of the role elections play and should play. Chief among them was the competitive model: it is the stimulus of elections and the presence of an alternative in the opposition that force governments to heed the wishes of the people. Many respondents produced concise formulations of the role of the election in the fashion of a civics textbook, like the Tasmanian skinclasser whom we have already encountered, who commented, 'Well, the elections are the voice of the people, aren't they? And what the people want they must get, or they [the politicians] don't get elected next time.' Of comparable popularity was a more sophisticated model in which the election served as an exchange point in a two-way flow of information: through election results the government could learn what the people wanted, while the campaign itself informed the people about rival policies, parties, leaders and candidates. Even those who discounted the value of elections recognised their role by inference: a typical model portrayed governments taking notice of the people only for the duration of the campaign, and then relapsing into an accustomed indifference or arrogance for the next three years. The actual function of elections is not in issue here: that is a matter discussed in a later chapter. What is important is the widespread sense that elections are crucial institutions in a democratic society — that without them, as more than one respondent asserted, we would have a dictatorship.

The Puzzle of Compulsory Voting

The notion that elections are fundamental to the polity carries with it the logical corollary that citizens ought to vote in them. Indeed, since turnout levels in most democracies greatly exceed the proportions reporting interest in politics it is very likely that the feeling a citizen ought to vote is responsible for bringing to the polls a large minority of the electorate who might not otherwise have bothered. In Australia compulsory voting is responsible for bringing most of the remainder — those whose belief that they ought to vote is offset by competing activities, faulty memory or simple inanition, those who do not share the belief at all, and those who do not like the choices offered them. But it is especially significant that compulsory voting is in no sense seen as an imposition on the electorate and resented by it.[21] On the contrary, public opinion polls have charted an impressive degree of support for the measure (Table 2.4).

These figures record attitudes toward compulsory voting at parliamentary elections; two further APOP questions in 1959 and 1965 found that support for compulsory voting in local government elections was lower, but still well above 50 per cent.

Respondents in the 1967 and 1969 surveys reported opinions that were well in keeping with the pattern discovered by Australian Public Opinion Polls. Asked in 1967 'Do you think that compulsory voting should be retained, or do you think that people should only have to vote at federal and state elections if they want to?', 74 per cent supported compulsory voting, 24 per cent opposed it, and 2 per cent had no opinion. In 1969 the distribution was 76 per cent, 23 per cent, and 1 per cent respectively, demonstrating in the context of the APOP findings an impressive solidity of opinion; 70 per cent of those interviewed both in 1967 and in 1969 gave the same answer on both occasions. And hardly anyone mentioned compulsory voting in 1969 as an aspect of government and politics in Australia that he disapproved of.

Interviewers also asked how strongly the respondents felt about the issue; by combining their answers to the two questions we can obtain a better understanding of the nature of attitudes to compulsory voting. The result is displayed in Table 2.5.

The intensity of feeling professed by those interviewed is remarkable. More than half claimed to feel very strongly about compulsory voting, and indeed only one in eight held their attitudes to be mild ones. Moreover, the proportion feeling very strongly about the matter was manifestly a good deal larger among those who supported compulsory voting than among those who opposed it. Nor was there much variation within the community

Table 2.4 Attitudes to compulsory voting

	1943 %	1955 %	1964 %	1965 %
Approve	60	71	73	67
Oppose	35	24	25	31
Undecided	5	5	2	2
Total	100	100	100	100

Source: APOP, questions 156, 1139, 1719, 1849.

21 Although it is fair to say that in federal politics compulsory voting was introduced by common agreement among the political parties as a means of reducing their campaign expenditures. See Colin A. Hughes, 'Compulsory Voting', *Politics*, 1, 1966, reprinted in his (ed.), *Readings in Australian Government*, Brisbane, 1968; Neil Gow, 'The Introduction of Compulsory Voting in the Australian Commonwealth', *Politics*, 6(2), November 1971.

in the extent to which compulsory voting was supported. Religion, education, class, age, residence, ethnic origin — none of these usually important sociological variables greatly affected the pattern of opinion. Compulsory voting was supported in much the same fashion by adherents of all parties. Those who supported it least were those with no interest in politics at all. And yet, as Table 2.5 shows, more than half of them were still in favour of it.

From the point of view of a civil libertarian, compulsory voting could seem a monstrous impertinence on the part of the state against the individual; one respondent, a British migrant, called it 'another form of dictatorship'. It is precisely the kind of authoritarian relationship that the Australian of myth and legend might be expected to jib at.[22] Yet the reality is quite otherwise. What accounts for it? A plausible explanation is that the great majority of Australians subscribe to the belief not only that they ought to vote, and that in general all citizens ought to vote, but that unless all citizens do in fact turn out and vote the framework of their democratic society will be in some danger. Many respondents gave reasons for their opinions (they were not asked to do so) and of these the great majority followed the line that without compulsory voting 'only a very small percentage would vote'. Some even welcomed a rod for their own backs, like the Brisbane manager's wife who remarked that 'if everyone was apathetic as me no-one would vote at all unless they had to'. But why *that* would be a bad thing she did not say; nor did those who feared simply that voluntary voting would lead to a small turnout. The explanation may be quite a simple one, and the corollary to the belief that all citizens should vote: that if all citizens *do* vote their democracy is not in any danger, and they may be excused any further attention to politics for the moment. Creighton Burns observed of his La Trobe respondents that while few of them thought that much depended on the outcome of an election there was at the same time an attempt to keep up the pretence that it meant something.

Table 2.5 Direction and strength of attitudes to compulsory voting, 1967

	In favour and feel			Opposed and feel		
	Very strongly %	Fairly strongly %	Not very strongly %	Not very strongly %	Fairly strongly %	Very strongly %
Those with no interest in politics	21	23	10	12	17	18
Whole sample	42	27	7	5	10	9

22 It can be argued on the other hand that the right to vote is a privilege to which conditions (such as the duty to vote whenever there is an election) may be attached, a proposition advanced by Hughes, 'Compulsory Voting', p. 228. But see W. Morris Jones, 'In Defence of Apathy: Some Doubts on the Duty to Vote', *Political Studies*, 2(1), 1954.

[They] still felt that something was required of them. They were required to vote; people were interested in their choice and their opinions. So they voted and talked as though it were a matter of some importance, even when they no longer expected anything to come of their activities. There was a ritualistic quality to their political behaviour; voting was a democratic rite.[23]

Compulsory voting is the rite sanctified and made universal.

The Character of the Demos

Even without compulsory voting it is likely that seven voters in ten would vote in federal and state elections.[24] But the proportion of those politically active is much lower, as we have seen. What kinds of people are they?

The answers are those that might be predicted from a study of the findings about political participation in other countries. High levels of interest in politics are associated with high levels of education and income, low levels of interest in politics with low levels of education and income; other things being equal, men are notably more interested in politics than women.[25] Some 55 per cent of the sample claimed at least 'some' interest in politics, but that proportion was only 36 per cent among women of low education (incomplete high school education or less) who had low household incomes. Among respondents with high education and high incomes the proportion having some interest in politics rose to 76 per cent, and among those who were readers of magazines as well, to 84 per cent.

High education and high income are often thought of as the principal identifying characteristics of the middle class. Magazine readership serves as a measure of information input, or perhaps of a readiness to seek information: the almost complete universality of newspapers, television and radio makes them useless as predictors, but only one-half of the sample subscribed to magazines or periodicals, or claimed to read them often.[26] That half, as might be expected, was disproportionately middle-

---

23 Creighton Burns, *Parties and People. A Survey Based on the La Trobe Electorate,* Melbourne, 1961, p. 137.

24 A 1955 APOP survey found that 77 per cent of those interviewed would vote even if it were not compulsory to do so. Hughes ('Compulsory Voting', p. 234) produced virtually the same figure from a Brisbane sample in 1963. In the four elections from 1913 to 1919, a few years before the introduction of compulsory voting in 1925, the average turnout was 74 per cent, a level comparable with that in Britain. There seems no reason, given the similarity of the British and Australian electorates on other indices of participation, to expect them to differ much on turnout in national elections.

25 An AID analysis, with 'interest in politics' as the dependent variable, was used to estimate the relative importance of various structural and psychological variables. The technique is used again in Chapter 7 and discussed in some detail there. See John A. Sonquist and James N. Morgan, *The Detection of Interaction Effects,* Ann Arbor, 1970. The program embodying the technique was made available by the Inter-University Consortium for Political Research.

26 *The Australian Women's Weekly* was the most frequently cited magazine, followed by *The Reader's Digest.* As proportions of the total the principal groups were women's magazines: 32 per cent; *The Reader's Digest:* 15 per cent; news magazines (*Time, Newsweek, Bulletin,* etc.): 12 per cent; news pictorial magazines (*Pix, Post,* etc.,) 7 per cent.

class.

As this discussion has implied, sex differences in interest in politics are pronounced among those with a poor educational background; or, putting it another way, high levels of education tend to minimise the differences between the sexes. Close inspection of the data suggests that a university education is especially important. Even then, however, there is an appreciable gap between the interest men and women take in politics. At every level, indeed, the data support the universal findings that men are more interested;[27] in the sample as a whole men were almost twice as likely to talk politics as women (40 per cent to 21 per cent) and much more likely to read about politics in the newspapers (51 per cent to 34 per cent), as well as to have some interest in politics (64 per cent to 46 per cent — a disparity of the same order, be it noted, as that between well and poorly educated).

In brief, class and sex are the principal shaping influences of one's interest in politics, and we do not have to search far for plausible explanations. For most of our female respondents, to have been born a girl was to be guaranteed a cultural conditioning that not even a middle-class family background and university education could entirely overcome, one in which politics was seen as 'man's business'. In maturity most of them were housewives, dependent on their husbands for much of their news about the world of social action. When asked whom they talked politics with, only 12 per cent of men nominated their wives and families; for women the corresponding proportion was 40 per cent.[28] Similarly, a working-class background has commonly been associated with a relatively short period of formal education, less surplus income to spend on newspapers and books — and less skill in using them, less confidence about personal efficacy in public affairs, and perhaps a narrower range of personal contacts. With these handicaps, a working-class voter is less likely to take an interest in politics than is one from the middle class,[29]

27 Milbrath (*Political Participation,* p. 135) calls this 'one of the most thoroughly substantiated [findings] in social science'. In the present data the only measure on which women head men is that of acceptance of identification with one political party rather than another (women 88 per cent; men 86 per cent), and here the male score is reduced because immigrants are less likely to accept a party label than the native-born — and immigrants are disproportionately male.

28 Cut off as they are from other sources of information and opinion, it is hardly surprising that many women follow their husbands in politics. A sixty-five year-old Newcastle housewife can stand for very many women in the sample, both in her account of her political involvement and in the apologetic way in which it was offered: 'I don't take much interest in politics; I mostly vote as my husband does. It is the wrong way to be, but it's a bit late to alter now. I don't think women take enough interest in politics.' The rapid growth of open-line radio programs, whose audiences are disproportionately female, suggests that isolation in the home is one of the chief causes of the greater apparent lack of political interest among women. See Don Aitkin and Ann Norrie, 'Talk-back Radio and Political Participation', *Australian Quarterly,* 45(2), June 1973.

29 Carole Pateman argues further that working-class voters are less interested because in their experience the workplace and political systems are not responsive to their desires, whereas this is less true of middle-class voters ('Political Culture, Political Structure and Political Change', *British Journal of Political Science,* 1(3), July 1971). This is a credible hypothesis, and most capably argued. But there is little support for it here. Working-class respondents

most especially where the working-class voter is a woman.

Yet sex, education and class do not by any means *determine* one's interest in politics. Nearly one in five poorly educated women talked politics with other people, and one in three followed news about politics in the press. Even among poorly educated working-class women nearly one in four followed politics in the press. To find the origins of interest in politics it is necessary to look into the childhood socialisation of voters, and at their first experiences of work and adult life. Here can be found events and circumstances that enable an awareness of politics to triumph over social handicaps or, conversely, that prevent such an awareness ever developing very far, no matter how nurturing the environment.[30]

It is clear that the middle-class nature of the *demos* has important consequences for the style and conventions of political life. And its small size poses something of a paradox, for although only one voter in four can be described as politically active, nine voters in ten accept that they have a preference for one party rather than for another. We shall see, moreover, that they generally follow this preference in voting. To resolve the paradox involves the extension of an earlier argument about the acceptance of the democratic myth. For the politically active an interest in politics is typically accompanied by a strong partisanship for one party rather than another: their greater information is a background for their preference, not a consequence of it. But partisanship, usually of a less passionate intensity, is also widespread among the politically uninterested, and for them it is the essential prerequisite for voting. Their preference for one party makes the act of voting meaningful as well as dutiful. For the great majority of voters, in fact, voting and party preference are twin: the one requires and expresses the other. It is to party preference, and its nature, that we now turn.

were not significantly less likely than their middle-class counterparts to give approving answers to questions about the political order, and they were equally satisfied about the state of government and politics in Australia. Their relative lack of interest in politics must therefore be attributed mainly to their poorer information and skills.

30 Of the interviews I conducted myself the most vividly remembered is that with the wife of a station-hand on a large grazing property 20 miles from Yass (NSW). A woman in her late thirties, of incomplete secondary education, and cut off from urban society since her marriage seventeen years before, she was nevertheless articulate, percipient and interested in politics, with a stock of opinions and judgments that would have done credit to anyone. She was clear about the origin of her interest in politics: a school class about parties and voting when she was eleven years old. The question of parental influence and example is discussed in more detail in Chapter 6.

3 Party Identification

Goodness, woman. I didn't know there were all these parties! I've never heard of some. (*widow, seventy-five, NSW country town*)

The notion that most voters possess a basic sympathy for one party rather than for another grew out of every-day experience and the discovery that the party shares of the vote at elections remained remarkably constant over a long period of time. It was of course possible to argue that voters made their decisions *de novo* at each election. There could be a great deal of movement in electoral politics, with voters changing their minds because of new candidates or new issues, or as a result of changes in life-style, or through sheer capriciousness: the similarity of one election result to another might be accidental. But the close inspection of election results suggested that most voters were likely to vote for the same party from one election to another. Even when issues were dramatically altered, or a famous local politician was replaced by a tyro, or economic disaster was visited upon a district, the pattern of party voting was very likely to stay the same. That such stability concealed a wholesale swapping of party preferences within an electorate was clearly unlikely; for most people, most of the time, party voting appeared to be a form of habitual behaviour.

Early surveys of political behaviour found ample evidence to support this proposition. Moreover, when asked by interviewers they were quite happy to label themselves as partisans of one party or another — 'Republicans', 'Democrats', 'Conservatives', 'Liberals'. Campbell and his colleagues, borrowing from reference group theory, termed this kind of psychological attachment 'party identification', and they demonstrated that it could persist 'without legal recognition or evidence of formal membership and even without a consistent record of party support'.[1] In

1 *The American Voter*, New York, 1960, p. 121. The concept was first introduced in George Belknap and Angus Campbell, 'Political Party Identification and Attitudes toward Foreign Policy', *Public Opinion Quarterly*, 15(4) Winter 1951-2, and its sub-

their model of the making of a decision to vote, party identification and its strength occupied a central place. Party identification became the basic determinant of vote, and was itself determined by the varying influences of upbringing, situation, education and life experience. A strongly held identification was very likely to result in a consistent pattern of support for the one party; a weakly held identification was less predictable. But identification was shown to be a great deal more stable than vote: a voter could cross party lines on polling day without feeling impelled to readjust his partisan loyalties, but if he did alter his view of the parties his vote would move in sympathy. It was party identification and the nature of its development and transmission that were responsible for the stability of the party system; victories and defeats — the immediate results of elections — were to be explained largely, though not entirely, in terms of contemporary forces acting on party identification.

The concept of party identification has proved a most powerful instrument for the analysis both of individual electoral behaviour and of the persistence of modern party systems. Its application outside the United States has suggested that in polities structured on the Westminster model, where voters are not offered a direct voice in the choice of the nation's chief executive, the correspondence of vote and identification is much closer than in the United States. Even a strong Democrat could vote for General Eisenhower in 1952 in good conscience; for a British Conservative in 1964 to vote for the Labour candidate in his constituency represented an act needing much more justification to the self, and could well herald a corresponding shift of his partisan self-image.[2] It might be expected, for want of evidence to the contrary, that party identification would be found to underlie much of Australian electoral behaviour; but the peculiarities of Australian politics — the number of parties, the federal system, and a large immigrant component in the population — make it clear that hypotheses from other polities must be tested afresh in Australia.

sequent discussion in the early Survey Research Center studies (A. Campbell, G. Gurin and W.E. Miller, *The Voter Decides*, Evanston, 1954; A. Campbell and H.C. Cooper, *Group Differences in Attitudes and Votes: a Study of the 1954 Congressional Election*, Ann Arbor, 1956) added little to its theoretical underpinning. The analysis of panel data reported in *The American Voter* demonstrated the stability of party identification over time and provided the evidence for the hypothesis that party identification was both logically antecedent to and more powerful than party choice in an election situation. It remains true, however, that the concept lacks close theoretical discussion, and, as Prewitt and Nie point out in their excellent critique of the SRC's electoral studies, it is a 'psychological attribute, uncomfortably close to the actual behaviour it is used to explain' (Kenneth Prewitt and Norman Nie, 'Review Article: Election Studies of the Survey Research Center', *British Journal of Political Science*, 1, 1971, p. 486). I use the term to mean no more than 'party attachment', and use it interchangeably with that term and others like it — 'partisan self-image', 'party loyalty', 'partisan stance', and so on. See also Ivor Crewe, 'Do Butler and Stokes Really Explain Political Change in Britain?', *European Journal of Political Research*, 2(1), 1974.

2 Butler and Stokes, *Political Change in Britain*, pp. 40-43.

The Extent of Identification

In exploring the partisan loyalties of the respondents the interviewers followed a pattern formed in the early Michigan studies. They asked 'Generally speaking, do you usually think of yourself as Liberal, Labor, Country Party or DLP?' Those who gave a positive answer were then asked whether their preference applied to federal politics, or state politics, or both. If they admitted to different preferences, another question asked for the reasons. A further set of questions sought to discover how strongly the respondents held their preferences, whether they had previously preferred a different party, and when and why they had changed. Those who had not offered a party label in answer to the first question were asked a series of questions to see if they had ever felt 'closer' to one party than another.[3]

Some seven voters in eight — 87 per cent — immediately agreed that they usually thought of themselves as partisans of one party rather than another. Eleven per cent said they did not, and the remainder either refused to say (0.7 per cent) or said they were not sure. These proportions are comparable to those obtained in other countries, and may be taken as characteristic of democracies in the Anglo-American tradition. The further questioning of those who did not at first describe themselves in party terms found that more than half of them either felt closer to one party than to others, or had felt this way in the past. If these admittedly half-hearted partisans are added to the others, party identification rises to 95 per cent of the sample, and the 'independents' fall to 5 per cent. On this basis the distribution of party identification among the sample was as follows: Liberal 45 per cent, Labor 40 per cent, Country Party 7 per cent, Democratic Labor 3 per cent, and no party identification 5 per cent. In addition seven respondents professed loyalties outside the four main parties: three self-styled independents, two Communists, a 'Republican', and a supporter of Liberal Reform — a group that was later to rename itself the Australia Party.

There are, of course, no independent or objective measures of party identification to compare these figures with. They are broadly in keeping with the pattern of party support in federal elections in the 1960s, although the sharp-eyed will notice that the level of identification for the minor parties is lower than their share of the vote, in the case of the DLP significantly so. This is a discrepancy that is discussed in Chapters 10 and 11.

Identification and Vote

Our next concern must be to establish the relationship between identification and vote. We should not expect a one-to-one correspondence, even if the two were virtually synonymous, because a voter's range of

---

3 Questions 35(a) to 35(j) in the 1967 questionnaire, and questions 37(a) to 37(i) in the 1969 questionnaire.

choice in any election is determined by the prior decision of the parties as to whether or not to present a candidate in his constituency. In the federal elections of 1969, for example, Liberal identifiers in twenty seats and DLP identifiers in sixteen were not provided with party candidates of their persuasion; given compulsory voting — and the widespread acceptance of the obligation to vote — such voters had the choice of voting for another party or of spoiling their ballots. In fact, scrutineers' accounts suggest that ballot spoiling is rare,[4] and that it has more than one cause; voting for the next-most-preferred party (a concept we shall discuss in a later chapter) is therefore the common way out.

With this proviso in mind, let us consider the disparities between the respondents' party identification as reported in 1967 and their account of their vote at the federal election in November 1966. To simplify discussion we shall restrict analysis to those who claimed to have either an attachment to one of the four major parties or no attachment at all. The data are set out in Table 3.1. In 1966 the non-Labor parties scored their greatest victory in the seventeen years since the coalition had come to power, and reduced the ALP to only 40 per cent of the popular vote, its lowest share since 1931. It was widely believed that one cause of Labor's poor showing was the party's campaign against Australia's involvement in the war in Vietnam, despite some support for that involvement among Labor voters and even among many active Labor supporters.[5] If this

Table 3.1   Party identification and vote, 1966

| 1966 Vote | Party Identification | | | | |
| | Liberal | Country Party | DLP | Labor | None |
	%	%	%	%	%
Liberal	96	24	15	8	51
Country Party	1	70	0	*	3
DLP	*	0	78	*	4
Labor	1	4	7	89	24
Other	0	1	0	1	2
Didn't vote/ Didn't remember	2	1	0	2	16
Total	100	100	100	100	100
(N)	(759)	(133)	(46)	(723)	(180)

Note: Party identification obtained in 1967; 1966 vote recalled in 1967.

* = less than 0.5 per cent

4 Informal voting, as we have noted, rarely exceeds 2 per cent, and manifest ballot spoiling presents only a tiny fraction of this. But it does exist. Along with contemptuous, obscene and acerbic epithets which scrutineers remember best are other more gentle indications of dissatisfaction. One of the respondents, a thirty-seven year-old stenographer in Sydney, confided to her interviewer, 'If I vote at all I vote Liberal. If I am displeased with both I just draw a little man. You can't be forced to *vote*.'

5 Useful summaries of the flow of Australian politics can be found in the regular 'Political Reviews' and 'Political Chronologies' of the *Australian Quarterly* and the *Australian Journal of Politics and History* respectively. For the impact of the war in Vietnam on Australian political attitudes see below, Chapter 14.

assessment had some substance to it we should expect the data to reveal a drift among Labor identifiers to the Liberal and Country Parties. Our expectation is borne out: some 8 per cent of Labor identifiers had voted for the Liberal Party. Since only 1 per cent of Liberal identifiers had voted Labor, and the parties' forces were of much the same size, the Liberal Party had much the better of the transfer.

Of the identifiers with the four parties, considered as a group, 90 per cent followed their attachment in their vote in 1966. Three years later that proportion was rather less — 81 per cent — and now the Labor Party was picking up votes from identifiers with other parties;[6] Table 3.2 provides the evidence.

Table 3.2   Party identification and vote, 1969

| 1969 Vote | Party Identification | | | | |
| | Liberal | Country Party | DLP | Labor | None |
	%	%	%	%	%
Liberal	76	13	19	5	28
Country Party	8	70	2	1	6
DLP	3	5	69	2	5
Labor	7	8	7	89	44
Other	3	1	2	2	4
Didn't vote/ Don't remember	3	3	2	1	13
Total	100	100	100	100	100
(N)	(738)	(127)	(58)	(788)	(107)

Note: Party identification and vote obtained in 1969.

Table 3.3   The relative stability of identification and vote, 1966/7 to 1969

| Party Identification 1967 to 1969 | Party Vote 1966 to 1969 | | |
	Same %	Changed %	Total %
Same	77	10	87
Changed	4	9	13
Total	81	19	100 (N = 1150)

Note: For the purposes of this table, and because the two parties were in coalition between 1966 and 1969, the Liberal and Country Parties have been treated as one party. Analysis is restricted to Liberal + Country Party, Labor and DLP identifiers.

6 If we allow Country Party voters to vote for the Liberal Party and Liberals to vote for the Country Party without regarding them as having departed from party loyalty (a justifiable decision given the fact of the coalition and the absence of the appropriate party candidate in many seats), this proportion rises to 93 per cent in 1966 and 86 per cent in 1969.

If nine out of ten voters have persistent party loyalties, and nine out of ten of them vote according to their loyalties, we have an immediate explanation for the stability of the party system itself. The problem then is to discover why these loyalties are so firmly based, and under what conditions they can be maintained while the vote changes.

The analysis so far has shown that party identification and party voting in elections are highly correlated but that a voter can identify with a party while voting for one of its opponents. But which is the more stable? The answer involves a comparison of the two variables over a period of time, and this is done in Table 3.3. Those who declared a party loyalty in 1967 are divided according to whether their party identification remained constant between 1967 and 1969, and again by whether the party they voted for in 1969 was the party they had voted for three years previously. The message of the table is one of great stability, both in identification and party choice for parliament: more than three-quarters remained steady. Thirteen per cent changed their identification, and in this group more than two-thirds changed their vote too. Yet the notable finding is that associated with those who changed either identification or vote but kept the other constant. Of these two-and-a-half times as many changed their vote but not their identification as changed their identification but not their vote. Party identification, it is clear, is the more stable disposition, and its vital role in maintaining the stability of the party system is strongly emphasised.

These Australian results bear an astonishing resemblance to similar findings for American and British samples, and the resemblance is

Figure 3.1 The relative stability of identification and vote over time: a cross-national comparison. The American data (1956-8-60) and the British data (1963-4-6) are drawn from Butler and Stokes, *Political Change in Britain*, pp. 41-2.

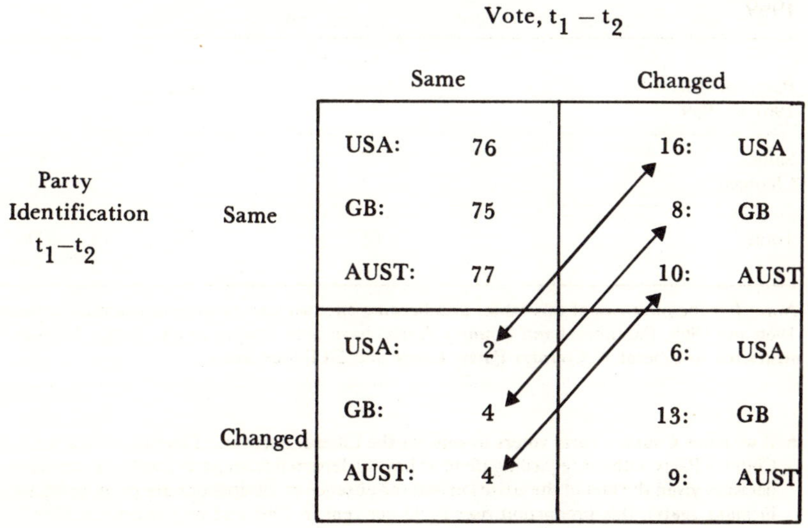

Vote, $t_1 - t_2$

powerful evidence to support a thesis that party identification is the cornerstone of Anglo-American party systems. The data are set out in Figure 3.1. In each case identification is more stable than vote, and in degree Australia lies between the two other polities. The greater relative stability of identification in the United States no doubt flows from the potential for vote-change induced by the election of President, while the slightly greater instability of identification in Australia than in Great Britain may reflect the added complication brought about by a federal system. It is likely, other things being equal, that the more electoral choices a voter is called upon to make, the more efficient a general political perspective is for him.[7]

Like any other psychological variable, identification is not something constant from one person to another, or indeed constant for one person over time. At any time some voters are passionate supporters of their party, some quite unenthusiastic; others wax and wane. *A priori* we would expect strength of identification to affect the likelihood of a party identifier supporting his party at election time. Table 3.4 displays the evidence. The small numbers of Country Party identifiers make it necessary again to combine them with Liberals and to treat the two parties as one for the purpose of voting; the DLP identifiers are too few to be subdivided by strength. Table 3.4 makes plain that the strength of attachment is a vital component of party identification. In 1966 the pressures to deviate from their party loyalty were much more intense upon Labor identifiers and, as strength of identification declined, more of them crossed party lines. The very strong Labor partisans kept their ranks close, and only 3 per cent voted for the government; but that proportion rose to 9 per cent among those who said their attachment was 'fairly strong', to 14 per cent among the 'not very strong' Labor identifiers, and to 27 per cent

Table 3.4   Strength and direction of identification, and 1966 vote

| | Party Identification | | | | | | | | |
| | Lib.-CP Identifiers | | | | None | Labor Identifiers | | | |
Direction of Vote, 1966	Very strong %	Fairly strong %	Not very strong %	Closer to %	%	Closer to %	Not very strong %	Fairly strong %	Very strong %
Lib.-CP	99	97	94	90	48	27	14	9	3
Labor	1	2	4	4	25	58	82	88	97
Other	0	1	1	4	6	3	2	1	*
Uncertain	0	*	1	2	21	12	1	1	0
Total	100	100	100	100	100	100	100	100	100
(N)	(260)	(418)	(200)	(50)	(110)	(270)	(276)	(153)	(33)

* = less than 0.5 per cent

7 There is a close discussion of the British and American findings in Butler and Stokes, *Political Change in Britain*, pp. 42-3.

— more than a quarter — of those who admitted only that they felt closer to the Labor Party than to any other. In fact in this latter category almost half as many had voted for the government parties as had voted for the Labor Party itself.

In short, defections are most common among those with a weakly held identification. Those whose attachments are strong are quite unlikely to deviate from their chosen party. What is more, the strong identifiers are much less likely to have doubts about how they should cast their vote. The respondents were asked how they would vote in a hypothetical federal election held 'tomorrow', that is September/October 1967, a time of relative electoral quiet (a Senate election campaign began at the end of the interviewing period). Table 3.5 presents their answers, using the format of the previous table.

By October 1967 the Holt government had lost some of the support it had enjoyed at the elections a year before, a result of its own actions as much as anything; and at the Senate elections at the end of the year the Labor Party appeared to have recovered some ground.[8] Figure 3.1 shows, as might be expected, that among Liberal-Country Party identifiers the propensity to vote Labor was largest among those with the weakest attachment. But it is the incidence of uncertainty that is the more striking. To be unsure of how one would vote may be, of course, a perfectly rational response, especially when party politics is quiet and one has no underlying party sympathy. Here it is abundantly clear that as the strength of party identification declines, the degree of uncertainty rises. Indeed, if the sample is considered as a whole, nearly 40 per cent of those who did not know how they would vote were those without any party identification, while those with the very weakest attachment made up another 11 per

Table 3.5 Strength and direction of identification, and 1967 vote

				Party Identification				
	Lib.-CP Identifiers			None		Labor Identifiers		
Direction of	Very	Fairly	Not very	Closer		Closer	Not very	Fairly	Very
Vote, 1967	strong	strong	strong	to		to	strong	strong	strong
Lib.-CP	95	92	75	72	20	14	11	4	1
Labor	2	3	13	10	30	61	80	91	97
Other	0	*	2	0	4	3	0	1	0
Uncertain	3	5	9	17	46	22	9	4	1
Total	100	100	100	100	100	100	100	100	100
(N)	(274)	(448)	(218)	(58)	(129)	(36)	(162)	(294)	(289)

* = less than 0.5 per cent

8 Because of the different electoral systems which apply in elections for the Senate and for the House of Representatives, Senate election results should be used with great caution as indicators of the mood of the electorate; they should never be used along with House results to establish points on a trend line.

cent; in short, one-half of the uncertain came from one-seventh of the sample. For the great majority of the remainder party identification provided a basis for appropriate action whenever an election was held.

A three-year period is a short span on which to base generalisations about the stability of identification or vote. But there are two other pieces of evidence to bring forward. The first is that the stronger the identification, the less likely the voter is to have altered it in the past: only one in eight of those who claimed a very strong identification said that they had ever preferred another party, while this was true of nearer one in four of those with weaker loyalties. The second is that strength of party identification is powerfully related to stability of voting (Table 3.6).

As strength of identification rises, so does the stability of party voting. Habitual voting can, of course, occur even when there exists no particular feeling towards the party supported. But where there *is* strong feeling the habit is much more common. Moreover, since some 30 per cent of the electorate can be credited with very strong attachments, and another 40 per cent with at least fairly strong attachments, the contribution of party identification to the stability of the party system is once again forcefully demonstrated: most voters have strong psychological ties to given political parties; these ties ensure that their votes will customarily be given to the candidates of their chosen parties; therefore the parties' shares of the vote do not change a great deal from one election to another.

Identification in a Federal Setting

Throughout this discussion we have been treating 'vote' as a single concept, as though Australia were a unitary state. But most Australians can cast votes at three separate levels of politics: for the national parliament at Canberra, for the state parliament in Sydney, Melbourne or one of the other state capitals, and for local government bodies — city, municipal or shire councils. Local government in Australia is altogether subordinate and will not be discussed here.[9] It is important, however, to consider the

Table 3.6   Stability of vote, by strength of identification, 1967

| | Strength of Identification | | | | |
	Very strong	Fairly strong	Not very strong	Closer to	None
Always voted for same party	84	73	66	41	36
Voted for different parties	16	27	34	59	64
Total	100	100	100	100	100
(N)	(562)	(738)	(372)	(115)	(50)

9 Local government in Australia was a relatively late creation of central government, and

extent to which voters treat the federal and state levels of politics as separate, or as part of one general political plane for which a single party identification is equally relevant. We start with two arguments whose tendencies are opposite. The first is that each state political system is recognisably part of the one family. In the late 1960s the four major parties functioned in each state; all states save Queensland have bicameral legislatures and all save Tasmania have preferential voting in single-member seats; in each state the parties secure much the same proportions of the vote in federal as in state elections; the transfer of state politicians to federal politics is not uncommon; in each party the state machines control endorsement of candidates for federal elections and the bulk of campaign finance. The grounds exist, then, for regarding federal and state politics as different arenas in which the same game is played, and the same spectators point their thumbs up or down.

But, second, it is not difficult to show that in given electorates the party shares of the vote can differ appreciably from state to federal election, and can maintain such a difference over time. Moreover, parliamentarians, party workers, journalists and academics have all at one time or another expatiated on federal/state *differences* in political behaviour and political issues: the different images of the federal ALP and a state Labor Party, the irrelevance of communism as an issue in state politics, but its importance at the federal level, the different calibre and vote-getting quality of federal and state politicians, the great importance of the personal following in state politics and the impersonality of federal politics, and so on. All these accounts and arguments imply that voters do or at least can vote differently at federal and state elections, and that they can have sensible and *persistent* political reasons for doing so.[10]

There are thus two questions to answer: what is the nature of federal/state voting patterns, and how are they related to party identification? The first question is answered in part by Table 3.7, which displays a summary of the party voting of the 1967 respondents both in the federal election of November 1966 and in the most recent state election at the time of interview (which was, for each state — Tasmania, 1964; New South Wales, South Australia and Western Australia, 1965; Queensland, 1966; and Victoria, 1967).[11] By summing the entries along

derives its powers from state legislation. Of the state capitals only Brisbane has a municipal arena large enough to attract thoroughgoing inter-party contests for power. Party politics in local government is generally subdued, and often formally non-existent.

10 This is to be distinguished from another type of argument, put forward by Joan Rydon, that voters may not be offered the same choice of candidates in the two contests: the DLP was more likely to offer candidates in federal than in state elections, for example, and the district held by a Country Party man in the state house may have a Liberal MP in Canberra. See Joan Rydon, 'The Electoral System' in Mayer, *Australian Politics*.

11 The respondents' report of their vote in 1966 is significantly different from the actual division of party shares of the vote at that election. In part the difference flows from the failure of many respondents to perceive any difference between the Liberal and Country Parties, in part from the amnesia of DLP voters. This apparent bias in the sample is discussed fully in Chapters 10 and 11 below.

the main diagonal we can see that at least 83 per cent of the sample had voted for the same party in the most recent pair of federal and state elections. The coalition's sweeping victory in the federal elections of 1966 unquestionably reduced the incidence of voting for the same party in both arenas: the greater Liberal support at the federal level obtained in each state as well as in Australia generally. Even so, Table 3.7 makes it likely that the overwhelming majority of Australians maintain a constant party preference whatever the nature of the election.[12]

Further evidence to support this hypothesis comes from Table 3.8,

Table 3.7   The pattern of federal and state voting in the mid-1960s

Federal Vote, 1966	State Vote					
	Liberal %	Labor %	CP %	DLP %	Other %	Total %
Liberal	40	4	2	1	3	50
Labor	1	35	*	*	1	38
CP	*	*	6	*	*	6
DLP	*	*	*	2	*	3
Other	*	1	*	*	2	3
Total	42	41	8	3	6	100 (N = 1804)

* = less than 0.5 per cent

Table 3.8   Stability in federal and state voting, 1967

Direction of Vote Federal Elections	Direction of Vote State Elections				
	Always Lib.-CP %	Always Labor %	Always DLP %	Different parties %	Total %
Always Lib.-CP	33	1	*	3	37
Always Labor	*	32	*	1	34
Always DLP	*	0	1	*	1
Different parties	3	4	*	21	28
Total	37	37	1	25	100 (N=1746)

* = less than 0.5 per cent

12 Recall of their vote in the 1967 Senate election was not nearly as sharp for the 1969 respondents as was recall of their vote in the 1966 House of Representatives elections, a discrepancy that has already been noted. Yet of those who remembered how they had voted in both elections, 66 per cent had voted for the same party.

which assembles respondents' answers to two questions about their past pattern of voting behaviour in federal and state elections.[13] We see yet another demonstration of massive stability in Australian party support as well as clear evidence that for most Australians the federal and state political arenas are one, at least to the extent that their own votes are involved. We can summarise Table 3.8 to make the point more clearly: in 1967

66 per cent had always voted for the same party in both federal and state elections.

1 per cent had voted consistently for one party in federal elections and for a different one at state elections.

5 per cent had voted consistently for one party in federal elections and for a number of parties at state elections.

7 per cent had voted consistently for one party in state elections and for a number of parties at federal elections.

21 per cent had voted for different parties in both federal and state elections.

The marginal frequencies in Table 3.8 tell us that Labor had enjoyed more consistent support in state elections than in federal, whereas for the coalition the levels of support were precisely the same.

It remains now for us to relate the discussion of voting stability to what has been learned about the patterns of party identification. We should expect that if few voters maintain different voting habits at the federal and state levels, then even fewer will support two separate party identifications, one for state politics, the other for federal. In fact, only 8 per cent of those who accepted a party label did so, and for most of them, it was clear, it was their federal party attachment that was the more important.[14] Much the most common pattern of double identification was Liberal or Country Party at the federal level and Labor at the state level; the next most frequent was a definite federal identification coupled with an uncertain state one. These two patterns reinforce what we have learned so far: that in the late 1960s Labor's advantage over the non-Labor parties lay in state politics, and that the pull of politics is essentially a national one.

Political Interest and Party Support

The trend of the argument so far has been that the electorate can be divided into groups of partisans according to each voter's underlying sense of belonging to one party rather than another. These attachments are long-lasting, and can persist even when an elector, for reasons peculiar to

13 Questions 43(d) and 43(c) in the 1967 questionnaire.
14 It is worth noting that the great majority of respondents appeared to relate to the federal party of their choice rather than to its state branch. In the free-answer comments made about the major parties obviously federal references outnumbered obviously state references by about 20:1.

a particular election, casts his vote in favour of one of his party's rivals. He is unlikely to do this at all if his attachment to his party is strong and, in fact, some three-quarters of the electorate claim that their attachment is either 'very strong' or 'fairly strong'. Are these degrees of attachment evenly distributed among the parties, or do some parties have more strong partisans than others? The answers to these questions are of considerable practical significance in the world of politics, since the greater a party's retinue of lukewarm supporters the more voters it will have at risk at any election.

The simple distribution of strength of identification within each group of party supporters is given in Figure 3.2, which shows that although the general balance of loyalty is much the same, there are some important differences between the parties. The Labor Party, for example, had a

Figure 3.2   Strength of identification within each party

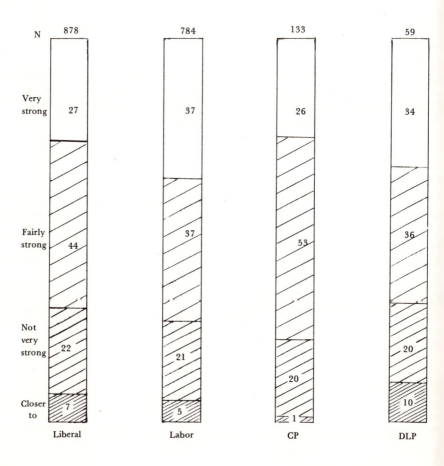

much larger proportion of 'very strong' identifiers than the Liberal Party,[15] and more than half of the Country Party supporters were 'fairly strong' identifiers. The distribution of partisans within the ALP and the DLP bore a close family resemblance. The further division of party supporters by sex (Figure 3.3) sharpens these differences. More than four in ten male Labor identifiers claimed to be very strong supporters of their party, a proportion otherwise approached only among DLP men. In both the ALP and the DLP the proportion of women identifying very strongly was much lower. In the non-Labor parties, by contrast, women were if anything more likely to be very strong identifiers than were men. The picture of the ALP as very much a party ruled by men and the Liberal Party as at least a sympathetic arena for the political activity of women is a familiar one; these party characteristics, it is clear, are echoed in a

Figure 3.3 Strength of identification within each party, by sex
M = male; F = female

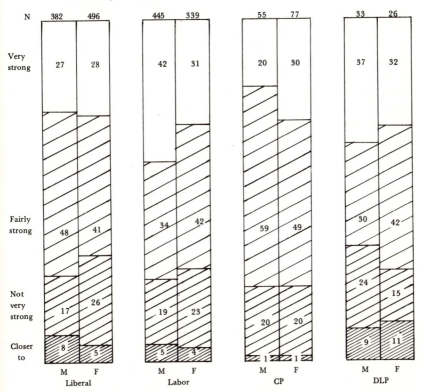

15 A study of Brisbane voters produced a similar finding: the proportion of 'wholehearted' supporters of the ALP was 38 per cent, compared with 26 per cent among Liberals. Paul R. Wilson and J.S. Western, 'Participation in Politics: A Preliminary Analysis', *Australian and New Zealand Journal of Sociology*, 5(2), October 1969, p. 107.

differential appeal of the parties to the sexes.

If we now recall our finding that interest and involvement in politics vary by class and sex it will also be clear that supporters are likely to be rather different from one party to another in terms of their awareness of day-to day politics. Table 3.9 shows, indeed, that at each level of strength of partisanship Liberal identifiers are likely to be more interested in politics than Labor identifiers — and that interest in politics is positively correlated with partisanship. More than one very strong Labor identifier in three admitted to only scant interest in politics; that is to say, one Labor voter in seven is both strongly committed to his party and almost indifferent to the flow of day-to-day politics. The equivalent proportion among Liberals is one in sixteen.

These patterns of attachment are of great moment. A man who has strong ties to his party but otherwise takes no interest in politics is hardly likely to leave the fold and vote for another party; he is, accidents or personal crises apart, unreachable and untouchable. Labor holds nearly two-and-a-half times more supporters of this kind than does the Liberal Party, and their impact is represented in the greater stability of the Labor vote. Eight of ten Labor identifiers have voted always for the Labor Party; among Liberals the corresponding proportion is seven of ten. And in the disasters that have befallen both parties since 1910 it is the Labor Party whose vote has held up best. In their blackest hour, even if they disagree about which faction is entitled to the label, Labor voters stick to their party; Liberals are quicker to desert. The cause, at least in part, is the greater interest in and exposure to politics characteristic of Liberals, who are thus more open to external influence.

Table 3.9   Interest in politics, by strength and direction of identification, 1967

Strength of Identification	Liberal Identifiers %	Labor Identifiers %
Very strong	78	63
Fairly strong	61	50
Not very strong	45	30

Note: Each cell contains the proportion within each category claiming at least some interest in politics.

4 Party Images

> Labor are only using the lower class to establish their image . . . If they
> could gain any benefit from going to the other side they would do so.
> (*pensioner, sixty-seven, Melbourne*)

What is it that people see in the parties that they identify with, and what
picture do they have of their rivals? The great majority of citizens have
little or no direct contact with any party. For them parties exist principally
in the mind, as more or less persistent images incorporating some history,
some policy, some ideology, and some personality, the whole bound
together by the attitudes and emotions of each individual. These images of
party change all the time, as fresh experiences are added to the pile and old
ones fade in importance, but they change slowly. To know why a person's
identification with a party remains so constant, it is necessary to know
something about his stock of party images.

The raw materials of these images come largely from the streams of
political statements, descriptions, comment and interpretation that issue
from newspapers, radio and television, in which political parties and their
leaders play the dominant role, and partly from each person's own
observation and conversation. Each party is concerned to build up a
favourable image of itself and an unfavourable image of its rivals; in
building these images an attempt is made to connect the needs and desires
of electors, the outputs of governments, and the abilities of the parties,
into one coherent, plausible and satisfying whole. The building of images
is thus one of the ongoing (and often unrecognised) functions of party
leaders and managers.[1]

---

1 There is a substantial literature on research into party images. The concept itself is
derived from the 'brand image' of advertising and closely resembles it. See John Downing,
'What is a Brand Image?'. *The Advertising Quarterly*, **2**, Winter 1964-5; Richard Rose,
Influencing Voters: A Study of Campaign Rationality, London, 1967; D.E. Butler and
Richard Rose, *The British General Election of 1959*, London, 1960; Jay G. Blumler and
Denis McQuail, *Television in Politics*, London, 1968. For Australian research, see Colin
A. Hughes and John S. Western, *The Prime Minister's Policy Speech: a Case Study in
Televised Politics*, Canberra, 1966; and Colin A. Hughes, *Images and Issues: the
Queensland State Elections of 1963 and 1966*, Canberra, 1969.

The image-builders operate under one crucial constraint, whose effect was caught in a striking metaphor by Graham Wallas: [2]

> The indifferent and half attentive mind which most men turn towards politics is like a very slow photograph plate. He who wishes to be clearly photographed must stand before it in the same attitude for a long time. A bird that flies across the plate leaves no mark.

If politicians wish to link their party with a certain quality or policy, they must keep at it. Yet they are likely to do so in any case, for the broad stands and attitudes that are at the core of each party's ideology are dear to the hearts of the faithful; to shift his party's emphasis elsewhere is a difficult and often dangerous business for a leader to undertake, and he succeeds, if at all, only over a long period and often by pretending to remain true to the old cause. [3] Thus Liberal-Country Party governments after 1949 presided over a vast increase in the size, power and functions of the central bureaucracy, while remaining firm believers — at least publicly — in both federalism and private enterprise. The ALP has abandoned for practical purposes the goal of nationalisation of industry, but prefers not to say so loudly or often.

There has been no major structural shift that might have altered the parties' attitudes to Australian society. The problems on the agenda for Australian federal governments have hardly changed since federation. Defence, immigration, industrial arbitration, federal-state relations and government intervention in the economy have remained the principal governmental issues around which parties have shaped their election policies. [4] To be sure, the details have changed, but party ideologies have accommodated these changes easily. Furthermore, the need to communicate with large numbers of potential supporters who are not interested in details causes each party leader to emphasise the most general aspects of his party's ideology and policy, and to deal with his opponents in similar fashion.

One consequence is that election rhetoric itself changes very little. When due allowance is made for contemporary crises and disagreements it remains true that an Australian politician of the twentieth century placed backwards or forwards fifty years would find the party lines in any election campaign since that of 1910 instantly recognisable. In 1910, to take that example, the great issues were defence and Labor's proposed land tax.

---

2 In *Human Nature in Politics* (London, 1908, p. 95), a remarkable book fifty years in advance of its time in its emphasis on what have since become the principal concerns of students of political behaviour.

3 Anthony Downs, in *An Economic Theory of Democracy*, (Chapter 7, and especially pp. 109-13) argues that consistency of this kind is forced upon parties by the logic of the party battle.

4 This is an observation which gains much support, for the period 1901 to 1949, from a reading of Geoffrey Sawer, *Australian Federal Politics and Law, 1901-1929* and *Australian Federal Politics and Law, 1929-1949*, Melbourne, 1963. Since 1949 these five issues have maintained their importance.

But much of the general debate centred on the nature of the Labor and Liberal parties, and what they stood for. According to Joseph Cook, the future Liberal Prime Minister, 'Labor was based on sectional legislation and class hatred'; to P.E. Tighe, the unsuccessful Labor candidate for North Sydney, the Labor Party 'stood for the workers so that they should receive the full fruits of their labour'.[5] Alfred Deakin contrasted the independence of Liberals with the caucus-bound restrictions placed on the actions of Labor MPs. Labor speakers responded that Liberals were simply the tools of monopolists. Liberals pointed to their record in government and pooh-poohed Labor policies as impracticable, expensive or 'visionary' (Deakin).

These shafts are among the perennial weapons of Australian party warfare, and they have been easily adapted to changing targets. In 1910, Labor candidates pictured the Liberal Party as the creature of the land monopolists; in 1919 the demon had become the wartime profiteers, in 1955 the large industrial companies and speculators, and in 1969 foreign-owned companies. The straight retort from the Liberal Party has undergone rather similar transformations. Liberals portrayed Labor MPs of 1910 as manipulated by caucus, unions or socialist agitators according to the predilection of the speaker. In the early 1920s the controllers' ranks were widened to include the IWW, Bolsheviks and Sinn Feiners. At the time of the 1955 split was added the international communist conspiracy, and in the mid-1960s, the 'thirty-six faceless men' of the ALP's federal executive.[6]

It is to be expected, then, that the images of the parties that voters possess will be formed principally from the account of each party's *raison d'être* given by its supporters and its opponents. And in the kinds of image they have of each party, the attributes, vices and virtues they associate with each, citizens reveal something about the values they hold to be important in politics as well as about the success of the parties in getting their messages across.

The information needed to build up an outline of party images was secured in a straightforward way. Early in each interview, before political parties had been much more than mentioned, the interviewer introduced the subject, and proceeded straight to a question that allowed the respondent to answer in any way he or she chose: 'Now I would like to ask you what you like and don't like about the political parties. Is there anything in particular you like about the Liberal Party?...Is there anything in particular you don't like about the Liberal Party?' Successive

---

5 *Sydney Morning Herald*, 19 and 24 March 1910. See also L.F. Fitzhardinge, *William Morris Hughes. A Political Biography* Vol. 1, Sydney 1964, pp. 240-6.

6 The continuity of theme is not restricted to party leaders. Henry Mayer has pointed out that newspaper editorialists' attitudes to strikes and union matters are utterly predictable, 'and if the leading articles of 1900 were reproduced in 1963 very few readers would note any difference'. (*The Press in Australia*, Melbourne, 1964, pp. 146-7).

questions were aked about the Labor Party, the Country Party and the Democratic Labor Party.[7] The interviewer endeavoured to write down the exact answer given to each question, and in general to collect as much information as the respondent had to give, by following up vague replies and clarifying ambiguity ('Could you tell me a little more about that?') The replies were later coded by means of a 100-item code whose entries were much the same for each party. The first five separate items in each answer were coded; only a tiny handful mentioned more than five items. The universe of comment that respondents made about each political party can be summarised under eight headings.

Leaders: references to past or present national, state and local party leaders, local MPs, and leaders or leadership in general.

Management of Government: the real or prospective quality of a party in power, its strength or lack of it, efficiency or inefficiency, competence, sincerity, honesty, pragmatism, selflessness, coolness, consistency, or their opposites.

Ideology: what the party is for and against, its ideas and stands, its philosophy and goals, its position on a left-right scale or a modern-traditional scale, whether it is humanitarian or not.

Foreign Policy, including defence and the party's stand on the war in Vietnam.

Domestic Policy, including concerns at the state and local levels as well as in federal politics.

Group-related Responses: the groups, interests and individuals that the party supports or opposes (or that support or oppose the party).

Party-related Responses: the quality of the party *qua* party, its unity or disunity, its freedom or lack of it, the kind of factions or influences that control it.

Other: a residual set of references, including historical events associated with the party and its origins.

There were, of course, some responses that did not fit easily into any one of the first seven boxes, and others that might well have gone into more than one. But in general coding did not prove difficult; respondents knew what they liked and disliked about the parties, and made their meanings clear.

However, they knew more, and cared more, about some parties than others. In 1967 the Labor Party attracted the greatest number of responses, the Country Party the lowest. Indeed, there was a clear division between the two major parties, on the one hand, and the two small parties, on the other, in the extent to which respondents were prepared to talk about them (Table 4.1).

In the case of the Country Party, the ambiguity of its separate status

7 Questions 6(a) to 9(b), and 12(a) to 14(b), in the 1967 questionnaire, and questions 8(a) to 11(b), and 14(a) to 16(b) in the 1969 questionnaire.

provides one explanation for the failure of many respondents to discuss it. As a Tasmanian bank manager's wife put it, 'Oh I was counting the Country Party and the Liberals together. Being not from the country I think they're the same, really.' But its self-imposed electoral remoteness from urban Australians is unquestionably the principal cause. Most Australian voters have never been offered a Country Party candidate in an election for the lower house, and the party's doings are poorly reported in the metropolitan press.[8] ('I never heard of them until I moved here', remarked a young married woman in a NSW country town who had spent most of her life in Sydney.) In the late 1960s the DLP was a national party in the sense that the Country Party was not, since it was organised in each state and contested most of the seats in the House of Representatives; its aspirations and persistence accounted for the wide recognition of it. Even so, for many respondents the name of the party was utterly without significance: 'Who are they?', 'Never heard of them', 'Are they new?' were frequent reactions. Some had trouble distinguishing it from the ALP ('I'm flat out working out which is the ALP and the DLP anyway', complained a Brisbane housewife); others clearly thought it was the Country Party or the Australia Party, while some twenty respondents — 1 per cent of the entire sample — suspected that the DLP was the Communist Party in disguise, a splendid irony.

In 1967 respondents were interviewed at a time of relative electoral quiet, and the power of party names to act as stimuli to comment, as demonstrated in Table 4.1, may have been at its weakest. Yet the heightening effect of an election situation, a time when politics is at its most pervasive, is notably great. A later discussion can be anticipated here: elections add a significant policy content to party images. But, as Table 4.2 shows, the distribution and balance of responses in 1969 was remarkably like that in 1967, despite the immediately past election and the fact that the sample was slightly smaller in size. Parties are securely located in the public consciousness.

That the Labor and Liberal parties attract the bulk of the comment makes sense in terms of their domination of electoral politics: the two

Table 4.1 Frequency of spontaneous responses, by party, 1967

	Favourable	Unfavourable	Total
Labor Party	1243	1668	2911
Liberal Party	1282	1448	2730
DLP	448	799	1247
Country Party	668	525	1193
Total	3641	4440	8081

8 Aitkin, *The Country Party in New South Wales*, pp. 299-300.

parties generally secure more than 80 per cent of the votes at federal elections. On the other hand, awareness of the Country Party and the DLP is relatively larger than their own shares of the votes would seem to warrant. The greater number of responses about the Liberal and Labor parties should not be attributed merely to the greater number of their supporters. Table 4.3 shows that the explanation is more complex. Approximately two-thirds of each group of each identifiers were prepared to bestow some praise on their own party, and much the same proportion of Liberals and DLP supporters criticised the ALP. In general the two major parties evoked comment from supporters of all parties, while the two minor parties were visible principally to their own supporters. Yet it should be observed that there are few cases in which the proportion saying something about a party drops below 25 per cent. Despite the lack of interest in politics displayed by a large minority of the sample, the readiness of the respondents to praise and criticise the parties is eloquent testimony to the great visibility of parties to the voter.

Table 4.3 suggests also that praise and criticism are distributed generally, save for the tendencies we have already noted. It appears, for example, that Country Party and DLP supporters alike find approx-

Table 4.2   Frequency of spontaneous responses, by party, 1969

	Favourable	Unfavourable	Total
Labor Party	1593	1809	3402
Liberal Party	1324	1794	3129
DLP	437	917	1354
Country Party	709	595	1304
Total	4063	5115	9179

Table 4.3   Responses about parties, by party identification, 1967

Party Identification of Respondent	Liberal Party		Labor Party		Country Party		DLP		N
	Like %	Dislike %	Like %	Dislike %	Like %	Dislike %	Like %	Dislike %	
Liberal	68	36	34	65	28	18	20	26	886
Labor	23	52	68	40	18	24	9	37	793
Country Party	38	33	25	57	64	20	14	22	138
DLP	57	58	37	70	25	32	72	18	60
None/NA	26	27	22	28	10	15	8	16	171
Whole Sample	45	42	45	52	25	20	16	29	2054

Note: Each cell displays the proportion of a group of party identifiers (row) giving at least one answer to the question 'Is there anything in particular you like [dislike] about the ... party?' (column).

imately the same amount to say for and against the Liberal Party. But these summaries are not adequate evidence of balance of opiuim Figure 4.1 provides a better analysis by measuring the extent to which any one kind of response is coupled with any other; the *phi* coefficients thus obtained allow us to picture the most important patterns of response. For this diagram fourteen variables were used, the eight responses concerning parties, and six concerning the three principal party leaders in 1967, Harold Holt, then Prime Minister, Gough Whitlam, newly elected Leader of the Labor Party, and John McEwen, the Country Party veteran.[9] Fourteen variables provide ninety correlations, and the nine largest of these (a number suggested by the distribution of the coefficients) are set out in Figure 4.1.

Figure 4.1 Patterns of response to parties and leaders

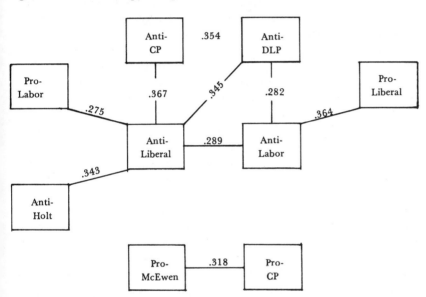

At its centre is a strong structure formed by pairs of hostile attitudes to parties (and the missing diagonal, anti-CP x anti-Labor, has a coefficient of .244, almost as large as some included in the diagram). Criticism of the Liberal Party is linked with five other types of response, and the anti-Liberal x anti-Labor link is stronger, we may notice, than the expected anti-Liberal x pro-Labor link. Criticism of the parties is to be expected, given the excess of blame over praise shown in Tables 4.1 and 4.2 — and also given the generally unenthusiastic attitudes the sample showed about 'the people running the government in Canberra'. Indeed, since most governments at most times necessarily attract more criticism than applause, it is understandable that the electorate should develop a

9 Questions 12(a) to 14(b) in the 1967 questionnaire.

generally critical attitude towards all parties.[10] But this criticism, as Figure 4.1 makes plain, is spread widely not selectively. Australian electors are not all myopic partisans. Many of them can see the warts in their own party's image as clearly as the highlights of rival parties.

Let us now consider the collective images of the four parties. We shall do this by contrasting in summarised form the two profiles, favourable and unfavourable, formed from the thousands of individual comments of the respondents, supplemented and illustrated by some of these comments themselves. It might be argued that these profiles are distorted, because of the failure of some respondents to answer the questions: may there not be tendency for non-answerers to possess different pictures of the parties?[11] In fact, that probability is low. We shall see that party images are remarkably constant from one group of party identifiers to another; futher analysis has demonstrated that *strength* of the party identification did not affect the kind of response given, although very strong identifiers were more likely to respond to these questions than were those who claimed no party attachment at all. Some of the non-responders were those with little or nothing to say about the party in question, while others were inhibited in answering some questions by their feelings of loyalty. But if all possible responses had been collected, it is abundantly clear, the profiles discussed shortly would have been much the same. Since the interviews were conducted in 1967, the party images are unaffected by the specific issues of an election situation, and can be thought of as the relatively abiding pictures of each party as held by the community. The nature of the change in the images brought about by an election forms the subject of a later chapter.

Let us first consider one respondent's replies *in toto*, partly to illustrate again the flow of the questions and answers, and partly to demonstrate that attitudes to parties ar not necessarily related in conventional ways. The respondent is a thirty-eight year-old electrician employed by the Tasmanian Hydro-Electric Commission; the interviewer, a paragon of the art, has managed to indicate stage directions as well as dialogue.

Is there anything in particular you like about the Liberal Party?
[Laughs] This is going to be a bit hard, isn't it? There *are* some things I like about the Liberal Party: I think their free enterprise system is...[O.K.] They're the best of a bad bunch I think at the moment.

---

10 See Campbell *et al.*, *The American Voter*, pp. 554-6.
11 Awareness of this problem has no doubt prompted the use of instruments administered to all respondents, such as the semantic differential (see, for example, Hughes, *Images and Issues*, and J. Trenaman and D. McQuail *Television and the Political Image*, London, 1961). Such techniques, however, bring in their train the problem of contrived data. The findings set out in this chapter suggest that the free-answer technique is at the least a perfectly valid means of building up an understanding of party images.

Is there anything in particular you don't like about the Liberal Party?
Yes, I . . . let me see. We'll have to get it right, won't we? I can't
say taxation because that's all right. They've got a free enterprise system
which I think is pretty good. I don't think they carry their social
services — pensions and so on — far enough. There's too much [control
of resources from?] outside Australia and not enough inside. Take the
Snowy River, for example. All this to be disbanded seems a crying
shame. Then there's the Ord River Scheme, Dr Patterson's scheme
in North Queensland, and the Murray River dam — all this that they're
not doing enough about.

Like about Labor?
Yes . . . there are some things I don't like for a start. I think socialism's
a good thing but I think it can be carried too far — such as when
they nationalised the banks. I don't agree or disagree about their policy in
Vietnam. The war's been going on twenty years or more there as I
understand it, and I think the Labor Party's right when they say it's
unwinnable.

Dislike about Labor?
   Their original idea about pensions and social services is good but they
should be increased considerably — although I don't think it's financially
possible to do away with the means test . . . I think they can give those who
are on it a lot more. [*Anything else?*] The Labor Party's idea on a
national shipping line is restricted. The Labor Party says they would
not disband the Snowy River [organisation], and would increase the
pensions, and do something about Northern Queensland — that's what
they say: I don't know if they would or not.

Like about Country Party?
   I like Mr McEwen. He always gives a fair and honest opinion . . .
we don't have a Country Party here and it's very hard to keep up with it —
there's nothing much in the *Mercury*. Mr Holt seems evasive . . . Put it
this way: I've got confidence in Mr McEwen as Minister for Trade . . .
he's about the only bloke I know who is a Country Party man, and he's the
Leader [langhs].

Dislike about Country Party?
   Well, I can't honestly say: I've never actually studied it. As I understand, it seems to be doing a change from a state to a national party, all
over Australia. Some of the publicity you read says the Country Party is no
longer a *country* party. Mr McEwen says he has to represent the people
in the city too. This came out at the beginning of the last election —
wasn't there a faceless group or something, backed by the Liberals,
trying to split the Country Party?

Like about the DLP?
Nothing.

Dislike about the DLP?
Yes, it's secretarian [*sic*; sectarian], just representing one class of people.
I watch Mr Watchamacallit's TV program — Mr Santamaria. He

seems to be always critical without having any suggestions about what to do.

This man is better informed than most of his fellow respondents, and very ready with his opinions. His own political stance is not immediately obvious from his attitudes; he described himself, as it happens, as very strongly Labor, and said of his father 'He's always been Labor, and a staunch trade unionist. That's where it comes from, doesn't it?' He himself was a member of the Electrical Trades Union, and claimed always to have voted Labor; he revealed a strong animus against his Liberal federal MP. Yet, and here he is typical of the sample, his strong loyalties do not prevent him from finding fault with his own party and bestowing some virtues on its rivals. And his adverse judgments on the Liberal Party come to some extent from his employment by 'the Hydro'; they are professional, rather than partisan, in origin. His subsequent comments on the three party leaders are in keeping with this even-handed approach: he has no time for Mr Holt, but he is reserved about Mr Whitlam — 'I don't know whether he is playing for Mr Whitlam or the Labor Party'; of the three he prefers Mr McEwen, of whom he has 'a very high opinion'.

The Liberal Party

We turn now to Table 4.4, which presents the favourable and unfavourable composite images of the Liberal Party, obtained by cumulating all the free-answer comments offered by the respondents in answer to the questions 'Is there anything in particular you like [dislike] about the Liberal Party?' Responses have been grouped by subject area, and specific remarks within those subject areas have been mentioned in italics where their frequency warrants it. Thus 'it serves the public interest' or remarks very like that, represented 4 per cent of all the favourable references to the Liberal Party, while all comments about the party's success in the management of government — including 'it serves the public interest' — accounted for 29 per cent. Other columns display the distribution of these classes of response amongst separate groups of Labor and Liberal partisans. A similar format is used later in the chapter for each of the other parties.

The Liberal Party's strength came in chunks of rather similar size: its perceived success in the management of the country, its general stance in politics, and its leaders, especially Sir Robert Menzies (who had in fact retired nearly two years before the interviews were taken). These three criteria account for 70 per cent of the responses favourable to the party. Apart from the reference to Menzies, however, and the linking of party to free enterprise, there was little that is specific in these attitudes.

A large proportion of the responses, from all sides, were couched in the most general terms: 'They've got some pretty good men', 'I like their ideas', 'They seem to know what they're doing', 'I think they do a good job', 'They only talk about what they can do', are some representative examples. The lack of detail in these judgments may be related to the party's continuous experience in government during a long period of general and rising prosperity. It benefited, as the party in power, from public pleasure at good times, but by implication rather than directly. Moreover to a large extent this image is the one that the party has itself put forward. The themes of experience, cautious pragmatism and progress have been its campaign stock-in-trade for a generation, and it is not

Table 4.4 The images of the Liberal Party, 1967

Image	Whole Sample %	Liberal Partisans %	Labor Partisans %
Favourable			
Management of Government	29	29	31
Honest, keeps promises	*5*	*6*	*5*
Serves the public interest	*4*	*4*	*5*
Ideology	21	23	13
Free enterprise	*3*	*4*	*2*
Leaders	20	18	22
Menzies	*9*	*8*	*13*
Domestic Policy	10	9	10
Group-related Items	8	9	6
Foreign Policy	7	7	10
Party-related Items	4	4	5
Other	1	1	3
Total	100	100	100
(N)	(1282)	(857)	(237)
Unfavourable			
Domestic Policy	26	29	23
Pensions	*8*	*10*	*7*
Group-related Items	19	11	22
Against the workers	*7*	*3*	*10*
Looks after big business	*6*	*4*	*7*
Foreign Policy	15	15	16
Vietnam	*9*	*8*	*10*
Management of Government	14	18	11
Looks after special interests	*5*	*7*	*4*
Dishonest, insincere	*4*	*5*	*3*
Ideology	12	11	15
Just after office	*3*	*4*	*3*
Leaders	9	10	8
Holt	*3*	*5*	*3*
Party-related Items	4	4	4
Other	1	2	1
Total	100	100	100
(N)	(1448)	(500)	(735)

surprising, given the party's long rule, that they are prominent in the electorate's own description of it.

The Liberal Party's wants and blemishes were a good deal more specific. They arose principally from its actions as the government, and suggest that the party has now a well defined corporate personality as a party. Its failure, or lack of success, in domestic and foreign policy and in management generally, made up more than half of all the adverse comments. The criticism of the Liberals in matters of domestic policy covered a wide range. The government's indifference to the aged, the sick and other beneficiaries of social service was a frequent complaint. 'I don't think bloody much of [them]', a young mother from a NSW mining town said with aggressive candour. 'Last budget they cut the pensioners out and that stuck in my gullet. They're pretty mean with child endowment, too.' But there were numerous criticisms also of the party's failure to 'get the economy moving', to keep prices down, to lower taxes, and to improve health services and education. In late 1967 the movement against Australia's involvement in the war in Vietnam had kept the question of involvement at the front of party politics (it had been a principal issue in the election of 1966); Vietnam was the subject of one critical reference in every eleven. Associated with it, through circumstance if not in each respondent's mind, was a feeling that the Liberals had tied Australia too closely to the United States. It is important not to make too much of this, since the great majority of the respondents later declared themselves in favour of close ties with America when asked that question directly. For many it was the style rather than the fact of the relationship that mattered: Mr Holt's unhappy pledge of 'All the way with LBJ' was remembered to his discredit.

Few had approved of the Liberal Party because of its relationship to groups and interests; indeed, those who talked in such terms did so usually to deny that the Liberal Party was that kind of party — it stood for everyone, for the public interest, rather than for any one group or section (another important component, of course, of the party's self-image). But group affiliations loomed quite large to those who found fault with the party. Many critics saw it as the party of and for big business, or, by corollary, a party opposed to the interests of the workers or the trade unions ('I don't think they're for the worker — all right if you've got plenty of money!'). Others saw it in opposition to old people and pensioners.

The negative public image of the Liberal Party also corresponds, of course, to a picture of the party that was constantly being marketed — the one put out by the Labor Party. Yet the distribution of responses among the two groups of party supporters makes clear that these images can co-exist within an individual's perspective. We have seen that Labor indentifiers were much less likely to find complimentary things to say about the Liberal Party than are Liberals. But when they did give praise, they did so in much the same fashion as Liberals themselves. Two differences only stand out from the columns of Table 4.1. Labor criticisms were twice as likely to centre upon the Liberal Party's associations with and opposition to groups, and Liberals were almost twice as likely to praise their party's philosophy and goals. We shall see that these contrasts have their counterparts with respect to other parties.

The Labor Party

Because the Labor Party has promoted itself from the beginning as the party of change, of policies, of ideas — as 'the party of initiative', to use a widely used phrase coined by W.K. Hancock — it might be expected that ideas and policies should form a prominent part of the favourable image of the party. In fact, such references were more frequently used of the Liberal Party. Labor's strength is its perceived role as big brother, or protector, or servant, of the worker (Table 4.5). It may be that many of those respondents who cited this relationship had in mind that the party could act efficiently on behalf of the working class only by bringing about changes in society, but that is not apparent from their responses. It is not legitimate, in fact, to suppose more than that such respondents possessed a simple 'interest' model of politics, in which the workers were represented, or looked after, by the ALP.

References to leaders and leadership qualities made up one response in five, a similar proportion to that for the Liberal Party. E.G. Whitlam was as widely and favourably perceived as Sir Robert Menzies, a considerable achievement for the Labor leader, who had been elected to his party's leadership only a few months before interviewing took place in 1967. As in the case of the Liberal Party, most of those who praised the Labor Party's goals and ideas did so in the most general terms; less than 2 per cent mentioned the party's stance as a radical group dedicated to change, and a like proportion saw it as a specifically humanitarian party dedicated to social welfare. The remainder of the responses, in all categories, tended to be general in kind, save that the party's attitude to the war in Vietnam was the principal item mentioned by those who talked of foreign policy; nevertheless, such responses amounted only to 2 per cent.

A quick comparison will show that the favourable image of each party is more general, less sharp in outline, than the unfavourable. This is especially the case with the Labor Party, whose negative image is rich in detail. The theme of 'leftness' linked many of these responses: the party was too far to the left, in favour of nationalisation, under communist influence, opposed to the war in Vietnam. Such criticisms made up one in four of the negative responses. For the first time in these analyses references to the party as a party emerge as important. It is hard to doubt that many respondents saw Labor as a good party ruined by communist influence and unity tickets, by union domination, or by internal fighting and disunity. Probably because of these sentiments, many respondents claimed that one could have no confidence in the party as a government, and others that Labor catered too much for union interests. To some extent this latter complaint is the other side of the Labor-looks-after-the working-class coin: it should be noted, however, that on this criterion the

Table 4.5 The images of the Labor Party, 1967

Image	Whole Sample %	Liberal Partisans %	Labor Partisans %
Favourable			
Group-related Items	30	19	37
For the workers	*26*	*16*	*32*
Leaders	22	35	16
Whitlam	*9*	*8*	*3*
Ideology	14	16	13
Management of Government	10	10	12
Honest, would keep promises	*3*	*3*	*3*
Domestic Policy	10	8	11
Party-related Items	8	9	5
Foreign Policy	4	1	5
Other	2	2	1
Total	100	100	100
(N)	(1243)	(387)	(736)
Unfavourable			
Ideology	24	25	20
Too far to the left	*10*	*10*	*8*
Nationalism	*4*	*5*	*1*
Party-related Items	21	20	26
Split, disunited	*10*	*8*	*14*
Union influence	*5*	*4*	*5*
Communist influence	*4*	*5*	*4*
Leaders	17	15	20
Calwell	*10*	*9*	*12*
Management of Government	16	17	14
No confidence in them	*5*	*6*	*4*
Won't be able to carry out promises	*3*	*3*	*3*
Foreign Policy	8	9	6
Vietnam	*5*	*5*	*5*
Group-related items	7	7	6
Looks after trade unions	*4*	*4*	*3*
Domestic Policy	5	5	6
Other	2	2	2
Total	100	100	100
(N)	(1668)	(924)	(457)

balance of opinion was overwhelmingly favourable to Labor. Finally, Labors' esteem sufered because of its past leader, Arthur Calwell. Of all the responses favourable to the ALP, only one in a hundred mentioned Calwell; but he was the subject of 10 per cent of the criticisms (while his successor drew fewer than a dozen unfavourable comments in nearly 1700).

The pervasiveness of Labor's positive and negative images is strikingly demonstrated by Table 4.5. The criticisms made of the Labor Party were much the same whichever party the respondents themselves supported (this was true even of DLP identifiers, save that they were, predictably, rather more likely to criticise Labor as being too far to the left). The kinds of praise awarded to the party revealed more variation. Labor identifiers were twice as likely as Liberals to link the party with the working class, while Liberals were twice as likely as Labor supporters to cite leaders and leadership. Yet even among Liberals Labor's role as the workers' party was the second most frequently mentioned item, as was leadership for the Labor identifiers. In short, the favourable and unfavourable images of the Labor Party are common property. Liberals can find virtues in it, and Labor partisans find fault; and all draw from a common fund of values and opinions. That common fund is an explanation in part of the persistence of the outlines of these images.

The Country Party

Since 1923 the Country Party has maintained a stable coalition relationship with the Liberal Party, at its most formal when the two parties are in government, but real enough even in opposition. The difference between the two parties in policy have been essentially of degree, and in country electorates the two parties receive support for much the same groups. Yet the structure of the images of the Country Party is more like that of the Labor Party than that of the Liberal Party.

More than one-third of the favourable responses connected the Country Party with a group — in the great majority of cases, with farmers or country people (Table 4.6). Its leaders received praise, and Mr McEwen, the party's Federal Leader from 1958 to 1969, was singled out for mention. It was judged to be experienced, honest and to be working in the national interest; it was praised for working well in coalition. One in nine responses acclaimed the party's ideas and stands, but without much detail. The considered judgment of one respondent could stand for many: 'I like somebody to have [at heart] the interests of the country minority who do a lot for the country nationally and who would be overlooked if there were not a specific party with their interests foremost; the rural people are in a minority numerically, you know.'

Like the Labor Party, the Country Party attracted criticism because of its nature as a party, but the substance of the complaint was quite different. One in four of the comments dismissed the Country Party as not a real party, or as a liberal front. One man, an English immigrant, used a comparison to make the point: 'In Britain in local government elections there are Conservatives, Independents, Moderates and such-like-but they're all Conservatives. I think this is an analogy for my feelings about

Table 4.6   The images of the Country Party, 1967

Image	Whole Sample %	Liberal Partisans %	Labor Partisans %	CP Partisans %
Favourable				
Group-related Items	39	35	41	51
For the farmer, countryman	*35*	*33*	*38*	*43*
Leaders	14	12	18	9
McEwen	*8*	*7*	*13*	*1*
Management of Government	14	13	13	16
Party-related Items	13	18	10	6
Association with Liberals	*5*	*8*	*2*	*2*
Ideology	11	13	8	13
Domestic Policy	5	5	5	4
Foreign Policy	3	2	3	1
Other	1	2	2	*
Total	100	100	100	100
(N)	(668)	(332)	(175)	(117)
Unfavourable				
Party-related Items	36	30	44	
Not a real party	*24*	*19*	*28*	
Wants more than fair share	*4*	*6*	*4*	
Management of Government	17	21	14	
Looks after special interests	*8*	*11*	*6*	
Ideology	17	15	8	
Just out for themselves	*5*	*5*	*6*	
Group-related Items	16	18	14	
Too interested in farmers	*6*	*4*	*7*	
Domestic Policy	6	8	3	
Leaders	4	4	3	
Foreign Policy	3	3	3	
Other	1	1	1	
Total	100	100	100	
(N)	(525)	(199)	(253)	

* = less than 0.5 per cent

the Country Party here.' A much smaller group objected that the party was greedy, that it took more (in ministries, for example) than its numbers warranted, or that it engaged in political blackmail; others saw it as just a means of keeping Labor out of office. The sectional theme implicit here was much more often made explicit. Thus the Country Party catered for special interests, and looked after farmers (again, with reference to the Labor Party and the workers, it is to be noted that the balance of opinion on this latter point was overwhelmingly favourable to the party).

These images were widely held across party lines. The legitimacy of the Country Party as the farmer's friend, and the importance of this role as the *raison d'être* of the party, are accepted on all sides of politics. The link is, of course, central to the party's own ideology, but that is not a sufficient explanation, for most of the respondents were not exposed to Country Party election propaganda. We may plausibly ascribe the acceptance of the link to two beliefs, the first that farmers are an important — and distant — element in Australian society, the second that important interests ought to be represented in politics. The same general explanation, substituting 'workers' for 'farmers', lies behind the similarly wide acceptance of the Labor-workers link.

It is worth noting that while both Labor and Liberal supporters thought highly of Mr McEwen, Labor supporters remarkably so, he was barely mentioned by Country Party supporters. The explanation most probably flows from the more limited perspectives of Country Party partisans. Of all the parties the Country Party is the least national in its structure, the state organisations being quite autonomous. Its supporters are therefore likely to be as aware of their state leaders as of the federal leader (a proposition hinted at in the data). But for Labor supporters and Liberals, who are more accustomed to see politics in national terms, the Country Party's Federal Leader is a man of significance. Tables 4.4, 4.5, and 4.6 each make clear that a party's supporters are less likely to mention its leaders than are supporters of other parties. It may well be the case that to a partisan his own party's leadership seems less important than its other positive qualities, while he can approve of another party's leader more easily than he can of its philosophy.

We have seen already that Country Party supporters were loath to criticise their own party, and the number of these criticisms is too small to justify a separate column; but in the broad their criticisms resembled in their distribution those of Liberal supporters. Again, the main lines of complaint were much the same in all parties. Labor supporters were most likely to deny the Country Party the status of a real party, but that was also the most frequent criticism made by Liberals. Conversely, Liberals were more disturbed by the Country Party's influence and activities in government, but that was important too for Labor supporters.

The Democratic Labor Party

The Democratic Labor Party, of all four parties, attracted the worst balance of favourable and unfavourable comment: there were almost two responses critical of the party to each one in praise of it. The tones of moderation and calm judgment that pervaded the responses about the Liberal, Labor and Country Parties were much less in evidence when the DLP was under scrutiny. Anger, bitterness, and contempt were frequent; we cannot doubt that the DLP, for most of those aware of its existence, represents the bad boy of Australian politics. A few extracts give something of the flavour of rejection:

NO — oh my goodness, no! They leave a nasty smell around the place! (*Melbourne housewife, fifty-eight, very strong Labor*)

I'd put a match to them! (*greenkeeper, NSW country town, thirty-one, very strong Labor*)

I hate the cows. They're rotten to the core. They're not worth two bob — a mongrel breed. (*retired boilermaker, Melbourne, sixty-seven, very strong Labor*)

They're not a political party in my opinion — just a church organisation. (*storeman, Sydney, forty-four, not very strong Labor*)

I don't believe in them at all, I don't think Mr Menzies should have made them a party at all — there were only one or two of them [in Parliament?] — and I'm not against Catholics! (*housewife, Victorian country town, seventy-six, very strong Labor*)

Even the praise had a negative flavour (Table 4.7). Eighteen per cent of the responses approved of the DLP because it was anti-communist ('They've got no commo instincts at all, really, have they?' offered an elderly Western Australian lady), while another 8 per cent enthused because it was anti-Labor. Specific positive virtues were infrequently named: the party's policies on education — principally government aid to independent (= church) schools — being the most important.

The main criticisms of the DLP resembled those made of the Country Party. The party itself was regarded as an impostor, a fraud, a useless object, and an anti-Labor device. But it also drew fire because of its link with Catholicism, both because it was thought to espouse Catholic ideas and because the church was seen as manipulating it. It has become conventional in Australian politics to deplore sectarianism (the aftermath of bitter sectarian politics in the early part of the century) and many respondents were obviously reluctant to be specific about what they disliked in the DLP although the tendency of their remarks was clear enough; the antipathy towards the Catholic-DLP link is therefore greater than is shown by Table 4.7. The matter is discussed further in Chapter 10.

If the Labor-workers and Country Party-farmers connections are seen as legitimate, why is the DLP-Catholic link condemned? If workers and farmers are allowed to be interests, why is the same status denied

Catholics? The short answer is that religion and politics are seen as separate spheres, that politics is agreed to be about the struggle for shares of a cake whose ingredients are nearly all economic. The DLP transgresses this rule by introducing essentially non-economic values into politics. Moreover, it rekindles the Protestant-Catholic antipathies that have subsided, or at least been kept out of sight, since the depression of the 1930s. We should note, however, that the links are not quite the same. Farmers and workers are seen as the intrinsically weak dependants, or

Table 4.7 The images of the Democratic Labor Party, 1967

Image	Whole Sample %	Liberal Partisans %	Labor Partisans %	DLP Partisans %
Favourable				
Ideology	43	41	39	43
Anti-communist	*18*	*19*	*16*	*14*
Party-related Items	14	19	13	8
Anti-Labor	*8*	*12*	*6*	*2*
Management of Government	13	14	19	11
Straightforward	*5*	*4*	*10*	*3*
Domestic Policy	7	4	8	13
Education	*3*	*3*	*2*	*6*
Leaders	6	8	3	4
Group-related Items	6	6	4	8
Foreign Policy	4	3	4	8
Other	7	5	10	5
Total	100	100	100	100
(N)	(448)	(234)	(92)	(79)
Unfavourable				
Party-related Items	42	40	45	
Not a real party	*15*	*17*	*13*	
Just anti-Labor	*11*	*6*	*16*	
Serves no purpose	*6*	*6*	*7*	
Run by the Catholic Church	*4*	*4*	*4*	
Ideology	28	31	24	
Catholicism	*11*	*10*	*12*	
Management of Government	12	11	12	
Leaders	4	4	4	
Group-related items	3	6	2	
Domestic Policy	1	1	1	
Foreign Policy	1	1	1	
Other	9	6	11	
Total	100	100	100	
(N)	(799)	(294)	(414)	

clients, of parties who will do their best for them when they are in power. But only a few of the responses objected to that kind of DLP-Catholic link. The majority connected the *church*, rather than individual Catholics, with the party (the Labor analogue would be 'domination by the ACTU') and their hostility seemed directed more at the Roman Catholic church as an institution than at individual Catholics. The point is made explicitly in this carefully toned-down remark of a Hobart academic: 'I do think they're a little too connected with the Catholic hierarchy. The hierarchy is all very well in its way, but I wouldn't say politics is its function.'

Throughout this discussion the point has been made that there is great similarity between the *kinds* of responses made about the parties, no matter what the partisan loyalty of the respondent, save only that partisans are less likely to criticise their own party and more likely to praise it. We may, therefore, argue on the evidence that perceptions of parties are only slightly filtered through the lens of personal attachment, or, to put it another way, that parties have to the electorate an objective reality that is only slightly distorted by partisan loyalties. [12] If this is the case, then a person's party identification cannot be responsible for the substance of his perceptions of the various parties. It may, indeed does, affect the extent to which he finds fault with his own party on virtues in its rivals, but that is the limit of its constraint.

Moreover, the timeless quality of these responses means that the images are likely to survive, relatively unchanged, for a long time. It is hard to doubt that some of the principal features of the images — Labor's protectorship of the workers, the Country Party's similar role with respect to farmers, the Liberal Party's zeal for free enterprise, the DLP's anti-communism — are as old as the parties themselves; other aspects of the images, Labor's disunity, or outside control, for example, are recurring themes in party warfare. The contribution of relatively persistent party images to the stability of the party system requires no emphasis. We need only observe that the general ideological flavour of the images can accommodate quite substantial real changes in politics and government. What the party supporters of 1910 and 1970 understood by 'government intervention in the economy' was no doubt very different, but party positions and images on the question are unlikely to have changed much.

Party identification and party image are two related aspects of a voter's view of the political world. We turn now to the way in which the voter combines the two — the ordering of his party preferences.

12 The similarity of response across partisan boundaries was not a chance phenomenon. A close analysis of these free-answer responses within class, religion, sex, age and other conventional groupings produced virtually no sharp differences. Middle-class respondents were rather more likely to refer to ideas, goals and policies, working-class respondents to parties as protectors of people and groups. Women were more likely to talk about leaders than were men, and less likely to remark on philosophy or goals. But, to make the point again, these differences were unremarkable: the striking aspect of the analysis was the similarity of response. The properties of the parties' images, it is clear, are in the public domain.

5 Ideology and Preference

I think some men in each party might be left, and so on, but I don't think of the whole party like that. (*orchardist, sixty-four, Tasmania*)

Parties are not chosen in a vacuum. However unthinkingly an elector identifies with a party it remains true that in choosing one party he has preferred it to others. And elections will make it clear, even to the most apathetic and ignorant, that parties are in competition with one another, that the essence of electoral politics is 'taking sides'. To enlarge our understanding of party identification we need to consider how far party choice can be construed as an ordered set of preferences, rather than as a simple blind allegiance. In doing so we can serve two other important analytic ends, one theoretical, the other empirical. We can decide the extent to which the Australian party system is perceived as being based on a single ideological continuum, classically from left to right, and discover how efficiently the preferential voting system, which has been in force for Australian federal elections since 1919, synthesises the millions of preference orders present in the electorate. The two purposes are of course related for, if there is a strong ideological basis to the Australian party system, we should expect to see it reflected in the way Australians construct their preferences. And it would provide a major contribution to an understanding of the stability of the party system.

The Recognition of Left and Right: a Cross-national Analysis
The notion that parties, policies, factions, politicians, trade unions and voters can all, for various purposes, be arrayed on an underlying continuum from left to right is one of the indispensable shorthand metaphors of political comment and discussion. What left and right stand for depends on the occasion, and very frequently remains unexplored by those using the terms. Conventionally, however, radicals, socialists, communists and Labor supporters, together with their goals and policies,

are located to the left of the continuum, while conservatives, anti-communists, supporters of private enterprise and Liberals, along with their goals and policies, are located to the right. Within parties and other groups the labels can be applied to those who follow policies which are either conservative or radical within the context of the group; it is this which allows commentators to describe certain unions or union leaders as right-wing or 'conservative',[1] or to talk of Labor's left and right wings. Within the Communist parties distinctions are made between 'right deviationists' and 'left sectarians'. The metaphor has the virtues of great simplicity and great plausibility. The real world provides many analogues of competitors facing one another across an open space, and in fact the obvious ones — a static war, as in the trenches in World War I, and field games such as football and hockey — are often used to provide other metaphorical language for politics. Voting in parliament can be seen as a continuum with MPs moving along the line from Yes to Abstain to No. The fabled 'swinging voter', who alternates between rival camps, obtains his name from another adaptation of the metaphor. In short, so much of the analysis of political conflict is supported by the notion of the ideological continuum that it is hard to think how discussion could proceed if the notion were to be declared bogus.

Yet there are two factors which should make us wary of accepting the notion as anything more than a metaphor. The first is that only a minority of respondents showed much concern with the symbols of left and right in their spontaneous comments on the parties. Perhaps one-quarter of the criticisms of the Labor Party had overtones of this kind, and the small number who praised the DLP often mentioned explicitly its hostility to communism. But the great majority manifestly had other criteria in the forefront of their minds, the parties' connections with groups, the quality of their leaders, and their competence in government being very much more important.[2]

The second is the convincing demonstration that in Britain, where left and right are also symbols of wide currency in political journalism and everyday discussion, these words are the intellectual property of the elite, and are barely recognised by the great mass of the electors. Indeed, when Butler and Stokes divided the British electorate into five groups in terms

1 One of the respondents, a university scientist, commented, 'I think I'd probably be to the left, but the Communist Party I'd regard as one of the most conservative on earth.' It need hardly be said that this is a most sophisticated use of the term. The Tasmanian orchardist quoted at the beginning of the chapter illustrates the tendency of much Australian political commentary to describe intra-party affairs in terms of left and right, but to avoid this usage when discussing the party struggle as a whole.

2 One possible explanation for the failure of the respondents to use these terms more frequently is that many are bewildered by them, a function in turn of inaccurate political commentary. I have argued elsewhere that newspapers use the terms much too indiscriminately, and often differ as to whether a given person, faction or policy is either left, or right, or neither 'Political Review', *The Australian Quarterly*, 39(3), September 1967).

of their recognition and use of the left-right framework, those who possessed what they called a 'fully elaborated dynamic interpretation' made up a tiny 2 per cent, and those who could use the terms at all sensibly were only 20 per cent. These proportions were remarkably at odds with the expectations of a number of politicians and journalists, who had guessed that perhaps 60 to 90 per cent of the electorate used these terms and their implications as a matter of course.[3]

The earlier discussion of the similarities between the British and Australian electorates in terms of participation might lead us to expect that in this matter, too, the two groups of electors would behave as one. The Australian data do not allow a full replication of the analysis made by Butler and Stokes,[4] but the available evidence is compelling. Table 5.1 sets out the comparisons, first in whether the respondents considered *themselves* as being to the left or right in politics, then (in widely separated parts of the interviews) in whether they saw the political parties as similarly located.

The proportions are very similar in the two countries, and for both questions; had it been possible to continue the analysis along the lines followed by the authors of the British study it seems reasonable to suppose that there would have emerged a similarly minute proportion of

Table 5.1   Recognition of left and right, a British-Australian comparison

	Britain			Australia	
	1963 %	1964 %	1966 %	1967 %	1969 %
Do you [British: ever] think of yourself as being to the left, the centre or the right in politics, or don't you think of yourself in that way?					
Yes	25	28	27	29	34
No	69	65	66	57	58
Don't know	6	7	7	14	8
Total	100	100	100	100	100
Do you ever think of the parties as being to the left, the centre, or to the right in politics, or don't you think of the parties that way?					
Yes	21	19	21	20	23
No	74	76	72	70	69
Don't know	5	5	7	10	8
Total	100	100	100	100	100

3 Butler and Stokes, *Political Change in Britain*, pp. 205-11. For evidence of very much higher levels of ideological awareness in Italy, see Samuel H. Barnes, 'Left, Right and the Italian Voter', *Comparative Political Studies*, 4(2), July 1971.
4 The Australian questionnaires did not include the semantic differential techniques that allowed Butler and Stokes to measure the recognition of left and right by those respondents who failed to react to these symbols in direct questions.

Australians whose grasp of the left-right framework was confident and secure. Even when the labels are used correctly, there is often a puzzlement as to what they mean. Such puzzled people possess a 'nominal recognition' of the framework, and are typified by a Snowy Mountains Authority engineer, who placed the parties from the left in the order Labor-DLP-Country Party-Liberal, and then reflected 'Really, I don't understand a great deal about this. The right leans towards Liberalism ... No-one has really explained right and left to me'. A Vaucluse receptionist, when asked whether she thought of the parties in terms of left and right, replied 'Yes — as red, pink and white'.

We have observed in Chapter 2 that knowledge about and involvement in politics are more characteristic of the middle class than of the working class, and, more specifically, of the better educated than the worse educated. Since to think of politics in terms of left and right is to further abstract what is already a highly abstract concept, we might reasonably expect the users of these terms to be found predominantly among the well educated and the middle class. This is indeed the case. Only one in sixteen of those without any schooling thought of themselves in left-right terms, and the proportion increased with every additional quantum of formal education to two in three of those who held university degrees. Understandably, the terms have more meaning to those interested in politics: 55 per cent of those who claimed a good deal of interest in politics also said they thought of themselves in terms of left and right, compared with only 1 per cent of those with no interest in politics. There was a comparable difference on each of the indexes of participation.

Given what we know already of the relationship between education, class and party, it is not surprising that these symbols have rather more currency for Liberals than Labor supporters: one in three Liberals, but only one in four Labor partisans thought of themselves in terms of left and right.[5] But since, in addition, the strength of one's identification with a party has a powerful effect upon one's involvement in politics, it is no more surprising that the recognition of left and right was greatest among those strongly committed to their parties. Within the Liberal Party, in fact, it ranged from 43 per cent among very strong identifiers to 25 per cent among the not very strong, and within the ranks of the ALP from 31 per cent to 18 per cent. Oddly enough recognition was greatest of all among DLP supporters, whose income and education were, on average, lower than those of Liberals. The explanation doubtless lies in the heavily ideological tone of DLP propaganda and the party's strongly anti-communist stance: to be DLP supporters means, for very many of them, seeing politics as a battle between the forces of Freedom and those of

5 But the proportions were higher amongst trade unionists than amongst non-unionists, suggesting that unionists are exposed to more ideological discussion than those who do not belong to unions. This matter is discussed further in Chapter 8.

Communism. Even so, we should notice that a *majority* of DLP supporters, like their counterparts in other parties, did not recognise these terms as applying either to themselves or to the party system. The left-right framework is familiar only to the sophisticated partisans in politics; most voters have no use for it.

One paradox stares out from Table 5.1. If some people derive their partisanship and their judgment of parties from an ideological perspective, why do we find greater proportions accepting the usefulness of the left-right continuum for themselves, than for political parties? Butler and Stokes have suggested that the answer lies in the purely nominal recognition of the terms by many voters, who know that, for example, the Labor party is said to be left, they are Labor supporters, and therefore they must be left too; but what this term means when applied to the Labor Party itself they have no idea. 'The elector who "knows" his own ideological location simply because he knows which party he supports stands in flat contradiction to our ideological model; he has stood on its head the basis of political choice which it assumes — his "ideology" follows his partisanship, not his partisanship his ideology.'[6] The interview schedules suggest that this description fitted many of our respondents, such as the sixty-eight year-old Hobart housewife, once a Belfast girl, who placed herself by saying 'Left — I'm a Labor one'.

Yet this may not be the only explanation. When asked to locate themselves on the continuum, Australians were much more likely to cluster around the 'centre' than the British (Table 5.2). The British sample divided evenly between left, centre and right, but the Australians avoided the left and preferred the centre. The explanations may lie in greater middle-class support for the British Labour Party than for the ALP, or in the greater disfavour that the word 'left' enjoys in Australia. We shall see shortly that the second explanation has some force to it.

The preference for the centre may conceal a lack of ideological awareness as often as display a nice sense of ideological distance. That is

Table 5:2   Ideological self-placement, a British-Australian comparison

Where would you say you are?	Britain 1963 %	Australia 1967 %
Left	33	10
Centre	33	56
Right	33	34
Other	1	0
Total	100	100 (N = 589)

6 Butler and Stokes, *Political Change in Britain*, p. 20.

to say, a respondent asked whether he thinks of himself as left, centre or right, and having indeed a minimal recognition of these terms, may be prompted to answer that he does. But when asked then to place himself the lack of meaning of the symbols for him asserts itself, and he plumps for the centre, a safe, middling place to be.[7] Support for this interpretation is available in the much smaller proportion of self-located 'centrists' than 'leftists' or 'rightists' who were prepared to place the parties on a left-right continuum: only 45 per cent did so, compared with 60 per cent and 70 per cent respectively for the other two groups. Some do see the centre as a way-station on the road from left to right (like the forty-four year-old Baptist builder in Tasmania who said 'Well, to be honest, I suppose I go to the right — though I'm starting to think more centre recently') but for many, it is clear the term has the fuzziest of references.

In Britain the combination of the Labour and Conservative parties and the intermediate position of the Liberals — more radical than the Conservatives but not as radical as the Socialists — allows little real disagreement about where the parties are placed along a left-right course. Even the Communist Party can be fitted easily into this system — by extending the continuum further left. And the fringe parties, the Welsh and Scottish Nationalists, may be disregarded because their share of the vote is still small nationally. In Australia the problem of the 'correct' placement of the parties is a great deal more serious, firstly because the minor parties together attract between 15 and 20 per cent of the vote, and secondly because of the ideological ambiguity of their stance in politics. It is true that the Country Party is a firm believer in private enterprise, especially that of farmers and graziers, but it is a firm believer also in government intervention in the economy, and its supporters share a traditional distaste for urban 'big business' and capitalists. At the end of World War II it was quicker than the Liberal Party to propose the banning of the Communist Party, but in recent foreign affairs, so far as it is possible to judge, it has been rather less 'hawkish' about Vietnam and less enthusiastically pro-American than its coalition partner. It has always seen itself as a centre party.[8] Is it then to be placed to the left or to the right of the Liberal party?

The DLP presents even greater difficulties. Rawson reminds us that

---

7 To nominate the centre may also be an implicit preference for peace and harmony rather than conflict, or be the logical consequence of having avoided a commitment to any party. The second is exemplified by the fifty-one year-old wife of a butcher, herself a small shopkeeper, who claimed a mixed voting history, and placed herself by saying '. . . the middle really. One political party doesn't interest me any more than another.' In a later chapter we shall see a decided tendency for Australians to place themselves as 'average' rather than 'upper' or 'lower' working or middle-class: there may be, in short, a tendency for Australians to avoid extremes; this is hinted at also in these data.

8 The ideology of the Country Party is discussed at some length in Aitkin, *The Country Party in New South Wales.*

'whatever one's political prejudices, hopes, fears, theories and expectations, one will find something in the history of the DLP to confirm them and something else to refute them ... No other Australian party at a similar stage has so resisted classification ...'[9] The party claims one of the symbols of the left in its name, and there is justice behind this in the focus of its social and economic policies, which reflect its origins in the Labor movement. But there is general agreement that it is the most anti-communist of the four parties in its foreign policies, and one sympathetic critic of the party has argued that 'one would judge the DLP *vote*, given the preferential system, as pro-Liberal and hence non-'left' whatever one might say about the DLP's policy as such'.[10] In short, there are no simple criteria for use in placing either the Country Party or the DLP in relation to the Liberal Party.

Nevertheless, few would argue that either minor party or the Liberal Party was to the left of the Labor Party in its domestic policy or general stance. Although our respondents differed greatly as to the relative positions of the Liberal, Country and Democratic Labor Parties, only a tiny handful of them put either the Labor or the Communist parties furthest to the right, and in no case did this seem to be the result of a self-conscious manipulation of the labels away from their accustomed positions. Such respondents were simply confused. They are represented by an English immigrant housewife, a university graduate who considered herself an independent. She answered the first question by saying 'I like to think of myself in the centre but I suspect I'm to the left, which is heredity — having been brought up by a very conservative mother'. A suspicion that she meant rather that she had rebelled against a conservative home environment is dispelled by her answer to the second question, in which she placed the parties from the left in the order Liberal-DLP-Labor-Communist, and commented: 'The Liberals are a bit on the left, a bit conservative. Communist and Conservative are the two opposites ... but I get confused between left and right.' In another part of the interview she referred to the preference of the middle class 'for the left'.

Most of those who answered the question were not confused, however, and, allowing for the difficulty of placing the two minor parties, drew up left-right continua that experienced political journalists would find sensible, even if they disagreed with them. Some 60 per cent placed the Liberal Party furthest to the right, 17 per cent the Country Party, and 16 per cent the DLP. (In Britain, 95 per cent considered the Conservative Party the most right.) The relative confusion among Australian electors compared to their British counterparts can be laid at the door of the greater number of essentially non-Labor parties in Australia. But that will hardly do for an explanation when we consider the difference between the two electorates in nominating the party furthest to the left (Table 5.3).

9 Rawson, 'The D.L.P. — "Get On", "Get Out" or Neither', in Mayer(ed), *Australian Politics* p. 425.
10 Duffy, 'The D.L.P. in the Seventies', in ibid., p. 409.

Both countries have minuscule Communist parties, of approximately the same electoral irrelevance (although Communists have been elected to the House of Commons). Why do British electors fail to bring their own Communist Party to mind in such a situation, while as many as two in every five of their Australian counterparts do so? One answer is that the Communist Party of Australia has played a more important role in union affairs than its opposite number in Britain, and although its electoral performance has usually been derisory, Communists have still to be taken seriously in politics.

Another, which flows from the first, is that in virtually all post-war federal elections in Australia, and in several before the war, domestic and external communism has been an issue in a fashion that has had no parallel in Britain. The vagueness of 'communism' as an issue is nicely demonstrated by the failure of respondents to react to it as a problem: only four in 1967, and three in 1969, mentioned it as a problem that the federal government should do something about. But it has flourished as a bogey. Labor partisans and academic critics alike have criticised post-war Liberal Party governments for 'kicking the communist can' as a transparent tactic aimed at discrediting the ALP — the tendency of such propaganda being that the Labor Party is heavily influenced by communists or the Communist Party. Table 5.3 suggests that in an election situation, where communists are generally absent, the Labor Party is relatively more conspicuous; even then, however, more than one in four of those who utilise the left-right framework put the Communist Party inside it.

Although the extent of communist influence within the ALP was always exaggerated,[12] the constant repetition of the communist theme has clearly had an effect upon the electorate (we shall see some more impressive evidence of this effect later in the chapter). By the mid-1960s,

Table 5.3   The party furthest to the left, Britain and Australia

	Britain 1963 %		Australia 1967 %	Australia 1969 %
Labour	95	Labor	51	61
Conservative	2	Communist	40	28
Liberal	2	DLP	7	7
Other	0	Liberal	1	3
Don't know	1	Other	1	1
Total	100		100 (N = 392)	100 (N = 419)

11 D.W. Rawson, *Australia Votes, the 1958 Federal Election*, Melbourne 1961, p. 5.
12 They were not entirely without foundation, however; as Rawson notes, 'The trouble with these allegations was that they were partly true' (*Australia Votes*, p.5).

when real communist influence in union affairs had fallen to a low level, Australia's involvement in the war in Vietnam kept the theme alive, even though the details changed. Communists remained the enemy, but they were now the Vietcong rather than the CPA (which had in fact broken into warring factions as a consequence of the Sino-Soviet split). In short, 'communist' and 'communism' have been the most important 'boo-words' of Australian politics, and they contaminate other words that have associations with them, especially 'socialist' or 'socialism', and 'left'. Here is one clue to the relative reluctance of Australian electors to label themselves 'left', and a further insight into one principal electoral handicap of the Australian Labor Party.

For those who could place the parties along a line from left to right, party identification made little difference to the likelihood that they would nominate a given order to the parties. There was in fact very close similarity between partisans of all parties in the proportions that placed the Communist Party or the Labor Party furthest left. At the other end of the scale, DLP partisans were more inclined to put their own party furthest right, while all other partisan groups showed clear majorities for the Liberal Party. It is possible to construct, from the several hundred separate continua described by the respondents, a compromise, or lowest common denominator, continuum, which reads from left to right Communist — Labor — DLP — CP — Liberal. We cannot, however, assume that this ordering represents the most common view of the party system.[13] To begin with, only one in five of our respondents claimed to see parties in left-right terms, whatever the precise ordering. And there was a good deal of disagreement as to the relative positions of the Liberal, Country and Democratic Labor Parties. However appealing such a construct is to a political scientist, therefore, he must remember that it has little to do with the way the mass electorate views the parties. Just how inadequate it is as a predictor of voters' *preference* we now proceed to discover.

'The Preferences'

It is the combination of compulsory and preferential voting that sets the Australian electoral system apart. These two constraints on an elector's freedom of action were introduced separately and for different purposes, but by 1962 they were universal in elections for the lower houses of Australian parliaments, state and federal.[14] Their consequence for the

13 Alford, in *Party and Society, the Anglo-American Democracies* (London, 1964, pp. 11-18) orders the parties Labor-DLP-Liberal-Country, an arrangement that would be approved by many Australian political scientists. Rawson, in *Australia Votes* (p. 53), suggests that whether the Country Party is more 'extreme' than the Liberal Party is an open question.

14 See Joan Rydon, 'Compulsory and Preferential', *Journal of Commonwealth Political Studies*. 6(3), November 1968; B.D. Graham 'The Choice of Voting Methods in Federal Politics, 1902-1918', in Hughes, *readings in Australian Government*.

nature of the electoral system is easy to exaggerate. Compulsory voting has brought to the polls the indifferent and the apathetic, including many women, but there is no evidence that one party has benefited disproportionately thereby. If anything, the most plausible hypothesis would be that the benefits have been shared, Labor attracting most of the uninterested, and non-Labor most of the women. The Country Party does not owe its favourable situation in politics to preferential voting but to the concentration of its supporters. While the DLP appeared able until 1972 to exercise a successful veto against a Labor government by the official direction of DLP voters' *second* preferences to non-Labor candidates, it is clear that this is only one of a number of tactics that the DLP could have employed. In a simple majority system, for example, the party would presumably have refrained from contesting marginal seats (where it would have urged its supporters to vote Liberal or Country Party) and reserved its electoral adventures for safe Labor seats, where the splitting of the non-Labor vote would be of no consequence. Preferential voting does make life easier for minority parties, since the inhibition of the 'wasted' vote is not present; but some minority parties have demonstrated a determined toughness even when the system is wholly antipathetic to them. In short, Rae's conclusion that 'the Australian system behaves in all its particulars as if it were a single-member district plurality formula'[15] has much force to it. Preferences are counted in perhaps one in five contests, and 'change the result' in only one in twenty.

If we shift our attention from the system to the citizen, however, it is clear that preferential and compulsory voting have a profound impact on the individual voter. As Joan Rydon has well put it,

> they alter the nature of the voting process. It is no longer a question of the elector voting for the candidate or the party he supports, or, in the absence of such candidate or party, not voting. He is required to indicate his order of preference for the available candidates, even though he may *support* none of them.[16]

Some voters find this process quite distasteful, often because they do not think of the parties in ordinal terms, or because they object to the lack of options open to them — a voter may not place more than one party last, for example. The circumstances of a by-election for the seat of Australian Capital Territory in 1970 provided another source of disquiet. For the first time Canberra voters were confronted with a candidate from the tiny National Socialist Party, one of seven offering, and some, in letters to the editor or in private conversations, expressed their objection at having to 'vote for' a Nazi at all, unable or unwilling to see that to place that

---

15 Douglas W. Rae, *The Political Consequences of Electoral Laws*, New Haven, 1967, p. 108.
16 Joan Rydon, 'The Electoral System', p. 128; my emphasis.

candidate seventh and last was decisively to vote *against* him. Preferential voting was frequently cited by respondents in 1969 as a feature of Australian government and politics that they disapproved of.

For most voters preferential voting forces the consideration of the parties along a most-favoured to least-favoured continuum, even if the result is a decision that the voter does not care at all about the minor places once he has placed 1 against his own party's candidate (this could be the most rational course of action for the great majority of Labor supporters, since Labor candidates are very rarely eliminated from the count). In practice, the parties come to the aid of their followers, because the ordering of the lengthy Senate ballot papers is of the utmost importance (both to ensure that the vote is a valid one and to prevent the drift of preferences), and appealing to supporters to follow the party's 'how-to-vote' cards is an ongoing process.

The parties' official orders are predictable enough. The Liberal Party puts the ALP last or, if there is a Communist candidate, second last. In country seats, the Country Party receives the Liberal Party's second preference, elsewhere the DLP is favoured. Labor shuns the Communist Party above all and generally tries to construct a preference order that does not lead to confusion. The Country Party and the DLP always give their second preferences to the Liberal Party, and prefer each other to Labor. Thus any voter may possess, in the polling booth, a number of preference orders, some set out on the how-to-vote cards he has been handed by party workers outside the building, and one his own summary of his likes and dislikes. His own, of course, may not coincide with any of the others.

Interviewers obtained the preference orderings of the respondents *via* the following series of questions:

If a federal election were held tomorrow, which party would you vote for?

And which party would get your second preference?

And which party would you put last? [17]

The interviewers were instructed to emphasise, if asked, that they were offering the respondents the widest possible choice of parties not just the set that they might expect in their own constituencies. But in any case the questions caused no difficulty, and do not appear to have been misinterpreted. It might have been thought, for example, that the second question would attract answers properly destined for the third, that is, that some voters would equate second and last, but the evidence suggests on the contrary that the logic of preferential voting is almost universally understood by the electorate. Nine out of ten could make a start with their first preference, while nearly eight out of ten could supply their

17 Questions 45(a)-(c) in the 1967 questionnaire and 44(a)-(c) in the 1969 questionnaire.

first, second and last preferences. It would have been possible to obtain more complete information by asking respondents to rank all the parties, but only at the cost of acquiring unknown quantities of spurious preferences. Knowledge of the first, second and last preferences does at least locate the main markers on the preference continuum. First preference, as defined here, is not necessarily the party identified with. The reason for the apparent shift in analysis can be simply explained. Firstly, preferences have such an application to an election situation that it seemed most sensible to treat them in this fashion. Secondly, by not equating party identification with first preference it was possible to use party identification in an analysis of the meaning of preference. We shall see in Chapter 12 that its use here was most productive.

The party system that emerges from the preference patterns is in many respects an expected one (Table 5.4). Country Party voters prefer the Liberal Party, and the compliment is returned. DLP voters are rather less enthusiastically pro-Liberal. Labor voters are sour on the DLP. Yet here are also surprises, the most arresting being the extent of the antipathy towards the Communist Party, which is introduced into the system only to be emphatically rejected, and on all sides. It is worth remarking that nowhere in the entire interview schedule do the words 'communist' or 'communism' appear. The general nomination of the Communist Party as Australia's most reviled party is a further striking example of the hold that anti-communism has upon the perception of the electorate, and a demonstration that recognition of the Communist Party as a menace is not restricted to those who see Australian politics in ideological terms. Moreover, the data present a fascinating jumble of preference orderings, with most possible combinations of the major parties represented by substantial groups of voters. The variety of preference orderings is so great, in fact, that it makes nonsense of the view that there is a single underlying dimension to party choice in Australia. The Australian party system, it is clear, occupies a multidimensional space.

The problem of the meaning of space and distance in a party system is an intriguing one, and it has known a long and distinguished debate.[18] Elegant unidimensional models of party systems have been shown to be inadequate representations of reality because of the failure of citizens to behave according to them. At the same time, mass perceptions of the party system are by no means wholly random: there are strong patterns

18 The models have been drawn primarily from economics. A summary of the literature is given in Butler and Stokes, *Political Change in Britain*, p. 201. See also Philip E. Converse, 'The Problems of Party Distance in Models of Voting Change', in M. Kent Jennings and L. Harmon Zeigler (eds.), *The Electoral Process*, Englewood Cliffs, 1966; Philip E. Converse and Henry Valen, 'Dimensions of Cleavage and Perceived Party Distance in Norwegian Voting', *Scandinavian Political Studies*, 6, 1971; and Michael Taylor, 'Review Article: Mathematical Political Theory', *British Journal of Political Science*, 1(3), 1971.

Table 5.4 Preference orders, by party, 1967

Liberal Supporters (N=698)

| Second Preference | Last Preference | | | | | All |
	Labor %	CP %	DLP %	Comm. %	Other %	%
Labor		4	11	16	*	*31*
CP	19		11	18	1	*48*
DLP	9	1		9	*	*19*
Comm.	0	0	0		0	*0*
Other	*	0	*	1		*2*
All	*28*	*5*	*22*	*44*	*1*	*100*

Labor Supporters (N=633)

| Second Preference | Last Preference | | | | | All |
	Liberal %	CP %	DLP %	Comm. %	Other %	%
Liberal		7	23	20	2	*51*
CP	7		12	3	1	*23*
DLP	12	2		7	*	*21*
Comm.	1	0	*		0	*2*
Other	3	0	2	*		*3*
All	*21*	*9*	*37*	*30*	*3*	*100*

Country Party Supporters (N=108)

| Second Preference | Last Preference | | | | All |
	Liberal %	Labor %	DLP %	Comm. %	%
Liberal		31	24	28	*82*
Labor	4		7	3	*14*
DLP	1	1		2	*4*
Comm.	0	0	0		*0*
All	*5*	*31*	*31*	*33*	*100*

DLP Supporters (N=53)

| Second Preference | Last Preference | | | | All |
	Liberal %	Labor %	CP %	Comm. %	%
Liberal		25	8	40	*72*
Labor	8		4	6	*17*
CP	0	8		4	*11*
Comm.	0	0	0		*0*
All	*8*	*32*	*11*	*49*	*100*

* = less than 0.5 per cent

Note: All respondents who named a party in response to each of the questions appear in these tables. Their first preferences define them as 'supporters': thus those whose first preference was Liberal are grouped in the first set. The rows and columns in italics illustrate the distribution, *within each set*, of last preferences and second preferences respectively: thus 31 per cent of Liberals placed Labor second, and 28 per cent placed Labor last. The figures not in italics display the proportions of Liberal supporters (Labor supporters, etc.) with given of preference in all party systems. The difficulty is that they cannot easily be reconciled without departing altogether from unidimensionality.

These patterns can be made to stand out more clearly from the data if we perform a simple reduction operation, and construct for each group of party supporters (defined for this discussion as those who would vote for that party 'tomorrow', that is September-October 1967) an index that shows the relative positions of the other parties on a scale running from -100 to $+100$. These positions are a summary of the perceptions of each group of party supporters, and are obtained by subtracting the proportion placing a given party last from the proportion placing it second — the italicised frequencies in Table 5.4. Where the first is the larger figure the result will be a minus quantity — that party is on balance seen unfavourably.

The end points of the scale have some meaning. If all supporters of Party A placed party B second, then none of them could have placed it last; therefore its score would be $100 - 0 = 100$. This is a measure of unity of opinion about the distance of party B relative to parties C, D...n, but not, alas, relative to party A. It could be possible for supporters of party A to be united in preferring party B as their second choice, but to see party B nevertheless as a long way from them, and close to the other parties, rather like this:

A   B   C   D   E . . . n

If party B is seen as a long way from party A, then the cause is presumably that in certain important respects the parties are significantly different: their ideologies may conflict sharply, or their electoral support may be very different, or their leaders may employ contrasting styles, and so on. If that is the case, then there is likely to be disagreement among supporters of party A about whether or not party B deserves second preference at all. To put it another way, the closer party B is seen to party A, in terms of policy, ideology, competence, leadership and other important attributes, the more likely it will be that supporters of party A make it their second choice.

It is reasonable to assume, therefore, that unity of opinion is to some extent an index of perceived relative distance.[19] If all supporters of A were to place B second, there would presumably be little of importance

combinations of preferences: thus, 19 per cent of Liberals placed the Country Party second and Labor last, while 16 per cent placed Labor second and the Communist Party last. The figures not in italics sum to 100 per cent.

19 This passage first appeared in a seminar paper in 1970, some time before I was able to read the article by Converse and Valen, and they too feel the force of this wholly intuitive deduction: 'there is an important sense in which consensuality of high or low ranks accorded by members of a particular party is being interpreted as a straight-forward function of some more underlying distance' ('Dimensions of Cleavage', p. 132).

Figure 5.1 Preference scales, by party, 1967. The arithmetic used in these scales would normally require that the positive and negative sides of each scale balance. They do not always do so, because Liberal Reform and other minor groups have been ignored.

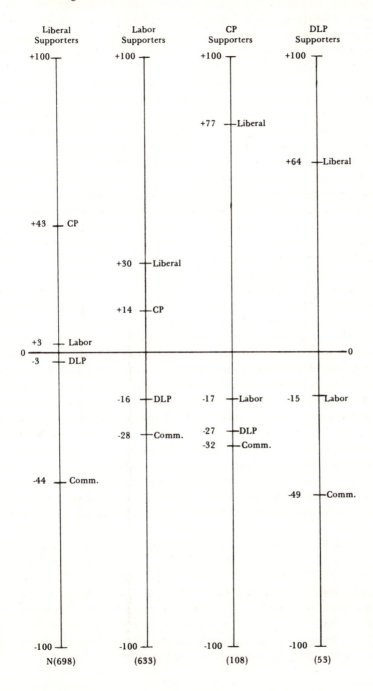

to separate the parties in their eyes. If in addition all supporters of B placed A second, we might find it reasonable as outsiders to conclude that in fact little does separate the parties. We cannot measure how little that little is, if only because 'distance' here is metaphoric, not real. But it seems possible to say that, if party B occupies the +100 position on the scale for supporters of party A, it is seen as being as close as another party could be. The opposite case, where everyone places party B last, describes party B, less precisely, as being as far away from party A as possible or conceivable. These limiting cases have some interesting properties. If everyone places party B last, then no-one can have placed any other party last, therefore all other parties will have positive scores, i.e. they will have been seen favourably. The reverse is true in the opposite case: all other parties will have negative scores.

The scales for each of the four principal groups are set out in Figure 5.1. We might first observe the lack of extreme cases. Only Country Party supporters see another party — the Liberal Party — close to their own position, and while the Communist Party is low on everyone's scale it is not, even for DLP supporters, way down at the bottom. The explanation is probably not hard to provide: there are more candidates for last place than for second. Thus Labor supporters, for whom in any case second preference usually holds little practical meaning, are divided by whether their aversion is to the DLP or the Communist Party; the DLP voters, their second preferences determined by the logic of their party's existence, have to choose between Labor and Communism for last place. Fifty years of coalition have the same effect on Country Party supporters who show in addition a surprisingly firm distaste for the DLP.

There are clear patterns, too. The Communist Party is a clear last within each group of party supporters, and the DLP second last outside the ranks of its own supporters, a position that surely makes the future expansion of the party unlikely. The Liberal Party is a firm second choice, the Country Party a consistent third. These summary preference lists give further meaning to the readiness of voters to see virtues in parties other than their own: in particular let us note that for Labor voters the Liberal Party is on balance the party next preferred. The explanation may be a simple one — that the other parties are detested more vehemently, or that they are seen as too small to be serious alternatives as governments, or that the general recognition of the Liberal Party at the time as a good manager of government implies that voters may value competence very highly, even when it conflicts with party loyalty. Whatever the reason, it is clear that in practice the electorate does not construct its preference systems in harmony with any simple ideological model. If anything, a more realistic representation would be that the majority of voters divide the party system into two, one half containing the three 'approved' parties, Liberal, Labor and Country, and the other the 'rejected' parties, the DLP and the Communist Party.

6 The Transmission of Party Loyalties

. . . politics is like religion: whatever you are born you stay. (widowed old-age pensioner, seventy-two, Sydney)

Politics, like society itself, is revealed to children by and through their parents. As commonsense and the now very extensive literature of political socialisation both tell us, the role of fathers and mothers in forming the basic political dispositions of their children is fundamental and very often decisive.[1] School, peer-group, church, television and other media can all make a contribution, especially if the parents are only mildly concerned with politics themselves and give few clues to their own political attitudes. And in general, as Jennings and Niemi remind us, the part played by parents will differ from one polity to another, across a spectrum ranging from those polities in which 'life and learning are almost completely wrapped up in the immediate and extended family to those which are highly complex social organisms and in which the socialization agents are extremely varied'.[2] It is likely that in Australia the role of the family remains predominant, for here the custom has been for the family to occupy its own separate house on its own block of land, and the children typically leave this home only at the time of their own marriage, while relatives — the 'great family' of grandparents, uncles, aunts and cousins — are the principal actors in family social interaction. Moreover, there is not in Australia, as there is in the United States of

---

1 Herbert Hyman, whose book *Political Socialization: a Study in the Psychology of Political Behavior* (Glencoe, 1959) provided the name and perhaps the beginning of this fast-growing field of research and theory, claimed that the family was the 'foremost' agency of political socialisation; the primacy of family, at least in the United States, has come under challenge from later writers. R.W. Connell provides a useful seventy-nine item 'introductory' bibliography in his 'The Origins of Political Attitudes', *Politics*, 2(2), November 1967. His own admirable *The Child's Construction of Politics* (Melbourne, 1971) is the major Australian study, and his critical article 'Political Socialisation in the American Family: the Evidence Re-examined', *Public Opinion Quarterly*, 36(3), 1972, is most important. See also A.F. Davies's chapter 'Political Socialisation', in F.J. Hunt (ed.), *Socialisation in Australia*, Sydney, 1972.
2 M. Kent Jennings and Richard G. Niemi, 'The Transmission of Political Values from Parent to Child', *American Political Science Review*, 62(1), March 1968, p. 169.

America, a highly developed tradition of teaching civics in school.[3]

Nevertheless, political socialisation in Australia is not simply, or even mainly, a matter of the semi-direct indoctrination of the young by the old; indeed, this seems to be a most atypical pattern. Rather is it the slow acquisition by the child of facts, unfacts and interpretations, assembled subconsciously from the mass media, personal observation, answers to questions, and overheard scraps of adult comment and conversation.

The means by which the child acquires his store of political inform- ation and prejudice, and the contents of that store, were not appropriate inquiries for the surveys. But respondents were asked about their parents' party preferences, occupations, religions and social classes, and also about the ages at which they themselves had first begun to hear about politics and to form likes and dislikes about the parties. Recall of such matters is likely to be imperfect, and it is important not to abuse the evidence by wringing too much from it.

Growing up within a family helps to fix some basic political dis- positions. Parents have much to do with the child's future partisanship and his interest in politics. Yet what is passed on can be critically affected by the times in which the family lives. A middle-class Catholic family in Victoria in the 1960s saw Australian party politics very dif- ferently from a similar family twenty years before. The impact of the Depression of the 1930s on political attitudes overcame the force of parental example in many families. If family influences seem unique and individual, generational influences are common and shared. This chapter looks at them both.

Politics and Parents

We can only guess at the kinds of political information the respondents first acquired. Connell's Sydney children in 1968, large consumers of television news and other fare, were by early adolescence putting together maps of the political system in which the main actors and their tasks, and the role of parties, were well delineated, and coloured by the beginnings of party loyalty. The great impact of television on these children[4] makes it doubtful that Connell's findings can be generalised to

3 Connell argues that the New South Wales pupil will acquire a respect for Queen and country in infants' school (ages 5-7) and some very basic civics, together with some actual experience in voting in class elections, in primary school (ages 8-11), at which his formal political education ceases. The main effect of this indoctrination, Connell suggests, 'is to propagate the tradition of conservative nationalism' ('Propaganda and Education', p. 162).

4 Nearly all of the children in his sample watched television news in the evening, many three or four times a week. 'Television news', in Connell's estimation, 'is in fact the main source of the children's knowledge of politics', and its primacy results in the children perceiving a political world which is a 'surface, a glittering mosaic of discrete images' (*The Child's Construction of Politics*, pp. 119-22).

the 1967 and 1969 samples, most of whom had grown up before television had become widespread in Australia. But Connell's argument that children tend to develop a party preference similar to that of their parents either because of a 'diffuse family loyalty' or because the parents hold a monopoly of information about parties, and their choice, in such a context, can only seem a reasonable one to the child,[5] is of quite general application.

Connell's data suggest strongly that party choice comes at a relatively late stage in the child's construction of politics, after he has developed a sense of what parties are for. On the whole, we should expect opinion to follow information: a child's strongly held party preference that flourished in the absence of any political information would be judged as bizarre and precocious. The data support such an expectation, for the great majority of the respondents reported that the age at which they began to form likes and dislikes about the political parties was somewhat later — often many years later — than the age at which they had begun to hear about politics. In contrast to the early political awakening of Connell's subjects, these grown-ups generally reported interest and partisanship in politics as having begun quite late in adolescence. One-half claimed that they had not begun to hear about politics until the age of about fifteen years, or later, while there were few who reported that their partisanship had begun earlier than eighteen years. A majority, in fact, remembered this as having occurred after they had reached voting age.

The most plausible explanations of this contrast lie in the fading memories of adults and perhaps in some differences in definition. There were a few who put quite precise dates to these events, and with good reason, like the old-age pensioner in a Brisbane suburb who said firmly, 'when I was twenty-two. That was when my husband began to talk to me about politics — then I went his way'. But in general it is the case that the older the respondents, the more likely they were to remember these events as having occurred at around adulthood or even later: fully one in four of those older than sixty placed the age at which they had formed likes and dislikes about the parties at twenty-five or more — that is, some years after they had acquired the right to vote. It is perfectly possible that growing affluence, the greater availability of political information, and higher levels of education among parents have all helped to reduce the age at which children become socialised into the world of politics. But it is no less likely that these rather diffuse 'events' are recalled with difficulty, and that the difficulty increases with age.

On the other hand, the young respondents were not so different from their parents' and grand-parents' generations. Nearly two in five of those who fell into the 21-30 age group reported that their partisanship had begun

5 Ibid., p. 81.

at twenty-one or later, and the same proportion placed it between age seventeen and twenty. Only one in five, then, claimed to have formed their partisanship relatively early (and only one in twenty remembered it occurring before the age of fourteen). Memory's efficacy may be suspect for these respondents too, but there is another possibility. While there can be no doubt that many of Connell's subjects had developed a party preference in childhood, it may be the case, nevertheless, that many voters' own *awareness* of this disposition is delayed until they enter an arena, such as their occupation, or the electorate, where their preferences will have consequences in action. An eighteen year old will very often have to decide whether or not to join a union, or what to say when a political conversation starts up in a group during the lunch-break; before very long he will have to cast a vote. It may be these events which he recalls, rather than undatable and often forgotten occasions in childhood or early adolescence.

If this argument is substantially correct, then one implication is that those who do recall an early introduction to politics and partisanship were brought up in homes where politics was a frequent subject for family comment and discussion (households where, we may guess, the parents' own partisanship was known). Some support for this hypothesis is contained in Table 6.1, which shows that the more respondents knew of their parents' own stance in politics, the more likely they were to recall that their own awareness of and concern about politics began in adolescence rather than later. No other factors seemed to play an important part. Girls took rather longer than boys both to become aware of politics and to identify with a party, but the trends were much the same. Class origins had but slight effect: of those who considered their family to have been middle-class when they were growing up, 66 per cent remembered hearing about politics before the age of seventeen, compared with 59 per cent of those from working class origins. The difference between the two

Table 6.1   Early awareness of and partisanship in politics, by knowledge of parents' partisanship, 1967[6]

Parents' Partisan- ship known	Heard about politics before age 17	Formed likes and dislikes about parties before age 17
	%	%
Both	68	16
One	61	14
Neither	48	8

6 Knowledge of parents' partisanship was obtained through questions 36 and 38 in the 1967 questionnaire. The Ns for each cell are, of course, different; but the approximate row variable Ns are 950, 450 and 650 respectively.

groups in the speed of acquiring a party preference was even slighter. The politicisation of the family, rather than sex or social class, appears to be the crucial variable.

When we remember that our body politic contains only a relatively small *demos* — those actively engaged in and concerned about public affairs — the contribution of the family environment acquires an added meaning. For the early learners were disproportionately to be found among those who took a good deal of interest in politics in adult life. Three in four of those who claimed to have formed likes and dislikes about the parties by the age of seventeen also reported that they now took a good deal of interest, or some interest in current politics. For those who acquired a party preference later, that proportion dropped to half.[7]

Political homes produce political children, and party homes produce party children. 'I grew up to Labor', explained a Victorian farmer. 'It's sort of traditional.' And a musician in Newcastle (NSW) commented, 'We were brought up Liberal'. Most children, if the respondents' recall of their own childhood is to be accepted, encounter either a united front of parental party loyalty — in which both parents are acknowledged supporters of the one side, or of no side — or a ruling orthodoxy maintained by one parent and acquiesced in by the other.[8] This last mode is well illustrated by a young clerk in the RAAF: 'Mother never said much, except that I believe she *was* Liberal. She let my father think she was going to vote how he told her, but I don't think she did. He was very strong Labor, and she said nothing, to keep the peace.' These common patterns help to explain some of the force of parental influence. Three in four of those who were born in Australia of parents who survived at least through the respondent's childhood recalled that their parents had either shared the same partisanship (53 per cent) or had appeared to have no partisanship at all (21 per cent).[9] Most of the remainder reported that one parent had had an explicit partisanship, the

7 Early awakening can occasionally have opposite consequences, as in the case of a widowed Salvation Army Officer, who remembered first hearing about politics when she was 'very small', and added drily: 'Father was a fanatic — which turned me off politics.'
8 This is a familiar finding. Berelson and his colleagues noted that 'many American families vote as a unit, making joint decisions in voting as in spending parts of the common family income' (B. Berelson *et al.*, *Voting*, pp. 92-3). Rawson found that most of the husband/wife pairs in his Parkes sample intended to vote the same way (*Australia Votes*, p. 182). The present data (in which information about the spouse was obtained from the respondent) are similar; they are discussed in Chapter 7. For studies of the Australian family, see S. Encel, 'The Family', in A.F. Davies and S. Encel (eds.), *Australian Society. A Sociological Introduction* (2nd ed.), Melbourne, 1970, and Harold Fallding, 'Inside the Australian Family', in A.P. Elkin (ed.), *Marriage and the Family in Australia*, Sydney, 1957.
9 The correspondence of parent-child party choice is so important to the general argument that we should remember it is based on recall data, and recall also of the attitudes of another person. It is quite possible that some respondents have endowed their parents with their own current party preferences. There is no reason to think that their number is large, or that such respondents are concentrated in the ranks of one party rather than another. But the possiblity remains, and it should lead to caution in making large claims for the implications of these data.

other not, and only a tiny 4 per cent told of parents with conflicting loyalties. The consequences of agreement and disagreement between the parents can be seen in Table 6.2. In the absence of united parental example, or when parents give no cues at all about parties, the new voter has been as likely to form an attachment to the Liberal Party as to the Labor Party.

As we might expect, cases where only one parent had an explicit partisanship form an intermediate region between the poles of united preference and united indifference. Where the partisanship of the parents was known and identical, 83 per cent of the children reported that their own first preference was for the party of their parents. Where the preference of only one parent was known, the followers declined to 63 per cent. The same effect obtains at the other end of the partisanship scale. Where the children knew the preference of *neither* parent, 18 per cent reported no definite early partisanship themselves; but where the partisanship of one parent was known, this proportion dropped to 6 per cent.

The influence of mothers and fathers in determining the party preferences of their children is by no means equal. To begin with, while 75 per cent of fathers were said to have had party preferences, this was true of only 60 per cent of mothers. Many respondents volunteered the information, in fact, that their mothers were quite apolitical: a Hobart butcher's wife, for example, commented, 'Oh, we never knew very much about Mum — she never discussed it: I couldn't say what her party was. She was never very politically minded.' Among the respondents themselves there were very many wives who confessed that they left 'all that' to their husbands. It would not be surprising to discover that in matters of political partisanship children tended to follow their fathers more often than their mothers. And indeed while 17 per cent followed their fathers' partisanship against their mothers', only 7 per cent took the opposite course. But if we now make allowance for the fact that the explicit partisanship of mothers was rather less common, a very different pattern emerges. Table 6.3 displays the proportion of Liberal adherents according to the joint preferences of the

Table 6.2   First party preference, by parents' partisanship, 1967

Respondents' Earliest Preference	Both Liberal %	Parents' Partisanship Divided[a] %	Both Labor %	None %
Liberal	86	44	10	32
Labor	8	41	83	40
Other[b]	2	8	1	10
None or don't know	4	7	6	18
Total	100	100	100	100
(N)	(313)	(66)	(435)	(265)

[a] Includes all parents with explicit but dissimilar party preferences
[b] Includes Country Party, DLP, other party

parents. Here it is abundantly clear that the mother's influence was the stronger. The table should be read by comparing equivalent rows (mother) and columns (father). Liberal mothers were more successful in directing their children's preferences than were Liberal fathers, and so too were Labor mothers compared with Labor fathers. A corresponding pattern appears if we study the proportion of early preferences for the ALP, rather than for the Liberal Party. The effect was strongest among boys, three times as many of whom followed their mothers' preference rather than their fathers' when the parents were in disagreement; among the girls the difference was less pronounced. The greater 'pull' of mothers than fathers in such situations has been observed also in Britain and the United States.[10] The explanation is most probably that, given the tendency in all three polities for women to be relatively uninterested in politics, a woman whose interest in politics is great enough to maintain a party preference in opposition to that of her husband is likely to be a woman of strong personality in many cases — perhaps most — stronger than that of her husband.

At the time of his first vote, then, the typical Australian is equipped with a store of political information and a recently formed preference for one party, a preference which is remarkably likely to be also that of his parents. But his inheritance from his parents does not stop here. His identification with one party is likely to remain with him for the rest of his life. We have seen that nearly 80 per cent of respondents suggested that they had always maintained the one party preference. Table 6.4, similar in form to Table 6.2, demonstrates how strongly the parental example persists in later life. Evident also is the relatively weaker hold of the Labor Party, of minor importance in Table 6.2, but now quite marked. The drift cannot be attributed wholly to the existence, after 1955, of the DLP: in fact, among

Table 6.3 Proportions of early preferences Liberal, by preferences of parents, 1967

Mother's Preference	Liberal %	Neither[a] %	Labor %
Liberal[a]	86	71	50
Neither[a]	59	28	22
Labor	32	19	10

Note: Each entry gives the proportion whose first partisanship was Liberal, within the category defined by the joint preferences of the parents.

[a] 'Neither' includes parents with Country Party, DLP, unknown or changing preferences

10 Butler and Stokes, *Political Change in Britain*, pp. 47-9; M. Kent Jennings and Kenneth P. Langton, 'Mothers *versus* Fathers: the Formation of Political Orientations among Young Americans', *Journal of Politics*, **31**(2), 1969.

children of Labor parents the drift to the DLP was only slightly stronger than the drift to the Country Party, and the drift to the Liberal Party was more than six times as strong. The stronger influence of the mother compared with the father, where parents differed in partisanship, was as true as at the time of the first vote. One implication of the lasting correspondence of parents' and children's party choices is that for some women their fathers' choices may be more important than their husbands'[11] — witness the testimony of a Perth barmaid, married for fifteen years: 'I always vote Labor. My father always voted Labor, and what's good enough for him is good enough for me.' It is not necessary to the argument, of course, that such positive loyalty to family be the cause of long-lasting partisanship. It is likely that for most voters life circumstances will reinforce early partisanship rather than undermine it, and this is a subject we shall study in a later chapter. But we may contrast the barmaid's explanation of

Table 6.4　Present party preference, by parents' partisanship, 1967

Respondent's Own Present Preference	Both Liberal %	Parents' Partisanship Divided[a] %	Both Labor %	None %
Liberal	79	48	21	33
Labor	10	38	66	44
Other[b]	4	6	6	11
None	7	8	7	22
Total	100	100	100	100
(N)	(331)	(65)	(474)	(338)

[a] Includes all parents with explicit but dissimilar preferences.
[b] Includes Country Party, DLP, Other Party

Table 6.5　Intensity of identification by parents' partisanship, 1967

Parents' Partisanship	Respondents' Intensity of Identification						
	Very strong %	Fairly strong %	Not very strong %	Closer to %	None %	Total %	(N)
Both parents partisan	34	40	18	4	4	100	(939)
One parent partisan	26	38	22	7	7	100	(435)
Neither parent partisan	22	36	20	6	16	100	(640)

[a] Includes those whose parent(s) died when the respondent was young, or who were immigrants.

11 A phenomenon observed by Davies and Encel, 'Class and Status', in *Australian Society*, p. 38.

her preference with this remark from a middle-aged Hobart stenographer: 'I've always voted Liberal, first of all because I was brought up to it, and more recently because I worked it out for myself.' [12]

Nor does parental influence stop at moulding the child's partisanship. The intensity of that partisanship is also affected. Those whose parents were both partisan were more likely to feel strongly about their own partisanship than those whose parents had appeared not to be partisan at all. Again, cases where only one parent had been partisan occupied an intermediate position. Table 6.5 sets out this finding in more detail; 'Closer to' refers to those who, while avowing no present party identification, agreed that in the past they had felt closer to one party rather than another. Three-quarters of those whose parents were openly partisan had become strong party identifiers themselves. But those from unpolitical families were much less likely to be strong identifiers — and one-sixth had no identification at all. The source of much of the stability in the Australian party system is thus the transmission of loyalties and interest from parents to children. As party supporters die and leave the electorate they are replaced by newly enfranchised voters sporting the same colours.

The Importance of Generation

Were nothing else than the transmission of party loyalty involved, there would be very little change in the size of the parties' supporting groups; and what change there was could be predicted from known fertility and death rates.[13] But although parental example and influence are fundamental, they are not everything. Even where parents are declared partisans for one party, their children may adopt, as we have seen, quite a different party preference. In some cases this is simply the other side of the happy-family coin: a child whose relationships with his parents are angry and rebellious may reject their political stance just as he rejects their standards in other matters. For how many respondents some such personal history was true we cannot say, but the number cannot have been large. Moreover, we may suppose that the pattern of angry rejection of the parents' choice of party is one that will occur in every generation, and on both sides of party politics: it probably has little effect on the stability of the system.

The influence of parents can be offset in quite a different fashion, however, and with marked variations according to age groups. Families do not inhabit a static world, however much it may appear so to them. In the twentieth century the social, economic and political environments by which families are surrounded have changed rapidly from one generation to another, and even within one generation. In quite short spans of time old social barriers become less relevant; new and different ones take their place.

12 Cf. 'I would never vote Liberal because my mother told me when she was eighty-seven never to vote Liberal; [that was] just before she died'.
13 For an attempt to do this in the British context, see Butler and Stokes, *Political Change in Britain*, pp. 263-74.

The scale of industry alters, old jobs become unattractive, new skills are sought. Party positions alter: the red-flag radicalism of one generation may be ho-hum orthodoxy to the next. Old political parties may even die, or become absorbed in new ones, while others spring fully formed from the grass roots. These changes are not always related; sometimes they are related only in subtle and indirect ways. And the child may interpret them differently from his parents.

Consider a young man on the verge of adulthood in rural New South Wales in the early 1920s. His parents have seen much change in the party system already — in twenty years they have voted successively for the Protectionist, Liberal and National Parties while supporting the same man. Now there is in the making a brand new Country Party, whose special appeal is to people like themselves. For the parents to change parties involves some sort of intellectual readjustment of their perceptions of the party system, and perhaps a conflict of interest over the problem of their favoured member of parliament. But for the son these inhibitions are much less powerful: to support the new party is for him a matter of the moment, and his perception of the new party is likely to be based on contemporary politics as he sees it, not on the past twenty years of Australian political history. By the time his own children have reached maturity the bestowal of his Country Party preference on them will have been a much more matter-of-fact business. For now the party system has changed again. In his part of the country the Country Party is the undisputed power within the non-Labor forces. His children may opt for the Labor Party, but unless they leave the district it is most unlikely that they will become Liberals.

To generalise, the transmission to the child of such parental values as party preference will occur most completely in times of apparent political stability, and least efficiently where there are dramatic and sudden changes in the economic, social or (especially) political environments. And since there is some change occurring at any time, the transmission of parental values can never be wholly efficient.

Before the contribution of a citizen's generation can be dealt with, there is an important prior problem of analysis to face. It is always difficult when using survey data to distinguish between effects arising from ageing and those arising from the different context in which each generation finds itself. It happens, for example, that of all the respondents the oldest were most likely to say that the Queen and the Royal family were very important to Australia: the proportion that felt this way increased steadily with age. What are we observing here? Is it that older people, being more conservative, are also more likely to value the symbols of political stability? Or is it that each new generation has found the monarch and Royal family decreasingly relevant to Australian society? Cross-sectional survey data can raise such questions, but they cannot help much in answering them; even an extensive analysis of these and other data can provide little more than suggestions. To observe the effects of ageing at all accurately would require a longitudinal study, in which respondents were quizzed at a number of points over a long period of time. Much the same procedure would be necessary if the goal were a major study of the effect of generation. [14]

Nevertheless, there is one dramatic illustration of the effect of generation, which is relatively unlikely to be contaminated by the effects of ageing: the party choice of respondents at their first election. We have seen that in the sixty years since the modern Australian party system began electoral support for the two main blocs has been very stable over time. Figure 6.1 displays Labor's proportion of the total valid vote in elections for the House of Representatives from 1922 to 1969, and the proportion of respondents who recall having voted Labor as first voters in those elections. The respondents who first voted in the election of 1919 and earlier years are too few in number to justify extending the graph backwards in time. However, they were predominantly Labor first voters both on average (58 per cent) and at each election.

We may first note that the two graphs bear only slight relation to one another: indeed, in more than half the intervals they move in opposite directions. It is true that during Labor's great decade — the 1940s — first voters were enthusiastically on Labor's side. But so were they in the early 1930s, when Labor was disunited and in disgrace, in the mid-1920s, when

Figure 6.1 Labor's share of the total valid vote, and of first voters' votes, 1922 to 1969

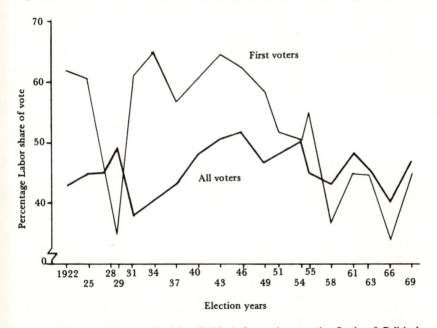

14 See William R. Klecka, 'Applying Political Generations to the Study of Political Behaviour: a Cohort Analysis', *Public Opinion Quarterly*, **35**(3), 1971, and Matilda White Riley, 'Aging and Cohort Succession:Interpretations and Misinterpretations', *Public Opinion Quarterly*, **37**(1), 1973.

the non-Labor Bruce-Page government was formed and returned to office, and to a lesser extent in the early years of the post-war Menzies governments. Up to the mid-1950s, in fact, the behaviour of first voters would seem to fit the widely accepted hypothesis that the young are more likely to be radical than the old. But not, clearly enough, thereafter. This contrast is more obvious if respondents are grouped into distinct 'generations'.

The use of this concept can be defended on commonsense grounds, but in addition it allows the separation of those respondents who were born or grew up in Australia from those who migrated to the country as adults.[15] Since there have been more than a million adult immigrants to Australia since the end of World War II and perhaps 50 per cent of them have become electors it is important that their contribution to Australian political behaviour be distinguished from that of Australians born and bred in the country. This is done in more detail in a later chapter. In the following analysis, which focuses on those respondents interviewed in 1967, immigrants form a residual group.

The native-born generations were defined by age and 'the election at which their members first voted, and the boundaries between generations were chosen after inspection of the data portrayed in Figure 6.1. The generations are as shown in Table 6.6.

These generations make sense historically. Generation V had not known, at least as voters, a party system that did not contain the Democratic Labor Party. Generation IV came to maturity during the early years of the post-war Menzies government. Generation III during Labor's heyday of the 1940s. Generation II is the 'Depression' generation.[16] Gener-

Table 6.6   Five generations in the Australian electorate, 1967

Generation	Born in the period	First voted in Federal Elections of the years	Age in 1967	Proportion of sample %
I	1874-1908	1901-29	59-93	16
II	1909-16	1931-37	51-58	12
III	1917-25	1940-46	42-50	14
IV	1926-33	1949-54	34-41	14
V	1934-46	1955-66	21-33	22
All immigrants who became electors after the age of 21				22
Total				100

15 Combining first voters in this fashion also smoothes out fluctuations in the graph that were due to sampling error and other technical causes. Although the general tendency of Figure 6.1 is robust enough, it would obviously be foolish to rest an argument upon the memory of first vote at any one election. Deaths and emigration may have distorted the sample's representativeness.

16 The characteristics of this generation — which are, broadly speaking, not dissimilar to those of the generations on either side of it — are investigated in Don Aitkin, Michael Kahan and Sue Barnes, 'What Happened to the Depression Generation' in Cooksey (ed), *The Great Depression*.

ation I is the most heterogeneous, for its members include some who played a part in colonial politics in the last decade of the nineteenth century, as well as some who first voted for Scullin in 1929. As Table 6.7 shows, these generations displayed notably different behaviour at the time of their first vote. Here is revealed one of the sources of Labor's consistent electoral strength until the mid-1950s. For at least forty years, it seems, Labor regularly attracted more than half of all those new voters who grew to adulthood in Australia. In some periods, notably World War II (Generation III), Labor was winning almost two new voters in every three. In the late 1950s and 1960s, however, Labor's attraction for young voters fell sharply.

In a first attempt to explain the Labor tendencies of first voters we might

Table 6.7 Proportion first voting Labor, by generation

	Native-born Generation					Immigrants
	I (oldest)	II	III	IV	V (youngest)	
	%	%	%	%	%	%
Proportion voting Labor at first election	56	59	63	58	43	44
(N)	(272)	(197)	(234)	(236)	(355)	(341)

Note: Only those who remember voting for a party are included.

Figure 6.2 Parents' Labor preferences and respondents' first votes, by generation

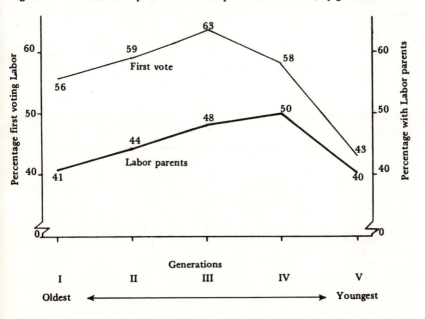

search for predominant Labor sympathies among their parents. There is a rough accord between parental sympathies and first voting preferences, as Figure 6.2 suggests. One reason why Labor voting among young voters increased so dramatically in the 1930s and 1940s was the fact that there were now more Labor parents within the community. By 1930 the modern party system, with its clear-cut choice between Labor and non-Labor (made only slightly uncertain by the entry of the Country Party in 1919) had been in operation for twenty years. Generation II was the first to grow up in the context of a simple two-party system; the parents of these voters (most of them born between, say, 1880 and 1900) grew up during the period when the Labor Party was establishing itself as a force in Australian politics.

Yet Figure 6.2 makes clear also that parental example cannot be the whole explanation. Generations I and II, for example, were far more strongly Labor than their parents; Generation V was hardly more so. Again, there is a marked decline in Labor support between Generations III and IV, but they report much the same proportion of Labor parents. One

Table 6.8   Proportion first voting Labor of those with Labor parents, by generation

		Generation		
	I (oldest) %	II %	III %	IV %	V (youngest) %
Proportion first voting Labor of those with Labor parents	88	91	94	83	73
(N)	(107)	(91)	(108)	(107)	(150)

Note: Consists of those having parents Labor or one parent Labor, and the other either no preference, preference unknown, or changing preference.

Table 6.9   Proportion first voting Labor of those whose parents were not Labor, by generation

		Generation		
	I (oldest) %	II %	III %	IV %	V (youngest) %
Proportion first voting Labor of those whose parents were not Labor	30	30	27	24	14
(N)	(137)	(110)	(129)	(124)	(219)

Note: Includes those having one parent Labor, the other a partisan for another party.

conclusion is hard to dispute: that the transmission of parental party preferences has been significantly less efficient at some periods than at others. Table 6.8 measures the differences for the Labor Party, by displaying the proportions first voting Labor of those with either two Labor parents, or a Labor parent and a neutral one. In the 1940s the tendency of children to follow the Labor sympathies of their parents was very strong indeed, but after Labor's defeat in 1949 the party's support among such potential Labor voters fell away. So did it also among those whose parents were not Labor, or who were divided in their partisanship (Table 6.9). Up until the middle of the 1940s Labor could rely on attracting perhaps 30 per cent of the first voters whose parents had not been Labor partisans. By the 1960s this proportion had dropped by half.

It is clear that at each election the cohort of new voters divides in much the same proportions as the rest of the electorate. But there can be substantial variations in this division, and at any time one party can profit handsomely. How persistent have these differences been? Some measure of the differential allegiance of generations can be obtained by comparing the proportions of each generation voting Labor in 1966 (Figure 6.3). This was commonly agreed to have been an election which reduced Labor's electoral support to its faithful; certainly the party's leader and policies appear to have found little enthusiasm in the electorate. The effect of generation was

Figure 6.3   The Labor share of the first vote, and of the 1966 vote, by generation

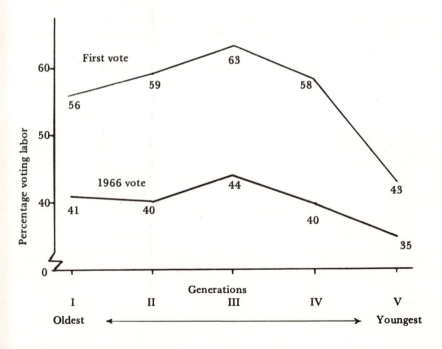

still present in 1966, but the curve is now a very gentle one. In 1966 no generation gave majority support to Labor, and there was only a 9 per cent difference between the strongest and weakest Labor generations, compared with 20 per cent between Generations III and V with respect to their first votes. As time passes, then, early generational differences are likely to be eroded by contemporary issues and other influences.

We can observe the erosion most directly in relation to Generation II, the members of which represent, in broad, the parents of Generation V. Approximately one in three of Generation II's early Labor voters had forsaken the ALP in 1966, and only 40 per cent of Generation V respondents claimed to have had Labor parents when they themselves were growing up. It seems likely, then, that Generation II's allegiance to the Labor Party was being eroded in the late 1940s and 1950s, a matter discussed in the next section of this chapter.

In short, the partisan preferences parents pass on to their children are accepted with a readiness that differs according to the temper of the times. When a party is at the height of its popularity it is likely to recruit very well among new voters, whether from its own supporters' families or otherwise. We may think of this as an intensification effect, and the converse also applies: when a party is in a slump it recruits relatively badly, despite the example of family. But that is not the whole story. At times, as during the Depression for the Labor Party, a party may attract new voters in disproportionate numbers in the face of indifferent support from the rest of the electorate. The causes of this phenomenon must be sought in part in the different perceptions of the parties and social reality by old and young; the lack of difference in 1967 between the images of party held by the old and the young should not cause us to rule out the possibility of its having existed at other times.

The data, finally, provide some insights into the electoral failure of the Labor Party in the 1960s. In 1955 and afterwards Labor polled poorly both among new voters and among immigrants. To some extent Labor's failure among new voters was an intensification effect: the party was also doing badly in the electorate at large. But we may also deduce that since Labor was not attractive to immigrants it was not attractive to their children either. Since new voters of Generation V together with immigrants constituted 44 per cent of the whole electorate, and 30 per cent of the respondents were descended from at least one immigrant parent, it is clear that Labor's electoral problem was of some magnitude.

The Development of Modern Party Politics: a Reconstruction

It is time to pause and consider the argument so far. What is it that distinguishes the politics of 1970 from those of 1870? The fundamental distinction is the existence in our own time and the complete absence a century ago, of a competitive party system, restricted to a small number of very stable teams, each of which enjoys the regular support of a large body of citizens whenever there is an election. Governments still fall, but they do so less often. Electors can support independents, or change their minds and vote for a candidate of another party, but few do so. It is still possible for a new party to engage in electoral politics, but it is manifestly difficult for it to break into the parliamentary arena. To do that requires the capture of a large body of electors. Not only are 90 per cent committed elsewhere, and their children already bespoken, but most citizens are not especially interested in politics: their party attachment is their principal link to the political process, and the complexity of that process in the twentieth century has given parties a useful role as simplifiers. While single issues still have power to draw citizens into active politics, it is hard to imagine a substantial body of electors now basing their political stance on a continuous review of problems and performance: life in a post-industrial society is too full to allow such a leisured political style. In short, Australian politics is now 'frozen' in the party mould. Parties have become to the world of politics what the limited liability company is to the world of business — a robust response to the need to overcome the unfortunate mortality of man. Short of a *coup d'état*, a permanently successful invasion, or the complete breakdown of the social and economic framework of the Australian polity, there seems every reason to suppose that Australian politics will retain its present shape for a long time. There is evidence (discussed in later chapters) to suggest that the Country and Democratic Labor parties will lose support and influence to a point where each will be absorbed into the Liberal Party; but this will only be to restore the situation to that which obtained in 1910 — a 'pure' two-party system.

The contrast with the political world of 1870 — parliamentary and electoral instability, uneasy and short-lived alliances between political notables, electoral contests in the name of roads and bridges — is marked. And questions arise. How did we get from there to here? And how quickly was the conversion to party politics accomplished? For twenty years lie between the great strikes of 1890, from which emerged the early Labor parties, and the general elections of 1910, in which Labor and Liberal candidates fought out the contest in virtually every electorate. Even in the 1920s parts of the countryside were still reacting to elections in the parochial fashion common half a century before. The change to party politics did not take place overnight.

The findings of the last few chapters help to illuminate the causes of change. Together with the body of writing on the politics of the Federation period, they point to three factors that deserve primary attention. The first was the fruitful soil of the 1890s. The long period of economic and social development that followed the gold rushes and agricultural expansion finished at the end of the 1880s in a wild boom, bitter strikes and a disastrous depression.[17] By then, and for the first time since the origins of

17 For the relevance of this experience to the emergence of the Labor Party, see Bede Nairn, *Civilising Capitalism: the Labor Movement in New South Wales, 1870-1900*, Canberra, 1973.

white settlement, each colony had become in potential a single society and a single economy — thanks principally to the telegraph and the railway. The failure of colonial governments, of politics as then constituted, to deal effectively with industrial strife and the Depression provided at least a climate of opinion in which new political responses to the challenge of government, new ideas about how society should be run, would be given consideration. The decision of trade unionists to enter politics as a group, rather than to persevere with the old dispensation, was appropriately the first major illustration that the old order was passing — appropriately, because workers' interests were not well served in either the Free Trade or Protectionist camps. But the electoral success of the early Labor Parties made clear to the old political hands that this new party way of doing things, though detestable, was not to be ignored, and thereafter they exploited and adapted those aspects of 'party' that suited their style.

The second factor was the effect of these changes upon electoral competition. Political notables, forced to see the advantages of party, moved to associate themselves more closely with one grouping or another; local party committees began to insist with more confidence that would-be candidates stick by party endorsement rules; the ease of communications made it possible for speakers and ideas to move quickly around the colony. Little by little the electoral choice of the voter was reduced, and determined, whether he liked it or not, by the readiness of each party to contest the electorate in which he lived. By 1910 anyone who intended seriously to sit in the Commonwealth parliament looked for party endorsement. If the electorate objected to the screen that had come between it and its elected representatives it gave no sign, for in the elections to the House of Representatives in that year candidates of the Labor and Liberal Parties won more than 95 per cent of the total valid vote, and the solitary independent who was returned, Sir William Lyne, was a former New South Wales premier standing in his rural fief.

Thirdly, with an effective choice increasingly restricted to the standard-bearers of two parties, campaigning on the same broad platform over the whole nation, it was natural that the electorate should begin to see the parties rather than the candidates as the true contestants, and to develop attitudes towards them. Since it was of the essence of political parties to appeal to the electorate in more or less ideological terms, the development among voters of an attachment to one party rather than to another was a relatively swift process, especially once it became clear that, for good or for ill, all governments were now party governments. In the years between 1890 and 1910 there would no doubt have been many voters who scorned these new parties, and stuck to Barton, Deakin, Kingston, Forrest or their local notable, but as the struggle between politicians became more and more a struggle between politicians-in-parties, such a strategy would have become less adequate. And whatever the parents' predilections, we may be confident that young men and women about to cast their first votes increasingly saw Australian politics as party politics, in which they had to make a choice between teams at least as much as between candidates. If their parents already possessed a party attachment this was likely to determine their own; if not, their place in society, economic interest, or some more muted aspect of family tradition would serve as well. Since the franchise was open to all adults almost from Federation, the spread of party attachments was very wide; after 1910 the scope for the emergence of new parties based on hitherto unattached groups was slight, and indeed the only two additional parties that have made a successful entrance into parliamentary politics have done so by hiving off under a different name coherent sections of the electoral support of one of the major parties.

At what point did party attachment become characteristic of the Australian electorate, as it is today? The way to an answer is suggested in a typically elegant paper by Philip Converse, who has employed a Markov chain procedure to demonstrate that approximately two generations after competitive party politics began most of the electorate would possess a stable partisan attachment.[18] His argument, applied initially to France and the USA, is easily transferred to Australia, and points to the 1920s as a time when some three-quarters of the electorate possessed such an attachment, a proportion not much less than that ruling today (see the short Appendix to this chapter). If the application of the Markov chain is appropriate in this situation then in 1970, some three generations after the beginnings of competitive party politics, Australia had reached the 'mature equilibrium' of partisan attachment, a situation in which the level of partisan attachment in the community had reached a relatively fixed point, above or below which it would not move.

So far we have been considering the system as a whole, and not the individual parties in it. We have seen that the logic of a parliamentary system in which simple majorities are decisive is to produce a party system in which gaining the magic 50 per cent plus one is the goal at elections. A more or less evenly divided electorate is the consequence. Within that electorate partisan stability is the rule. But there are exceptions: 21 per cent of the 1967 sample said that they had once preferred a different party and, while some of these respondents had moved from Liberal to DLP or had moved elsewhere within the bounds of the non-Labor camp, a clear 17 per cent had crossed the major party boundary. The direction and timing of these movements are set out in Table 6.10. There is impressive evidence of a long-term drift of Labor supporters away from their party, a movement at its peak in the 1950s because of the DLP fracture. The electoral importance of this drift is not to be denied: in terms of net profit the non-Labor bloc's advantage was of the order of 5 per cent. Yet it was a net advantage only. At all times there was a smaller drift *to* the Labor Party, and in fact in the year

18 Philip E. Converse, 'Of Time and Partisan Stability', *Comparative Political Studies*, 2, 1969.

following the 1966 elections (a bad year for the coalition government) the drift to Labor was almost twice as great as the drift away from it.

In the long run, therefore, these movements of party identification are likely to have a self-cancelling effect, even though in the short run they can represent the difference between electoral defeat and victory. Moreover, their absolute scale is quite small: most voters stay with the one party. But the small scale and the self-cancelling nature of changes in party identification are an important aspect of our understanding of political stability, and reinforce what we have learned already.

Appendix

Converse noted that there was a striking similarity between France and the USA in the extent to which a voter's possession of party identification was related to a similar disposition in his father. He then used his findings to show how intergenerational transmission of party loyalty holds the key to the stability of the modern party system. The argument can be illustrated with Australian data. Let us assume that in the mid-1890s children were very likely, on coming of age, to adopt a partisan stance if their fathers possessed one (not necessarily the same one), and that a smaller proportion would do

Table 6:10   Changes in party identification over time

Direction of Change	1948 and earlier	Period of Change Between 1949 and 1961	Since 1961
	%	%	%
Labor to non-Labor	69	81	55
Non-Labor to Labor	31	19	45
Total	100	100	100
(N)	(64)	(114)	(100)

Table 6.11   Party attachment, by father's attachment, a cross-national comparison

	Father Identifies with a Party			Father Does Not Identify with a Party		
	Australia %	USA %	France %	Australia %	USA %	France %
Respondent identifies with a party	92	82	79	75	51	48
Respondent does not identify with a party	8	18	21	25	49	52
Total	100	100	100	100	100	100

so where their fathers did not have a party attachment. These situations represent the effects of parental example, on the one hand, and the pressure of the times on the other — new voters could not avoid party politics as easily as their parents could. We can provide estimates of these proportions by extrapolating from the 1967 survey — a procedure that Converse defends. These estimates are set out in Table 6.11, with the American and French equivalents for comparison,[19] and they can be regarded as conditional probabilities that a child will develop a partisan attachment, given his father's partisan stance or lack of it, and as entries for transition probabilities in a Markov chain picturing the transmission of party loyalties from one generation to another.

If these transition probabilities remain constant then the system will move towards a fixed point or equilibrium. In the Australian case we can start with the assumptions that in the mid-1890s 5 per cent of the electorate possessed a partisan attachment (a conservative estimate, given that Labor won between 15 per cent and 30 per cent of the vote in the four largest colonies in elections between 1891 and 1894), and that a 'generation' was twenty-five years. In 1920, after one cycle, approximately 75 per cent would, according to the transition matrix, have possessed a partisan attachment. In 1945, after two cycles, the proportion was 88 per cent; in 1970, after three, 90 per cent. These latter proportions are, of course, supported by the 1967 sample, in which 87 per cent owned to a party identification. On this argument the conversion to partisan politics in Australia was a swift and decisive one — and a good deal faster than was the case in either France or the USA.

There are difficulties, which Converse concedes, in the application of the Markov chain procedures to such a situation (one is that the mathematics require transition probabilities to remain the same at all times, which is an improbable account of the real world), and he goes on to develop a most ingenious regression model which obviates them. But for our purposes, for a polity whose long experience of a democratic party system is yet unbroken, the simple Markov chain is a useful and illuminating model.[20]

---

19 Ibid., p. 145.
20 For a helpful introduction to Markov processes see J. Kemeny *et al.*, *Introduction to Finite Mathematics*, Englewood Cliffs, 1957.

PART II The Context of Stability

7 Party and Society

Like about Liberal Party? I think they have a better class of man to rule the country ...

Dislike about Labor? Not a good class of people — they're not educated. Oh, there are exceptions, but the majority of them aren't. (*wife of retired banana-grower, eighty, NSW*)

In Part I we have seen that, like his counterparts in other Western democracies, the Australian citizen combines a rather tepid interest in politics with a firm attachment to party. Although a good deal of conventional political rhetoric still places great importance on the links between the citizen and his parliamentary representative, it is the party, not the MP, that most citizens support with their votes. Parties outlast their individual parliamentary members, and provide a stable element in politics and government; their ability to survive through the generations depends in turn upon the preparedness of citizens to go on voting for them, and upon the fact that citizens tend to inherit such partisan loyalties from their parents. Finally, to close the circle, voters behave in this way because parties continue to minister to the needs of voters, both in the short term, as formulators of acceptable policies, and in the long term, as bearers of broad ideologies and views of society, which are important and satisfying to their supporters. At one level, then, party politics can be seen as a nicely balanced, self-contained system, and susceptible to analysis in its own right.

But the party system seems to be connected in more ways than this to the society of which it forms a part. The number of parties, and their relative importance, point to the social, economic, ethnic or regional cleavages in the nation. Parties remain fresh and relevant to citizens because their ideologies accord with the voters' experiences of social and economic life, and their hopes and fears. Party policies are proposals to change or maintain aspects of the social and economic fabric of society; and so on. So pervasive do these links appear that any examination of the stability of politics must concern itself with the possibility that political stability is simply an expression of an underlying social and economic stability — or if that is too determinist, a partner of that stability. The exploration of that possibility, and of the links between party attachment and society, are the principal tasks of the second part of this book.

But where to begin? As anyone who has made even a cursory analysis of the social basis of electoral support knows only too well, most sociological attributes — sex, age, income, education, occupation, and so on — are related in some degree to voting intention or party loyalty. What is more, nearly all of these attributes correlate with one another. The need is for a sorting device, and statistics offers a variety of multivariate techniques which allow the analyst to sift through a set of variables, discover the important ones, and estimate their relative importance in accounting for the characteristic under examination.[1] For our purposes, the most useful, because of the illuminating clarity of its results, is the Automatic Interaction Detector (AID) developed by Morgan and Sonquist of the University of Michigan.[2] The AID program searches, among a set of attributes nominated by the analyst, for the attribute most like another attribute whose nature is being explored. Having found it, the program then measures the extent to which the first attribute could be considered a substitute for the second. Imagine a society (like Northern Ireland) in which religion and politics are very largely co-terminous: to know a person's religion is to be able to predict, with a small chance of error, which party he will vote for. Imagine further that within one of the religious denominations there is a growing disagreement about the stance of that church in politics, and that this disagreement is one in which the old oppose the young. The application of the AID program to appropriate survey data from that society would reveal that religion was of all attributes the one most like party preference, and that it accounted for a large proportion of the variability of party preference (that is, the variability between people in party preference is usually associated with differences in religion). It would also reveal that in religion A there was an important relationship between age and party preference, and this added something further to an understanding of the variability of party preference. The systematic branching that is characteristic of the AID program has led to the description 'tree analysis' being applied to it: the more important the attribute, the closer it is to the base of the tree.

The application of tree analysis to data from the 1967 survey is set out in Figure 7.1. The aim was to test the relative strength of the influence on identification with the Australian Labor Party, of fourteen sociological characteristics possessed by respondents: state, region (town or country), age, sex, length of residence at current address, house ownership, religious denomination, church attendance, education, nationality at birth, income of head of household, occupational grade (manual or non-manual) of head

---

1 A useful introduction is John P. Van de Geer, *Introduction to Multivariate Analysis for the Social Sciences*, San Francisco, 1971.
2 John A. Sonquist, Elizabeth Lauh Baker, and James N. Morgan, *Searching for Structure*, Ann Arbor, 1971. The Computer program was made available by the Inter-University Consortium for Political Research.

of household, occupational grade of father, and union membership in household. This list of attributes includes most of those conventionally held to have some relationship to partisan choice.[3] Many of them, such as occupational grade, education and income, or father's occupational grade and respondent's education, are obviously related to one another as well as to Labor identification.

Of all these variables, the one most strongly related to the distribution of Labor identification within the sample was the occupational grade of the head of the household: 58 per cent of manual and 26 per cent of non-manual respondents identified with Labor.[4] That split reduced the variance by 10.5 per cent — that is to say, the tendency of manual respondents to identify

Figure 7.1   A tree analysis of Labor identification, 1967

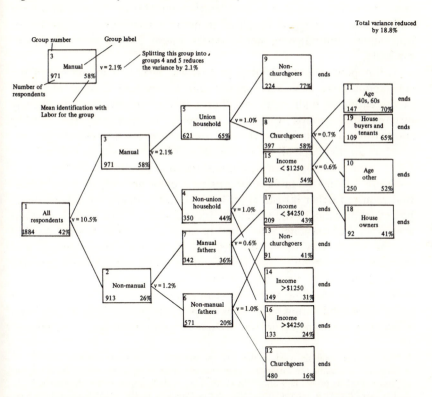

3 No information was obtained on material possessions other than a house. But in a society where virtually all households possess a car, a refrigerator, and television and radio receivers, the utility of these indices as discriminators is small.

4 A few respondents for whom information about occupational grade was not obtained were grouped by the program with the non-manuals, which increased the apparent level of Labor identification in that group from 25 per cent to 26 per cent. It is possible, of course, to remove from the data set all respondents for whom any such information is missing, but the cost is substantial reduction in the size of the data set. Accordingly, that procedure was not followed; the cost is a small degree of fuzziness in the group means.

with Labor and of non-manuals to identify with other parties accounted for a little more than 10 per cent of the variability in Labor identification.[5] Given the traditional importance of occupational status as the basis of the Labor/non-Labor division, a figure of 10 per cent is low, and we shall shortly consider why.

At the next step in the searching process each of these first two groups was further subdivided, manual respondents according to whether or not a member of the household belonged to a trade union, and non-manuals in terms of the occupational grade of the respondent's father. Here we see interaction at work. For those in the manual group, father's occupational prestige was not nearly as important as union membership, and for those in the non-manual group, union membership was much less important than father's occupational grade. These four groups were then subdivided into eight, providing a range of Labor identification of from 77 per cent among manual non-churchgoers who lived in union households to a bare 16 per cent among churchgoing non-manuals whose fathers were also non-manuals.

At this point the subdividing process was near its end: several of the sub-groups were now very small, and others had a level of Labor identification so high or so low that a further subdivision into sharply differentiated groups was most unlikely.[6] In fact only two further subdivisions took place, and the end product was ten discrete sub-groups, which accommodated all the respondents; the groups are set out in Table 7.1. The entire sorting process reduced the total variance by 18.8 per cent.

Figure 7.1 and the table summarising it point not only to the variables that require further investigation but also to the degree of independence possessed by some of the variables. Income, for example, was important even when occupational grade had been accounted for; but the *level* of income which was important differed as between non-manuals and manuals. Churchgoing was important in both occupational prestige groups,[7] but house-ownership was not. These groupings were not a matter of chance, a quirk of the particular sample interviewed in 1967. At only one point in the subdividing was the selection of sub-groups likely to have been affected by sampling error: the division of group 8 by age. Here income

---

5 The variance analysis used in the AID program is a repeated one-way analysis of variance. 'Reducing the variance' can be thought of as being equivalent to 'reducing the error in making predictions about the value of one variable given certain information'. In this case, knowing whether the respondents belonged to the manual or non-manual categories and the mean for each category reduced the error in predicting the level of Labor identification by 10.5 per cent.

6 Analysis of any sub-group ends when the number in the group falls below a certain point, or when no division of much consequence can be made of the sub-group. These limits are set by the analyst, and are necessary to prevent the remorseless generation of smaller and smaller sub-groups.

7 The two categories called 'non-churchgoers' are slightly different. Group 9 includes those who claimed to go to church less than once per year, while group 13 is restricted to those who 'never' went.

contributed almost as much as age to the reduction of variance. Otherwise, the tree produced by Figure 7.1 may be thought of as a strong plant.

And what is its fruit? That the most important variables underlying Labor identification are those which relate to what is commonly termed the voter's 'class situation' — occupational grade, income, union membership,

Table 7.1 The partisan battle-lines in Australian electoral politics, 1967

Group	(N)	Percentage of sample	Percentage Identifying with Labor
A Manual non-churchgoers in union households	(224)	12	77
B Manual churchgoers, in their 40s or 60s, in union households	(147)	8	70
C Manual housebuyers and tenants, from non-union households, and with incomes less than $1250	(109)	6	65
D Manual churchgoers, not in their 40s or 60s, in union households	(250)	13	52
E Non-manuals with manual fathers, and incomes less than $4250	(209)	11	43
F Manual houseowners, from non-union households, and with incomes less than $1250	(92)	5	41
G Non-manuals with non-manual fathers, who are non-churchgoers	(91)	5	41
H Manuals from non-union households with incomes greater than $1250	(149)	8	31
I Non-manuals with manual fathers, and incomes greater than $4250	(133)	7	24
J Non-manuals with non-manual fathers who are churchgoers	(480)	25	16
Total	(1884)	100	(mean 42)

Note: In this analysis wives have been grouped according to the occupations of their husbands.

house-ownership. In comparison, church attendance or age have puny explanatory power. These relative importances do accord, of course, with the relative importance of the parties themselves; the DLP, to take one example, attracted only one vote to every sixteen polled by the Labor and Liberal Parties.

Let us return to the puzzle of the relatively small gain in accuracy of prediction provided by the AID dissection of the data in Figure 7.1. Fourteen important social-structural variables reduce the error in predicting at random an individual's Labor identification by less than 20 per cent. How is this to be explained? If political parties have their roots deep in Australian society, and express politically the fundamental cleavages in that society, why do social-structural variables account for so little in estimating party identification? A clue to the answer can be seen in the range of sub-group means in Figure 7.1. The first split, into non-manual and manual groups, accounts for more than half of the reduction in variance (10.5 per cent, of 18.8 per cent). But each of the new sub-group means has moved only 16 per cent from the sample mean. Occupational prestige may be the most powerful variable at our disposal, but it is not, to anticipate a theme of the next chapter, especially powerful. Had 70 per cent of manuals and only 13 per cent of non-manuals identified with Labor — proportions that might have been suggested by some versions of conventional wisdom — then that first split would have reduced the variance by 33 per cent. And what is true of the first split is true also of those which follow it: there are no very sharp differentiations in the tendency to identify with Labor. In consequence, the reduction in variance is relatively small. For a full understanding of the origins of party identification in Australia we would have to push a long way past social structure.

In this respect Australia is similar to Great Britain, Canada and the United States. A recent comparative survey, employing a similar AID analysis for fifteen societies, makes clear that social structure plays a relatively small part in 'explaining' party identification in the Anglo-American polities (Table 7.2). In contrast, in the Scandinavian countries social structure is a good deal more important, while in the Netherlands the power of religion in reducing variance is more than twenty-five times greater than it is in Australia. There are nations in which social structure has a great deal to do with the direction of partisanship, but Australia is not one of them. The reasons will become clear as this section progresses.

In the next few chapters we shall pay attention to most of the variables used in the tree analysis, investigating both their relationship to party identification and their contribution to social and political stability. But two of them, age and sex, we should consider now.

Age should not detain us long. We have already seen that voters of the youngest generation were in 1967 least likely to identify with Labor, and close examination of the AID analysis confirms that this was very generally true, no matter what the sub-group being analysed. However, the differences were not large enough to overshadow other variables except in one case, that of sub-group 8, manual churchgoers from union households. Here the searching procedure discovered the best division to lie between those in their forties or sixties, and everybody else, a split which is of no apparent theoretical or historical significance. But a simple regrouping into those younger than forty and those forty and older provides a very similar differentiation: 64 per cent of the older group identified with Labor compared with 51 per cent of the younger.[8]

As an explanatory variable sex proved in one sense very much like age. At every split, in every sub-group, men were more likely than women to identify with Labor, but the differences were not as large as those manifest in other variables. As it happens, the range of difference was commonly between 5 per cent and 15 per cent which, in terms of the AID procedure, is not large enough to matter. But as Goot and Reid have pointed out, in a spirited

Table 7.2   Social structure and partisanship, a cross-national comparison[9]

| Country | Reduction in Variance due to | | | Total[a] |
	Occupation %	Religion %	Region %	%
Netherlands	0	50.1	0.4	51.2
Austria	12.0	30.3	2.9	46.0
Sweden	32	0	0	37.9
Norway	24.3	3.9	2.2	37.9
France (4th Republic)	4.9	28.4	1.4	34.4
Finland	31.8	0	0	33.2
Italy	0.3	21.9	1.5	28.3
Denmark	19.4	n.a.	n.a.	27.7
Belgium	n.a.	23.2	n.a.	23.2
West Germany	2.1	12.0	0	19.7
Canada	1.7	8.0	2.9	15.0
Australia	8.9	1.8	0	14.6
USA	3.0	5.5	4.5	12.8
Great Britain	3.3	0	0	12.0
Ireland	0	0	0.5	3.1

[a]Other sources of reduction in variance are included.

Source: Adapted from Richard Rose (ed.), *Electoral Behavior: a Comparative Handbook,* New York, 1974, P. 17.

8 It should be clear that the splitting process can produce groups that do differ with respect to the dependent variable, but do so for no reason that is clear to the analyst. This is most likely to occur at the end of the analysis, when the sub-groups are small and the opportunities for random variation correspondingly increased. It can be argued that if the independent variables are known to be important, any such unexpected finding deserves particular attention. The AID program allows the researcher to constrain the predictors so that they cannot be divided except in an ordinal fashion. This was not done here, since age is, as we have seen, an index of two quite separate variables, life-cycle and generation.

9 The tree analysis used in this chapter differs from that illustrated in Rose's *Electoral Behaviour,* for which contributors were required to work to given outlines. But the results are similar, and the reduction in variance of the same order.

critique of the research on women and political behaviour, these differences do require attention.[10] The fact that lower Labor identification among women was thoroughly pervasive suggests that it is not a consequence of some hidden aspect of social structure. Nor do these data lend much support to the belief that for the most part the greater apparent conservatism of women is due to the fact that women live longer and that old people are more conservative. In Australia old people are not more conservative, and although there are more old women than old men (in the 1967 sample, among voters over sixty there were 112 women for every 100 men) these partisan differences cannot be explained so easily. Table 7.3, which groups respondents according to national origin as well as age and sex, provides the evidence. In every group save the foreign-born over sixty (where the difference is in any case negligible), women were less likely than men to identify with Labor.

The finding cuts across the discovery of the previous chapter that wives and husbands tend to share the same partisanship. For if women tend to be more conservative than men in terms of party preference, it would follow that in general wives were less likely to be Labor partisans than their husbands. This is indeed the case. Table 7.4 provides the data, first a comparison of husbands' accounts of their own partisanship with what they thought their wives, partisanship to be, and then a comparison of wives' accounts of their own party preference with what they thought their husbands' preferences were.[11] The analysis is restricted to husbands whose preference was reported to be either for Labor, or for the Liberal or Country Parties. In both parts of Table 7.4 there is impressive similarity of party preference within the marriage, yet there is also a clear indication that the

Table 7.3   Labor identification, by age, sex and national origin, 1967[a]

Age Group	Native-Born		Foreign-Born	
	Men %	Women %	Men %	Women %
21-9	41	34	53	39
30-9	47	31	44	25
40-9	52	44	47	36
50-9	55	39	39	32
60+	52	32	38	40
(N)	(690)	(762)	(214)	(161)

[a] Each cell contains the proportion identifying with Labor, of those with some party identification

10 Murray Goot and Elizabeth Reid, *Women and Voting Studies: Mindless Matrons or Sexist Scientism?* Sage Professional Papers in Contemporary Political Sociology, Beverley Hills and London, 1974.

11 Spouse's party preference was obtained from questions W1(b) and H7(b) in the 1967 questionnaire.

tendency of a wife to support the Liberal or Country Parties when her husband is a Labor supporter is much greater (approximately three times greater) than the tendency for a non-Labor husband to have a Labor wife. The contrast between the two parts of the table also suggests strongly that some non-Labor wives married to Labor husbands keep their partisan leanings to themselves, a possibility we have encountered before.

We shall see that church attendance seems to play some part in producing these male-female differences, but on the whole the data allow us only to point to a phenomenon to be explained. Explanation must be left to others.

Let us proceed now to a consideration of the links between party identification and the structural variable which by general agreement lies at the heart of the Australian party system, social class.

Table 7.4 Party preferences of husbands and wives, 1967

Wives' Preferences according to Husbands

Wives	Husbands	
	Lib.-CP %	Labor %
Lib.-CP	92	13
Labor	6	87
DLP	2	0
Total	100	100
(N)	(212)	(165)

Husbands' Preferences according to Wives

Wives	Husbands	
	Lib.-CP %	Labor %
Lib.-CP	95	23
Labor	4	76
DLP	1	1
Total	100	100
(N)	(279)	(244)

8 Class and Party

> Friendly people are middle class. Hotel types are lower class. Upper class are snobs. (*housewife, forty-four, NSW town*)

The pre-eminence of occupational grade in the tree analysis comes as no surprise to any student of Australian politics. The association of the two main parties with two broad occupationally related classes of Australian society has been taken for granted by most writers on Australian politics and buttressed by comparisons, impressionistic or systematic, which show Australia to be high on the list of class-based polities.[1] Moreover, there has been a pervasive tendency in Australian historiography to picture Australian history as the working out of class conflicts, or the rivalry of different sets of class values, or the vicissitudes of the attempt to create a new, classless society in the Antipodes.[2] In all these accounts the working class, first that in the bush and then its urban successor, has been granted an honoured initiating role; and this has been extended to its political expression, the Australian Labor Party.

In supplying this emphasis Australian historians have had the backing of a procession of foreign observers, who have commented on and made much of the distinctive qualities of the Australian class structure.[3]

A pre-occupation with class has occurred also because no other cleavages seem, on the face of it, to have the same importance. Race has been of

---

1 See, for example, Alford, *Party and Society*.
2 A short list of references might include Russel Ward, *The Australian Legend*, Melbourne, 1958; Robin Gollan, *Radical and Working Class Politics*, Melbourne, 1960; Brian Fitzpatrick, *The British Empire in Australia: an Economic History 1834-1939*, Melbourne, 1941, and *A Short History of the Australian Labor Movement*, Melbourne, 1944; Ian Turner, *Industrial Labour and Politics, Dynamics of the Labor Movement in Eastern Australia, 1900-1921*, Canberra, 1965. The pre-eminence of the class theme has not gone unchallenged: D.W. Rawson dismissed it as pseudo-Marxist in an important review of Gollan's book (*Quadrant*, 5(1), Summer 1960-1, pp. 81-3). For two other counter-attacks from very different perspectives, see Henry Mayer, 'Some Conceptions of the Australian Party System 1910-1950', *Historical Studies*, 7(27), November 1956; and Humphrey McQueen, *A New Britannia: An Argument Concerning the Social Origins of Australian Radicalism and Nationalism*, Melbourne, 1971.
3 The list is very large. Better known representatives include Albert Métin, *Le Socialisme sans Doctrines, la question agraire at la question ouvrière en Australie et Nouvelle-*

negligible significance, since the Aboriginal population is tiny; Australia has been overwhelmingly European for more than a century, and of British and Irish stock until the 1960s. Religion was once important, but sectarian passions have cooled, a change emphasised by the easy public acceptance of government financial subsidies to church schools after 1963. Urban-rural differences have added colour and variety to Australian politics — but most Australians live in cities, and have done so for several generations. In social analysis, class is king, undisputed.

Perhaps just because of the undeniable primacy of class few of those who have written about it in Australia have spent much time asking exactly what class is, or in what fashion it is translated into politics. In general only Marxists have used class terms in a clear-cut fashion, but conventional Marxist categories are inadequate to describe a society that has not known a distinct upper class for more than a century, and in which five-sixths of the workforce are employees, but only half the votes go to the workers' party. 'Working-class' has been used to mean all workers, all workers in blue-collar jobs, all unionised workers, and all those who consider themselves working-class. The basis of class distinction has been no less slippery: sometimes occupation, sometimes income, sometimes social prestige, sometimes life-style, sometimes a state of mind, and sometimes a combination of these elements and others. The uncertainty is pardonable, for investigations of the concept of class itself always attest to its complexity and its variety.[4] But these very qualities make suspect any analysis of the nature of party politics that relies heavily on social class, for this is to explain *obscurum per obscurius*; we do not get far in understanding one phenomenon by advancing a second the meaning of which is even less clear.

These problems are obvious to anyone who looks hard at the bases of support for political parties, and it says much for the hold that class has on the sociological and historical imagination in Australia that they are generally ignored. Indeed, the explanatory power of class has sometimes been accepted on the evidence of data that give only faint support to the claims. Encel, for example, claims that 'the correspondence between class identification and voting is so close in the survey results that the two may be regarded as largely alternative measures of the same general social outlook'. This sweeping assertion rests on survey data that show one-third of the 'Upper Middle Class' rejecting the Liberal and Country Parties, and the same proportion of the working class rejecting the ALP; a further survey

---

Zélande, Paris, 1901; James Bryce, *Modern Democracies*, London and New York, 1921; D.H. Lawrence, *Kangaroo*, London, 1923; Thomas Wood, *Cobbers*, London, 1934; Egon Kisch, *Australian Landfall*, London, 1937; J.D. Pringle, *Australian Accent*, London, 1958; Jeanne MacKenzie, *Australian Paradox*, Melbourne, 1961. It ought to be pointed out that these critics have not always agreed about what *is* characteristic of class in Australia.
4 See especially A.F. Davies, *Images of Class: an Australian Study*, Sydney, 1967, and for a good theoretical discussion, Ralf Dahrendorf, *Class and Class Conflict in Industrial Society*, London 1972.

cited as evidence reports that 'just over half the "middle class" [voted] Liberal'.[5] It is difficult to escape the feeling that the obsession with class has been in part an ideological one — that many Australian historians and sociologists have been committed to a view of Australian society and politics in which class concepts play the predominant part. This viewpoint has provided a means of organising their material as well as allowing a critique of contemporary society;[6] but it has rarely come under much examination. Class is nearly always the independent variable, not the thing to be explained.

Because the analysis of social class has been impaired by a failure of scholars to agree on terms — a common experience in the social sciences — it is important to make clear what the underlying assumptions of the following discussion are. This is not the place for tightly argued theoretical definitions. Let us propose rather that the importance of class to politics will be the greater the more that inequalities in wealth, financial security and occupational status produce feelings of class awareness or class consciousness expressed in organisations which either operate in party politics themselves or are affiliated to other groups which do.[7] The links in this chain may be expressed in diagrammatic shorthand thus:

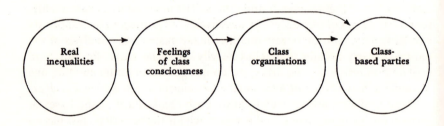

5 *Equality and Authority*, Melbourne, 1970, pp. 96-7. A similar argument appears in the first edition of A.F. Davies and S. Encel (eds.), *Australian Society. A Sociological Introduction*, Melbourne, 1965, p. 37. Encel's reluctance to abandon his hypothesis in the face of his data is the more strange in that the passage quoted follows an admirable account of the complexities involved in the concepts of class, status and power.

6 Davies's remarks on students of class apply also to not a few Australian historians, political scientists and sociologists: 'Not only have most writers on class been against it...but most accounts have been thrown together by writers concerned to promote particular large views of society, which, in their turn, were thought efficacious in persuading us to act (or to refuse to act) in particular ways which seemed good — and urgent — to them.' ('Concepts of Social Class', *Australian Journal of Politics and History*, **2**(1), November 1956, p. 84). Compare the recent argument of S.M. Miller ('The Future of Social Mobility Studies', *American Journal of Sociology*, **77**(1), July 1971) that the American pre-occupation with social mobility studies reflected a desire to criticise the bourgeois society of the Eisenhower years. He notes a corresponding failure to look at the lack of fit between theory and data.

7 The starting point for this discussion is Giovanni Sartori's important paper 'From the Sociology of Politics to Political Sociology', in S.M. Lipset (ed.), *Politics and the Social Sciences*, New York, 1969. An earlier and less complete version was published in *Government and Opposition*, **4**(2), Spring 1969.

Class-in-politics therefore has three elements: inequality, consciousness and competition. It is clear that the intermediate link is all-important in understanding the importance of class, for while no modern society is free of systematic economic inequalities, not all possess class-based parties. Let us begin, then, by examining the nature of class consciousness in Australia.

Class Consciousness in Australian Society

Elizabeth Bott, writing of a small group of families in London, reflected that 'people disagree profoundly in their views on class, so much so that we sometimes wondered if they were talking about the same society'.[8] Alan Davies' *Images of Class* ten years later showed that perceptions of class in Australia were complex phenomena also. Yet as practically all surveys on the subject have shown, the word 'class' means something to most people, and they use it confidently about themselves and others.

In 1967, respondents to the first survey were brought into discussion of class through the following question: 'Some people say that there are social classes in this country. Others disagree. Do you think there *are* or *are not* social classes in Australia?' Those who gave a firm answer for or against the presence of classes were asked why they felt as they did. Nearly eight in ten said that there were social classes in Australia; one in seven said there were not, the rest were not sure. Although this distribution suggests that the vision of Australia as a classless society has not been realised in the contemporary world, the examples people used in illustrating the existence of class raise other doubts. Table 8.1 displays their answers, grouped in

Table 8.1   Perceived origins of class, 1967

		Per cent
I	Classes are natural groupings arising out of innate human differences (birds of a feather flock together), snobbishness or laziness	52
II	Class is based on money, wealth, income, occupation	31
III	Classes are the result of politicians seeking votes, editors seeking greater circulation (social pages), trade unions seeking members	9
IV	Classes result from the circumstances of one's birth (2 per cent), or education (3 per cent)	5
V	Other	3
	Total	100
		(N = 1304)

8 Elizabeth Bott, *Family and Social Network: Roles, Norms and External Relationships in Ordinary Urban Families*, London, 1957, p. 159.

what seemed to be the most meaningful categories. The most striking aspect of Table 8.1 is the relatively small proportion that saw classes arising out of economic inequalities, let alone out of relations to the means of production. The Polish immigrant glass worker who summed up class tersely with 'One class hold the positions and one class work for them' and the young Scottish machinist who (in answer to a subsequent question) defined the working class as 'The ones who work for the middle class' are two of a very small band. Moreover, the great majority of those who used money or income as examples referred not to how people *earned* their money, but to how they *spent* it. And they were outnumbered, by almost two to one, by respondents who saw class as the result of human differences, real or supposed.

Further questioning might in some cases have produced agreement that these human differences arose out of or reflected differences in access to wealth; but there is no warrant for us to assume this, and in very many cases the respondent had something else in mind altogether. An Air Force NCO who had lived on the one base for fourteen years became aware of class 'when a couple of women who would not talk to my wife talked to her when I became a sergeant'. A retired university teacher remarked 'Well it [class]'s easily formed. [Take] for instance Mr and Mrs A and their family, growing up. They entertain people — but they aren't going to invite Mr and Mrs X because they aren't used to going to that kind of house.' A Sydney stenographer was quite emphatic that 'You will always have classes no matter where you live. It's only wishful thinking to think you will have equality: people are not made the same.' Finally, an elderly retired grocer spoke in the same vein: 'Individuals are like fingers: they're not all the same.'

Native-born Australians, members of one of the world's most homogeneous societies, have little opportunity to set their views of class in Australia against an experience of class in any other society. In consequence, a particular interest attaches to the comments of immigrants, especially the British. The following remarks give us some comparative insight, and their variety may be typical:

I never see no snobbery or nothing. That's one thing. Everyone's very nice to me. (*housewife, sixty-eight, formerly Belfast*)

... The classes [here] are rather different from the UK. Here it's mostly income followed by educational status ... [I remember] the very posh road we were taken up when we first came to Perth in Western Australia, and were told 'The bookies live here'. They were the elite, followed by the doctors and lawyers. (*housewife, thirty-five, formerly England*)

... there's *very much* class consciousness in Australia. Canberra strikes you right between the eyes *there*: you've got to show your pedigree to play golf at the Royal Canberra. (*engineer, sixty formerly England*)

Reading the social pages in *The Advertiser* drives me up the wall. I put this down to the fact that the morning paper I read in Britain was a national paper and the social news in that was at the Royalty level. (*housewife, twenty-eight, formerly England*)

Apart from the almost complete lack of reference to economic inequality, there is no connecting thread in these extracts. They illustrate, if anything, the variety of experience that people have of class divisions and the varying weight they place on them. In this the immigrants seem no different from the native-born.

The great majority not only accepted that there were classes, they seemed equally clear about which class they themselves belonged to. Only 4 per cent of those who said that there were classes located themselves outside either the middle class or the working class. Those that said there were no classes in Australia were subsequently offered a card on which four class names — upper, middle, lower, and working — were printed, and told that these were the names that some people used for social classes. If they were asked to say which of *these* social classes they belonged to, which would they choose? Some 8 per cent remained obdurate that there were no social classes; and another 4 per cent were uncertain about where they would place themselves. But of the remainder virtually everyone chose the middle class or the working class. The final distribution of the sample over these class categories is given in Table 8.2

There is nothing surprising in the overwhelming nomination of middle class and working class, of course. 'Middle' and 'working' are the only two adjectives that are commonly used to qualify class. 'Upper' and 'lower' both have strongly pejorative overtones (as in the extract at the beginning of the chapter) and are rarely used descriptively. Both might be thought to offend against the conventional image of Australia as a society that has escaped the class extremes of the Old World, in a fashion that 'middle' avoids because of its safe vagueness and 'working' because of its functional and almost universal reference. Nor is there anything uniquely Australian about that. The avoidance of 'upper' and 'lower' was just as marked in the British surveys already referred to.[9]

Table 8.2 Class self-placement, 1967

| Upper | Percentage in Class Category | | | Other | Refused | DK | Total |
	Middle	Lower	Working				
71	51	1	43	1	2	2	100 (N = 1988)

9 *Political Change in Britain*, pp. 66-7 and Appendix.

Table 8.2's revelation of an Australian middle class that is rather bigger than the working class is in keeping with the findings of Broom, Jones and Zubrzycki, whose 1965 national survey produced a middle class of 49 per

Table 8.3   Descriptions of class characteristics, Australia and Britain

	Australia 1967 %	Britain 1963 %
What sort of people would you say belong to the middle class?		
Occupation: non-manual, white-collar, skilled, professional, employers, self-employed	42	61
Income and level of living: wealthy, rich, comfortably off, good housing	31	21
Educational level or intelligence: well educated, brains, university or public school background	9	5
Manners and morals: social graces, moral standards	6	5
Attitudes and hierarchical location: snobbish, superior, aristocratic	3	5
Family background, breeding	1	1
Political: supporters of Liberals (Conservatives), right wing	*	1
Ordinary, decent, plain-living, average people	6	} 1
Other	2	
Total	100	100

What sort of people would you say belong to the working class?		
Occupation: manual, semi-skilled and unskilled, people who work for a living, employees	57	74
Income and level of living: poor, low-income people, people who live in slums, poor housing	22	10
Educational level and intelligence: poorly educated, unintelligent, left school early	5	3
Manners and morals: lack of social graces, low moral standards	5	7
Attitudes and hierarchical location: humble, subservient, lower class people	2	5
Ordinary, decent, plain-living, average people	6	} 1
Other	3	
Total	100	100

* = less than 0.5 per cent.

cent and a working class of 44 per cent, with similarly tiny proportions opting for 'upper' or 'lower'. As they noted, proportions of this kind make Australia seem perhaps the most middle-class country in the world, and certainly more middle-class than Great Britain or even the United States.[10] We shall consider shortly the extent to which such self-placement is congruent with the distribution of occupational prestige, income, housing and the like. But it will be evident that the preference for a middle-class location cannot be a simple function of employer or self-employed status, and that it poses an important problem about the meaning of class self-placement.

Some further insight into the meanings of class can be gained by pursuing what respondents said about each of the two main classes in response to the questions 'What sort of people would you say belong to the middle [working] class?' To give the discussion some comparative perspective Table 8.3, which displays the answers, includes the equivalent responses from the 1963 British survey conducted by Butler and Stokes.[11]

Table 8.3 has two important messages. The first is that in Australia as in Britain, *specific* classes are defined very much by reference to occupation and income. The second is that occupation is not as important as a defining characteristic in Australia as it is in Britain, and that income is more important. In general, there is little doubt that classes are seen more sharply in Britain: not only is occupation there almost a single index of class position, but virtually none of the British sample resorted to the descriptions 'average', 'ordinary', 'decent' and the like, which some in the Australian sample used for both the middle and working classes — a certain sign of the lack of definition of class images.[12]

These cross-national differences are consistent with Alford's picture of the greater salience of class in Britain, and they are reinforced by an examination of the relationship between class self-placement and economic inequalities. Since occupation was the most frequently mentioned class discriminator we begin with it, using two of the measures of occupational grade developed since 1965 by Broom and his colleagues, the non-manual/manual (white-collar + managerial/blue-collar + service) dichotomy employed already in the tree analyses, and a six-fold classification in which the categories are styled professional, managerial, white-collar, skilled manual, semi-skilled manual and unskilled manual.[13] Table 8.4 displays the distribution of class self-placement among the six categories of occupational grade.

10 L. Broom, F.L. Jones and J. Zubrzycki, 'Socal Stratification in Australia', in J. Jackson (ed.), *Social Stratification*, Cambridge, 1968.
11 *Political Change in Britain*, p. 68.
12 The use of these bland, careful terms was characteristic of people talking of their own class, not the other one.
13 See Leonard Broom, F. Lancaster Jones and Jerzy Zubrzycki, 'An Occupational Classification of the Australian Workforce', *Australian and New Zealand Journal of*

It is clear that there is more to class self-placement than occupational status. The two measures come close to correspondence only among professionals, but at the other end of the scale one unskilled worker in three[14] considers himself to be middle-class. Furthermore, although occupational rank can be sensibly dichotomised, the distribution of Table 8.4 suggests that a three-fold or even a four-fold measure of occupation would also be appropriate; but that fits uneasily with the plain implication of the earlier discussion that Australians recognise only two classes in their society.

Table 8.4   Occupational grade and class self-placement, 1967

Class Self-placement	I Professional %	II Managerial %	Occupational Grade III White-Collar %	IV Skilled Manual %	V Semi-skilled Manual %	VI Unskilled Manual %
Middle	91	66	68	45	38	34
Working	9	34	32	55	62	66
Total	100	100	100	100	100	100
(N)	(290)	(396)	(283)	(355)	(321)	(311)

Table 8.5   Middle-class self-placement, by occupational grade and income, 1967

Income Level	Occupational Grade Non-manual %	Manual %
High (>$6251)	92	70[a]
Medium ($2251-6250)	53	44
Low (<$2250)	58	29

Note: Each cell contains the proportion describing themselves as middle-class within categories jointly defined by occupational grade and income.

[a] fourteen cases

Sociology, 1(2), October 1965, Supplement. This paper reported the development of a 10/-item occupational scale from 348 occupational titles used in the 1961 Census of Australia. From this scale Broom and Jones devised a sixteen-category occupational prestige scale (Leonard Broom and F. Lancaster Jones, 'Career Mobility in Three Societies: Australia, Italy, and the United States', *American Sociological Review*, 34(5), October 1969) which can be further reduced in a number of ways. Farmers and graziers are here distributed over the first two of the six categories, and are classed as 'non-manual'.

14 Or his wife, since wives are grouped according to the occupation of their husbands. In general women were rather more likely than men to give themselves a middle-class label, but that does not explain the data reported here, since the proportions of each sex, among unskilled workers and their wives, reporting a working-class self-placement were men: 69 per cent, women: 64 per cent.

Since members of the sample regarded wealth and income as an important component of class distinctions, and since income appeared twice in the tree analysis, it makes sense to consider occupation and income together. Table 8.5 shows that something is gained by doing so. Among those with non-manual occupations and high incomes there was an overwhelming tendency to see one's place as being in the middle class. High incomes of this order, however, were earned by only 8 per cent of the sample. For the remainder income differentials had some effect among manual workers, but not elsewhere, while occupational grade tended to affect whether or not low-income earners considered themselves middle-class. Yet we are left with the fact that three of every ten poorly-off manual workers consider themselves middle-class. Perhaps the range of incomes in Australia is not wide enough for feelings of class consciousness to emerge strongly, except at the wealthy extreme; certainly this is part of conventional wisdom.[15]

The same puzzle emerges from an analysis of the contribution of educational background to class self-placement. The longer the experience of formal education, the more likely the person was to describe himself as middle-class; and this is particularly true of those who went to university, 96 per cent of whom placed themselves in the middle class. Yet there remain large discrepancies: 34 per cent of those who had only primary school education considered themselves middle-class, and the proportion was 26 per cent even among primary-educated manual workers. Nor did housing prove to be much help as a discriminator. Australia is a nation of house-owners and house-buyers, and three-quarters of the sample fell into one of these two categories. Among those with non-manual occupations, owners and buyers were hardly more likely than tenants to describe themselves as middle-class; among manual workers, 42 per cent of owners and buyers labelled themselves middle-class, compared with 33 per cent of tenants. It is the lack of difference which is remarkable.

In sum, the class in which people locate themselves is not fully predictable from a knowledge of their economic and social circumstances. And if that is the case, then we are entitled to a strong suspicion that class labels are worn lightly by many Australians. This hypothesis is confirmed by an examination of the stability of class self-placement, firstly in response to different questions at the one time, and secondly over the two

---

15 In 1964-5 the top 2.5 per cent of taxpayers earned 12 per cent of all income and 56 per cent of the taxpayers earned between $1800 and $3400 p.a. (Bruce Macfarlane, *Economic Policy in Australia*, Melbourne, 1968, p. 205). Real poverty is not typical among wage earners and is most commonly experienced by pensioners. There is some evidence to suggest that since 1960 the narrow range of incomes in Australia has begun to broaden significantly, but it is probably true that Australia is still among the most egalitarian nations in terms of the distribution of personal income. See Bruce M. Russett *et al.*, *World Handbook of Political and Social Indicators*, New Haven, 1964, pp. 243-7.

years between the two sets of interviews. In 1969 respondents were asked both a free-answer and a forced-choice question about their class self-placement.[16] The free-answer question produced a set of descriptions very similar to those offered in 1967, with a great concentration on middle and working class. Confronted with the labels upper, middle, lower and working, most of those who had previously denied that there were classes, or who were unsure, now chose a class. But there was also a significant rethinking on the part of many of those who had already nominated their class. Indeed, one-seventh of those who had previously described themselves as upper, middle, lower, or working now changed their minds (principally in equal trading between middle and working class). But between 1967 and 1969 the impermanence of class descriptions was even more marked, as Table 8.6 shows.

The erosion of both the working class *and* the middle class makes it clear that we are not witnessing the psychological effect of real social change (during these two years the economy remained buoyant and unemployment low)[17] but rather the arbitrariness of the original and successive self-placement. For of those who had described themselves in 1967 as middle-class or working-class, 32 per cent two years later had either abandoned one class label for another or denied the existence of class altogether. But if class labels are as inconsequential as this, we are entitled to assume that a similarly large proportion maintained the *same*

Table 8.6   The stability of class self-placement, 1967 to 1969

| Class Self-placement in 1969 | Class Self-placement in 1967 | |
	Middle %	Working %
Upper/middle	67	22
Lower/working	18	63
Other	3	4
None	4	3
No such thing	4	3
Don't know	4	5
Total	100	100
(N)	(734)	(596)

16 Questions 58(a) and 58(b) in the 1969 questionnaire.
17 Close inspection of individual histories over the two years showed that changes in self-placement were unrelated to changes in income and occupation. But this examination produced one interesting finding: self-placement was much more stable where objective and subjective class locations were congruent. For example, 84 per cent of manual workers who had called themselves working-class in 1967 stuck to their label in 1969, compared with only 60 per cent of self-styled middle-class manual workers; among non-manuals, 86 per cent of the middle class so described themselves two years later, compared with 62 per cent of the non-manual 'working class'. It seems that 'deviant' class self-placement is less confidently held.

class self-placement at the two interviews quite by chance. In short, although most people will readily place themselves into a social class, for perhaps two-thirds of them class labels carry little meaning or permanence.

There is one final piece of evidence that bears on this point, a measure of the relative importance of class in comparison with other attributes, as seen by those interviewed. In 1969 respondents were offered a randomly ordered set of cards on which were printed 'terms we might use to describe ourselves'. Common to each set were Australian and British subject; another card contained the name of the appropriate state as an adjective and a fourth the name of the respondent's town or district (e.g. resident of Melbourne). The fifth card showed working-class on one face and middle-class on the other, and was given — appropriate face up — to those who had already placed themselves in one or other of these two classes (the others were not offered the class card). Respondents were then asked to reject the card 'least important to you in describing who you are', and to repeat this process until there was only one card left. The relative importance of these attributes is set out in Table 8.7, which displays each attribute's share of first, second and subsequent placements. Table 8.7 shows that in comparison with the other attributes class had clearly the weakest salience — much less than such an 'old-fashioned' description as 'British subject'. Only 6 per cent saw class as most important — the lowest proportion of all five descriptions — and 41 per cent regarded it as least important, making class much the most popular choice for last place. The indifference towards class was more pronounced among the middle class than among the working class: 3 per cent of the former placed class first compared with 9 per cent of the latter. But even among the working class, as the figure of 9 per cent suggests, the class attribute was of small importance (and 61 per cent of the working class placed it last or second last).

These data should not be asked to support too heavy an argument, if only because class, of all the attributes available to the respondents, was the only one that related immediately to politics. It is possible that had the

Table 8.7 The relative importance of selected attributes, 1969

Ranking	Australian %	British Subject %	State %	Town %	Class %
Most important	63	11	10	10	6
2nd	20	22	33	14	10
3rd	10	20	32	22	17
4th	5	30	17	27	26
Least important	2	17	8	27	41
Total	100	100	100	100	100
(N)	(1842)	(1839)	(1836)	(1837)	(1806)

sample been offered religion, for example, or party identification, as additional or alternative attributes, class might have looked more impressive. Yet in the context of the earlier discussion these data confirm that class is of little importance to most Australians: one's town, one's state and even one's status as a British subject appear to loom larger. These attributes may be labels too, but they are manifestly labels of more significance than class.

Class and Party Identification

What political functions, then, do class labels serve? For a minority of voters classes may serve as meaningful reference groups, and the terms 'middle-class' and 'working-class' as proud banners in what is seen as a great social and political struggle. But for most it seems clear, class is a concept of merely nominal value: it is simply the term used to subsume the manifold differences in occupation, income prestige, residence, life-style and education that characterise social life in a complex urban industrial society, and to place a person, in the broadest terms, in the social hierarchy. The general use of class labels demonstrates a sidelong awareness of social and economic differences, but not necessarily a sense of that solidarity of political interest which is called class consciousness. Furthermore, class labels are not terms of passion, and they are not especially reliable as a mark of people's social location. Given all this, we should be unwise to expect to predict accurately a person's party identification from a knowledge of his social position, however that is defined. Tables 8.8 and 8.9 display the joint frequencies of party identi-

Table 8.8   Party identification, by class self-placement, 1967

Party Identification	Middle-class %	Working-class %
Lib.-CP	70	34
Labor	27	62
DLP	3	3
Total	100	100
(N)	(951)	(772)

Table 8.9   Party identification, by occupational grade, 1967

Party Identification	Non-manual %	Manual %
Lib.-CP	72	39
Labor	25	58
DLP	3	3
Total	100	100
(N)	(851)	(967)

fication and social class, first using class self-placement, then occupational grade, as measures of class. The frequencies of Table 8.9 will be familiar from the tree analysis in Chapter 7.

These measures give much the same result: about seven in ten of the self-designated middle class and of those in non-manual occupations identify with the Liberal and Country Parties, and about six in ten of the working class and of those in manual occupations identify with the Labor Party.[18] These relationships are not at all powerful, and the correlation between accepting a working-class label and identifying with the Labor Party is especially weak. Something is gained if the two measures are considered simultaneously (Table 8.10), but the gain is not remarkable. And if only 69 per cent of manual workers who think of themselves as working-class identify with the Labor Party, there is hardly any justification for describing a failure to identify with Labor among such voters as 'deviant' behaviour.

The nebulousness of the class-party link is emphasised and illustrated when we consider what the respondents thought to be the partisan

18 Class self-placement and occupational rank by no means match each other, as has been shown (Table 8.4). So the similar distribution of Tables 8.8 and 8.9 pose an interesting problem, especially as the two measures of class can be used almost interchangeably in a wide range of other analytic situations as well. Philip Converse has noted the same similarities in American data ('The Shifting Role of Class in Political Attitudes and Behaviour', in Eleanor Maccoby, Theodore Newcomb and Eugene Hartlye, *Readings in Social Psychology*, New York, 1958, pp. 391-3). Crossing the two measures of class produces the following distribution:

| Class Self-placement | Occupational Rank | | Total |
	Non-manual	Manual	
Middle	34	22	56
Working	12	32	44
Total	46	54	100 (N=1680)

The balance of this table provides a starting point for a plausible explanation of the similarity between the two measures of class. We can conceive of each measure as encompassing three elements: those whose objective and subjective class locations are in sympathy, those whose class locations are for good reasons in conflict, and those whose subjective class locations are a matter of chance. The first group is common to both measures, the second is presumably small and probably of much the same size in each class, and the third is by definition distributed between classes in proportion to the relative sizes of the classes. Since the two classes are of approximately the same size, we should expect this third group to be divided more or less equally between them. This model does not require that membership in any category be fixed, nor that the categories maintain the same size. The crucial condition rather is that at any time the two measures of class divide the electorate in approximately the same proportion. If this condition is satisfied then either measure of class can be used in analysis, with much the same results in the great majority of cases.

allegiances of the two classes.[19] Less than a quarter thought that the middle class voted mainly for one party (and of those some 10 per cent thought it voted Labor!), but nearly six in ten thought the working class did; of these nearly everyone thought it voted Labor. In fact, as we have seen, the middle class is more solidly Liberal-Country Party than the working class is Labor.

The data must be ransacked to turn up even faint traces of a class-conflict belief, in which there are two opposed classes and two opposed parties bearing their standards. A respondent who did express his attitudes to parties and leaders in this fashion was a man from Yass (NSW), whose terse answers contain the outline of a class-conflict perspective.

Is there anything in particular you like about the Liberal Party? I don't think they're for the worker. They're all right if you've got plenty of money.

Don't like about the Liberal Party? If we had a lot of money we'd probably be for them.

Like about Labor? They're for the worker. A working person must vote Labor.

Don't like about Labor? No.

Like about Mr Holt? He's no good for the worker. All right for the money man...

Like about Mr Whitlam? Yes, I like Mr Whitlam. I think he will be good for the worker...

Like many respondents, he used 'the worker' rather than working class, as did the Tasmanian skin-classer from whose articulateness we have already benefited:

...the Liberal Party is a party more or less for the — how would you put it? — more or less for the economic divisions of the country, and Labor is for the workers, and the others more or less fight against each other — though I've never had much to do with them.

The simplicity of his vision of the Labor Party and the confusion surrounding the *raison d'etre* of the Liberal Party are noteworthy; we shall

Table 8.10   Labor identification within class categories

Class Self-placement	Occupational Grade	
	Non-manual %	Manual %
Middle	18	41
Working	44	69

Note: Each cell displays the proportion identifying with Labor within a category defined by the two measures of class.

19 In reponse to questions 55(a), 55(b), 56(a), and 56(b) in the 1967 questionnaire.

return to this contrast shortly. A few respondents appeared to see a clean equation between Labor and the working class, but found nothing elsewhere. The finality of this remark from a Queensland woman, the wife of an electrician and herself in employment, is most expressive: 'Well, I suppose I'm Labor and that's all there is to it. I'm a working woman and working-class and that's all there is to it.' But persuasive evidence of the presence of developed class-conflict beliefs was lacking.

The statistical evidence can be marshalled quickly. In both classes, those who saw their own class as supporting one party were more likely to support it themselves than those who saw it as evenly divided. A similar firmness of allegiance was characteristic of those who saw the *other* class as supporting one party. Among the working class, those who saw the middle class as solidly Liberal were themselves 65 per cent Labor, compared with 55 per cent Labor among those who thought the middle class was evenly divided; among the middle class, 71 per cent of those who thought the working class was Labor-supporting were Liberal-Country in their own allegiance, compared with 59 per cent of those who thought it was evenly divided. These differences are not striking and they demonstrate how few voters look at politics from any kind of a developed class-conflict perspective.

Class conflict may play some part as one of the myths of Australian politics, but it is not obviously relevant to partisan choice. In 1967 only one in four believed that there was bound to be conflict between different social classes, a proportion common to both the working class and the middle class.[20] If class conflict were seen as real and important we might expect those who felt this way to be more sharply polarised than those who did not. We should expect, that is to say, that those in the working class who saw class conflict as inevitable would be more likely to support the party of the working class than those who did not; and that there would be a corresponding firming of Liberal allegiance in the middle class. In fact this belief had no effect upon party identification in either class. Not only that, but over the two years from 1967 to 1969 there was a massive change in individual responses to this question, and the general randomness of direction in these changes suggests that the question had not tapped profound attitudes towards Australian society. Much the same can be said of the belief that it is very difficult to move between classes, which ought also to help polarise party allegiance, if class conflict were real and important. It is true that working-class respondents were more likely than middle-class to say that movement between classes was very difficult (24 per cent, compared with 14 per cent), and the middle class was more

20 In 1969 the proportion jumped to two in five, the result presumably of the conflict-emphasising circumstances of the preceding election campaign. In Britain there was a similar increase between 1963 and 1964 in the proportion seeing class conflict as inevitable.

insouciant about class conflict generally. But the effects of these attitudes upon party identification were trivial, and the lack of permanence of the attitudes themselves was pronounced.

If party allegiance in Australia is not greatly affected by notions of class conflict, class may nevertheless be important in the sense of social network: people who meet together are likely to act together (this is what more than a half of the sample seemed to think class was all about). Social contacts could be important in two ways: friends and neighbours (or more generally one's local community) could separately influence one's political attitudes.

The class location of friends proved to be similarly patterned for the middle and working classes. Almost half of those who called themselves middle-class claimed to have mainly middle-class friends, a slightly smaller proportion to have friends from all classes, and the balance (7 per cent) to have mainly working-class friends. There was a corresponding distribution in the working class save that rather *more* than half of those who described themselves as working-class said they had mainly working-class friends. Table 8.11 relates these patterns to party identifications, and suggests that social milieu has an important effect upon those who consider themselves middle-class: middle-class people with working-class friends tended to identify with the ALP. But there seemed to be no equivalent effect upon the working class. In fact Labor identification was highest (though the differences are slight) among those with mainly middle-class friends.

Neighbours ('people who live around here') also appear to have some influence on the middle class, although the effect is more subdued (Table 8.12). In both classes Labor identification increases as the proportion of working-class neighbours increases; the effect is, however, rather more pronounced in the middle class. It seems fair to argue that social milieu is more important as a political context to the middle class than to the working class; yet, perhaps to state the obvious, social milieu as it has been defined here need have nothing whatever to do with social or economic inequality.

Let us draw this discussion of class and party identification to a close by inspecting the stability of class self-placement and of party identification,

Table 8.11   Labor identification, by class self-placement and friends' class

Respondent is	Mainly Middle-class %	Friends are Mixed %	Mainly Working-class %
Middle-class	22	60	57
Working-class	70	60	63

displayed simultaneously. It is clear that the broad socio-economic divisions within the community are more useful in explanations of the stability of political behaviour than of short-term political change. [21] If these socio-economic divisions were defined in terms of class location to be followed (much of the time, at least) by changes in party loyalty. Table 8.13 tests this hypothesis by displaying movements in class self-placement and party identification among those who were either middle-class or working-class and either Liberal-Country Party or Labor in both 1967 and 1969. To begin with, party identification was significantly more stable than class self-placement: twice as many changed their class as changed their party. But what is most striking is that only 4 per cent changed their class and party allegiance together — not all of them in sympathy. Twice as many changed parties but not classes, and *five* times as many — one-fifth of the entire sub-sample — maintained a constant party identification but altered their class description.

It is apparent that we do not need notions of class consciousness or class awareness to explain the party loyalty of Australian voters, if by class is meant anything more than a vague feeling of placement in the social hierarchy along with people like themselves. Even that does not account

Table 8.12 Labor identification, by class self-placement and neighbours' class

Respondent is	Neighbours are		
	Mainly Middle-class %	Mixed %	Mainly Working-class %
Middle-class	23	26	40
Working-class	51	60	63

Note: Each cell contains the proportion identifying with Labor, of those with some party identification.

Table 8.13 The stability of class self-placement and party indentification, 1967 to 1969

Class Self-placement	Party Identification		
	Stable %	Varied %	Total %
Stable	68	8	76
Varied	20	4	24
Total	88	12	100 (N = 1032)

21 Warren E. Miller, 'The Socio-Economic Analysis of Political Behaviour', *Midwest Journal of Political Science*, 2, August 1958, p. 241. The argument is one of the principal texts in Campbell *et al.*, *The American Voter*.

for Labor partisanship among the working class. More realistic, and no less adequate, is a simple 'interest' model of party choice, in which the great majority of citizens support the party than seems most likely to better their lot; and their lot is generally, though not always, defined in economic and material terms. There is no empirical warrant for importing into this model the notion that people first see themselves as belonging to a class, and that the party represents the interests of that class. Certainly some voters do think like this, and the concept is basic to analysis and discussion on the left of politics. But for the great majority of the electorate, class labels are devoid of much partisan implication. This does not mean that we should avoid using the terms 'working class' and 'middle class' — probably an impossible prescription in any case — but rather that we should recognise that they denote, in the world of D.W. Rawson, the 'uncertain and fluctuating' division between 'those who think of themselves as "ordinary people", who stand to gain by the levelling of incomes and prestige, and those who feel that they stand to lose by this process'.[22]

Yet a paradox remains. If class is so barren of precise meaning and consequence, why are class labels so widely accepted, why is the Labor Party so frequently referred to as the party of the working class, why, in sum, have the terms such currency in both academic and popular discourse? The answer requires us to consider the relationship of class and party from a different vantage point. It is conventional to see class as preceding party and indeed this is the only commonsense assumption when class is defined objectively — for we would not normally expect people to choose a job or seek a certain income level in response to their feelings of loyalty to a political party. But there is a persuasive conjectural argument set forth most lucidly by Giovanni Sartori, reformulating Lenin, that parties and other political institutions may be *responsible* for the development and maintenance of class awareness.[23] In this account parties act as 'class persuaders' by playing on 'class appeal', and such a role is necessary because ideologies require powerful organisational backing if they are to take hold.

> The party is not a 'consequence' of the class. Rather, and before, it is the class that receives its identity from the party. Hence class behaviour presupposes a party that not only feeds, incessantly, the 'class image', but also a party that provides the structural cement of 'class reality'.

Parties are not the sole providers of such organisational sub-structure: in the case of the working class the same function can be performed by trade

22 D.W. Rawson, 'Labour, Socialism and the Working Class', *Australian Journal of Politics and History*, 7(1), May 1961, p. 76. One respondent, a Hobart man in his late thirties, argued that the middle class voted for the Liberal Party because 'it's the party of "no change" rather than "change", and if you're in a favourable situation you'll naturally vote for no change...'

23 Sartori, 'From the Sociology of Politics to Political Sociology', p. 84.

unions.

We do not have to accept this argument in its entirety to note that it makes sense of one perplexing aspect of the class in Australian society: the much greater sharpness and clarity of the image of the working class. By contrast the middle class is an imprecise and residual category. In talking about parties and leaders (Chapter 4), a large proportion of respondents described the working class as the basis of the Labor Party's support or as its very *raison d'être*; few linked the middle class to any party, or spoke of it either favourably or unfavourably. In describing the two classes (Table 8.3) respondents needed fewer attributes for the working class than for the middle class. And they were very much more likely to see the working class as a monolithic voting bloc than to see the middle class as one. The simplest and most plausible explanation for these differences accords with Sartori's argument. The employment of class terms in Australian politics is confined generally to the left, and to its principal organisational expressions, the ALP, the trade unions, and the Communist parties. If the Liberal Party is the political projection of the middle class, it must be said that the party does not use explicit class appeals in its election campaigns; indeed it argues that class politics are divisive, and claims to be above regional, sectional and class interest. [24] And the trade union movement has no ideological equivalent on the right. The Chambers of Commerce and of Manufactures, and the other peak institutions of industry, commerce and finance, even the Institute of Public Affairs, the financial backstop of the non-Labor parties in the 1930s and 1940s, defended private enterprise, not the middle class.

The middle class lacks a champion, and it is not surprising that its image is so diffuse and its boundaries so uncertain. This is a further reason for doubting the relevance of class consciousness in determining party choice, for we have seen that 'middle-class' people, without the benefit of *class* evangelisation from the Liberal and Country Parties, are more strongly non-Labor than the working class, organised both by a major party and the union movement, is Labor.

It would be easy to retrace the argument of this chapter and, following Sartori, to rework the data to show the influence of party upon class: among manual workers, for example, 72 per cent of Labor identifiers but only 39 per cent of Liberals placed themselves in the working class. But this is at least premature. We should first consider the relationship of trade unionism — more precisely, membership of a trade union — to both class self-placement and party identification.

---

24 The fullest analysis of the Liberal Party's ideology is Tiver, 'Political Ideas in the Liberal Party'. The only sustained use of explicit appeals to the middle class occurred during R.G. Menzies's efforts to construct the Liberal Party during the mid-1940s — a period of Labor ascendancy. See his collection of speeches of that time, *The Forgotten People*, Sydney, 1943, especially Chapter 1.

The Contribution of Unionism

The parliamentary Labor Parties in Australia are historically the creation of trade unions, and unions as a whole will exercise considerable influence within the ALP through their representation at state conferences and councils of the party and through the subsequent election of union representatives to the party's federal conference and executive. Although the actuality of these relationships is subtle and complex, it is part of conventional wisdom, especially on the right, that the ALP is to a greater or lesser extent controlled by the unions, or at the very least that it is an extension of the union movement. The confident summary of Sir Frederick Eggleston may be regarded as the classic statement:

> It must always be remembered that the Labour party is first and foremost a Trades Union party. The Trades Union is its fundamental basis; its strength arises from the power of the organised Trades Unions; the Unions give it enormous electoral advantages, for most members vote as a matter of course for the candidates selected by the Trades Union party. The party supplies the personnel who come up for election, while experience in the movement has been found to be excellent training for Parliament. [25]

Certainly the sheer size of the union movement is impressive. In 1969 there were 324 separate trade unions in Australia, and their 2.3 million members represented 50 per cent of wage and salary earners; union membership was rather more common than in Great Britain and much more so than in the USA or Canada. [26] The peak association of the trade unions, the Australian Council of Trade Unions (ACTU), represented through affiliation some three unionists in four, [27] and occupied an influential position in the penumbra of Australian national government. Although the ACTU was not affiliated to the Labor Party (only individual unions may affiliate, and they may do so only at the state level) two unionists in three belonged to unions affiliated with the ALP, [28] and union affiliation fees were an important source of party revenue. Only one union, the Federated Clerks Union, was affiliated to the DLP, and

---

25 F.W. Eggleston, *Reflections of an Australian Liberal*, Melbourne, 1953, p. 37.

26 D.W. Rawson and Suzanne Wrightson, *A Handbook of Australian Trade Unions and Employees' Associations*, Canberra, 1970, pp. 4, 18, n. 1, see also the second edition, with D.W. Rawson as sole author, Canberra, 1973, pp. 8-9. The difficulties associated with classifying unions and enumerating their membership and affiliations are lucidly explained by Rawson. In the first third of the twentieth century union membership in Australia was proportionately greater than in any other non-communist country. The Australian proportion, which fell steadily from a peak of 61 per cent in 1954 to 50 per cent in 1970, has since risen to 53 per cent in 1972, but remains less than in Sweden or Norway. See also Alford, *Party and Society*, p. 292, n. 1, and Trevor Matthews, 'Australian Pressure Groups', in Mayer and Nelson, *Australian Politics*.

27 Rawson and Wrightson, *Handbook*, p. 12.

28 D.W. Rawson, 'A Note on Union Affiliations with the A.L.P.', *Politics* 6(1), May 1971, p. 95.

that in Victoria only. On the face of it, trade unions, individually and together, are the bulwark of the worker and a great source of organisational strength for the ALP.

The massive organisational structure of unions is nevertheless far from complete, for approximately one-half of the workforce is not unionised. Moreover, as the survey data reveal, Australians share a widespread distrust of unions, a sentiment expressed by many unionists as well as nonunionists. In both 1967 and 1969 respondents were asked whether they thought trade unions had 'too much power or not too much'. On each occasion those thinking that unions had too much power were the largest single group — and a clear majority in 1969; on each occasion one in three unionists felt this way. If unions are not popular, strikers are even less so, and strikes are the activity of unions that most directly impinges on the general public. Only one respondent in six in either 1967 or 1969 would say that his sympathy was generally with the strikers when he heard of a strike. The remainder were evenly divided into those who were generally hostile to strikers and those who thought their attitude would depend on the circumstances of the strike in question. In this matter also the attitudes of unionists were not much different from those of nonunionists (only one in five in 1967 and one in four in 1969 were favourably disposed towards strikers, and one in three was hostile).

Certainly the recent history of industrial relations is an important context in which to discuss these attitudes, and the late 1960s saw a sudden increase in industrial strife.[29] Yet these findings usefully serve to introduce a discussion of the impact of unionism on party identification. For in 1967 only 61 per cent of unionists identified with Labor: one unionist in three was a supporter of the Liberal and Country Parties, and another one in twenty supported the DLP. Unionists' allegiance to the ALP, then, was of the same order as that of the self-described working class and of manual workers.

But of course, the group of union members is in no way co-terminous with either manual workers or the working class; indeed, in recent years the principal development of unionism has been among white-collar workers, whose unions now represent about one-third of all white-collar workers.[30] Accordingly, we can obtain a better feel for the association of union membership with Labor identification by looking at it within occupational rank cateogries and for male heads of household only (Table

29 Working days lost through strikes per employee, which had been stable around 0.20 throughout most of the 1960s, rose to 0.28 in 1968 and to 0.46 in 1969, the highest level of the index reached for more than fifteen years. They were to rise much higher still in the 1970s. For 1955 to 1968, see D.W. Rawson, 'Strikes', unpublished seminar paper, Department of Political Science, RSSS, Australian National University, 1970; the 1969 index figure has been computed from data in *Labour Report*, No. 54, 1968 and 1969.
30 Matthews, 'Australian Pressure Groups'. See also R.M. Martin, *Whitecollar Unions in Australia*, Sydney, 1965.

8.14). Since only twelve members of Category I belonged to unions the analysis is confined to categories II to VI. In each category union members were more likely than non-unionists to identify with the Labor Party, and this was especially so among semi-skilled and unskilled manual workers: the association is clear.

But which is the cause, and which the effect? Does the impact of union membership induce workers to think of themselves as Labor supporters, do Labor supporters seek out unions, or do both kinds of behaviour occur? Let us consider the first possibility. The union principle is the conversion of individual claims and demands into those of the group, and the opposition of the numerical strength of the union to the economic strength of the employer. If unions are to radicalise the political outlook of their members, an almost indispensable mechanism for this change should be the development of heightened class awareness on the part of the union member. We are, of course, faced immediately with another problem of causality, for it is possible that class-conscious workers would seek out unions as an expression of an already existing set of attitudes. But this is much less of a problem, for union membership is forced upon many workers whether they seek it or not: two-thirds of the unionist respondents believe that union membership was necessary in their job,[31] and many of the remainder may have joined their unions because they believed that 'it was the thing to do'.

Are unionists more class-conscious than non-unionists of the same occupational level? The answer is a cautious 'yes'. Among manual workers, 71 per cent of unionists placed themselves in the working class, compared with only 51 per cent of non-unionists. But given the frail stability of class self-placement that has been demonstrated already, it is clear that this is not powerful evidence to support the argument that union membership

Table 8.14   Labor identification among male heads of household, by occupational rank and union membership, 1967

	II Managerial %	III White-Collar %	IV Skilled Manual %	V Semi-skilled Manual %	VI Unskilled Manual %
Non-unionists	27	24	50	54	44
Unionists	50	52	62	81	75

Note: Each cell contains the proportion identifying with Labor of those with some party identification.

31 Legally enforced compulsory unionism was not the main cause (indeed, no state now has such legislation on its books, though it was in force in Queensland and New South Wales for many years), but rather *de facto* compulsion arising out of individual industrial agreements, union vigilance and social pressure. The number of workers legally obliged to join unions cannot be determined with any accuracy, but it is not large.

generally produces heightened class consciousness.[32] The greater preference of unionists for Labor has other causes.

Let us consider the alternative possibility that union members are
Labor because Labor workers feel the need to express their partisan
loyalty in union membership. We have a measure of willingness to join
unions: unionists were asked whether membership of their union was
compulsory for people in their job and, if so, whether they would have
joined the union otherwise. Hypothetical questions like the last must be a
little suspect, as they can reflect the respondent's state of mind at the time
of the interview as much as that when he joined his union. We should note
at once that three-quarters of Labor unionists believed that their membership was compulsory whereas half the Liberal and Country Party unionists
were volunteers — but the explanation of this unexpected finding is that a
much larger proportion of non-Labor unionists have white-collar jobs,
and white-collar unions have not been able to bring about a situation in
their employment areas where union membership is virtually universal.

If the compulsory unionists are considered alone, 70 per cent of the
'willing conscripts' (those who would have joined anyway) were Labor
supporters, whereas only a little over half of the unwilling were; these
proportions were much the same in both 1967 and 1969. To express the
relationship in this way, however, is to suggest that attitudes to union
membership precede partisan loyalty, whereas the reverse is surely more
likely. Table 8.15 displays the proportion in both 1967 and 1969 of
compulsory unionists who would have joined their unions without such
compulsion, within the two major categories of party identification. In
both years Labor partisans were more favourably disposed to joining their
unions, and this finding lends weight to the proposition that for some
unionists partisan attitudes precede union-based attitudes.

But the fact that half of the Liberal and Country Party identifiers
would still have joined their unions suggests also that unionists need not
see unions as deeply involved in party politics — that they can keep their

Table 8.15   Preparedness to join union, by party identification, 1967 and
1969

Party Identification	Would have joined Union	
	1967 %	1969 %
Liberal-Country Party	50	54
Labor	75	77

32 It cannot even be argued that union membership leads to a notably greater devotion to
the ALP among Labor supporters. It is true that 46 per cent of Labor trade unionists
considered themselves 'very strong' Labor partisans — but so did 35 per cent of Labor
non-unionists. Again, the difference is not remarkable.

union membership and their party identification in separate compartments of the mind. Indeed, the data show that the affiliation of unions with the ALP and union activity in party politics generally are widely unpopular. In 1967, 89 per cent of those who thought their unions should have close ties to the ALP were Labor supporters themselves — and they made up only 60 per cent of Labor supporters; the remainder thought unions should stay out of politics altogether. In 1969 the question was reworded. [33] Only 30 per cent of Labor unionists could be found to agree with the proposition that their union should be affiliated with the ALP; Liberals were opposed almost to a man. All respondents were asked whether they thought unions should usually support one party or should avoid doing so. Supporters of union alignment in politics were greatly outnumbered by opponents of such a course of action, even in the working class (63 per cent to 22 per cent) and among Labor identifiers (57 per cent to 30 per cent). [34] If unions are generally thought to have too much power, and to have no place in politics, their role as creators of class consciousness must be at best a small one. And if Labor sympathies can give people a favourable view of trade unions, they can also lead people to think of themselves in class terms.

Although the notion of an Australian class consciousness must be severely qualified, this does not mean that we can dismiss the partisan implications of placement in the social hierarchy. But henceforward we will measure that location, whenever necessary, by using not self-placement but other more objective measurements, in particular the manual/non-manual dichotomy. And in doing so we will assume, unless evidence suggests otherwise, that the link between such placement and partisan loyalty is in most cases a direct one — that the bricklayer's labourer who thinks of himself as Labor, the Liberal solicitor, the Country Party farmer, possess such loyalties because they see their party as most likely to serve their own interest best. Most voters do not appear to generalise their loyalty into that appropriate for a group to which they belong, and of those who do, very few generalise their feelings to encompass those of a class, strictly defined. Australian politics is the politics of parties, not of classes, and it is on parties that Australians focus.

33 Questions 77(i) in the 1967 questionnaire and 77(j) in the 1969 questionnaire.
34 It is probably the case that, like the British workers surveyed by Goldthorpe and his colleagues, Australian workers tend to see their unions as instrumental in terms of improving their wages and working conditions, and not as agencies of social change. See John H. Goldthorpe *et al.*, *The Affluent Worker: Political Attitudes and Behaviour*, Cambridge, 1968, p. 28 and generally.

9 Mobility and Migration

There's a difference in the working class today than what was termed the working class years back...when my parents were young [about 1920]. There was a definite difference then. Now people are better off. You might say that there is now that middle part, whereas it was more like the servant and master idea before. (*housewife, twenty-nine, Hobart*)

There is much in the remarks of the respondents to suggest that the class-party link has undergone a major change during the twentieth century. It would be sensible to expect some change to have occurred: since Federation, Australia has much more than doubled its population, it has become an affluent, urban, industrial society, and in the last twenty-five years it has taken in more than two and a half million immigrants. It is true that this massive reshaping of a political community has not impaired the capacity of the major parties to attract and retain supporters. Industrial changes, like wars and depressions, are events that modern party systems can take in their stride. Yet there have been changes to the whole society and they have had their effects on patterns of behaviour in the body politic. This chapter explores them.

The Effects of Social Mobility

Changes in the industrial structure of a community have an initial impact on the individual by affecting his choice of occupation and his expectations of it. Later they will affect the extent to which he pushes his children towards similar or different occupations. The occupational mobility within and between generations that these changes stimulate can have obvious consequences in change of income and life-style, and, in some cases, of political outlook. For all these reasons, social mobility is a recurring theme both in creative writing and in academic discussions about the nature of contemporary society. In tracing the relationships between party choice and social mobility we move onto some well tilled ground.

The most important change that has occurred to Australia's occupational structure in the last sixty years has been the failure of rural employment opportunities to keep pace with the increase in population. In consequence, farmers and farm workers have become an ever smaller proportion of the workforce. In 1911, graziers, farmers and farm workers, the whole rural sector, made up 28 per cent of the male workforce; in 1966 they were only 11 per cent. The movement of rural workers and their children from farming occupations to other jobs has introduced an element of structural or 'forced' mobility. [1] But the broad division between the non-manual and manual occupational sectors has not changed very much in the twentieth century. Table 9.1, [2] which summarises the occupational distribution of the male workforce in six of the seven censuses between 1911 and 1966, indicates that there has been only a slow growth in the *proportion* of non-manual jobs, although their number more than doubled between 1911 and 1966. Indeed, most of the increase occurred between 1933 and 1947, and the proportion of non-manuals actually declined between 1947 and 1961, though it increased again over the next inter-census period.

Since farmers and graziers have been defined here as 'non-manual', and have generally made up much more than half of the rural workforce (the typical form of rural industry is the family-owned and family-run farm), it is clear that the slow movement in the proportion of non-manual and manual jobs conceals some other important changes that have occurred within these broad classifications. Farmers, graziers and small pro-prietors have declined in importance, but professionals and clerical workers have greatly increased. Among manuals, farm workers were once the second largest group; by 1966 they were insignificant, and miners had also declined in importance. But craftsmen were more numerous, as were

Table 9.1   Occupational change in the Australian male workforce, 1911 to 1966

	1911 %	1921 %	1933 %	1947 %	1961 %	1966 %
Non-manual	31.1	32.0	33.6	38.8	36.3	37.5
Manual	68.9	68.0	66.4	61.2	63.7	62.5
Total	100.0	100.0	100.0	100.0	100.0	100.0
(N millions)	(1.47)	(1.74)	(2.11)	(2.39)	(3.13)	(4.42)

1   L. Broom and F. Lancaster Jones, 'Father-to-Son Mobility: Australia in Comparative Perspective', *American Journal of Sociology*, 74(4), January 1969, pp. 333-42.

2   Adapted from an analysis of census results presented in F. Lancaster Jones, 'Occupational Change in Australia, 1911-66', *Indian Journal of Sociology* 2(2), September 1971. Encel (in *Equality and Authority*, pp. 115-23) assembled other evidence to reach much the same conclusions. The emphasis on the *male* workforce here is deliberate, and follows from the finding that husbands and wives in the two samples were very likely to have the same party preference. To the extent that party preference is associated with occupation, therefore, the husband's occupation has been the important item for analysis. From the vantage point of the mid-1970s it seems likely that, in future, analysis will need to be broadened to take account of the wife's occupation also. It should be noted that the inclusion of the female workforce in Table 9.1 would have resulted in a lowering of the non-manual proportions, since women are disproportionately employed in factory and other process jobs.

factory hands. These changes imply that social and occupational mobility between generations has been most complex, and that the broad similarity between past and present occupational structures may mask considerable movement between jobs.

This was the finding of Broom and Jones,[3] and it is confirmed by the data of the 1967 and 1969 surveys. Table 9.2 displays the inter-generational occupational mobility of the male breadwinners in the 1967 sample, that is, it compares their occupations with those of their fathers. It should be remembered that while the 1967 breadwinners are represent-ative to some degree of the male workforce in 1967, their fathers are not similarly representative of any past workforce: Table 9.2 reveals occu-pational mobility over almost a century, since the fathers of the oldest respondents were at work in the 1870s, many of them in other countries. Moreover in most cases the occupations of fathers were those they had when the respondent was growing up[4] — that is, when they were towards the peak of their careers — whereas the sample contains many young men at the beginning of their working lives. We cannot, therefore, meaning-fully compare the recall of fathers' occupations with early census dis-tributions.

Table 9.2 is thick with numbers, and this very thickness is its first important characteristic. Every cell is filled; only seven of the 36 cells contain less than 1 per cent, and only one cell contains more than 10 per cent.[5] There is considerable and wide-ranging mobility here, and it is by

Table 9.2 Turnover of occupational grade from fathers to sons, 1967

Father's Occupational Grade	Son's Occupational Grade							
	I %	II %	III %	IV %	V %	VI %	Total %	(N)
I	2.1	1.9	1.0	0.9	0.9	0.9	7.7	(69)
II	2.9	13.5	3.3	3.2	3.7	3.8	30.4	(270)
III	1.2	1.9	2.5	1.5	0.9	0.7	8.7	(77)
IV	1.5	2.9	2.6	4.0	3.8	1.9	16.7	(149)
V	0.7	2.5	2.4	3.9	3.8	3.0	16.3	(145)
VI	0.5	3.3	1.9	4.6	4.6	5.4	20.3	(180)
Total	8.9	26.0	13.7	18.1	17.7	15.7	100.0	
(N)	(79)	(231)	(121)	(161)	(158)	(140)		(890)

Note: See Table 8.4 for an explanation of categories.

3 'Father-to-Son Mobility', especially Table 3.
4 See question 83(a) in the 1967 questionnaire. It will be noted that the sample is rather more non-manual in character than the 1966 census. The explanation is that the sample is one of *voters*, while the workforce includes non-naturalised immigrants as well, who are disproportionately concentrated in unskilled and semi-skilled occupations.
5 The welter of numbers need not obscure the meaning of the Table 9.2. 2.1 per cent of the males in the sample, for example, were professionals whose fathers were also pro-

no means only in an upwards direction. The direction of mobility is best illustrated by collapsing Table 9.2 into the familiar non-manual/manual categories, as in Table 9.3. There has been a small net increase in the non-manual proportion of sons, compared with their fathers, but it has been accompanied by considerable movement between the non-manual and manual sectors, both upwards and downwards. Indeed, while two sons in three have remained in the broad occupational rank of their fathers, those that have moved have been almost as likely to move downwards as to move up, a consequence required of course by the small change in the total manual/non-manual distribution shown in Table 9.1. The partisan implications of these three possibilities — immobility, upward mobility and downward mobility — are charged with significance for an understanding of electoral stability.

Before we explore them, however, there is a paradox that requires explanation. Each respondent was asked also about his perception of his family's social class when he was growing up. If this social class position is compared with the respondent's present sense of his own social class, a dramatic change in perceived class structure of Australia appears to have taken place. Table 9.4 illustrates the shift, using the format of Table 9.3. Here, in contrast to Table 9.2, there is little downward mobility, while almost one in four report an improvement in social class. Two in three of the sample remember growing up in a working-class family, but the sample is now predominantly middle-class.

Part of the explanation of the difference between these two measures of social mobility is already available: the nomination of one's own social class is a haphazard business for many Australians, and Table 9.4

Table 9.3 Turnover of occupational grade from fathers to sons, summarised

| Father's Occupational Grade | Son's Occupational Grade | | Total |
| | Non-manual | Manual | |
		%	%
Non-manual	30.3	16.4	46.7
Manual	18.1	35.2	53.3
Total	48.4	51.6	100
			(N = 890)

fessionals, 1.9 per cent were managers whose fathers were professionals, and so on. A comparison with the comparable table (it displays turnover of occupational rank between *respondent's* father and head of household, i.e. between wife's father's occupation and husband's occupation as well as between father's and son's) in Butler and Stokes, *Political Change in Britain*, p. 96, is full of interest. In the British example, ten cells of thirty-six contain less than 1 per cent, and three contain more than 10 per cent; manual immobility is pronounced.

contains a good deal of chance. But it is likely also that many respondents were remembering a change in fortune. In the thirty years from the late 1930s to the late 1960s Australian society grew rapidly wealthier; gross national product per head more than doubled between 1938/39 and 1968/69.[6] There can be few Australians over the age of thirty, pensioners aside, who could not report that in material terms they were better off than were their parents at a similar age. Since class is seen by many as related to income and access to material goods, it would not be surprising, given the lack of definition of 'class' that we have observed, if Australians interpreted a substantial rise in income as equivalent to a change in class position — or perhaps that class barriers which had once depended on income differentials had now fallen. The young Hobart housewife whose remarks on the changing nature of class appear at the head of the chapter voiced a not uncommon theme. 'It's all changed since I was a girl', a Brisbane pensioner told her interviewer, while a Victorian dairy farmer's wife allowed that there were classes, 'but not as much as previously, though; people aren't as poor as they used to be'. A farmer in the same

Table 9.4 Turnover of social class, from parents to respondent, 1967

| Family's Class[a] | Respondent' Class | | |
	Middle %	Working %	Total %
Middle	31	5	36
Working	23	41	64
Total	54	46	100 (N = 1825)

[a] When respondent was growing up.

Table 9.5 Labor identification and occupational mobility, 1967

| Father's Occupational Grade | Son's Occupational Grade | |
	Non-manual %	Manual %
Non-manual	23	55
Manual	43	68

Note: Each cell displays the proportion identifying with Labor among those with some party identification within categories jointly defined by son's occupational grade and father's grade.

6 E.A. Boehm, *Twentieth Century Economic Development in Australia*, Melbourne, 1971, Table 22 (p. 84). These years saw Australia's fastest ever economic growth per head, and followed an almost standstill thirty-year period, after 1909/10, when real gross national product per head rose by less than 3 per cent. The contrast is a powerful one.

state dismissed classes as things of the past: 'Since the war there's been no class.' It is hard to escape the feeling that the continuation of prosperity and the passage of the generations have taken the sting out of class, that class lines have become vaguer.

Whatever the case, it is clear that any *embourgeoisement* hypothesis about the political consequences of upward social mobility — that more affluent workers will desert Labor for non-Labor as the political expression appropriate to their new social position — will need very careful examination.[7] Let us then consider the evidence. Social mobility has two faces, *inter*-generational (the son's movement away from the occupational status of his father) and *intra*-generational (a person's change in occupational status with respect to his first job). We start with fathers and sons.

Table 9.4 demonstrated that two in three sons held the same broad occupational rank as their fathers and that those who had moved had been almost as likely to move down as up. The partisan accompaniments of such mobility and immobility are set out in Table 9.5, which shows the proportion claiming Labor identification among male breadwinners, defined by their own occupational grade and that of their fathers.[8] We would expect Labor identification to be most frequent among manual sons of manual fathers, and least among non-manual sons of non-manual fathers, and this is indeed the case. In the upwardly and downwardly mobile groups, Labor identification was of intermediate strength. Current occupational rank, rather than father's rank, is the more powerful. And whatever their father's occupational grade, most manual sons were Labor, just as most non-manual sons were non-Labor. There is no suggestion at all in these data that in their politics the upwardly mobile become more middle-class than the middle class.[9] The relationship between inter-generational social mobility and party choice can be expressed simply as follows: downward mobility is associated with an increase in Labor identification while upward mobility is associated with a decrease in Labor identification.

The movements are of approximately the same order. For the downwardly mobile the increase in Labor identification was 21 per cent (non-manual fathers were 34 per cent Labor, while their manual sons were 55 per cent Labor) while for the upwardly mobile the *decrease* in Labor identification was 17 per cent (manual fathers were 60 per cent Labor while their non-manual sons were 43 per cent Labor). The similarity in the

7 The original hypothesis related to British conditions, and has been the subject of close investigation (which found little support for it). See Goldthorpe *et al.*, *The Affluent Worker*.
8 The sample was reduced in this fashion in order to allow the best possible test of the relationship between mobility and party choice; women, as we have observed, are often as influenced by the partisan legacy of their fathers as they are by the gift of their husbands.
9 A favourite theme in American political comment of the 1950s and 1960s. For some comparable American data, see Campbell *et al.*, *The American Voter*, p. 459.

size of these shifts is an important aspect of the political consequences of social mobility. For if, as conventional wisdom reports, there had been a steady 'middle-classing' of the Australian electorate in the past half-century we should expect to find it associated with a corresponding decline in the Labor Party's share of the vote. In fact, of course, the Labor Party has held on to its electoral following, despite many years in opposition. The explanation for the paradox is twofold: the extent of upward social mobility (defined in occupational terms) has been exaggerated, and there has been considerable downward mobility as well. [10] In sum, to the extent that partisan choice is affected by occupational rank, it appears very likely that in the electorate as a whole changes in the structure of the workforce have had no systematic effects.

Why, then, has it been so commonly assumed that social mobility goes only one way — up? The answer is no doubt a complex one. Part of it is locked in the Australian value system. As Zubrzycki has put it, 'upward mobility . . . is regarded in Australia as a social right, as least in the sense that government should provide many more opportunities and ways of achieving it'. [11] Increasing affluence is certainly important, since middle-class self-placement has become more common. Because material success is one of the ruling values of Australian society it is likely both that the downwardly mobile will tend not to advertise their condition and that people will find it an uninteresting and perhaps unpalatable subject to read about. It seems also that those who have experienced upward mobility will be more eager to write about it, and more capable of doing so, than those who have suffered a downward shift in occupational rank. Whatever the explanation, it is not generally realised that one Australian male breadwinner in six is working in a job of lower occupational rank than his father, and that this proportion virtually offsets the upwardly mobile.

Does social mobility have political consequences because it is associated with an increasing awareness of class? The data suggest that such a sequence was not important. The tendency for respondents to report a change in social class from the time when they were growing up to the time of the survey seemed little affected by actual changes in inter-generational occupational grade. There was a slight net increase in working-class self-placement among the downwardly mobile, it is true (62 per cent

---

10 It is tempting to add that downward mobility appears to produce Labor conversions more easily than upward mobility produces non-Labor conversions, a process that would probably cancel out the effect of small net upward mobility; but the differences in Table 9.5 are too slight to support such a hypothesis strongly.

11 Jerzy Zubrzycki, 'The Relevance of Sociology', *Australian and New Zealand Journal of Sociology*, **9**(1), 1973, p. 10; cf. 'Australians also tend to think of such social mobility as a climb up the social scale: they think of it in terms of how easy it is for a man to "get on".' (Craig McGregor, *Profile of Australia*, London, 1966, p. 111). McGregor goes on to argue that in fact there is almost *twice* as much downward mobility as upward mobility — a guesstimate that is not borne out here. But it was a good hunch.

reported that their family had been working-class, while 64 per cent so described themselves), but the vagaries of the relationship are well set out in Figure 9.1.

Among the upwardly mobile sons there has been a very large net movement also in upward class self-placement — 37 per cent. This movement is only half as large (19 per cent) among the manual immobile — but the surprise is that it has occurred at all: certainly it is not related to a major shift in occupational rank. We have a further indication that class

Figure 9.1   Class self-placement among sons of manual fathers, 1967

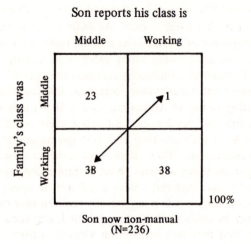

awareness is not especially helpful in understanding party choice. To adapt a remark of Ferdynand Zweig when reflecting on social mobility, 'a man would seem to be thinking primarily about himself, about the individual aspect of the problem, and not about the social situation or the social structure'.[12]

Mobility within the one generation requires separate consideration. To begin with, a common work experience for men has been to start in a manual occupation, and to move into a non-manual job after acquiring experience. Although 46 per cent of the male breadwinners in the sample held non-manual jobs at the time of the interview, only 23 per cent had begun their working life in such a job — a proportion that was substantially lower than that of fathers in non-manual jobs. Secondly, patterns of mobility have been correspondingly affected: most of the mobile experienced upward mobility. While 24 per cent of the male breadwinners had moved from a manual first job to a non-manual job at the time of interview, only 6 per cent had moved downwards from a non-manual job. The partisan associations of these movements are full of interest, as Table 9.6 reveals. The downwardly mobile have become even more Labor than those whose work experience has remained entirely blue-collar: indeed, the downwardly mobile within one generation represent one of the most solidly Labor groups that are encountered throughout the analysis. And those who have moved into non-manual occupations are only slightly more likely to be attached to the Labor Party than those who started in the non-manual sector and remained there.

Table 9.6 suggests in predicting party identification, not much is gained once the present occupation of a man is known by knowing also the first full-time job that he had. Nevertheless, the strong Labor partisanship of the downward movers is provocative. We cannot explore its implications here, save to note that downward mobility is *not* associated with heightened class awareness. Despite their greater Labor loyalty a smaller proportion of the downward movers (59 per cent) thought of themselves as working-class than was true of the manual immobiles (65 per cent).

Table 9.6 Labor identification and intra-generational mobility, 1967

Respondent's first job was	Respondent's present job is	
	Non-manual %	Manual %
Non-manual	28	73
Manual	31	62

Note: Each cell displays the proportion identifying with Labor of those with some party identification, within categories jointly defined by occupational grade of the respondent's present and first full-time jobs. The analysis is confined to male breadwinners.

12 *The Worker in an Affluent Society: Family Life and Industry*, London, 1961, p. 134.

These findings add an important dimension to our understanding of the causes of electoral stability in Australia. We have seen that occupation, or perhaps occupational milieu, is a most salient component of party choice: were the occupational structure of the society to change we should expect these changes to affect the party balance, other things being equal. There has been great change in the occupational structure since the turn of the century, but not in ways which have had direct consequences on the party system.[13] Despite the common view that Australian society is moving, and has been moving, towards a condition in which all men will have clean, 'nice', white-collar jobs, the reality is that during this century there has been for men only slight upward. movement in the ratio of non-manual to manual jobs. One condition of partisan stability is therefore clear. There is a second: occupational mobility between generations has been very common, and it has been almost equally distributed between upward and downward movers. Each of these movements has partisan consequences — and of approximately the same importance: downward movers pick up Labor attachments in about the same proportion as upward movers develop non-Labor attachments. In short, the process of social mobility has been a balancing one, and the net party advantage (to the non-Labor parties) has been very slight. Slight advantages of this kind are not, of course, unimportant, since Labor's defeat in 1961 was accomplished by only a handful of votes, but they will not support a theory of *embourgeoisement*, at any rate as a factor affecting the rise and fall in party support.

The extent of the experience of social mobility (it was known by more than one-third of males) should cause us to look again at the relationship between occupation and party choice. If mobility is common, and leads to a weakening of the former class-party tie for each mobile person, then the links between class and party in Australia must have weakened. To test this hypothesis we need a single statistic that expresses the relationship between class and party: we find it in Alford's 'index of class voting'. The index is derived by subtracting the proportion of non-manuals voting Labor from the proportion of manuals voting Labor.[14] If the classes were completely opposed, the index would be 100 (100-0), while a random relationship — each class splitting evenly — would produce an index of 0 (50-50). To obtain a measure of the change in the relationship we can employ the generational categories introduced in Chapter 6, and test four measures of party affiliation — party identification, first vote, vote in 1966, and intended vote in 1967. The results are given in Figure 9.2.

13 The decline in the rural sector has, of course, been of poignant interest to the Country Party, a matter that is discussed in a later chapter. The great increase in the entry of women into the workforce (they represented a little under a third of the entire workforce in 1966) has not yet had an effect on the party system.

14 Alford, *Party and Society*, pp. 79-80. This statistic is similar in its import to the 'index of status polarization', in Campbell *et al. The American Voter*, pp. 344-6.

The fact that these four measures of partisanship are closely related to one another explains the strong pattern of Figure 9.2. But for an explanation of the *shape* of the pattern we must look elsewhere. Let us first note that the differences in class voting, however measured, between generations I and V are slight, and do not support a hypothesis that the

Figure 9.2   An index of class voting, by generation

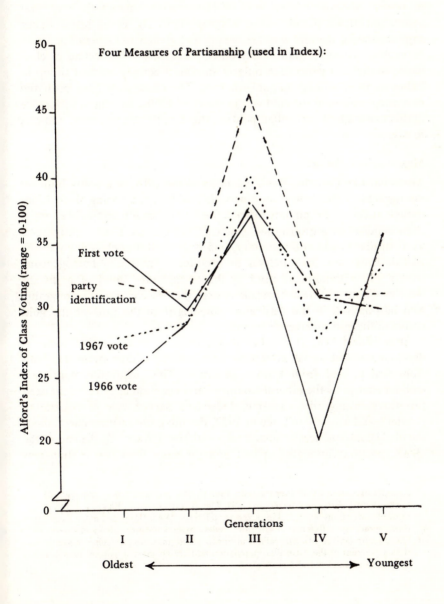

class-party link is weakening.[15] And secondly, as we would have expected from the evidence of Chapter 8, the extent of class voting is relatively low — it is much closer to 0 than to 100. In sum, Figure 9.2 is consistent with the general argument already advanced: that in the long run there has been a balanced relationship between class and party, with social mobility contributing, not to the 'middle-classing' of the society, but to the maintenance of a low level of class voting.

The high and low points of Figure 9.2 require some attention. Generation III first began to vote in the 1940s, during Labor's longest period in power, and the higher level of class voting characteristic of that generation flows mainly from disproportionately enthusiastic Labor support among manual workers, which was greater in Generation III — on each measure — than in any other generation. The decline in class voting in the next generation reflects an almost equally marked slump in Labor support among manual workers. The cause may have been the mounting tension of the cold war in the early 1950s, and the transference of this tension into Australian politics; the data do not, however, allow us to say.

Migrants and Politics

Australia, like Canada, New Zealand, and the USA, is a polity built on immigrants.[16] The flow of new arrivals has been unceasing since 1788, though at times of economic distress the inflow has sometimes been more than matched by a disgruntled exodus. Until the late 1940s immigration to Australia, forced and voluntary, had originated overwhelmingly in the British Isles, and had helped to produce a culturally homogeneous society which thought of itself as the transplanted child of a distant 'Mother Country'. Most Australians were the descendants of immigrants who had arrived in the Australian colonies from the time of the gold rushes of the mid-nineteenth century.

After World War II the Labor government, as an act of national development, set about attracting immigrants in large numbers, both from Britain and from Europe generally. This policy was continued without change by the Liberal-Country Party coalition after 1949 (the need for heavy immigration became, indeed, a sacred cow of Australian politics), and was still in force in 1972, despite growing uneasiness about the likely consequences of sustained population growth. By the end of the 1960s, post-war immigration had brought more than two million new

---

15 Alford's analysis of APOP over the years 1942 to 1961 produces a slow and slight decline in class voting (*Party and Society*, p. 103). The data displayed in Figure 9.2 differ from those already published in Aitkin, Kahan and Barnes 'What Happened to the Depression Generation'; the differences result from redefinitions and some tidying of categories.

16 Our concern here is with Australians of European origin, since Aborigines make up less than 1 per cent of the Australian population and are far more important as a political issue than as an electoral force.

settlers to Australia, rather less than half of whom had come from Great Britain. The remainder came from all over Europe, but especially from Italy, Germany and Greece; and there were substantial contingents of Poles, Dutch, Hungarians and Yugoslavs. At the 1966 census those born outside Australia represented 18.4 per cent of the whole population, a proportion that had been growing steadily since 1947.

The effect of migration upon the electorate has been somewhat less pronounced than on the society as a whole, because non-British immigrants cannot be naturalised for five years and not all choose to acquire Australian citizenship when they are free to do so. Some 574,000 persons were granted citizenship by naturalisation between 1945 and 1968. While the number of migrants enrolled as voters is not known, the proportion of the 1967 sample born overseas was 22 per cent.

A great deal has been written about migrants and Australian society; but little of it relates to politics — and this itself is a warning that the impact of immigrants upon Australian politics is hard to measure.[17] The lack of writing on migrants and politics points also to a paradox: the numbers of immigrants have been very large, and migrants for the most part have entered Australian society from the bottom, as unskilled labourers, most often lacking command of English and capital as well as a marketable skill. Yet the post-war period has produced no Tammany Hall, no migrant political parties or groups, nor even a notable individual politician of immigrant stock who relies on an electoral base of quondam migrants. It is not that the Australian political parties have successfully gone out after migrant members and voters; in fact the parties have ignored immigrants almost entirely.[18]

The likely explanation of the absence of a 'migrant politics' is a multi-faceted one. To begin with most migrants have come to Australia in response to governmental planning and many of their needs are catered for by an elaborate public service apparatus. Many, too, have come in a process of family chain-migration from parts of Italy and Greece, and are able to rely on friends and relatives already resident in the new country for

17 In most of the books that have been written about the migrant experience, 'politics' and 'political parties' are not even index entries. Notable exceptions are Alan Davies's chapter 'Migrants in Politics' in Alan Stoller (ed.), *New Faces. Immigration and Family Life in Australia*, Melbourne, 1966 and Paul R. Wilson, *Immigrants and Politics*, Canberra, 1973. See also Michael Kahan's unpublished Ph. D thesis (University of Michigan, 1970), 'Some Aspects of Immigration and Political Change in Australia since 1947'.

18 Jupp cites scathingly the example of officials of an ALP branch in an area holding several thousand Greeks, who 'wouldn't have a bar of them. We are here to help Australians' (*Arrivals and Departures*, Melbourne, 1966, p. 86). But the more typical attitude is one of indifference and ignorance. For the Greek worker's attitude to his union and to unionism generally, see Petro Gergiou 'Migrants' Unionism and Society, *Australian and New Zealand Journal of Sociology*, 9(1), 1973. Al Grassby, formerly Labor MP for Riverina, is the one notable parliamentarian who has learned a smattering of other languages in order to communicate with his constituents. His electoral success did not apparently inspire any imitative behaviour on the part of his parliamentary colleagues.

information, contacts and jobs. The British have moved easily into a
political culture that bears a marked resemblance to the one in which they
grew up. And above all, post-war immigration has been cushioned by (and
has in part stimulated) continuously burgeoning prosperity. There has
been little overt friction between Old and New Australians that has had
political outcomes, and no more between different ethnic groups among
the immigrants. It is fashionable now to talk of Greek and Italian ghettos
in parts of Sydney and Melbourne, but there are in fact very few
parliamentary constituencies where the concentration of immigrants from
a single country is heavy enough for the 'migrant vote', other things being
equal, to be decisive there.

In Australian politics immigrants have adopted a very low posture, and
their most characteristic political trait is non-involvement. Alan Davies
has remarked that 'Migrants are people whom politics has already failed:
their apathy runs deep.' [19] Yet in this respect they have only behaved like
Australians. We have seen (Chapter 2) that for at least two in three
Australians politics is a most peripheral activity. Considered as a group
the same can be said of immigrant Australians. Indeed, if we divide the
sample into four groups — Australians born of Australian parents,
Australians born of migrant parents, British migrants, and non-British
migrants — a rather unexpected pattern emerges. Table 9.7 repeats some

Table 9.7   Political participation, 1967, and national origin

	Australians born of Australian parents	Australians born of migrant parents	British migrants	Non-British migrants
Percentage who . . .				
follow politics on the radio	15	21	18	17
talk much about politics with others	31	27	35	33
follow politics on television	33	35	40	38
follow politics in the newspapers	42	44	48	44
care which party wins elections	61	63.	61	44
think there are social classes	82	77	78	59
know neither the name nor the party of their federal MP	27	33	38	56
know neither the name nor the party of their state MLA (MHA)	28	32	46	62
belong to trade unions	26	21	27	38
think that what the government does makes a difference to how well off you are	56	55	60	40

19 Davies, *Migrants in Politics*, p. 114.

of the tests of political participation used in Table 2.2, this time comparing the native-born with the foreign-born. On the first tests the four groups are practically indistinguishable. But on the indices of awareness and involvement which follow, it is clear that non-British migrants are distinctive: they are less concerned, less involved, and less knowledgeable, despite the fact that a greater proportion belongs to trade unions than of any of the other three groups.

A smaller degree of involvement is accompanied, appropriately enough, by a smaller degree of use for party labels — and by a relative coolness towards the ALP (Table 9.8). Non-British immigrants were the most indifferent of all to the claims of the ALP, less than a third of them affirming any kind of attachment; and nearly one in five possessed no party loyalties at all. [20] British migrants were in this, as in political participation generally, much more like native-born Australians than their fellow migrants from Europe: among the migrants it was the Europeans who showed an interest in the DLP — the British almost ignored it. Labor's lack of appeal is the more striking in that among the immigrant males in the sample manual workers outnumbered non-manuals by almost two to one. Table 9.9 shows that even amongst manual workers Labor's drawing power was not very great.

The greater attraction of the DLP for immigrants deserves some additional consideration. Between 1947 and 1951 Australia took in

Table 9.8 Party identification, 1967, and national origin

Party Identification	Australians %	Australians born of migrant parents %	British migrants %	Non-British migrants %
Lib.-CP	49	46	46	38
Labor	38	41	39	30
DLP	2	2	2	6
Other	*	0	1	*
None/don't know	11	11	12	26
Total	100	100	100	100
(N)	(1222)	(294)	(230)	(194)

* = less than 0.5 per cent

20 Paul Wilson (*Immigrants and Politics*, pp. 30-1) reports great difficulty in interviewing Italians on the subject of politics. Marilyn Cleggett ('Migrants in the DLP; A Study of the Involvement of a Group of Migrants in the Democratic Labor Party in Victoria', unpublished MA thesis, La Trobe University) reports similar difficulties in interviewing migrants from Eastern Europe. The interviewers in 1967 and 1969 had more profitable experiences, and relatively few migrant respondents refused to discuss their political attitudes. The most likely explanation is that both these samples are of voters, and the migrants among them had been in Australia for at least five years (most of them longer). They were, presumably, more at ease in their political culture than Wilson's respondents, many of whom were not citizens.

170,000 displaced persons from the refugee camps of Europe. Many of them were from Eastern Europe, and fiercely anti-communist. Some observers have argued that the DLP's manifest and militant anti-communism appeals to such voters, and aggregate analysis of electoral statistics has added some weight to the hypothesis.[21] Secondly, immigrants from Catholic Europe might be expected to look upon the DLP as a church party akin to those they had known in their homelands.[22] The sample is too poorly endowed with migrants for this question to be settled conclusively, but by dividing immigrants into Northern, Eastern and Southern Europeans it is possible to construct the beginnings of an argument (Table 9.10). DLP support appears to come in similar proportions from Southern and Eastern Europeans. Further analysis suggests that DLP identification among migrants is confined almost entirely to manual workers: the middle class prefer the Liberal and Country Parties.

The survey data allow us to do little more than speculate about the causes of partisan choice among immigrants. No doubt many adapted their old party preferences to the new political culture where that was possible (as it was, very generally, for British migrants). But two general factors seem especially important. The first is that immigrants hope to do well in their new country, and to do so through their own efforts. Their interest in politics, therefore, is bound to be affected by the extent to which these hopes can be realised. Since the economic climate in Australia from the end of World War II has been generally favourable to such small-scale individual endeavour, it ought not to be surprising that migrants have been only faintly interested in Australian politics ('failed'

Table 9.9   Labor identification, 1967, by national origin and occupational grade

	Non-manual %	Manual %
Australians	25	59
Australians born of migrant parents	29	60
British migrants	23	56
Non-British migrants	21	46

Note: Each cell displays the proportion identifying with Labor of those with some party identification.

21 James Jupp, *Victoria Votes*, Sydney, 1961, p. 22; Cleggett ('Migrants in the DLP', p. 53) reports that Polish leaders claimed that 75-95 per cent of Poles supported the DLP, but argues that sophisticated Poles would vote Liberal, in order to distinguish themselves from the peasants.

22 Cleggett and others argue against this notion on the ground that in Australia there is tension between the Irish and Italian strains in the Catholic Church, and that the church has only a weak hold over the Italian Catholics anyway.

migrants can always return home, as many have done). Given all this, the migrant preference for the coalition parties can be seen as a consequence of relative indifference, and the coalition's very longevity provided in itself an explanation for continuing migrant support: when things are going well, and one has no long-standing attachment to a party, what is the point in changing? As a middle-aged Italian housewife explained it,

> Look, I tell you the truth. We came here in the Liberal Party — I think it was always the Liberal Party. We came here sixteen years ago and we have not experienced any other party.

She was echoed by an Old Australian, whose Labor sympathies did not cloud his perception:

> New Australians in particular vote for the government. That's under-standable — they've been brought out here by the Liberal-Country Party. They've had such bad times in their own country they think it's a wonderful government.

Secondly, the Labor Party could all too easily be portrayed, not only as a party sympathetic to communists and communism, but as one which would in government be antipathetic to the kind of private enterprise context in which many migrants hoped to make good. In contrast the Liberal Party could appear as the party most likely to benefit migrants: 'they give assurance of freedom and security — that's most important', said a Polish storeman in Melbourne (a very strong DLP identifier).

Yet we should not make too much of these partisan differences between Old Australians and New. In 1967 the Labor Party was only just beginning (with considerable help from the Holt government) the upward movement that would place it in government in 1972. At that time the balance of opinion within the electorate favoured the non-Labor parties, and the stronger preference of migrants was a difference of degree only. It was, of course, a difference in degree that had profound electoral effects. Immigrant citizens made up some 22 per cent of the electorate in 1967,

Table 9.10 Party identification, 1967, and European origin

Party Identification	Southern Europeans %	Eastern Europeans %	Northern Europeans %
Lib.-CP	41	40	56
Labor	30	28	27
DLP	8	7	4
Other	0	0	2
None/don't know	21	25	11
Total	100	100	100
(N)	(77)	(53)	(45)

and the government's lead within that group was at least 2 per cent, and probably 3 per cent — a very handy insurance in a close election.

But this pattern of partisan choice is clearly alterable. Migrants are less strongly attached to political parties than are native-born Australians. They are, therefore, presumably more responsive to the contemporary political climate. It seems very likely that had the Labor Party been in office without pause after 1949 it would have benefited (though perhaps not quite to the same degree) from the migrant vote. Had it survived, the Whitlam government might in due course have attracted as Labor supporters most of those migrant voters who were not strongly committed to the other side.

Social mobility has failed to disturb the equilibrium in the party system, and the massive immigration of the twentieth century has had no powerful effect. Migrants have accepted the party choices offered to them without demur, with only marginal benefit to the non-Labor bloc. In the long run even that advantage may disappear, and immigrants emerge, rather like the young, as voters rather more subject to electoral tides than the rest of the electorate, and thus a potential resource to each side.

10 The Two Faces of Religion

> There's too much religion in Australian politics. If you're Catholic you support the DLP, and if not that, the ALP. (*truckdriver, forty-five, Scottish migrant, Traralgon, Victoria*)

White Australia is an Anglo-Celtic, rather than an Anglo-Saxon, society, and it has been so since the beginnings of settlement. Although the great majority of its inhabitants are descendants of setters, free and convict, from the British Isles, the English are now somewhat under-represented, and the Irish are overrepresented. The evidence to support this claim is mostly circumstantial, since records of place of birth for the settlers of the nineteenth century do not exist in any number; following others on the same quest, we rely instead on the census evidence about religious denomination.[1] That for 1966 is given in Table 10.1 and in its broad shape bears a striking resemblance to the distribution of religions in

Table 10.1 Religious denominations of the population, 1966

	%
Church of England	33.6
Catholic and Roman Catholic	26.3
Methodist	9.7
Presbyterian	9.0
Other Protestant [a]	6.4
Other Christian [b]	3.3
Non-Christian [c]	0.7
Indefinite	0.3
No religion	0.8
No reply to the question	9.9
Total	100.0

[a] Principally Lutheran (1.5 per cent), Baptist (1.4 per cent), and Church of Christ (0.9 per cent).

[b] Principally Orthodox (2.2 per cent).

[c] Principally Hebrew (0.6 per cent).

1 For example, K.S. Inglis, 'Religious Behaviour' in Davies and Encel, *Australian Society*, 2nd edition, pp. 437-8, and Ward, *The Australian Legend*.

the colony of New South Wales in 1851.[2] Australia is and has been nominally Christian, and the Christian community is divided into a Protestant majority and a large Catholic minority (rather like that of the United States of America). But the Catholic proportion in the United Kingdom plus Eire is probably not greater than 15 per cent, while the Anglican proportion is as high as 60 per cent. The large Irish-Catholic minority (Catholics from other countries, notably Italy, are still a small proportion of the Catholic community) has been a factor of quite pivotal importance in Australian political history, and before embarking on a discussion of the present relationship between religion and politics we should first consider its history.

The Sectarian Inheritance

No one who reads the history of religious conflict in Australia can fail to be impressed at how important the link between religion and party politics once was. Although sectarian animosities have cooled, or at least been driven out of public debate ('I can't understand how you can mix religion and politics and still feel comfortable', said one respondent), the social base of each party's electoral support reveals much evidence of the role that religious affiliations played in the party's formation.

At the turn of the century religion, politics, class and national background represented four overlapping dimensions of Australian society.[3] The Irish settlers in Australia, whether of convict origin or free, were on all accounts disproportionately concentrated in the working class, and overwhelmingly Catholic. The pastoralists of the inland and the urban bourgeoisie dominated the governmental and political structures of the colonies, and were overwhelmingly Protestant (Presbyterian in the countryside, Anglican in the cities). Between Catholics and Protestants there lay a century of opposition, and this had been intensified by disputes over the shape of public education in the 1870s.[4]

Leaders of the Roman Catholic Church, the colonial operations of which had begun in the face of official disapproval, felt harassed by liberal proposals to set up a free, secular and compulsory education system that could cope with rapidly increasing demands for education. Their response was a demand for an equivalent share of public expenditure for their own schools. When this was refused, the church proceeded rapidly to establish a parallel system of parochial schools paid for from church funds and from the pockets of the parents of the children educated in them. Catholics were at first unenthusiastic about these schools, and it was not

2 When Catholics were 30.4 per cent and Presbyterians 9.7 per cent; the balance were mostly Anglicans (ibid., p. 47).

3 Hans Mol, *Religion in Australia: a Sociological Investigation*, Melbourne, 1971, especially Chapter 12, provides a good account of the historical links between religion and occupation.

4 There is an excellent summary in Encel, *Equality and Authority*, pp. 164-83.

until religious sanctions were threatened (in a pastoral letter from the Australian bishops in 1879) that enrolments in the parochial schools began to rise. By 1890 possibly one half of all Catholic children were attending church schools, and the proportion grew to two-thirds in the 1930s and four-fifths in the 1950s.[5] Separate educational systems institutionalised and perpetuated the religious cleavage, and the constant problem of paying for its schools gave the Catholic Church a standing grievance against the state, a grievance that lost force only after the reintroduction of state aid to church schools in the 1960s.

The denominational division in the Australian colonies was so pervasive and so powerful that the developing party system could not escape from its influence. The Labor Party did begin as a movement in which class loyalties were supreme and sectarian differences deplored — indeed, there was a ban on religious discussions at party meetings.[6] In these early years Protestants, Catholics and rationalists worked harmoniously enough in building the new party, and Catholics were by no means dominant. Methodism, for example, was very strongly represented among miners: the mining town of Broken Hill was 30 per cent Methodist in 1890, and the population of Newcastle, another centre of Labor activity, was also notably Methodist.[7] But once Cardinal Moran, the leading Australian prelate, had given the Labor movement his approval, and other clerics and the Catholic press encouraged the faithful to join the party and become active in it, the influence of Catholics within the Labor Party began to grow. In 1891 only one in twelve of the newly elected Labor MLAs in New South Wales was Roman Catholic; ten years later the proportion was three in ten, and ten years later again it was four in ten.[8]

The role of the church itself in bringing about this result ought not to be overemphasised. The Labor Party was the natural political home of the Irish-Catholic working man. Quite apart from his economic interest in supporting a party representing the claims of the worker against the boss, he would have been attracted (as Moran was) by the anti-British nationalism of the party, and by Labor's pronounced intention of breaking up large landed estates to provide opportunities for landless men to become small farmers, a matter of symbolic concern for the land-hungry Irish. In addition, there was the undeniable linkage between the

5 K.S. Inglis, 'The Australian Catholic Community' in H. Mayer (ed.), *Catholics and the Free Society*, Melbourne, 1961, p. 12.
6 I.E. Young, 'A.C. Willis, Welsh Nonconformist, and the Labour Party in New South Wales, 1911-33', *Journal of Religious History*, 2(4), 1963, p. 304.
7 Walter Phillips, 'Religious Profession and Practice in New South Wales, 1850-1901: the Statistical Evidence', *Historical Studies*, 15(59), 1972.
8 Celia Hamilton, 'Irish Catholics of New South Wales and the Labor Party, 1890-1910', *Historical Studies*, 8(31), 1958, p. 265; R.N. Spann, 'The Catholic Vote in Australia', in Mayer, *Catholics and the Free Society*, pp. 117-21. For Moran's role see also Patrick Ford, *Cardinal Moran and the A.L.P.*, Melbourne, 1966.

Protestant churches and the non-Labor parties.

The Church of England regarded itself, if not as the established church, then at least as the church of the establishment, and it did not publicly engage in politics. But members of it, together with leading clergymen of the Nonconformist denominations, were prominent in such political organisations as the Christian Citizens' League and the Temperance Alliance.[9] In placing the blame for society's ills on drink or immorality the spokesmen for these organisations avoided discussion of the economic and social causes of poverty and unhappiness; the political position of these organisations was essentially conservative. Moreover, their dedication to the virtues of the puritan ethic, hard work, thrift and sobriety, was not generally shared by the Catholic community — to the regret of Catholic bishops, who had somewhat middle-class aspirations for their flock. The Temperance Alliance had acted simply as an electoral pressure group, endorsing those candidates who supported its aims. As the suspicion grew that the Labor Party was becoming tainted with popery, the support of the Alliance became more selective: in the NSW elections of 1904, sixty Liberals received Alliance support but only eleven Labor candidates and thirteen others gained it; and the Protestant churches actively called on their adherents to vote for temperance candidates.[10] The polarisation of churches and parties went a step further on the occasion of the fusion of the rival non-Labor parties, which was marked in New South Wales by the request of two prominent Catholic non-Labor politicians to join the Labor caucus.[11]

By 1910, then, the modern party system was established with a ready-made suit of denominational clothing: the Liberal Party contained few Catholics either in the parliaments or in influential positions outside, and the Labor Party contained a very important Catholic element. At the parliamentary level, Catholics began to dominate the ALP within the next decade, as a result of the conscription controversies of the Great War. The harsh measures used by the British in putting down the Easter rebellion in Dublin in 1916 helped to produce the last efflorescence of Irish sentiment in Australia, a sentiment that took on a strongly religious colour because of the outspokenness of the leading Melbourne prelate, Dr Mannix. When the Labor government of W.M. Hughes decided later in the year to proceed with a plebiscite on whether Australians should be conscripted for military service, the opposition to conscription was fiercest among Irish-

9 Ronald Lawson, 'The Political Influence of the Churches in Brisbane in the 1890s', *Journal of Religious History*, 7(2), 1972; J.D. Bollen, 'The Temperance Movement and the Liberal Party in New South Wales Politics, 1900-1904', *Journal of Religious History*, 1(2), 1960.
10 Ibid., p. 171. See also his *Protestantism and Social Reform in New South Wales 1890-1910*, Melbourne, 1972.
11 Hamilton, 'Irish Catholics of NSW', p. 264; Bruce Mansfield, *Australian Democrat. The Career of Edward William O'Sullivan 1846-1910*, Sydney, 1965, pp. 302-4.

Australians, and in Victoria was led by Dr Mannix. The government's decision broke the ALP in two. Hughes and the twenty-three who followed him were expelled from the party; twenty-one were non-Catholics, and most crossed to the other side of politics or retired from the arena altogether. The result was a further coming together of political and religious lines: the parliamentary ALP became as dominated by Catholics as the non-Labor parties already were by Protestants. And the next ten years witnessed, in New South Wales at least, occasional flare-ups of sectarian politics, at a pitch that had not been known for half a century. [12]

These Labor = Catholic, non-Labor = Protestant equations persisted until the mid-1950s, when the Labor Party endured another split, this time as a result of Catholic fears of communist domination of the country (and, on the left, of corresponding fears of Catholic dominance). [13] The result was the formation in 1955 of the Australian Labor Party (Anti-Communist), soon renamed the Democratic Labor Party. The DLP, it was generally conceded, was a party supported very largely by Catholics, but its share of the vote was too small for that to represent a majority of Catholics. The fundamental denominational alignment within the party system had been dented, not destroyed.

It is important not to attach too much *religious* significance to the links between Catholics and the ALP: the attraction of the Labor Party for Catholics was determined by the facts of social structure, not by religious doctrine. And throughout the ALP was tinged both by atheism and socialism; until the mid-1960s it was opposed to state aid for church schools, not in favour of it. Although the bulk of Catholics were supporters of the ALP, and although the party's leadership was often dominated by Catholics, the ALP remained a coalition, in which it was bad form to raise 'the sectarian issue'.

It is probably true that the relationship between denomination and party remained constant but lost much of its emotional force, at least until the mid-1950s. Part of the reason for the decline in feeling has been that until recently state aid to church schools was accepted as an issue that had been settled once and for all, and no other important sectarian issue had arisen to take its place. At the same time, denominational labels have

12 An example was the so-called 'Ne Temere' bill of the Fuller National government in New South Wales, which made it an offence for anyone to declare that a legally contracted marriage was not a proper marriage — a move seen by Catholics as an attack upon their church's doctrine of marriage. The story of this bill (which was not in fact made law) is told with great gusto in J.T. Lang, *I Remember*, Sydney, 1956, pp. 181-5.

13 Eggleston recalls a leader of the ALP saying to him, probably in the 1930s, 'that there was no Labour Party in Australia but only a branch of the Catholic Church' (*Reflections of an Australian Liberal*, p. 51). 'The split' is the best documented event in modern Australian politics. See Robert Murray, *The Split: Australian Labor in the Fifties*, Melbourne, 1970; T.C. Truman, *Catholic Action and Politics*, Melbourne, 1959; Paul Ormonde, *The Movement*, Melbourne, 1972; and Niall Brennan, *The Politics of Catholics*, Melbourne, 1972.

been as stable within the electorate as party affiliations, at least across the great Protestant-Catholic divide. Marriage within the faith has been a fact of social life, and children have received from their parents their denominational place in life, and much of what it implied, just as they have done a host of facts and opinions about the political and social economic worlds. Of the 1967 sample, the proportion of Nonconformists married to Catholics was around 6 per cent, and it was only 11 per cent among Anglicans. Separated from kindergarten to the end of their schooling (and very often after that, for the Catholic Church maintains a rich variety of social organisations that allow the devout to avoid social contacts other than with those of their own faith) Catholics and Protestants live together in Australia in an atmosphere of relatively cordial indifference.

Denomination and Party Choice

The denominational basis of party identification is set out in Table 10.2, which reveals a marked denominational pattern. Of all the major religious groups Catholics are the only one in which more than half identify with the ALP, and alone contain more than a negligible number of DLP adherents. Protestant denominations are the home of supporters of the Liberal and Country Parties, and that support ranges between 58 per cent among Anglicans and an impressive 70 per cent among Presbyterians; support for the DLP is negligible. The confidently non-religious (2 per cent of the sample compared with 1 per cent in the census, plus 10 per cent who declined to answer the question) included both the highest proportions of Labor adherents of any group and the sample's only communists.

Yet denominational differences in partisan preference are not extreme ones, save that Presbyterians and Catholics tend to be found on opposite sides. Since we know that denominational distinctions were once socio-

Table 10.2   Denomination and party identification, 1967

	Anglican	Roman Catholic	Presby- terian	Metho- dist	Other [a] Protestant	Orthodox	Jewish	None
	%	%	%	%	%	%	%	%
Lib.-CP	58	38	70	60	64	60	57	42
Labor	42	51	29	40	35	38	43	53
DLP	*	11	1	*	1	2	0	0
Other	*	*	*	*	*	0	0	5
Total	100	100	100	100	100	100	100	100
(N)	(700)	(463)	(217)	(210)	(149)	(48)	(23)	(55)

Note: Includes only those with some party identification.

* = less than 0.5 per cent.

[a] Mainly Baptist and Lutheran.

economic distinctions in different clothing, it is important to inspect the link between religion and party when the influence of occupational grade is allowed for; this is done in Table 10.3. The Catholic-Presbyterian disparity is present within both occupational groups. Catholics of either occupational grade were more likely to identify with Labor than were equivalent groups in any other denomination, while Presbyterians were least likely to do so. The relative lack of success of the Liberal and Country Parties in attracting Catholics was even greater than Table 10.3 suggests, since Catholics provided in addition practically all the DLP identifiers. Table 10.4 supplies the proportions of manual and non-manual Catholics supporting the three major party groups. Even among non-manuals, only a little over half identified with the Liberal and Country Parties. In contrast 84 per cent of non-manual Presbyterians, and 77 per cent of non-manual Anglicans preferred the Liberal and Country Parties, and among manual workers 54 per cent of Presbyterians and 49 per cent of Methodists chose the non-Labor parties.

In sum, the occupational basis of party choice is not as powerful for Roman Catholics as it is for members of other denominations. Middle-class Catholics are less likely to support the Liberal and Country Parties, and Catholic support for the Democratic Labor Party comes in similar proportion from both occupational groups. It is difficult to reject the conclusion that this broad pattern of party support has historical roots:

Table 10.3 Labor identification, denomination and occupational grade, 1967

	Anglican	Roman Catholic	Presbyterian	Methodist	Other Protestant
	%	%	%	%	%
Non-manual	23	33	15	30	17
Manual	59	64	45	50	53

Note: Each cell displays the proportion identifying with Labor within categories jointly defined by denomination and occupational grade.

Table 10.4 Party identification and occupational grade among Roman Catholics, 1967

	Non-manual %	Manual %
Lib.-CP	53	26
Labor	33	64
DLP	14	10
Total	100	100
(N)	(188)	(262)

Roman Catholics, members of an important community, still display in their party choice a preference forged in the early years of the twentieth century. The Protestant domination of the Liberal and Country Parties may still be a source of distrust; certainly, few Catholics have made their way to the top in the non-Labor parties, even after seventy years.[14] A community memory of a time when nearly all Catholics were underprivileged workers may also be a factor. But it would be a memory only: Catholics in the sample were only a little more likely than Protestants to be in manual occupations, and the same finding has been presented elsewhere.[15]

Middle-class Catholics who think of themselves as Labor, and working-class Presbyterians who shun that party, are demonstrating the power of upbringing in shaping partisan preference. That they see these preferences as persistently relevant emphasises again that party identification can be an ideological badge whose wearer's vote is an affirmation of his general view of the world. The two rarely change, and their constancy contributes to the stability of the political order.

The solidity of such a party identification can be gauged by inspecting the effect of an issue which was basic to it — state aid for church schools. The state aid issue was such a powerful grievance of the Catholic Church for nearly a century that its settling in the 1960s ought to have worked some important changes to the religion-party link. This was especially the case because one condition of the change in policy was the belief within the Liberal and Country Parties that hitherto Labor-supporting Catholics would be attracted to the non-Labor parties if an attractive state aid policy were produced; the Labor Party's quick response to these non-Labor initiatives demonstrated that it too saw important electoral consequences in state aid and wanted the issue taken out of electoral politics.[16] The speed with which a settled policy that state aid was not possible became a settled policy that state aid was right and proper was indeed impressive. Although the DLP had called for assistance to church schools from its foundation, the Country Party was the first major party to propose a general departure from established practice, in 1961. Sir Robert Menzies followed on behalf of the Liberal Party in 1963, and the Labor Party, after

---

14 J.A. Lyons, UAP Prime Minister from 1931 to 1939, is the best known non-Labor Catholic — but he was an ex-Labor man. Phillip Lynch, Liberal Deputy Leader from 1972, and Sir John Cramer, Army Minister from 1956 to 1963, are more recent examples. The Federal Parliamentary Country Party has rarely contained any Roman Catholics, and in 1962 only 8 per cent of the members of the Country Party in New South Wales were Roman Catholics (Aitkin, *The Country Party in New South Wales*, p. 140).

15 Some 58 per cent of Catholics were in manual occupations (or married to manual workers), compared with 53 per cent of Anglicans, 49 per cent of other Protestants, 52 per cent of adherents of other religions, and 50 per cent of those professing no religion. See also Mol, *Religion in Australia*, Chapter 12.

16 Henry S. Albinski, 'The ALP and Aid to Parochial Schools Controversy', *Pennsylvania State University Studies*, 19, 1966.

some agonies, came up with a bid in 1966. These party moves caused much public disquiet within and outside the Protestant churches, and in 1969 a lively pressure group, the Council for the Defence of Government Schools (DOGS) presented candidates in a number of marginal seats, without much effect. State aid was the new orthodoxy, and accepted as such: a Gallup poll in 1955 had found a divided electorate, with only 51 per cent in favour of aid to church schools; seventeen years later that proportion had grown to 68 per cent.[17]

The impact that the state aid question had on voters can be explored in the survey data for 1967, when the early lead of the non-Labor parties in proposing state aid might have been remembered. There can be no doubt that Catholics were united in approving of state aid, as Figure 10.1 illustrates, and that members of other denominations were less en-thusiastic (the distribution of responses in 1969 to the same question was almost identical). The very degree of Catholic support suggests that the question could hardly be a fine discriminator of Catholic political partisanship. And so it proved. Among Catholics, those who were completely in accord with state aid were 50 per cent Labor; those who were less than wholeheartedly committed to the policy were 54 per cent Labor.

Figure 10.1   Attitudes to 'government aid to schools', by denomination

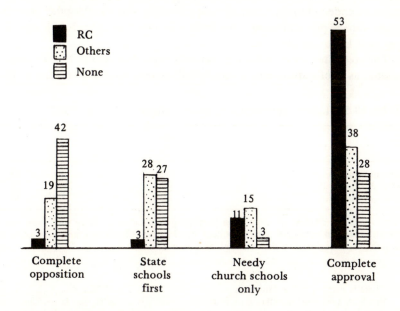

17 In 1972 the question had a different form: 'In your opinion should government aid for non-government schools be increased — or left unchanged — or reduced — or cut out altogether?' Some 11 per cent had no opinion, 37 per cent wanted aid increased, and 31 per cent wanted it unchanged.

The differences are very slight, and are matched by equivalent stability among Protestants: those who were wholly opposed to state aid were only marginally more Labor than those who were wholly in favour of the policy. State aid may have had some electoral consequence in 1963 and 1966 (although there is no evidence that this was the case), but it appears to have had little or no effect on fundamental partisan perspectives.[18] Party identification, to make the point again, is rooted in the individual's life experience and ancestry, and cannot easily be affected by issues of the day.

Churchgoing and Conservatism

One of the important discoveries in Mol's thorough analysis of contemporary religious belief and behaviour in Australia was the clear correlation between regular attendance at church and political conservatism,[19] a relationship that existed within every denomination. Mol's finding is completely confirmed by the 1967 survey. In the tree analysis at the beginning of this section, churchgoing emerged as the most important predictor of partisan loyalty for manual unionists and for the non-manual sons of non-manual fathers. But in fact churchgoing was of importance at almost every stage of the analysis: in the sample as a whole regular churchgoers (defined as those who attend church at least once a month) were 33 per cent Labor, compared with 58 per cent Labor for those who never attended church; manual trade unionists who were regular churchgoers were 58 per cent Labor, but those who never went to church were 80 per cent Labor; and so on.

The frequency of churchgoing varies a good deal across the denominations, as Mol's study and some APOP surveys have shown; again, the

Table 10.5 Labor identification, by churchgoing and sex, 1967

	Men %	Women %
Attend regularly	33	33
Attend occasionally	45	35
Never attend	60	44

Note: Each cell displays the proportion identifying with Labor, of those with some party identification, in categories jointly defined by the respondent's sex and regularity of churchgoing. 'Regularly' is defined as at least once a month.

18 There is nothing in the data to disprove a hypothesis that the differences that do exist flow from partisanship rather than from issue orientation, that is, that Labor Catholics were likely to look with less favour on state aid than non-Labor Catholics. References to state aid were very sparse in both 1967 and 1969 as reasons for liking or disliking parties and leaders, and few respondents nominated it as one of the important problems governments should do something about.

19 Mol, *Religion in Australia*. Chapter 44.

1967 survey provides corroborative evidence. Roman Catholics provide the most regular churchgoers, while most Anglicans are purely nominal adherents; members of smaller Protestant denominations occupy an intermediate position.[20] Churchgoing is also very much a female activity — nearly two regular churchgoers in three were women, while nearly two in three of those who never went to church were men. Is this then, one possible explanation for the greater conservatism of women? For some of it only — Table 10.5 supplies the evidence. Among regular churchgoers men and women are equally antipathetic to Labor, but the influence of church upon men is clearly much more powerful than it is upon women. Women who never go to church are much less likely to identify with Labor than are their male counterparts.

Churchgoing varies too by class: going to church is rather more a middle-class than a working-class activity. There are plenty of manual workers in the nominal lists of all denominations, but while 42 per cent of non-manuals were regular churchgoers, only 32 per cent of manual workers were — and the proportion of quite nominal church adherents among the manual workers exceeded that among non-manuals by a similar margin. The joint effects upon Labor identification of church-going, denomination and occupational rank are displayed in Figure 10.2.

The message of these data is that Labor identification increases as church attendance decreases, and it does so within each of the three broad denominational groups and the two occupational groups. At the same time, however, the independent effects of denomination and class are not washed away: Catholics are always more likely to think of themselves as Labor than Protestants, as are manual workers compared with non-manuals. Given that among regular churchgoers a majority of manual workers in each denominational group preferred the non-Labor parties, and that even among occasional churchgoers Protestants were unenthusiastic about Labor, the importance of churchgoing as an influence

---

20 The distribution was:

	Catholic %	Other Protestant %	Anglican %	Whole Sample %
Regular	60	38	19	35
Occasional	29	48	58	44
Never	11	14	23	16
Total	100	100	100	100
(N)	(461)	(572)	(691)	(205)

See also Mol, *Religion in Australia*, Chapter 2. The distribution is very similar to that of a British sample in 1963, set out in Butler and Stokes, *Political Change in Britain*, p. 125, n.2

upon parties in Australia can hardly be underestimated.

It is probable that churchgoing has this effect because it represents a cluster of mutually reinforcing influences on the political outlook of the citizen. At the most fundamental level, to follow Troeltsch's typology, the major Australian denominations are all 'churches', accepting the world and its social order and benefiting from a secure position in it (as, for example, landowners whose church and school lands are not subject to rates or taxes). [21] It would be understandable if regular churchgoers picked up a generally conservative attitude to the temporal world from

Figure 10.2 Labor identification, by denomination, regularity of churchgoing, and occupational grade

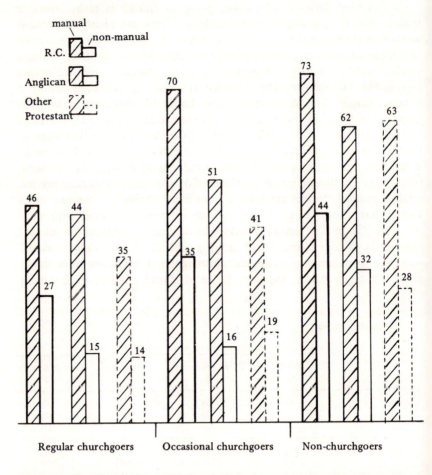

21 The contrast is with the 'sect', whose attitude to politics and society is hostile and potentially revolutionary. See E. Troeltsch, *The Social Teaching of the Christian Churches*, 2 vols., London, 1931 and David Martin, *A Sociology of English Religion*, London, 1967.

their experience of their church, even in the absence of explicit commentary from church leaders. This attitude would be reinforced by frequent contact with likeminded people in the church community, especially when the churchgoer took an active part in the lay organisations associated with the church. Opposing, radical, points of view would therefore be less frequently encountered and perhaps consciously avoided. It is particularly important to note that only 34 per cent of manual workers who were good churchgoers were also members of a trade union; among manual workers who never went to church the proportion was 69 per cent, and it was still high — 60 per cent — among occasional churchgoers.

Accompanying their confident and generally conservative attitude to the political order, all of the Australian churches have been no less conservative about issues of personal morality — drink, sexual behaviour, gambling, and censorship. It is true that the Catholic church has been more relaxed about gambling (and it derives some of its revenue from lotteries and bingo). Political parties have been chary of initiating major changes in the legal status quo in these areas, and when they have done so have generally followed the results of plebiscites or allowed backbench members to sponsor private members' bills. Nonetheless, in the twentieth century it has generally been the case that the outspoken parliamentary defenders of 'proper moral conduct' have been found in the ranks of the non-Labor parties, while most of the occasional champions of change and liberalisation in the laws governing such conduct have stood up from the Labor benches. Labor has often been portrayed (as in the elections of 1972) as a party of atheists and permissives, and while this characterisation ignores both the considerable Catholic element in the party and its Noncomformist wowsers, it is likely that the charge has had some effect among regular churchgoers: the fabled association of socialism with free love dies hard.

This account is highly speculative, and there is only circumstantial evidence to support it. But there is no mistaking the conservative attitudes of churchgoers in fields other than party preference. Compared with those who never went to church, churchgoers were less sympathetic to strikers, much more antagonistic to a proposal that people should be allowed to read and see what they liked, more eager that hotel opening hours should be reduced and even, save for Catholics, better disposed towards the Royal connection. [22] To the extent that party attitudes in these matters have been distinguishable in principle if not in practice it can be said that church-

22 Questions 74, 25a, 27 and 18 in the 1967 schedule. In one traditional test of conservatism — attitudes to capital punishment — regular churchgoers proved less toughminded than either occasional churchgoers (who were most in favour of hanging) or non-churchgoers. On this matter, in fact, party preference was a more significant predictor: in every denomination, and at all levels of churchgoing, Labor partisans were clearly less in favour of hanging than Liberals.

goers' attitudes accord with those of the Liberal and Country Parties, and non-churchgoers' with those of the Labor Party. This too is a long-established association.

The conservative churchgoing third has been and remains an important factor in party and electoral politics. There is little evidence to suggest that its size is decreasing, despite the commonly expressed view that religious observance is on the wane. Data collected in the nineteenth century suggest that church attendance in New South Wales and Victoria then was not much higher than in the middle or late twentieth century. [23] From 1861 to the present Church of England services seem to have attracted about one Anglican in six. Catholic church attendance increased during the nineteenth century to include perhaps one-half of the faith. Methodist and Presbyterian congregations were relatively more numerous in the mid-nineteenth century and have declined slowly since. But the chief impression, over more than a century, is of stability; churches are accepted social institutions of some influence, and they clearly satisfy a widespread demand.

The role of the family in funnelling new members to the churches is most important. Neither of the two surveys explored the churchgoing habits of the respondent's family when he or she was growing up, but data of this kind were collected by Mol. Table 10.6 presents a reanalysis of

Table 10.6   Churchgoing among respondents and among their parents, 1966

| Parents' attendance was | Respondents' attendance is | | Total |
| | Regular | Irregular | |
	%	%	%
Catholics (N = 498)			
Regular	56	19	75
Irregular	11	14	25
Total	66	33	100
Anglicans (N = 723)			
Regular	9	25	34
Irregular	5	61	66
Total	14	86	100
Others (N = 704)			
Regular	28	27	55
Irregular	7	38	45
Total	35	65	100

23 See Mol's summary of nineteenth century data (*Religion in Australia*, p. 11) and of Gallup polls from 1947 to 1962 (p. 14).

Mol's figures; it will be noted that the denominational groupings and churchgoing boundaries are slightly different from those already used in this chapter. In all three groups parents are remembered as having been rather more devout in their time than their children are now; if we allow for some exaggeration caused by filial piety the survey evidence is consistent with a picture of slowly declining church attendance. The role of the family in boosting churchgoing is very clear: five faithful Catholics in six, and four faithful Nonconformists in five, came from regular churchgoing families, and even among Anglicans the proportion was two in three. Patterns of family indifference to church are equally plain. At the same time, the churches do not wholly rely on parental examples. In all three groups there is a small contingent whose attendance at church is regular, but whose parents were not keen churchgoers; they balance to some extent the backsliders from pious families — the more so if that piety has been exaggerated in the remembrance.

To some extent, denomination and churchgoing represent the past and present faces of the great religious cleavage that has characterised Australian society since the early nineteenth century. Their consequences for partisan choice are plain, and important, and the decline in their joint and separate influence is only a slow one. They have contributed very greatly to the stability of the pattern of Australian politics, and can be expected to continue to do so.

The Mystery of the DLP

From the time of its genesis in the great 'split' of 1954-5, the Democratic Labor Party has remained an enigma. In the beginning the puzzle centred around its objectives. Was this yet another breakaway faction of the ALP, destined in time to be reunited with the main party? Or was it, as some of its early leaders declared, a new and lasting 'third force' in Australian politics, that might even supplant the ALP as the major political party of ordinary people? After ten years of life the DLP was manifestly neither a reunitable faction nor an embryonic major party: aided by the pro-portional representation system it had established a small beachhead in the Senate, where its leader was dignified with the status of Leader of a recognised party, but in general elections for the House of Representatives the party's vote continued to fall in each election after a modest high-point of 9.4 per cent in 1958.

Throughout its existence the DLP offered another puzzle: what kinds of people supported it in elections? That most of them were Catholics seemed hardly in doubt, if only because of the historic connection with the party of the National Civic Council, a lay organisation of the Catholic Church, the open support accorded it by the long-lived Dr Mannix, and by other church leaders, and the fact that nearly all those members of parliament who defected from the ALP and campaigned (mostly unsuccessfully) under the banner of the new party were Catholics. At the same time, the

DLP never received anything approaching the full support of Catholics —
that would have given DLP candidates a handy 25 per cent of the vote in
most seats, whereas even in Victoria and at the height of its success the
party was hard pressed to poll much better than 15 per cent. And while
DLP support varied widely from state to state, the Catholic proportion did
not, save that Catholics were relatively fewer in South Australia and
Tasmania.

The identification of the supporters of the DLP has therefore been a
persistent goal of political scientists. Rawson noted in his study of the
1958 federal elections that support for DLP candidates was not obviously
related to any important variable, and argued that only survey research
could provide hard evidence.[24] But the DLP's share of the vote has always
been so small that the number of its supporters produced in a national
sample of even 2000 has been hardly adequate for close analysis.
Moreover, its support has been spread so evenly across electorates that
little could be gained by heavy sampling in areas where the party is strong.
Investigators have had to rely on the national samples of APOP, and these
have tended to report lower than expected levels of DLP support.[25]

The 1967 and 1969 samples were expected to illuminate some of these
problems, if only because the sampling had been very carefully controlled.
The 1967 sample's report of its members' vote in the federal elections of
1966, however, was a rude disappointment: only 3 per cent remembered
having voted DLP at elections only twelve months previously, when in fact
the DLP had polled 7.4 per cent. [26] Close inspection showed that
the proportion of DLP votes in the sample was low everywhere — in
individual seats, in groups of seats, and across the states. This was
puzzling, to say the least, for on grounds of sampling variability there
should have been a few seats from which there was greater than expected
report of DLP voting. In other ways, moreover, the sample was splendidly
representative of its population (see Appendix). Shortly after the 1967
interviews were taken there occured a Senate election, in which the DLP
secured 9.8 per cent of the vote; interviewed two years later, only 3.2 per
cent of those who had voted in that election remembered having supported
the DLP.

What of those who *did* remember? In the 1967 sample they possessed
two distinctive characteristics. Almost without exception, they were DLP
identifiers as well as DLP voters: and virtually all of them were regular
churchgoing Catholics. It was hard to accept that either description could
be true of the mass of DLP voters. As we have seen in Chapter 3, the

24 Rawson, *Australia Votes*, pp. 237-43.
25 A point remarked on by Alford (*Party and Society*, p. 205), who made very good use of
    APOP data in analysing the social and religious base of the DLP. See also Reynolds,
    The Democratic Labor Party, pp. 48-71.
26 Some of the following material and argument was first presented in 'Tracking Down the
    DLP Voter', *Australian Quarterly*, **44**(3), 1972.

pattern of party support for the other parties includes both a solid body of party identifiers and a tail of past supporters of other parties. Surely the DLP had attracted such people too, especially because of its intermediate 'position' between the two major parties. But where were they? Equally, Labor claims that the DLP represented only an unrepresentative Catholic rump had been indignantly denied by DLP spokesmen, who asserted that the party was supported by many Protestants and people of no denomination attracted by the party's stand on communism and by its foreign and domestic policies. The undeniable fact that the DLP's attitudes often received support from conservatives generally, as well as Catholic conservatives, lent conviction to this defence. But where were the Protestant supporters of the DLP?

The most plausible hypothesis suggested by the survey data was the following: the 1967 sample was a genuine microcosm of the whole electorate, and the avowed DLP voters in it represented the confident and committed supporters of that party, who were almost exclusively Catholics in good standing with their church. They made up approximately half of the DLP's electoral support. Three broad possibilities could account for the failure of the remainder to admit to their past DLP support: (i) they might have been reluctant to do so; (ii) they might have forgotten it altogether; or (iii) they might have regarded their vote as 'really' a Labor or a Liberal vote because their effective preference was for another party.

The first alternative should not be discounted entirely. The discussion in Chapter 4 leaves no doubt that the DLP is a disliked object in Australian politics, and a Protestant who had voted DLP on policy or other grounds might well be conscious of the reaction of other Protestants should this be known. The unforced answers of the respondents when the DLP was mentioned suggest that sectarianism is not far below the surface of Australian politics. An elderly clerk from Traralgon (Victoria) gave a typical response: 'They seem to be a sort of subversive mole — not entirely in the open. You don't know exactly whether they represent the church or not.' A fellow clerk from Melbourne was less charitable: 'They receive their so-called platform from Mr Santamaria's group — which is of course the Roman Catholic church. That's the trouble: they want to ram it down my throat as a political belief.'

The 1969 survey provided an opportunity to test the hypothesis that a substantial proportion of the DLP's support was subject to severe memory lapses, since interviewing in this survey began on the Sunday immediately following polling day. Respondents were now being asked to recall a vote they had cast only days, rather than months, before. In 1969 the DLP secured 6.0 per cent of the vote, and 5.2 per cent of the sample reported having voted for it — an excellent fit. Since the 1969 sample included surviving members of the 1967 sample, supplemented only to take account of the deaths, comings-of-age and naturalisations that had occurred in the interim, the disparity in recall of the 1966 and 1969 DLP vote could not be due to inter-sample variability. The cause lay in the patterns of response of those interviewed.

The good match of the 1969 report with the actual result at once disposed of the possibility that a large proportion of DLP voters were too embarrassed by their preference to admit it. It seemed much more likely, indeed, that responsibility for the 1967 result could be laid at the door of Time, the great eraser. To begin with, while the reported DLP *vote* moved from 2.8 per cent to 5.2 per cent between 1967 and 1969, DLP *identification* moved from 2.9 per cent to only 3.2 per cent. That is, the increase in DLP voters was made up almost entirely of people whose fundamental party attachment was to other parties or to none, the majority of them Liberals (there were approximately two Liberal or Country Party supporters to every one Labor identifier). Secondly, few of the 'new' DLP voters were regular churchgoing Catholics. Table 10.7 compares the DLP voters in both samples to illustrate the change in apparent support between 1966 and 1969. In fact, fifty-three of the sixty DLP voters in 1966 were Catholics; forty-eight voted DLP again in 1969, and they were joined in doing so by ten Catholics who had not been in the 1967 sample — eight of whom were regular churchgoers. Thus fifty-eight of the ninety-one DLP voters in 1969 were Catholics but they now represented a much smaller proportion of the total.

It would be wrong to jump to the conclusion that most of the Protestant remainder were among those who had failed to report their DLP vote in 1966: there is simply no evidence available to confirm or disprove such an assertion. But the most plausible argument points the other way. Since nearly all of those who had voted for the DLP in 1966 and were not DLP identifiers had forgotten less than a year afterwards that they had voted DLP, it is reasonable to suppose that the cause of their having departed from their customary loyalty was not deeply embedded. *Ergo*, there seems no very good reason to assume that most of the new DLP voters in the 1969 sample were other than first-time recruits.

Table 10.7   Reported DLP voting, 1966 and 1969, by denomination

	1966 %	1969 %
Church of England	3	13
Roman Catholic	88	64
Presbyterian	3	6
Methodist	2	8
Other Protestant	2	4
Other religion	2	3
No religion	0	2
Total	100	100
(N)	(60)	(91)

The implications of this analysis can now be drawn together. In the late 1960s the DLP possessed a solid core of committed voters who were regular churchgoing Catholics; they made up about 3 per cent of the electorate and about half of those who voted for the DLP. Most of the other DLP voters were Liberals and Protestants, and it is likely that their defection to the DLP was temporary only; the second preference of these voters for the Liberal Party, their former home, helps to give the DLP its solidly anti-Labor aspect. But the DLP has failed to attract them as permanent supporters and this is part of the cause of the party's downward electoral trend. The other part is the party's relative failure to recruit young voters as supporters. We have seen that the principal mechanism underlying the continuity of party life is the transmitted inheritance of party loyalty from one generation to another. But the DLP has not grown large enough for inheritance to be important.

Those who broke away from the ALP to form what was to become the DLP unquestionably had a fierce emotional loyalty to the new party which would have erased their former attachments. The failure of the DLP to win or retain more than one or two lower house seats in any parliament has deprived it of the advantage of incumbency — of being a legitimate choice for the less politically involved in a constituency. At the same time, its partisans are drawn equally from the non-manual and manual strata (Table 10.4) and from the foreign born and their children as well as from native Australians (Table 9.8). It may be doubted whether the struggle against communism, both in Australia and abroad, can provide a sufficient vehicle for the inter-generational transmission of a DLP preference. Migrant children grow up in another land, where the communist threat, whatever the rhetoric, is a distant and subdued one; and the stories of struggles within the union movement in the 1940s and 1950s must quickly acquire an antiquarian irrelevance to young voters growing up in a later world. The prognosis for the DLP is electoral extinction, and its failure to contest House of Representatives seats in states other than Victoria in May 1974, and its abysmal performance in the December 1975 elections, are signs that the end cannot be far away.

11 Town and Country

[The Country Party] are here to help the country man, and I'm all in favour of helping the country man because he is the backbone of the country. (gardener, fifty-four, Queanbeyan, NSW)

There are two good reasons for paying particular attention to the urban-rural dimension in Australian politics, despite its minor contribution to the tree analysis. The first is that the dimension is represented politically in the continuing existence of a major party, the National Country Party (until 1974 the Australian Country Party). The second is that tensions between town and country have been an important aspect of Australian society and politics from the beginning. Agrarian parties are not common in the party systems of the world, but urban-rural tensions are — to the point indeed, that Lipset and Rokkan incorporated them as an integral part of their general schema of party-system formation. [1]

The urban-rural cleavage, and the political consequences that flow from it, provide only a special case of a more general phenomenon: man lives in communities, and his community is likely to affect his opinions, attitudes and behaviour. The differences between communities provide much of the variety in social life, and the movement of people from one community to another is an indispensable part of the process of social change. This chapter explores the ways in which partisan choice is related to where people choose to live.

Political scientists know less than they would wish about how the influence of a community operates on an individual member of it. There are two plausible scenarios: people can be motivated to conform to the perceived standards of the community they live in; and people can be powerfully affected by informal social contacts at the local level, and by more formal participation in voluntary associations. There are, however, other possibilities that reduce the primary influence of the community — it may, for example, be made of likeminded people who choose to live among people thought to be like themselves; in general, and for those interested in political behaviour, the question has hardly moved from the

1 Lipset and Rokkan, 'Cleavage Systems, Party Structures and Voter Alignments'.

stage of speculation.[2] For all that it is hard to doubt that the role of the community can be important: there is some evidence to suggest that, other things being equal, when a community possesses a strong partisan loyalty to one party, many of its members will cleave to that party, rather than to the one more appropriate to their religion or class position. And the more homogeneous and tightly knit a community, the more powerful its influence will be. An excellent example is the political behaviour of voters in mining and resort seats in Britain, where the local political environment operates to reduce the expected effects of social class: compared with their counterparts elsewhere, working-class voters in seaside resorts are more likely to support the Conservative Party, while middle-class voters in mining seats are more likely to support Labour.[3]

Australia possesses few areas as homogeneous in their social composition as the British mining or resort seats. But the influence of the local political environment is still discernible. Table 11.1 compares the degree of Liberal party identification of voters in two groups of seats, encompassing respectively 'middle-class' and 'working-class' suburbs in Sydney and Melbourne. The seats were selected with the object of creating two groups as unlike as possible in terms of social character, real-estate value, and prestige.[4] The two groups of seats were, of course, very different in their

Table 11.1 Liberal identification in middle-class and working-class seats, by occupational grade, 1967

Respondents' Occupational Grade	Middle-class Seats %	Working-class Seats %
Non-manual	79	47
Manual	61	30
(N)	(184)	(253)

2 The message of Gordon Herbert's excellent MA thesis, 'A Social Geography of Voting Behaviour in Sydney and Melbourne' (Australian National University, 1972), which provides a useful summary of the literature and the problems of methodology. See also the chapters by Erwin K. Scheuch, Kevin R. Cox, and David R. Segal and Marshall W. Meyer in Mattei Dogan and Stein Rokkan (eds.), *Quantitative Ecological Analysis in the Social Sciences*, Cambridge (Mass.), 1969, and Robert D. Putnam, 'Political Attitudes and the Local Community', *Amercian Political Science Review*, 60(3), 1966.

3 Butler and Stokes, *Political Change in Britain*, pp. 144-5.

4 The seats included were, *middle-class*: Mackellar, Bradfield, Wentworth (Sydney), Isaacs, Higinbotham, Chisolm, Higgins, Kooyong (Melbourne); *working-class*: Dalley, Grayndler, Blaxland, Reid, Werriwa, Lang, Kingsford-Smith (Sydney), Wills, Yarra, Scullin, Gellibrand (Melbourne). The sample design reduced to two in three the number of seats available for selection. The other capital cities were excluded on the ground that none was large enough to provide the suburban homogeneity sought. For some guidance as to suburban ranking, see F.L. Jones, *Dimensions of Urban Social Structure*, Canberra, 1969, and A.A. Congalton, *Status and Prestige in Australia*, Melbourne, 1969.

partisan allegiance, and part of the reason is that they contained notably different electors: in the middle-class group the proportion of non-manual workers was 70 per cent, well above the average, whereas in the working-class group the proportion of non-manuals was 30 per cent, almost as far below the average. But these differences in occupational grade by no means explain the differing party loyalty of the two groups of seats. Those manual workers who lived in the expensive suburbs were twice as likely to think of themselves as Liberals as were their counterparts who lived in the industrial suburbs. And, in those latter areas, the Liberal Party could not even gain a majority among non-manuals. We cannot jump from these most suggestive data to the explanation that we are seeing the 'contagion' effect of a community. It is plausible, for example, to suppose that many non-manuals who think of themselves as Labor may often choose to live in a strongly Labor environment, or that many manual workers who live in exclusive suburbs are the descendants of working-class families and live where their families always lived. There may even be differences in the kinds of manual workers concerned. But there is clearly something to explain.

A moment's reflection on the nature of such communities provides a clue to another source of stability in the political system. Communities do not change quickly, even though their members may come and go, grow to maturity and die. Many of Sydney's suburbs, for example, have retained the same character for a century or more: Vaucluse, Pott's Point and the harbour foreshores generally have always been middle-class preserves, while Surry Hills, Woolloomooloo, and the outer western suburbs have never been other than working-class. [5] The industrial mode, population distribution and social character of many country areas have been determined as long. [6] Mining and industrial cities like Newcastle, Wollongong, Broken Hill, Mount Isa may grow in size, but their special character does not desert them, and survives the passage of generations. A person who spends his whole life in such a community is likely to have his perception of social and political reality affected, perhaps powerfully, by the fact that nearly all his social contacts will be with members of the same community. The political outlook of farmers, to take perhaps an extreme example, seems to owe its character principally to the fact that most farmers' friends and neighbours are other farmers.

Beneath the homogeneity of Australian society there is an important diversity, the product of the historic experience of different communities. It is to these variations that we now turn.

---

5 See, for example, the familiar association of class and suburb in nineteenth century Sydney portrayed in Cyril Pearl, *Wild Men of Sydney*, London, 1958.
6 Aitkin, *The Country Party in New South Wales*, Chapter 1.

Regional Variations

In a federally organised polity the component states or provinces are an obvious source of variation, since diversity is implied by the federal compact itself. Such expectations are well borne out in the United States, or in Canada, or in West Germany, or even in the USSR. But they are not realised in Australia. There is a similarity between the Australian states, and between their inhabitants, that makes the analyst search almost in vain for significant differences.[7] Each of the mainland states possesses a relatively moist coastal strip and a dry inland; the population distribution of each state is an example of 'metropolitan primacy', with a single capital city possessing no true rivals and containing a large proportion of the state's population;[8] each state has a strong primary industry sector; and, the effects of climate apart, there are no marked inter-state variations in dress, style of life, or speech.[9] There are, of course, differences of degree. Two in every three South Australians live in Adelaide, but only one in three Tasmanians lives in Hobart. Mining is vastly more important in Western Australia than in Victoria; wheat-growing is not important in Queensland or Tasmania; large factories are concentrated in Sydney, Melbourne and Adelaide; Tasmanians and Western Australians are more 'state conscious' than their fellow citizens in other states, and so on.[10] But these differences have not been translated into variations in the social or political context. The mean occupational grade of the respondents in the 1967 survey, grouped by state, ranged from 3.5 in Victoria and Tasmania, through 3.6 in NSW and Western Australia, to 3.8 in South Australia and Queensland.[11] Apart from the

---

7 See S.R. Davis's useful comparative chapter 'Diversity in Unity', in his *The Government of the Australian States*, Melbourne, 1960. His comment on p. 717 can serve as a text: 'In terms of certain items such as area or population wide disparities exist between States. However, in most of the measures which can be made of various aspects of the "social constitution" of the States of Australia the more remarkable feature is the degree of uniformity.' See also Ward, *The Australian Legend*, p. 6.

8 A. James Rose, 'Metropolitan Primacy as the Normal State', *Pacific Viewpoint*, 7(1), May 1966.

9 Though see Bruce Petty, *Australia Fair*, Melbourne 1967, for a brilliant cartoonist's view, and J.W. Berry, 'The Stereotypes of Australian States', *Australian Journal of Psychology*, 21(3), 1969.

10 Only 10 per cent of the respondents in 1969 placed state first — as the attribute most important in describing who they were; but another 33 per cent placed it second (see Table 8.7). There was substantial inter-state variation, with 30 per cent of Western Australians and 25 per cent of Tasmanians placing state first; thereafter the state scores were: South Australia 17 per cent, Queensland 15 per cent, Victoria 6 per cent and New South Wales 4 per cent — a distribution almost in inverse ratio to size of population. The order of states in terms of first plus second ranking of state was Western Australia 68 per cent, Tasmania 63 per cent, South Australia 62 per cent, Queensland 51 per cent, Victoria 38 per cent, New South Wales 30 per cent.

11 This index was obtained by multiplying for each state the number of respondents in each of the occupational grades 1 to 6 by the rank's number (e.g. forty respondents in grade 2 = 80), summing these products, and dividing the total by the number of respondents in the state. The lower the index number, the higher the mean occupational rank. There was little variation in the proportions of each rank across the states.

failure of the Country Party to survive in South Australia and Tasmania, and the much greater success of the DLP in Victoria than in the other states, the four parties have flourished to much the same degree in each of the states. It is sometimes argued that the particular nature of the industrial structure of a state will lead to corresponding attributes in that state's policies: thus, Tasmania is thought to have a more 'right-wing' or 'moderate' ALP because the state lacks heavy industry; or New South Wales to be more militant than Victoria because of its greater numbers and concentration of miners, wharf-labourers and railwaymen. Plausible as these generalisations can be, the industrial structure of the states is only one factor in the explanation. New South Wales has had a conservative, Catholic-dominated Labor Party since the 1940s, despite the potential for militancy, while Victoria's Labor Party, as a result of the split, was particularly left-wing from 1955 to the early 1970s.

In any federal election there will be variations in the support gained by each party from state to state, but that for the two major parties has not varied much either across states or over time. [12] That for the ALP, over the seven elections between the years 1955 and 1972, is set out in Table 11.2. Of all the states New South Wales, the largest in population, shows the least variability in support for the ALP. The poorer showing of the ALP in Victoria is directly attributable to the greater success of the DLP in that state, and ALP showing may be expected to improve (as it did in 1972) as the DLP declines. Otherwise, the message of Table 11.2 is that with respect to the Labor Party, the six states are close kin. The same uniformity is present in the pattern of Labor identification, which in 1967

Table 11.2   The Labor share of the vote at elections for the House of Representatives, by state, 1955 to 1972

Year	NSW %	Vic. %	Qld %	SA %	WA %	Tas. %	Australia %
1955	50	37	42	49	52	46	45
1958	47	40	37	48	35	47	43
1961	52	42	48	52	41	54	48
1963	48	40	46	52	39	52	46
1966	41	35	42	41	43	52	40
1969	48	41	48	52	50	53	47
1972	52	47	47	51	46	59	50
Mean 1955-72	48	40	44	49	44	52	46
Coefficient of Variation	7.7	9.5	9.3	8.4	13.9	8.5	7.2

Note: Each figure represents the Labor proportion of the formal, first-preference votes cast in that election.

12 Western Australia is the one state where the trend often runs counter to that in the rest of the nation. See Malcolm Mackerras, 'The Swing: Variability and Uniformity', in Mayer, *Labor to Power*, p. 238.

was 46 per cent in Queensland, South Australia and Tasmania, 44 per cent in New South Wales, 38 per cent in Western Australia and 37 per cent in Victoria. The source of all these variations lies in the complex interactions of social, economic and political variables; in most cases the differences are so slight that the data available can be of little help in teasing out causes. We can note, nevertheless, that if each state closely resembles its sisters in its social composition, economic basis, population distribution and party structure, the movement of people from one state to another is unlikely to result in changes in partisan identification.

The Case of the Country Party

Inter-state variations are a minor puzzle to the researcher, and a good subject for cocktail party conversation; urban-rural political variations are altogether more important. Some of them stem from differences in the distribution of social and economic attributes: [13] the countryside contains no large cities, little heavy industry, and all the nation's primary production. But that is not all. Those who live in the country have had less formal education than their city cousins, they are more likely to be Protestants, to be good churchgoers, and to be conservative in their social attitudes. [14] The population of some rural areas is an older one, because of the outward migration of the young in search of work or a less restricted life, a process now almost a century old. Rural communities tend to be well defined geographically, inward-looking, slow to accept new ideas, and relatively stable in membership. Their influence on their members, therefore, can be expected to be greater than that of an urban community.

The partisan consequences of urban-rural differences in Australia are well known. Country electorates have rarely been a source of strength for the Labor Party, and aggregate voting patterns in the country have been less volatile than in the city. [15] The greater political conservatism of the country is revealed at the individual level too. In the dozens of comparisons of urban and rural voters made possible by the tree analysis, the rural group was less likely, in every case but one, to support Labor than the urban group. The single exception was the group of manual trade unionists, 68 per cent of whom in the city identified with Labor, compared

13 The evidence bearing on this point has already been presented in Chapter 5 ('Rural Society') of my *The Country Party in New South Wales*. It is only summarised here.
14 J.M.L. Woods, in a comparison of conservatism in an urban and a rural sample, concluded that the differences in degree were slight, and could be attributed largely to age, sex and education variations in the samples ('Conservative Political Attitudes', BA (Hons.) thesis, University of Sydney, 1972). No close analysis of conservatism was possible in the 1967 and 1969 surveys, but the evidence suggested that rural residence contributed something to the greater conservatism of the country-dwellers, even when age, sex and education had been controlled for. In the clearest case, attitudes to capital punishment, the attitudes of city respondents varied a good deal by age and education, but those of country respondents did not and were appreciably more conservative.
15 Don Aitkin, 'The United Country Party in New South Wales, 1932-1941, a Study of Electoral Support', MA (Hons.) thesis, University of New England, 1960.

with 73 per cent of their rural fellows. The exception to the rule is easily explained. Trade unionism is much better organised in the city than in the country, and therefore draws into its net many manual workers who would not normally join a union. In the country, by contrast, such workers are not recruited, and union membership includes a higher proportion of those who would want to join a union anyway — Labor partisans.

All of this is consistent with higher non-Labor support in country seats. But it does not explain the existence of a special party whose clientele are drawn entirely from the country. I have argued elsewhere that the Country Party's existence and survival must be seen as the product of a successful ideology rooted in the social experience of country people in the nineteenth and early twentieth centuries, and in the historical importance of Australian governments both in providing social capital for the development of the rural areas and in controlling the marketing of primary products.[16] The ideology rests on the obvious differences in life-style, pace and cultural values that exist between country and city communities, differences that are in no way peculiar to Australia.[17]

At the same time, there *is* something special about the political behaviour of Australian farmers. The Country Party's very existence, of course, is one item of evidence — it has few counterparts elsewhere in the world, and farmers' groups that were for much the same reasons similarly active in North America at the turn of the century failed to produce viable political parties.[18] American farmers, according to Campbell and his associates, are in comparison to city dwellers less stable and less committed in their party preference, less involved and interested in politics, and more likely to vote in reaction to changing economic conditions.[19] In the Australian context these farmer/city dweller contrasts dwindle and even vanish. Farmers and graziers are, for example, *more* interested in politics than almost any other group, they are not obviously more volatile in their party preference — nor are they less committed to their party. Nor do they vote in simple reaction to economic conditions: Figure 11.1 suggests that throughout the 1950s and 1960s, when farmers experienced first a drop in income from wool, then after a short period of prosperity, a drop in income from wheat — all in the context of steadily growing domestic prices — the Country Party's share of the vote remained very

16 *The Country Party in New South Wales, passim.*
17 See, for example, the discussion of the urban-rural cleavage in Norwegian society, in Stein Rokkan and Henry Valen, 'Regional Contrasts in Norwegian Politics: a Review of Data from Official Statistics and from Sample Surveys', in Erik Allardt and Yrjö Littunen, *Cleavages, Ideologies and Party Systems*, Helsinki, 1964.
18 Graham, *The Formation of the Australian Country Parties*, Chapter 1.
19 Campbell *et al.*, *The American Voter*, Chapter 15. See also S.M. Lipset, *Agrarian Socialism: the Cooperative Commonwealth Federation of Saskatchewan*, Berkeley, 1950; and for a useful bibliography, Bradley M. Richardson, 'Urbanization and Political Participation: the Case of Japan', *American Political Science Review*, 67(2), June 1973.

stable. [20]

It is likely that through its ideology the Country Party has been able to subdue class hostility in the country to some extent, and thus attract as members and supporters men and women whose preferred party elsewhere would be Labor. But the evidence is not compelling. The Liberal Party also has its share of rural seats, which it appears to hold as comfortably as does the Country Party its own electoral possessions. Moreover the two non-Labor parties have fought one another on and off for half a century, and the results have been quite inconclusive, save that where the urban population of a seat is growing, the Liberal Party appears to have an edge.

What, then, is the cause of the pattern of party representation in country electorates? The answer is an historical one. The country parties made their electoral breakthrough in the years around 1920, and their early successes were impressive, especially in grazing and wheat-farming seats. Very soon, however, their parliamentary representatives were forced to decide the party's parliamentary strategy, and one by one, beginning with the Federal Country Party in 1923, they chose to join non-Labor

Figure 11.1   Farmers' prosperity and the Country Party's electoral performance. *Source: Quarterly Review of Agricultural Economics,* 1950 to 1970.

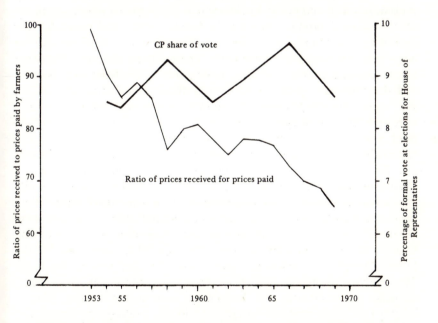

20 Figure 11.1 is, of course, a very crude measure of the relationship between economic conditions and party voting, since the economic indicator does not take into account farmers' capacity to overcome cost/price problems by increasing productivity. Moreover, throughout the period of Liberal-Country Party government (1949-72) the coalition did its best to ensure that farmers were protected from adverse general economic conditions. Nevertheless the lack of correlation between the two curves is important in itself.

coalitions. The price of a share in power, set in a succession of electoral pacts, was the end of further attempts at large-scale electoral expansion. The pacts held the Country Party to those regions where it had been immediately successful; the others it has been able to enter only occasionally and without conspicuous success. As a result its electoral representation in the 1970s strikingly resembles that of the 1920s. In parts of the countryside the Country Party has become the hegemonic non-Labor Party, benefiting from inheritance of party loyalties, the development of stable party organisation and the persistence of community power structures. In other parts these factors work in favour of the Liberal Party. Partisan representation in the country is therefore frozen in the mould of the 1920s.

There is little in the electoral experience of the Liberal and Country Parties to suggest that they attract different groups as supporters, and little in their generally amicable relations in coalition to suggest that they possess widely different attitudes to politics, policies or administration. It is true that, as we saw in Chapter 4, the images of the parties are substantially different, but they are not directly competitive, and there is strong reason to think the identities of the parties are very often not separately perceived in the country. The evidence arose from the same poor fit of recall and reality in 1966 which led to the identification of the DLP's electoral support. In 1966 the Country Party had polled 9.7 per cent of the vote, but only 5.8 per cent of the sample, interviewed a year later, remembered having voted for it. There was no obvious explanation for the discrepancy: the primary sampling units — the federal divisions — included the correct proportions of rural divisions and divisions in which the Country Party had presented candidates; response rates in these areas were high. If a bandwaggon effect were operating it should have benefited the Country Party as well as the Liberal Party.

The first move, clearly, was to examine the recall of the respondents who lived in country electorates, especially those contested by Country Party candidates. In 1966 the Country Party contested twenty-seven seats, of which nineteen fell into the sample; in seven seats, the Country Party candidate faced a Liberal as well as a Labor candidate; and five of these fell into the sample. In all, 111 respondents claimed to have voted for the Country Party; but in addition eighty-five claimed to have voted for the Liberal Party in seats *where no Liberal candidate had presented himself*. The interview protocols of each of these respondents now came under scrutiny; particular attention focused on each person's voting history, length of residence in the electorate, sex and age, strength and direction of party identification, views about parties and leaders, knowledge of the local members of parliament, and expectations as to which party would win the seat.

Four of the eighty-five respondents had arrived in their constituencies recently enough to make it likely that they had voted elsewhere in 1966.

Two of the remaining eighty-one may well have voted Labor instead of Liberal. But seventy-nine of the eighty-five were almost certainly Country Party voters. [21] Why had they told the interviewer that they had voted Liberal? Three broad explanations stand out in the interview records.

(i) *The two parties were seen as one.* Thirty-three of the respondents made it clear that they saw no essential difference between the parties: 'I take the Liberal and Country Parties together', remarked a thirty-nine year old Queensland truck-driver. Some saw the two parties as fused, or as the city and country wings of the same party; others regarded the Country Party as the policy force, or the moral presence, inside the Liberal Party — 'a solid backbone for the Liberal Party', as another Queenslander, a sixty-three year-old woman, put it. About half of them had voted for 'the Government', for 'Holt' or for 'the L-CP'. In their terms these voters were not wrong in their account of their vote in 1966: the coding system was overelaborate, in that it distinguished objects when they saw no need to do so.

To them should be added another twenty-nine whose voting histories suggested that they too saw no particular difference between the two parties, but whose free answer comments about the parties and leaders contained no statements to that effect. Consider, for example, the case of a forty year-old NSW civil engineer, who had lived in the same town since the age of sixteen. He claimed to be a 'very strong' Liberal, and always to have voted Liberal in both state and federal elections since his first vote in 1949. Had an election been held tomorrow he would have voted first for the Liberal Party and then for the Country Party; but he expected the Country Party to win the seat. He knew the names and parties of his state and federal MPs. In his electorate, Hume, the Country Party and the ALP have fought close contests between themselves since the 1920s; in recent years a Liberal candidate had offered only once, in 1954, and then ran a poor third. Were there only one such case it could be ignored, and the cause put down to interviewer error. But since there are more than two dozen, we must assume for want of a better explanation, that when such respondents answered 'Liberal' they meant 'the candidate supporting the Liberal government'.

(ii) *The respondent was a newcomer.* Seven of the respondents had taken up residence in their constituencies within the past five years. All had Liberal-voting backgrounds; most were ignorant of the names and parties of the local MPs; most thought the Liberal Party would win the

---

21 The addition of these seventy-nine respondents to the Country Party's tally, and subtraction from the tally of nine 'pseudo-Liberals' (respondents who claimed to have voted for Country Party candidates in seats where no Country Party candidate stood) brings a corrected estimate of the Country Party's 1966 vote very close to its actual proportion. In 1969, when interviewing followed hard on polling day, the recalled Country Party vote was 9.1 per cent, compared with 8.6 per cent actually secured by the party.

seat, or had no idea. It seems reasonable to suppose that these respondents, lacking an awareness of local political circumstances (for whatever reason), were thinking about voting either in terms of past contexts or with their eyes on national concerns — i.e. 'for the government'.

(iii) *The respondent was young and/or uninterested.* These respondents, some young, some old, revealed a low level of interest in politics and a correspondingly small fund of political knowledge. Though claiming solid Liberal voting histories, most put their strength of identification with the Liberal Party only at 'not very strong'; one denied any such attachment at all. Such voters may have assumed that the Country Party candidate *was* a Liberal, or have forgotten such details by the time of the interview, though aware of them on polling day.

The Country Party's electoral support, then, contains a large minority, as much as 40 per cent, who see no real difference between the Country and Liberal Parties. Indeed, that proportion may be a good deal higher, for the 40 per cent consists of those who were quite unable to recall having voted for the Country Party one year after having done so — a very strong test of failure to perceive differences between parties. [22]

The existence of such a large group attests to the importance of pacts between parties in preserving a minor party's electoral strength. But it tells us also that few non-Labor citizens are likely to feel lost for a proper political home should they move from country to city or in the other direction. Nonetheless, continued residence in a community is likely to be a source of individual partisan stability, and departure from that community is at least a potential cause of instability. We look now at the other side of the coin.

Population Movements

Australians are a mobile people. In any year, perhaps one voter in seven changes his address; [23] of the sample only ten per cent had never moved, and nearly half had moved at least once in the previous ten years. Limitations on the data collected from the respondents prevent a thorough analysis of the direction and frequency of residential shifts, and for the

---

22 Analysis of a survey of Country Party *branch members* in 1962 suggested that 45 per cent of them saw their party as simply an anti-Labor party (Aitkin, *The Country Party in New South Wales*, pp. 285-6).

23 A measure of residential mobility can be derived from changes to the electoral roll, which are summarised each year. In 1966, for example, approximately 9 per cent of the electorate moved from one electoral division to another (this figure represents the proportion of names removed from the rolls less the proportion of the adult population known to have died, adjusted to take account of the deaths of adult non-citizens). In addition, a further 3 per cent changed addresses within the same divisions. Since these are the changes known to have occurred it is very probable that the actual proportion of address changes each year is rather higher, perhaps as much as 15 per cent in all. But the estimate of 20 per cent previously given in Aitkin and Kahan, 'Australia', in Rose, *Electoral Behavior*, is probably too high.

most part our attention will focus on the movement from the respondent's place of birth to his place of residence in 1967, a rough index only.

Comparing these two places provides, nevertheless, some findings of great interest. The first is set out in Table 11.3. Most population movement in Australia in the period has occurred *within* states: indeed the four most populous states have retained precisely the same fraction of their native-born electoral population — seven-eighths. Moreover, the movement across state borders was to the net advantage of New South Wales and Victoria — and to Victoria especially with respect to Tasmania, which lost more than a quarter of its native-born and attracted few from elsewhere.

Table 11.3 Internal migration in Australia: from state of birth to state of residence in 1967

Now Resident in	Born in							
	NSW	Vic.	Qld	SA	WA	Tas.	O/seas	Whole Sample
	%	%	%	%	%	%	%	%
NSW	87	7	9	6	7	7	30	35
Vic.	4	87	3	4	4	15	31	29
Qld	5	3	87	1	2	4	12	14
SA	2	3	1	87	3	1	12	11
WA	1	1	1	2	84	0	11	8
Tas.	1	*	0	0	1	73	3	4
Total	100	100	100	100	100	100	100	100
(N)	(578)	(446)	(203)	(153)	(122)	(85)	(454)	(2042)

* = less than 0.5 per cent

Table 11.4 Internal migration in Australia: region of birth to region of residence in 1967

Now Resident in	Born in		
	Metropolitan Areas	Non-metropolitan Cities and Towns	Rural Areas
	%	%	%
Metropolitan Divisions	77	32	38
Urban Divisions	6	21	12
Rural Divisions	17	48	49
Total	100	100	100
(N)	(658)	(373)	(556)

Note: The respondent's region of residence in 1967 has been defined by electoral division. 'Metropolitan' comprises the six state capitals, 'urban' the divisions in other large cities and towns (such as Newcastle, Wollongong, Townsville, Bendigo and Launceston) and rural to the remainder. Region of birth has been defined by the place and not by the division, and was obtained by the question 'Where were your parents living when you were born?'

Within each state, the principal population movement has been the drift from the country to the city. Table 11.4 sets out its consequences, summarised for Australia as a whole (inter-state variations are minor). Both non-metropolitan cities and the rural areas have lost heavily to the metropolis, and there has been substantial movement to the country from non-metropolitan cities as well. Three-quarters of those born in the capitals were living there in 1967, but only half of those born in the country were still living there. These movements, together with immigration from overseas, have had a profound effect on the shaping of the electorates in the three broad regions (Table 11.5).

The electorate of the capital cities includes one voter in four who was born in another country and another one in five who was born in the rural areas of Australia.[24] The rural electorate contains a smaller proportion of immigrants, and its pull from the metropolis has been weak; but one in four of its voters were born in non-metropolitan cities. Given that the historic cleavage has been between the metropolis and everywhere outside it, it is notable that the urban and rural electorates are similarly composed: two in three were born outside the capitals, and very similar proportions came from the capitals and from overseas.

What partisan consequences have followed from these major shifts of population? Campbell and his colleagues have pointed to three kinds of situations in which residential mobility could be accompanied by political change.[25] In the first, movers retain their partisan loyalties but change the net partisan balances both in the place they leave and in the place they go to. For such changes to be significant the departures or arrivals have to be skewed politically, as when a new coal mine, or a major industrial development, commences in an otherwise purely rural constituency.

Table 11.5   The regional origins of the electorate, 1967

Region of Birth	The Metropolitan Electorate %	The Urban Electorate %	The Rural Electorate %
Metropolitan	45	18	17
Urban	10	35	27
Rural	19	32	41
Overseas	26	15	15
Total	100	100	15
(N)	(1126)	(217)	(663)

24 A Melbourne sample of unknown representativeness contained, in 1971, 26 per cent who had lived on a farm in their youth and another 29 per cent who had lived in the country at some time. The evidence suggested also that many city-dwellers retained an emotional attachment to country life and values. See John Barrett, 'Melbourne and the Bush: Russel Ward's Thesis and a La Trobe Survey', *Meanjin Quarterly*, 31(4), December 1972.

25 Campbell *et al.*, *The American Voter*, pp. 442-3.

In the second case, a set of circumstances that leads to a person's changing his party allegiance leads also to his changing his address. The paradigm is that of the man whose promotion into the ranks of the bosses supplants his former working-class loyalty, and his change of status and partisan outlook is marked also by a move to a 'better' suburb. The third case reverses the causality: a move to a new environment breaks down old buttresses of one erstwhile party loyalty and provides strong enough stimuli for the mover to develop a new one.

Each situation is plausible, and anyone interested in politics can give examples that appear to fit the case. Indeed, respondents occasionally proffered their own case histories: a middle-aged school teacher in Queensland reflected:

I was brought up in a Labor Party atmosphere, and lived in an area where the ALP was represented. Moving to an area where a Liberal man is in, and finding the member is open-minded and does a tremendous amount for the voting constituents, I changed my voting habits.

Some consequences of residential mobility, of course, are very clear: the drift to the city has almost halved the Country Party's share of the vote in forty years (Table 1.1). But has Labor been the principal beneficiary or has the Liberal Party? To asses the net advantage and disadvantage to the parties requires some knowledge of the kinds of people who move.

As might be expected age proved to be the most important predictor of mobility. Almost one-third of those in their twenties had moved within the previous two years, and more than half had moved within the past five. By contrast, only one in twenty of those in their sixties had moved in the past two years, and one-half had lived where they were interviewed for more than twenty years. The greater mobility of the young is probably a characteristic of the life-cycle; both men and women are likely to be most mobile in the period between leaving their parents' home and establishing one for the next generation in the family. And occupational class is not an important consideration. Those with non-manual occupations were more likely to move than manual workers, but the difference was slight — 31 per cent compared with 28 per cent.

Since we know already that the younger respondents were disproportionately non-Labor in their partisan loyalties, it is not surprising to find that movers were more likely to be non-Labor. But in fact recent movers were more likely to be non-Labor at the time of the interview whatever their age (Table 11.6). Again, the differences are not large; and there is no consistent pattern — Labor identification does not progressively increase among the stay-puts.

Table 11.6 cannot tell us whether mobility caused a change of identification or simply accompanied it. The only available evidence that bears on this point is information about the respondents' changes in party preference. A close examination of these data provides no support for a hypothesis that recent movers are more likely to be preference changers. Young movers, whose party loyalty might be thought *a priori* to be doubly at risk, were if anything rather less likely to report changing their party preference than anyone else. The age group in which preference-changing was most commonly reported was 40-49, and in this case preference-changing seemed quite unrelated to moving residence. Only one datum emerged as a footprint in the sand: those who had changed their party preference very recently were more likely to have moved in the past ten years than to have stayed put. This was true whether the shift had been from Labor to Liberal or in the opposite direction. Labor's revival in 1967, and the coalition's great years from 1963 to 1966, appear to have been more effective in producing converts among the mobile than among the immobile; and that presumably takes us back to the influence of long-standing community ties, a subject discussed at the beginning of the chapter.

That these ties are an important ingredient in shaping party identification is emphasised by an analysis of the stability of party preference in three different kinds of seat: traditional working class seats, traditional middle-class seats, and the rapidly growing suburban seats on the fringes of the metropolis. Studies made of residents of the 'new outer' suburbs attest to widespread indifference to politics.[26] And a good *prima facie* case can be made that pioneering citizens who left a community behind will wait years before a new one grows around them: in parts of Melbourne and Sydney suburban populations have grown from a few hundred to several hundred thousand in the space of fifteen years. Citizens in these suburbs, we can argue, will lack the community ties that relate the social

Table 11.6   Residential mobility, age and Labor identification, 1967

Age Group	0-2	3-5	Years since last move 6-10	11-20	More than 20/ never moved
	%	%	%	%	%
21-29	36	43	37	29	38
30-39	32	40	39	39	41
40-49	37	50	46	46	46
50-59		36		44	41	52
60-69		22		36	36	48
70+			38		45	41

Note: Each cell contains the proportion identifying with Labor, of those claiming some party identification, in categories jointly defined by the respondent's age and the number of years since he last moved.

26 See Davies, 'Suburban Political Styles'.

experience of a group to a 'proper' party preference at the individual level. Their party preference, formed before they come to the new suburbs, is more likely to be affected by short-term forces than that of their former friends who stayed behind.

The instruments available to test such a hypothesis are coarse; we know whether the respondent has ever preferred a different party, and whether he or she has ever voted for different parties. These tests of the effect of living in the new suburbs are shown in Table 11.7, and they are consistent with the hypothesis. There is clear evidence that the transfer to the new suburb is associated with a greater fragility of party identification. We cannot, of course, know to what extent the fragility was present *before* the move, but the pattern of Table 11.7 at least suggests that this is not common. The same tendency is present in the greater likelihood of the new suburbanites having voted for different parties, but the gap is much smaller. Party identification, we might argue, is a broad disposition which has many other manifestations besides voting, and can be acted upon by community pressures, seen and unseen. Voting, on the other hand, is a private act, and is insulated to some extent from community pressures.

These findings are somewhat unsatisfactory, and they suggest the need for further research into the political consequences of residential mobility. Yet some tentative generalisations can be advanced. Preference-changing is not common in the Australian electorate, and it is not much more likely to happen among those who move about than among those who do not. But if we consider only those who say that they once did prefer another party, then length of residence is important. In all, 37 per cent of those who had changed their preference had done so in the previous five years, but that proportion was 46 per cent among the recent movers and 29 per cent among non-movers. Moreover, the movement does not necessarily benefit one party more than another. It happens that in the 1950s and

Table 11.7 Stability of identification, and of voting in federal elections, by type of seat, 1967 [22]

	Type of Seat		
	Traditional Working Class %	Traditional Middle Class %	New Outer %
Once preferred another party	12	17	27
Have voted for different parties	23	28	29

27 Analysis was confined to Sydney and Melbourne, and the following seats were included: *traditional middle-class*: Bennelong, Bradfield, Mackellar, Wentworth, Chisolm, Higgins, Kooyong; *traditional working-class*: Dalley, Grayndler, Kingsford-Smith, Gellibrand, Scullin, Wills; *new outer*: Hughes, Mitchell, Bruce, Deakin, La Trobe. See also note 4 in this chapter.

early 1960s the non-Labor parties profited, but then they profited also among young voters at the same time; there was a secular tide in favour of the coalition. In 1967 the Labor Party's revival started, and it began to benefit from changes of heart among those with relatively loose ties to a local community — as it did increasingly among young voters.

One strong implication of this argument is that residential mobility affects partisan attachment mostly by taking away the reinforcing contribution of a favourable local environment. Since the differences which have been isolated are quite small, it is clear also that most movements of people from one state to another, or from country to city, represent transfers of partisans. Before we conclude the chapter we should consider, as far as the inadequate data will allow, what consequences these transfers may have had.

Again, we must resort to a movement of people from their region of birth to the region in which they were interviewed in 1967. Since the decision to move will have been affected in many cases by family circumstances, a first strategy might be to see whether the occupational rank of the respondent's father was related at all to the movement of the son or daughter; the results are set out in Table 11.8.

The data of Table 11.8 ought not to be subjected to too great a weight of argument, for the link between father's occupational rank and that of his children is not at all a complete one, as we have seen. Yet there are

Table 11.8   Internal migration and father's occupational grade, 1967

Respondent's Region of Birth	Region of Respondent's Present Residence		
	Metropolitan %	Urban %	Rural %
Metropolitan	57	45	60
Urban	52	65	48
Rural	52	61	42

Note: Each cell contains the proportion having manual fathers.

Table 11.9   Internal migration and Labor identification, 1967

Respondent's Region of Birth	Region of Respondent's Present Residence		
	Metropolitan %	Urban %	Rural %
Metropolitan	45	49	34
Urban	38	55	35
Rural	49	49	36
Overseas	41	45	36

Note: Each cell contains the proportion identifying with Labor, of those with some party identification.

persuasive suggestions here of a pattern in internal migration, in which the countryside has lost much of its working class, especially to the non-metropolitan cities, and retained its middle class (a pattern quite consistent with the decline in rural employment since the beginning of the century). There is a familiar similarity in the rural and urban patterns, and a dissimilarity between both of them and the metropolitan pattern, which is of the export of non-manuals to the non-metropolitan cities and of manual workers to the countryside.

The partisan accompaniments of these movements are set out in Table 11.9, using the same format, but adding immigrants in this case. The striking finding is that place of origin is of little importance in the country, where Labor's share of the electorate is uniformly low. Given that much of the metropolitan movement into the rural areas has been of working-class origin, the weakness of Labor identification among that group says something for the resocialising effects of country residence upon newcomers. Those who have left the country are much more likely to be Labor identifiers than those who stayed behind, and we have seen also that they are more likely to have come from working-class backgrounds.

We are now in a position to put into place another piece in the jigsaw of stability. The relative size of Australia's rural population has been falling steadily since before the end of the nineteenth century, except for a short-lived surge at the time of the Great Depression, when unemployed men took to the road. Part of the cause has been the replacement of men by machines in the rural industries: in 1933, for example, rural production absorbed 25 per cent of the workforce, but in 1966 its share was only 9 per cent. Most of those who left the country, then, will have been members of the rural working class. They were not, as we have seen, solid Labor partisans, but the transfer to an urban environment, and to manual work in a unionised setting, unquestionably converted many of them to Labor supporters. The drift to the city has thus been to Labor's advantage.

At the same time, the rural electorates they left behind have become relatively more non-Labor in their complexion. And it is probable that the sway of Country Party and Liberal values grew disproportionately, as the one possible opposing force decreased in size. By 1968 there were nearly three farmers or graziers to every one rural worker, and Labor's electoral clientele in the countryside was now the country townsman, not the rural worker. But in the towns industries were of small scale, and unionism poorly developed. The drift to the city has thus had the additional consequence of strengthening the rural electorate for the non-Labor parties: a Labor gain has been balanced by a non-Labor gain.

12 The 'Preferences' and Their Correlates

> Well, if there was a Country Party they'd get it [my second pre-
> ference], but this would be because I don't want to give a second
> preference anywhere so I'd waste it as far as possible. (*scientist,*
> *thirty-nine, Hobart*)

So far we have been considering the social context and historic origins of
party identification. But, as the discussion in Chapter 5 made clear, the
party to which a citizen gives support at elections and a measure of loyalty
between them represents only the first level of his view of party politics.
There are other parties in the political world: some he may see as tolerable
alternatives, some he has no time for. In an electoral system in which
preferential voting is practised, these likes and dislikes can have crucial
implications. How far do their origins lie in the contemporary political
environment, how much in the voter's social and economic background?
What determines these preference orders?

We call tree analysis to our aid once again. To subject to examination
each of the thirty principal combinations of first, second and last
preference would be an unrewarding task because of the small numbers
involved in many cases. Instead, we shall concentrate on pairs of first and
second, and first and last preferences, within the two groups of Liberal
and Labor supporters. In doing so the inter-relatedness of the data must
be kept in mind. We can only guess at some of the priorities in these
preference orderings. Do Labor supporters give their second preferences
to the Liberal Party residually, because of their hatred of the DLP and
distrust of the Communist Party, or purposefully, because it seems the
party most like their own, or because of a combination of these motives?
The first hypothesis may seem the most attractive, but there is no way of
proving it from the survey data. Accordingly, the search is for the
correlates of preference, not for its causes.

The small numbers of Country Party and DLP supporters make them
ineligible for extensive multivariate analysis, but some simple ground-
clearing is possible. Occupational class, for example, was irrelevant in
determining the direction of Country Party voters' second and last
preferences.[1] In the case of DLP supporters, however, it was of some
importance: all those DLP supporters who placed the ALP second thought
of themselves as working-class, and working-class DLP voters were also

much less likely to place the Liberal Party second and the Communist Party last. Few other social-structural variables appeared to have much impact. Metropolitan DLP voters showed a deep antipathy for the Communist Party, while rural DLP voters tended to nominate Labor for last place. Presbyterian Country Party voters were most likely of all to reject the DLP. The variable that seemed most important of all was interest in the outcome of elections.[2] Nine of ten DLP *and* Country Party supporters who cared a good deal about which party won elections gave their second preferences to the Liberal Party (or, in the case of the DLP, to the Country Party as well), compared with only six in ten of those who didn't care. And those who didn't care much which party won were most likely to give Labor their second preferences. To a degree, orthodoxy in following official how-to-vote advice by supporters of the minor parties appears to be related to involvement in politics generally, not, as might plausibly be suggested, to a *lack* of interest in politics.

The correlates of the preference patterns of Liberal and Labor voters are a good deal more varied than those of Country Party and DLP voters (Table 5.4) and the use of AID analysis to locate them is amply justified. For purposes of evaluation we shall concentrate not on the twelve trees that were produced in analysing the principal patterns for each group of party supporters, but on the polar groups — those most likely to nominate a given party and those least likely to do so.[3] The justification for doing so is a simple one. There are few theories that account for preference orders, and indeed apart from these surveys there is little information *about* preference orders at all except for those whose votes are commonly subject to preference counting — Country Party and DLP voters. In the absence of both data and theory a close analysis of the whole range of correlates of preference might seem premature. An examination of the polar groups, on the other hand, emphasises those variables most strongly related to given preference orderings; theory-building might reasonably start from here.

Table 12.1 presents the polar groups for three principal classes of Liberal voter: those who favoured the Country Party as their second preference, those who favoured the Labor Party, and those who favoured the DLP. Since the largest single group of Liberals (48 per cent) placed the Country Party second, that party is the first to be treated. It was the choice most characteristic of Protestant Liberals in the rural areas of New South

---

1 As in the earlier discussion on preferences (Chapter 5), *first* preference here is defined as the party the respondent would have supported 'tomorrow' (question 45a, 1967 questionnaire).

2 Question 48 in the 1967 questionnaire. An almost identical set of results came from cross-tabulating second preference with interest in politics (question 30 in the 1967 questionnaire).

3 Twenty-seven predictor variables were used in these analyses: the social-structural variables used previously (Chapter 7), plus measures of political participation (Chapter 2), membership in organisations, self-placement in social class, feelings of relative prosperity, and number of magazines and newspapers read.

Wales, Victoria and Queensland (79 per cent) and indeed among rural Protestant Liberals everywhere (70 per cent). There is, of course, nothing mystifying in this finding: we should expect the Country Party to be most salient to Liberals in country seats in states where the party is firmly entrenched. And we have already observed that both the Liberal and Country Parties are disproportionately Protestant in their membership and parliamentary representation.

Those Liberals least likely to see the Country Party as the next preferred choice were in part those with opposite characteristics — Catholics who lived in the state capitals and other cities and were tenants or house-buyers. As the Country Party had no notable housing or rental policies that might have angered voters it is safe to assume that these tenants and house-buyers are in fact more usefully described as younger, lower income-earning or working-class Liberals.[4] Such Liberals, whatever their

Table 12.1 Variations in second preference among Liberal voters, 1967

Party Chosen as Second Preference	Highest Support Among	%	Lowest Support Among	%
Country Party (mean for all Liberals 47%)[a]	Rural Protestants in NSW, Victoria, Queensland	79	Urban Catholics who are tenants or house-buyers	13
	Rural Protestants	70	Urban tenants or house-buyers	27
Labor Party (mean for all Liberals 31%)	Labor identifiers and those with no party identification	78	Non-Labor identifiers who care a good deal which party wins the election and who expect to be worse off economically or the same in a few years' time	16
	House-buyers who don't care much which party wins the election and who identify with parties other than Labor	64	Non-Labor identifiers who care a good deal which party wins the election	22
Democratic Labor Party (mean for all Liberals 19%)	Urban Catholics	41	Rural voters in states other than Victoria or Tasmania	5
	Urban non-Catholics with a good deal of interest in politics	35	Rural voters	8

[a]The means given in this and the following tables are based on those respondents who were able to give specific second or last preferences, and are thus larger than those given in Table 5.4.

4 Both income and occupational grade contained enough internal variation to be suitable as categories to split at this point of the analysis — but not quite as much as the variable owner/buyer/tenant.

denomination, were not likely to see the Country Party as next best, partly, we may expect, because as city-dwellers they did not see or hear much of it, and partly, as voters who were relatively poorly off, because they associated it with landed wealth. If we defer consideration of Liberal second preferences for Labor for the moment, and move to the DLP, we can see that in some respects the DLP and Country Party attracted opposite kinds of Liberals: the one was the choice of the urban Catholics, the other the choice of the rural Protestants. The case of the DLP is, however, more complex. Where urban residence and Catholicism go together, the choice of the DLP was more than twice as likely as it was among Liberals as a whole. Yet the nomination of the DLP was also very common among urban non-Catholics who claimed 'a good deal' of interest in politics, suggesting that among Liberal sophisticates the DLP's religious affiliations were not important, or that those Liberals who did not take much interest in politics were frequently unaware of the DLP's existence.

Nearly one-third of the Liberals chose the Labor Party as their second preference, and those overwhelmingly likely to do so were either Liberal voters who still thought of themselves as Labor or those who had no party identification at all. The Labor identifiers demonstrate the importance of the independent status of party identification, *vis-à-vis* party support in elections. When a voter moves from supporting one party to supporting another, while *retaining* his former identification, it is understandable that he reserves a high place for his former choice. It is as though he were saying 'I'm really Labor at heart, but just for the moment I'm voting Liberal' and he gives his second preference to his old party. In 1967, when the Liberal Party was still dominant, there were enough Labor identifiers who were voting Liberal for the group to show up in the tree analysis. But the same phenomenon occurred on the other side of politics: in the much smaller group of Labor-voting Liberals, 73 per cent gave the Liberal Party their second preference, compared with 51 per cent for Labor voters as a whole. Party identification plays a major part also in determining the group least likely to place Labor second: non-Labor identifiers who saw election outcomes as important, that is, those who saw sharp differences between the Labor Party and the coalition. Those of that group who were not optimistic about their future prosperity (and were presumably apprehensive about the financial consequences to them of a Labor government) were even less likely to place the Labor Party second.

There is a pattern in these Liberal second preferences, and we should expect it to be related in some way to the parties that Liberals were least enamoured of (Table 12.2). Again we consider three parties, but this time the Communist Party replaces the Country Party, which few Liberals placed last. The communist Party was rejected most wholeheartedly by South Australian Liberals, and firmly by politically-interested urban Liberals in New South Wales, Queensland and Western Australia. It was relatively ignored, on the other hand, by rural Liberals in those states and by Victorians and Tasmanians.

The case of South Australia is a fascinating but explicable one. Until factional disputes within the Liberal Country League in 1972 destroyed its carefully nurtured and long established unity,[5] South Australia had possessed perhaps the closest approximation of a two-party system in Australia: the Country Party was virtually non-existent and the DLP very weak in numbers and in electoral support.[6] Furthermore, both the LCL and the Labor Party have demonstrated an ability to attract the votes of at least half the electorate — admittedly in separate electoral arenas (the LCL in the federal elections of 1966, the ALP in the state elections of 1962, 1965 and 1968). The South Australians in the sample were nearly all either Liberals or Labor supporters, and each group tended to give second place to the other's party. For Liberals, in consequence, the Communist Party was a very common nomination for last; Labor voters were also emphatic in rejecting it, but, as elsewhere, the devil on the left had to compete with the devil on the right. The relative indifference of rural Liberals to the Communist Party may be due to the rarity of Communist candidates in rural electorates; that of Victorians to their greater distaste for the

Table 12.2 Variations in last preference among Liberal voters, 1967

Party Chosen as Last Preference	Greatest Rejection Among	%	Least Rejection Among	%
Communist Party (mean for all Liberals 44%)	South Australians Urban voters in NSW and Qld who follow politics on television	70 62	Victorians and Tasmanians Rural voters in NSW, WA and Qld	23 35
Labor Party (mean for all Liberals 28%)	Voters 61 years and older in NSW, SA and WA Voters 61 years and older	60 44	Voters between 21 and 60 in NSW, SA, WA and Qld with incomes greater than $2251 Voters between 21 and 60 in NSW, SA, WA and Qld	18 21
Democratic Labor Party (mean for all Liberals 22%)	Victorian tenants and house buyers Manual workers in states other than Victoria	37 33	Non-manual Catholics and nonconformists in states other than Victoria Non-manuals in states other than Victoria	10 15

5 For one account, see Steele Hall *et al.*, *A Liberal Awakening*, Adelaide, 1973; and for background, Neal Blewett and Dean Jaensch, *Playford to Dunstan*, Melbourne, 1971.
6 The Country Party and the Liberal Party merged in 1931 as the Liberal Country League; the Country Party made some efforts to revive its own organisation in the late 1960s, but without much success. South Australia has the smallest proportion of Catholics of all the states (20 per cent in 1966 compared with 26 per cent for Australia), and the DLP has been less successful electorally there than in any other state.

Democratic Labor Party, which is strongest in that state.

Age was the important dimension concerned with antipathy towards the Labor Party: old Liberals were more likely to put Labor last, especially in New South Wales, South Australia and Western Australia, while young Liberals were more divided in their dislikes. Here the explanation may lie both in the politics of the Depression and later immediate post-war years, when the party system was simpler and the temperature of politics perhaps higher. Antipathy towards the DLP was greatest among working-class Liberals, especially in Victoria; middle-class Liberals were more concerned with the threats of the ALP and the Communist Party.

There is nothing tidy about these preference patterns. Variables important in one relationship are overshadowed elsewhere; it is impossible to juggle the pieces so that a single, meaningful picture emerges. But it is clear that there were a number of powerful influences on the second and last preference of Liberals. Religion (but not churchgoing) was one, urban or rural residence another; state differences were important, as were class and age. Some of these are variables that we have seen to affect identification itself, and it is not surprising that they affect the whole preference order of the voter. Others, such as state, are clearly linked to a

Table 12.3   Variations in second preference among Labor voters, 1967

Party Chosen as Second Preference	Greatest Support Among	%	Least Support Among	%
Liberal Party (mean for all Labor voters 51%)	Urban voters in NSW, SA and Tasmania who don't care much which party wins the election	80	Rural voters in Vic., Qld and WA who have lived in the same area for six years or more	28
	Urban voters in NSW, SA and Tasmania who care a good deal which party wins the election, and are aged 21-40	71	Urban men in Vic., Qld and WA who have lived in the same area for six years or more	38
Country Party (mean for all Labor voters 23%)	Rural regular church-goers in NSW, Victoria and Western Australia	54	Urban voters, aged 21-50 outside Victoria	6
Democratic Labor Party (mean for all Labor voters 20%)	Catholic voters in Victoria, SA, Tasmania and WA	41	Non-Catholics with a good deal of interest in politics	7
	Catholics	29	Anglicans, non-religionists and others[a] who don't care very much which party wins the election and who have moderate or no interest in politics	9

[a]Principally Orthodox and Jewish.

specific contemporary political situation. Tables 12.3 and 12.4 show that much the same mixture of ingredients is relevant in the case of Labor voters.

Reading quickly downwards in Table 12.3 suggests that for Labor voters the Liberal Party was the second choice of the city-dweller, the Country Party of the countryman, and the DLP of the Roman Catholic. Closer inspection only polishes this trichotomy. Those least likely to put the DLP second were non-Catholics with a good deal of interest in politics — here religion and sophistication combine in opposition against a perceived Catholic splinter group. It was easier for Labor voters to put the Liberal Party second if they did not care much which party won the election, or, if they did care, if they were forty or younger — those whose adult lives had been spent wholly or largely under a non-Labor federal government. Regular churchgoing combined with rural residence boosted the attraction of the Country Party as the next most preferred party.

The complex groupings of states in Table 12.3 have some simple causes. There is not, as we have observed, a strong Country Party organisation in either South Australia or Tasmania, and Labor voters in these states rarely included the Country Party in their scheme of preferences. In Victoria, on the other hand, a historic alliance between the Country and Labor Parties existed throughout much of the 1930s and 1940s, and the memory of a somewhat radical farmers' party lives on. For Victorian Labor voters, then, the Country Party was very often the preferred alternative, even in Melbourne. The DLP is strongest of all in Victoria, and it is not surprising that Victorian Labor Catholics should place it high; Catholics in South Australia and Tasmania have fewer alternatives, and the DLP profits accordingly. The Liberal Party consequently appears as a residual choice. The discussion of Chapter 5 may usefully be recalled here: on the face of it the Labor supporter has a difficult choice in a preferential system, in that all the other parties in the system are antagonists with whom formal alliances are out of the question or most unlikely. But the Communist Party is nevertheless no alternative at all, and virtually no Labor voter awarded it his second preference.

In analysing last preference we once again replace the Country Party by the Communist Party (Table 12.4). The latter was the bane of Labor voters in the capital cities of four states. Religion was important in the case of the DLP, which was rejected most enthusiastically by politically interested non-Catholics. The Liberal Party was the last choice of poorly educated non-churchgoers, and, in Victoria alone, of well educated Catholics and Nonconformists — a surprising double contrast. Once again, rural residence was associated with a relative indifference to the Communist Party, and the same attitude was shown by Victorians and Tasmanians, whether Labor or Liberal voters.

It is difficult to summarise this material. But its very complexity enriches our understanding of the process of party choice. We have seen ample evidence tht voters are not the one-eyed spectators of the political world that they are often portrayed; it is entirely appropriate that their total view of the party system should be rich in variety. The great mixture of preference patterns, and the diversity of social and psychological attributes with accompany them, help us to understand why the battery of predictor variables used in the tree analysis in Chapter 7 had so little power in reducing variance. Party identification in Australia is determined by the interaction of a large number of variables which can combine in many ways; it can be explained in simple terms only at the cost of severe distortion.

There remains one further possibility to explore: that in directing their second preferences voters are influenced by considerations of policy or ideology — a hypothesis advanced by Converse and Valen.[7] Family loyalty or social situation may, according to this argument, determine a man's

Table 12.4   Variations in last preference among Labor voters, 1967

Party Chosen as Last Preference	Greatest Rejection Among	%	Least Rejection Among	%
Democratic Labor Party (mean for all Labor voters 37%)	Nonconformists, non-religionists and others with a good deal of interest in politics	69		
	Voters with a good deal of interest in politics	35	Voters with moderate or no interest in politics in states other than Victoria or Tasmania	25
Communist Party (mean for all Labor voters 30%)	Urban voters aged between 21 and 60, in NSW, SA, WA and Qld	49	Victorians and Tasmanians	13
			Rural voters, aged between 21 and 60, in NSW and WA	16
Liberal Party (mean for all Labor voters 21%)	Non-churchgoers in NSW, Victoria, WA and Tasmania, with primary education or less	45	Anglicans, non-religionists and others,[a] with secondary education or more	9
	Catholics and Nonconformists with secondary education or more, in Victoria	40	Catholics and non-conformists, with secondary education or more, outside Victoria, who have lived in the same area for ten years or more	12

[a]Principally Orthodox and Jewish

7 'Dimensions of Cleavage and Perceived Party Distance in Norwegian Voting', p. 128.

party identification, but once that is decided his second choice goes to the party whose policy stands are closest to his own. We know enough now about the quantum of interest in politics present in the electorate to be able to guess that such voters are unlikely to be very numerous — what is envisaged is a sophistication and awareness that could be true of no more than one citizen in three. But what is the evidence? Consider Table 12.5, which presents an analysis of the relationship between the direction of second preferences among Labor and Liberal voters and their attitudes about strikers.

The propensity of Liberals to direct their second preferences to Labor, and of Labor voters to direct theirs to the Liberal Party, is related to their attitudes about strikers: the more sympathy with strikers the more Liberals choose Labor, and the less Labor voters choose the Liberal Party. The differences are more pronounced among Liberals than among Labor voters. A similar pattern exists with respect to attitudes to trade unions, at least among Liberals: 29 per cent of those who thought that unions had too much power gave their second preferences to Labor, compared with the 44 per cent of those who were much more relaxed about union power. (Among Labor voters an attitude to union power was simply irrelevant to the direction of second preferences.) And again, Liberals who were hawkish on Vietnam were rather less likely to choose Labor as next preferred party than Liberal doves.

Table 12.5   Attitudes to strikers, and second preferences, among Liberal and Labor voters, 1967

| | Attitude to Strikers | | |
	Generally For %	Depends %	Generally Against %
Liberal Voters			
Second Preference to			
Labor	55	38	26
CP	23	44	54
DLP	22	18	20
Total	100	100	100
(N)	(40)	(301)	(369)
Labor Voters			
Second Preference to			
Liberal	49	55	61
CP	29	22	21
DLP	22	23	18
Total	100	100	100
(N)	(134)	(313)	(173)

But over the whole range of policy items about which opinions were sought, the links between policy stand and second preference were generally slight or non-existent. And even where they were not, we cannot ignore the fact that some of the linkage was a function of a pre-existing party tie. Former Labor supporters might quite understandably have an untroubled feeling about unions or an anti-war stance on Vietnam that was a legacy of their old attachment and not a position independent of party ties. The case for policy or ideology playing a major part in the choice of next best party is a weak one. The principal determinants for the great majority of citizens seem to be the same ones which affect party identification itself — those to do with the citizen's social situation, broadly conceived.

PART III The Context of Change

13 The Pattern of Change

> I have no personal likes or dislikes of the various political parties. I vote as my conscience guides me. (*retired engineer, sixty-six, Sydney*)

In this chapter and those following it we move to a consideration of the nature of electoral change. Electoral stability in Australia we have seen to be the result of a complex interaction between attitudes to politics and government, the process of family socialisation, and slow, balanced, alterations to the social and economic fabric of the nation. What accounts for the electoral changes that do occur? Although there is an equilibrium in the party system, party strengths are so finely balanced that quite small movements in popular support can be enough to tip a governing party out of office. Are these movements random or purposeful? Are they slow-moving or fast? The answers to these questions are of interest in their own right and they touch on matters of concern in democratic theory. But in addition they form a necessary part of the analytic purpose of this study: to understand stability we must be able to account for change.

It will be clear that something more is needed than a discussion of the 'swing' between one election and another. However ingeniously estimates of swing are determined,[1] they compress many different phenomena into the one statistic. Our need is to separate these phenomena, and examine them individually. Figure 13.1 illuminates the problem. An 'electorate' is a body of voters at a point in time, and its membership undergoes continual change. Voters die or emigrate, new voters are enfranchised by coming of age or through naturalisation or through changes in the definitions of citizenship. In a society with a relatively static population, the gains and losses will be matched: if parties gain and lose voters in equal proportion then the party balance will not be disturbed. In a society with an expanding population, such as Australia, the gains will out-number the losses, and a disparity in the gains and losses may therefore be more important in determining the party balance.

---

1 There are useful discussions of swing in Aitkin, Hall and Morgan, 'Some Facts and Figures', in Mayer and Nelson, *Australian Politics*, pp. 267-8, and Malcolm Mackerras, *Australian General Elections*, Sydney, 1972, pp. 267-80.

The process of gaining and shedding voters we can describe as 'replacement'.[2] At an election held at time t_2 the electorate has lost a proportion of its strength since the election at t_1 (the voters in the thin rectangle *a*)[3] and gained new recruits who have never voted before (those in the rectangle b). One time period later, at t_3, the electorate has lost another section of its voters (c) and gained still more to replace them (d). The replacement of b for a, and of d for c may have important partisan consequences which are obscured in simple swing calculations; they must be investigated.

Those voters who were in the electorate at two points in time—t_1 and

Figure 13.1   The change in an electorate over time

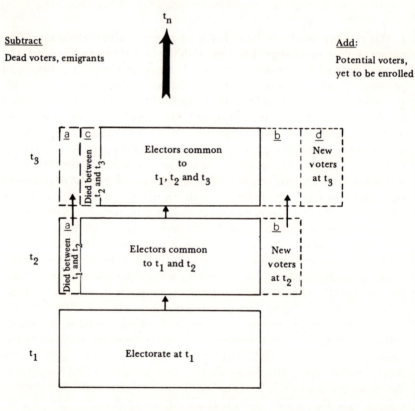

2 Following Butler and Stokes, *Political Change in Britain*, Chapter 12. The technique used in this chapter departs in some small ways from that used by these authors, and the interested reader is referred to their Chapter 12 for a very full account of the process used.

3 Death is the only significant cause of departure from the electoral roll that can be precisely estimated. Emigration of citizens is not immediately followed by their elimination from the roll, and many Australians permanently resident overseas continue to vote. Imprisonment for a term longer than one year and lunacy are the other major causes; neither is significant for our purposes.

t_2, or t_2 and t_3, or t_1 and t_3 — can have done a great variety of things at the two elections. They may have voted or not voted, supported one party twice, moved from one major party to its rival, moved from a minor party to a major one, or vice versa, and so on. Each of these paired actions has partisan consequences, each requires attention. The universe of possible moves, or pathways, between two elections is set out in Figure 13.2, in which each cell represents a unique combination of paired actions.[4] By placing respondents in the appropriate cells we can come to estimates of the importance of each type of electoral movement to the total result.

The shaded cells in Figure 13.2 represent those who supported the same party on each occasion, or did not vote. The unshaded cell at the bottom of the diagonal we can ignore hereafter, since it contains people who had no chance to vote, having been non-voters at t_1, and having died before t_2; in a three-year cycle of elections they are in any case numerically

Figure 13.2   Pathways of electoral change

		t_2					
		L–CP	DLP	ALP	Other	Non-v.	Dead
t_1	L–CP	▨	P_{12}	P_{13}	P_{14}	P_{15}	P_{16}
	DLP	P_{21}	▨	P_{23}	P_{24}	P_{25}	P_{26}
	Labor	P_{31}	P_{32}	▨	P_{34}	P_{35}	P_{36}
	Other	P_{41}	P_{42}	P_{43}	▨	P_{45}	P_{46}
	Non-voter	P_{51}	P_{52}	P_{53}	P_{54}	▨	$p56$
	New voter	P_{61}	P_{62}	P_{63}	P_{64}	P_{65}	

4 It will be clear that a transition matrix which contained all possible pathways, that is, separate rows and columns for all party groups both elections, would be very large. There have been usually around ten different groups contesting recent federal elections. Few survive to fight again and judicious summary is therefore necessary. All tiny parties, single-issue groups and independent candidates appear as 'Other', and the Liberal and Country Parties have again been grouped together. The non-voter group includes those respondents who were uncertain of which party they had supported or would support, a combination discussed below.

negligible. The shaded diagonal we would expect to contain most voters, and the proportion of voters placed on it is an index of electoral *stability*. But to examine change we need to compare the pairs of cells that contain each party's gains and losses. The rows of the table represent what happened to each party's electoral support *after* t_1, the columns represent the source of each party's support *at* t_2. Labor's losses to the Liberal and Country Parties, for example, appear in cell p_{31} (the subscripts are identification numbers, the first denoting the row, the second the column), while Labor's gains appear in cell p_{13}. There are five pathways in which we have a particular interest:

1. *Straight conversion.* The direct movement of voters from one major party to the other is what is commonly meant by the term 'swing', especially in the phrase 'swinging voter'. In terms of the Labor Party's advantage, it can be expressed as Labor's gains from the coalition minus its losses to the coalition, or $(p_{13} - p_{31})$. However, a single vote won in this fashion is actually worth two: it reduces the first party's score by one vote as well as increasing the second party's score by one vote. So the contribution of straight conversion to a party's advantage is actually twice its apparent value; in the case of Figure 13.2, $2(p_{13} - p_{31})$. Written in this form a positive result denotes a Labor lead, a negative result a lead for the coalition.

2. *The circulation of DLP voters.* By 1966 the DLP had become virtually a non-Labor auxiliary and, as we have observed, it served as an alternative repository of votes for a small proportion of Liberals. Nevertheless, it attracted support from erstwhile Labor voters too, and there was substantial drift in and out of the party's ranks during the period under consideration. Since our interest is principally focused on the extent to which this drift favoured one of the major parties at the expense of the other, we monitor it by obtaining the balance of the losses to and gains from the DLP experienced by both major parties, and subtracting one from the other. In terms of Figure 13.2,

$$(p_{23} - p_{32}) - (p_{21} - p_{12})$$

The result is not doubled, since a DLP voter who switches to the Liberal Party does not reduce the *Labor* Party's share of the vote.

3. *The circulation of minor party voters.* As Table 1.1 reminds us, the votes garnered by candidates outside the four principal parties have rarely been considerable, and have not exceeded 4 per cent since the establishment of the DLP. Nevertheless by 1969 one of these minor parties, the Australia Party, had developed to the point where it appeared to have a chance of making inroads into the support of the Big Four. Which party would have suffered most? We monitor the contribution of minor party supporters by using the same logic already described for DLP voters, or

$$(p_{43} - p_{34}) - (p_{41} - p_{14})$$

4. *Differential turnout and uncertainty.* It is common to assume that

compulsory voting in Australia removes the need to worry about turnout,[5] and the fact that the total vote is rarely more than 95 per cent of the enrolled electorate is ascribed (when it is noticed at all) to inefficiency in the rolls. But 1 per cent of respondents in both 1967 and 1969 were prepared to say that they had not voted at all; we shall see that the partisan consequences of staying away from the polls were not unimportant.

Uncertainty about one's past behaviour is by no means the same thing as refraining from voting, and it is placed in this category for the sake of convenience. Respondents who were unsure about which party they had supported in 1966 or 1969 were about as numerous as those who reported that they had not voted. In 1967, however, respondents were asked about what they would do in a hypothetical election held 'tomorrow'. In such situations the proportion of uncertain respondents typically rises greatly, and the past behaviour of such voters is of especial interest.

Following the logic already described, we obtain a measure of the contribution of non-voters and the uncertain to the major-party struggle by the formula

$$(p_{53} - p_{35}) - (p_{51} - p_{15})$$

5. *Replacement*. Between 1966 and 1969 the electorate grew from 6,193,881 to 6,606,243, or by 6.7 per cent — a little over 2 per cent per year. But this was a net increase. Every year approximately 1.2 per cent of the electorate died, and another 3.3 per cent were newly enrolled, of whom three in every four had come of age; the others were naturalised immigrants or British immigrants entering the roll after a statutory six months' residence in the country. We have already observed that throughout most of the 1950s and 1960s the Liberal and Country Parties profited from new enrolments. By 1969 there were signs that the disproportionate share of the support enjoyed by the coalition among new voters had begun to wane. But little was known of the partisan consequences of death. We look at the importance of replacement — the balance of losses and gains due to deaths and new enrolments — by means of the formula

$$(p_{63} - p_{36}) - (p_{61} - p_{16})$$

To obtain the *net* effect of all of these contributions to one party's advantage over the other, we simply add them up. The result will be positive when the tide has turned in Labor's favour, as it did between 1966 and 1969, and negative when the non-Labor parties are in the ascendant.[6]

---

5 See, for example, R.G. Cushing and R.W. Gibberd, 'Sources of Swing in the Election', in Mayer, *Labor to Power*, p. 272. I have used the same escape route myself in other writings, but repentance is always possible!

6 The sharp-eyed will have noticed that the five pathways of change examined plus the 'stability diagonal' do not exhaust the cells of Figure 13.2. But those that remain do not affect the major party balance: if a non-voter or a new voter supports a minor party or the DLP he does not directly affect the strength of either major party. The counting of preferences can cause his vote to have an effect, but the numbers are small enough for this complication to be disregarded.

Let us now study the movements which did take place, first between 1966 and 1967, when the respondents were first interviewed, then between 1967 and 1969, the time of the second interview, and finally between 1966 and 1969.

A Little Chronology

The period marks the start of Labor's electoral recovery, which was to place it in power following the elections of 1972, after twenty-three years in opposition. The resignation early in 1966 of Sir Robert Menzies, the Leader and founder of the Liberal Party, was followed at the end of the year by the greatest win then ever recorded by the coalition, under its new Leader, Harold Holt (see Table 1.1). Here the important factors seemed to have been the general public support for intervention in the Vietnam war (decided upon by the government in 1965 and opposed by the opposition) and the lack of popular regard for the Leader of the ALP, Arthur Calwell.[7] From the high point of November 1966 the coalition's relative advantage declined quickly, partly because of the replacement of Calwell by his younger and more impressive deputy Gough Whitlam, and partly because of the ineptitude of the government itself, which allowed a series of minor political events to blossom into crises.

By the end of 1967 the coalition's share of the vote had dropped very greatly, and there were moves within the Liberal Party to replace Holt. But in December the Prime Minister was drowned while surfing, and the new Liberal Leader, John Gorton, revived his party's spirits and fortunes until he, too, began to make m istakes of political judgment that caused public questioning of his leadership.[8] At the elections held in October 1969 the Liberal-Country coalition managed to survive, but its majority was cut from forty to seven; Labor's share of the vote increased by 6.9 per cent. In the following parliament the Liberal and Country Parties failed to regain the initiative, and in March 1971 John Gorton voted against himself after a tied result in a party vote of confidence; he was replaced as Leader and Prime Minister by William McMahon. The new Prime Minister was not loved either by his party or by his coalition partners in the Country Party (their former leader, Sir John McEwen, had vetoed his succession to the leadership after the death of Holt), and the last eighteen months of the Liberal-Country Party government were marked by the kind of public disunity that had formerly been characteristic of the Labor Party. On 2 December 1972 the government was defeated, and Labor was returned to

---

7 No major study was carried out of the 1966 election, but there is much useful commentary in the regular political chronicles published in the *Australian Quarterly* and the *Australian Journal of Politics and History*.

8 Apart from the two journals cited in note 7 above, essential reading on this period is Alan Reid, *The Power Struggle*, Sydney, 1969, and his later *The Gorton Experiment*, Sydney, 1971.

office with a majority of nine; its share of the vote had increased by 2.7 per cent.[9]

On 18 May 1974 the Labor government survived a double dissolution election, forced on it by an obstructionist Senate controlled by the opposition, and continued in office with a majority of five in the House of Representatives; it remained in a minority in the Senate.[10] This election saw the end of the DLP's representation in parliament. A few weeks before the election one DLP Senator (V.C. Gair, Queensland) accepted a post as Ambassador to Ireland, and resigned: his four colleagues failed to retain their seats as Senators in the election following the double dissolution, an election that was precipitated by the uproar surrounding Gair's appointment.

The election result did not put an end to confrontation between the government and the Senate, and in late 1975 the Senate threatened to reject supply at a time when the Labor government's public standing seemed low. The Prime Minister, Mr Whitlam, chose to continue in office rather than resign; since the Liberal opposition in the Senate remained obdurate a financial crisis seemed inevitable. This impasse continued for some weeks, and was suddenly resolved when the Governor-General, Sir John Kerr, dismissed Mr Whitlam, appointed the Liberal Leader of the opposition, Malcolm Fraser, as caretaker Prime Minister, and dissolved parliament. In the ensuing elections the Liberal-Country Party coalition enjoyed a comfortable victory. Though the Labor Party was greatly reduced in parliamentary numbers its electoral support remained well above that recorded in the disasters of 1931 or 1966 (Table 1.1).

In retrospect, it is plausible to explain the Labor advance after 1966 as a steady progression towards power, made possible both by the failure of the Liberal Party to solve the problem of the succession to Menzies, and by Gough Whitlam's ability to weld the Labor Party within and outside parliament into a credible alternative governing party. In this process the three years after 1966 count more towards Labor's return to power than the three after 1969, and the timing of the interviews — September-October 1967 and October-November 1969 — was usefully, if fortuitously, arranged. Yet as Figure 13.3 suggests, there was a revival in the government's standing in the electorate after the election of John Gorton as Leader of the Liberal Party, and much of it had subsided by the time of

9 For the 1969-72 period and the 1972 elections, see L. Oakes and D. Solomon, *The Making of An Australian Prime Minister*, Melbourne, 1973, and Mayer, *Labor to Power*.

10 The Australian Constitution (Sec. 57) provides for the dissolution of both Houses of the Parliament if the Senate twice fails to pass a bill approved twice by the House of Representatives. For the 1972-4 period, and the 1974 elections, see C.J. Lloyd and G.S. Reid, *Out of the Wilderness — The Return of Labor*, Melbourne, 1974; Peter Blazey and David Campbell, *The Political Dice Men*, Melbourne, 1974; and Laurie Oakes and David Solomon, *Grab for Power: Election 74*, Melbourne, 1974.

the 1969 elections. The survey data do not allow us to say much about this revival, as it began and ended between the two sets of interviews. Nevertheless, the patterns of change that can be identified are full of interest.

Figure 13.3   The changing party lead, according to APOP, 1966 to 1969. The DLP is not included in the figure; its support was generally estimated at 7 per cent. Support for other parties and independent candidates (including the Australia Party) rose from an estimated 1-2 per cent in early 1967 to an estimated 3-4 per cent in late 1969.

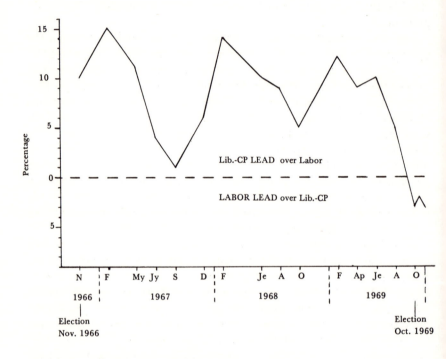

The Great Liberal Slide, 1966 to 1967

Table 13.1 (p. 218) gives estimates of the variety of electoral decisions made in 1966 and 1967.[11] In less than twelve months the commanding

11 Some explanation of the derivation of the entries in the table (and in Tables 13.3 and 13.4 below) is in order. First, the marginal totals of the row for new voters and the column for the dead were estimated from census and immigration data. Second, the distribution of new voters across their row was determined by examining the preferences of respondents interviewed in 1967 who were not eligible to vote in 1966. Third, the distribution of dead voters down their column was determined by applying known mortality rates to groups of respondents defined by age, sex and party identification. Fourth, the DLP's share of the vote has been built up to the levels appropriate for 1966 and 1967 (estimate of support in an election for the House of Representatives) by subtraction from the Lib.-CP and ALP 'stable' cells, in the proportion two Lib.-CP votes for every ALP vote. Fifth, the entries for cells elsewhere in the table come from a cross-tabulation of 1967 survey data (questions

lead of the Liberal and Country Parties over the Labor Party, of 9.5 per
cent, had declined to 1.3 per cent — a position of near parity. The
contributions that each of the five sources of change made to this decline
were as follows:

Straight conversion	2 (4.1 — 1.2)	+5.8
Circulation of DLP	(1.6 — 1.6) — (3.0 — 2.7)	—0.3
Circulation of other	(0.7 — 0.6) — (* — 0.6)	+0.7
Differential turnout and uncertainty	(0.3 — 1.9) — (0.3 — 4.1)	+2.2
Replacement	(1.1 — 0.5) — (1.3 — 0.5)	—0.2
Net change in Labor's position	(9.5 — 1.3)	+8.2

* = less than 0.1 per cent

Two-thirds of Labor's gross improvement came from straight conversion,
from 1966 Liberal and Country Party voters who were prepared ten
months later to support the Labor Party. Most of the rest came from the
much greater tendency of non-Labor than Labor supporters to be
uncertain as to which party they would support — a striking indication of
the loss of standing suffered by the Liberal and Country Parties in 1967.
And although the non-Labor parties managed more than to hold their own
in terms of replacement and the circulation of DLP voters, these gains
were relatively insignificant.

At the same time the Labor Party by no means kept the loyalty of all
those who had voted for it in 1966. Former Labor voters went over to the
ranks of the government, the DLP and minor parties, and others moved
into the category of uncertain. Table 13.1 and the two that follow make
plain that electoral movements are never wholly one way. Parties gain
supporters even when they are losing others.

But what changes the relative positions of the parties is the *rate* at which
they do so. Compare the Lib-CP and ALP rows in Table 13.1. We can
reanalyse the data by expressing the cell entries as percentages, not of the
whole sample, but of Lib-CP and ALP voters in 1966. The result appears
in Table 13.2. Labor retained 85 per cent of those who had supported it in
1966, the Liberal and Country Parties only 75 per cent. The non-Labor

42c and 45a). Sixth, the entries in the table have been adjusted so that the marginal totals
of the first six rows would agree with the relative proportions voting for the various parties
in 1966 as disclosed by election returns, adjusted to take account of sample estimates of
non-voting and census and immigration estimates of new enrolments (the procedure is
described in Frederick Mosteller, 'Association and Estimation in Contingency Tables',
Journal of the American Statistical Association, **63,** 1968, pp. 1-28).

With minor changes, most of them related to the different Australian situation, the
procedures used to estimate the entries in each cell are those adopted by Butler and
Stokes, *Political Change in Britain,* p. 283, n.2. A similar caveat is offered: because of
the various kinds of adjustment undertaken, because of problems of recall, and because
of the sample size, too much reliance should not be placed on the exact figures used.

parties lost proportionately more than the Labor Party to the DLP, proportionately more former non-Labor voters were unsure of what they would do, and the non-Labor parties lost more than they gained from Labor in the straight exchange of supporters. To some extent, of course, this is the likely fate of the dominant party at any time. As we have already seen, its supporters at the point of its greatest success will include very many who have been attracted from its rival, and may be expected to slip away as soon as the dominant party begins to lose its appeal. This was the situation in 1967. The Labor Party, by contrast, had already been unusually reduced (1966 was the ALP's worst election since 1931), and was not likely to lose as great a proportion of its supporters as were its opponents.

Labor Creeps Ahead, 1967 to 1969

The death of Harold Holt and the election of John Gorton slowed down the rate of Liberal decline, but did not reverse it, as Table 13.3 reveals. Over

Table 13.1   Pathways of change, 1966 to 1967

1966	1967 Lib.-CP %	DLP %	ALP %	Other %	Non-v. %	Dead %	Total %		Percentage of 1966 Electorate Voting
Lib.-CP	35.7	2.7	4.1	0.6	4.1	0.5	47.7	⎫	49.9
DLP	3.0	2.2	1.6	*	0.2	*	7.0	⎬—9.5	7.3
ALP	1.2	1.6	32.4	0.6	1.9	0.5	38.2	⎭	40.0
Other	*	*	0.7	1.6	0.2	*	2.6		2.7
Non-voter	0.3	*	0.3	*	0.5	*	1.1		
New voter	1.3	0.2	1.1	*	0.8	*	3.4		
Total	41.5	6.7 —1.3	40.2	2.9	7.6	1.1	100.0		
Percentage of 1967 Electorate Voting	42.0	6.8	40.6	2.9	7.7				100.0

Source: 1967 sample. (N=1913)
* less than 0.1 per cent

Table 13.2   The change in party support after 1966

Party Preferred in 1966	Party Preferred in 1967 Lib.-CP %	DLP %	ALP %	Other %	Non-v. %	Dead %	Total %	(N)[a]
Lib.-CP	75	6	9	1	8	1	100	(913)
ALP	3	4	85	2	5	1	100	(731)

[a] These Ns are derived from the marginal totals of Table 13.1, and therefore adjusted, rather than actual.

the two years Labor picked up a further 4.7 per cent, and moved from a position of relative disadvantage to one of relative advantage. In 1969 the Liberal and Country Parties needed the assistance of the Democratic Labor Party to retain office; they had not needed it (though they received it) in 1966. The sources of Labor's strengthened position were as follows:

Straight conversion	2(5.8—5.0)	+ 1.6
Circulation of DLP	(1.0—0.8)—(1.5—0.9)	− 0.4
Circulation of other	(1.7—1.1)—(0.4—0.8)	+ 1.0
Differential turnout and uncertainty	(3.6—0.3)—(2.6—1.7)	+ 2.4
Replacement	(3.3—0.8)—(3.7—1.3)	+ 0.1
Net change in Labor's position	(3.4 + 1.3)	+4.7

Not only was the size of Labor's advantage reduced between 1967 and 1969, but its origins were very different. Conversion, which had been responsible for most of Labor's gains between 1966 and 1967, now accounted for less than a third. The explanation was not that Liberals had ceased to flow to the Labor Party but that there was an almost corresponding flow in the opposite direction. Although we cannot be sure of the causes, it is certainly reasonable to argue that many of those who had ceased to support the government in 1967 because of its errors in leadership were attracted back when there was a change of leader. The largest single contribution to Labor's improvement was differential turnout and uncertainty. More than half of those who had been unsure in 1967 eventually preferred Labor, and in addition, almost 2 per cent of

Table 13.3   Pathways of change, 1967 to 1969

1967	Lib.-CP %	DLP %	ALP %	1969 Other %	Non-v. %	Dead %	Total %		Percentage of 1967 Electorate Voting
Lib.-CP	28.3	0.9	5.8	0.8	1.7	1.3	38.8		42.0
DLP	1.5	3.5	1.0	0.2	*	0.1	6.3	−1.3	6.8
ALP	5.0	0.8	29.5	1.1	0.3	0.8	37.5		40.3
Other	0.4	*	1.7	0.6	*	*	2.7		2.9
Non-voter	2.6	0.2	3.6	0.4	0.3	*	7.1		7.7
New voter	3.7	0.3	3.3	0.3	*		7.6		
Total	41.5	5.7	44.9	3.4	2.3	2.2	100.0		
		3.4							
Percentage of 1969 Electorate Voting	43.4	6.0	47.0	3.7					100.0

Source: Panel. (N=1477)

* less than 0.1 per cent

1967 Liberals finally did not vote at all, compared with less than a fifth of that number of 1967 Labor supporters. Once again the non-Labor parties profited from the circulation of DLP supporters, and from new enrolments; but that latter gain was offset by a greater proportion of non-Labor deaths.

We cannot, of course, add together all the contributions from both time periods in order to establish a summary for the period 1966-9. To discover this we must construct a third set of pathways, which appears in Table 13.4.

Change, 1966 to 1969

In the three years from the election of 1966 to that of 1969 the Labor Party converted a relative deficit of 8.7 per cent into a lead of 3.4 per cent — an improvement all told of 12.1 per cent. Its sources were these:

Straight conversion	$2(8.2 - 3.4)$	+9.6
Circulation of DLP	$(1.4 - 1.1) - (3.0 - 2.1)$	−0.6
Circulation of other	$(1.9 - 0.9) - (* - 1.6)$	+2.6
Differential turnout and uncertainty	$(0.8 - 0.3) - (1.3 - 1.5)$	+0.7
Replacement	$(4.0 - 1.5) - (4.3 - 1.6)$	−0.2
Net change in Labor's position	$(8.7 + 3.4)$	+12.1

* = less than 0.1 per cent

Table 13.4 presents an analysis of the movement between the two elections of 1966 and 1969. Uncertainty ceased to be important; replacement we already know to have been of little net advantage to either

Table 13.4   Pathways of change, 1966 to 1969

1966	1969							Percentage of 1966 Electorate Voting
	Lib.-CP %	DLP %	ALP %	Other %	Non.-v %	Dead %	Total %	
Lib.-CP	29.0	2.1	8.2	1.6	1.5	1.6	44.0	49.9
DLP	3.0	1.9	1.4	*	*	0.1	6.4	7.3
ALP	3.4	1.1	28.1	0.9	0.3	1.5	35.2	40.0
Other	*	*	1.9	0.5	*	*	2.4	2.7
Non-voter	1.3	*	0.8	*	0.3	*	2.4	
New voter	4.3	0.6	4.0	0.5	0.1		3.5	
Total	41.0	5.7	44.4	3.5	2.2	3.2	100.0	
Percentage of 1969 Electorate Voting	43.4	6.0	47.0	3.7				100.0

DLP / ALP / Other grouping: −8.7

3.4

Source: Panel. (N=1528)
* = less than 0.1 per cent

side. Three quarters of Labor's improvement came from straight conversion, and most of the rest came from the circulation of minor party
supporters. The Liberal and Country Parties gained a little from the
circulation of DLP voters, and marginally from replacement.

Tables 13.1, 13.3 and 13.4 enable us to reconstruct the changing
disposition of the Australian electorate between 1966 and 1969. Labor's
impressive improvement in popular support can be seen to have occurred
mainly because the party attracted across former supporters of the
coalition. They came in two waves, the first between 1966 and 1967, the
second between 1967 and 1969. In the first period Labor lost few of its own
supporters to the non-Labor parties, but in the second there was a
considerable flow, and Labor's net advantage was only small.

The second important contribution came from the movement of voters
between the major parties and the minor parties and independents. Here
the principal component was the flow of Liberal and Country Party voters
(mainly Liberals) to the ranks of the Australia Party, which made its entry
into national electoral politics in 1969. The data suggest that the Australia
Party gained two Liberals for every Labor supporter that it attracted.
Finally, Labor benefited in 1969 from the decision of some 1966 Liberals
not to vote at all. We may see this as an inevitable cost suffered by a party
which is losing popularity. Compulsory voting rules out this alternative for
most voters, but not, it is clear, for everyone.

Although the Liberal and Country Parties managed to hold a slim lead
over the ALP as a result of replacement, in historical terms this was a very
good result for Labor. For most of the 1950s and 1960s, as we have seen in
Chapter 6, the non-Labor parties had profited handsomely from new
enrolments, and even though they probably lost through deaths, the much
greater number of new voters ensured a continuing insurance against
defeat. A reasonable estimate of the Liberal-Country Party advantage
from replacement in the period 1963-6 is 1.5 per cent.[12] As for the DLP,
its vote declined between 1966 and 1969, and the non-Labor parties were
the beneficiary, a finding that comes as no surprise after the discussion of
Chapter 10.

There is an instructive comparison between these tables of electoral
change and the equivalent British examples presented by Butler and
Stokes.[13] In Britain the contribution of straight conversion to the
changing lead of one party over the other was much less than in Australia,
and the contribution of differential turnout and replacement much more.
Part of the explanation is no doubt contained in the particular time
periods chosen in each case, but it is possible that part arises from the

---

12 Cushing and Gibberd provide ('Sources of Swing in the Election', pp. 273-4) some
   admittedly crude evidence that suggests that between 1969 and 1972 Labor did very well
   from replacement, almost as well, indeed, as from straight conversion.
13 *Political Change in Britain*, pp. 283-92.

consequences of compulsory voting in Australia and the lack of it in Britain. Between one fifth and one quarter of the British electorates pictured in these tables chose not to vote, but *constant* non-voting was characteristic only of one tenth. In other words, between 10 per cent and 15 per cent of the British electorate were moving at any time from or to a position of non-voting. In a period of changing party fortunes these movements would have a powerful impact on the party balance, which could often exceed that of any other source of change.

In Australia, setting aside the 1 per cent who do choose not to vote, and the 2 or 3 per cent who forget or who are unable to vote for accidental reasons, non-voting is not an option, and a voter who is dissatisfied with his own party must either suppress his feelings or vote for another or for an independent candidate. We have seen in Chapters 4 and 5 that a large proportion of those who identify with the major parties are at least aware that the party they do not themselves support is nevertheless a party of some worth and potential. Half of the Labor partisans in the 1967 sample, and one-third of the Liberals, actually placed the other major party second in their set of preferences. It is possible, then, that many Australian voters do not find it hard to make the jump across the party board, while British voters are not forced by the system to make the choice of whether or not to jump — they can always do nothing. It would be understandable, then, if straight conversion were to play a larger role in electoral change in Australia than in Britain; whether it actually does so can be determined only when many more sets of pathways, from both polities, are available for study.

Change and the Nature of Stability

The pathways of change discussed in this chapter have illuminated one aspect of the nature of stability that is of central importance to this study. The common use of the pendulum metaphor in describing electoral change has led to the posing of questions like 'why are swings (or movements) between elections so small?' In fact, as Tables 13.1, 13.3 and 13.4 make plain, electoral movements between two points in time are quite considerable in size, but they are to a large degree self-cancelling. Party gains from all sources tend to balance party losses, and a comparison of the aggregate election statistics can tell us only the net consequence of these movements. Table 13.5 emphasises this point by comparing the proportion of voters who changed positions between two points of time with the net swing to Labor over the same periods. There is not a constant relationship between these estimates, but at least it can be said that in each case there was substantially more voting variation than was implied by the change in Labor's position relative to that of the coalition.

What is more, much of the electoral movement can be *directly* self-cancelling or compensatory. Between 1967 and 1969 5.8 per cent of the electorate moved from supporting the Liberal and Country Parties to supporting Labor. But they were almost matched by another 5.0 per cent who moved the other way. The analyst who observes a very small movement in party strengths and sets out to discover why it was so small may be chasing the wrong hare. We need to look at the universe of swinging voters — all those who changed from one major party to another, not simply those who changed from the loser to the winner — to understand the dynamics of any particular election result.

The data do not allow us to explore the electoral behaviour of 'swinging voters' very far, since we need at least three elections in a series to observe anything more than a simple change of party preference. We have already observed of course, in Tables 3.5 and 3.6, that those strongly committed to a party are most unlikely to vote for its rivals, and that conversely, those with no fixed party attachment are quite likely to change or to be uncertain as to what they will do. These truisms gain significance when we realise that fixed party attachments are very common in Australia; although it is possible for any voter to change sides, much of the change comes from those who are weakly linked to the parties.

The primary task of the next three chapters is to investigate the concomitants of that change, to determine to what extent these movements in party fortunes were related to events and changing situations in contemporary Australian politics. In doing so we look at the separate contributions made to electoral change by contemporary issues, by attitudes to leaders, and by the election campaign itself, the three most important immediate influences on any election situation.

Table 13.5   Voting movements and the swing to Labor, 1966 to 1969

Time Period	Proportion of Voters [a] who Changed Position %	Net Change in [b] Labor's Position %
1966-7	24	+ 8.2
1967-9	31	+ 4.7
1966-9	32	+12.1

[a] The values in this column are derived from the diagonal cells of Tables 13.1, 13.3 and 13.4, and represent adjusted data rather than actual survey data. New enrolments and dead voters are not included in the bases on which the percentages are taken.

[b] The values in this column are derived from the marginal totals of Tables 13.1, 13.3 and 13.4.

14 Issues and Electoral Change

Dislike about Labor? At present, the conflict with the Vietnam business. I agree with the government, as during the war overseas I got a fair idea of what the communists could do, and I think Vietnam should be supported by the Australians. (*sheet-metalworker, forty-six, Newcastle*)

Issues — disputes about alternatives — occupy an important place in one traditional account of the electoral process. They form the stuff of election campaigns, in which spokesmen for government and opposition debate before the nation about what should be done (or who would do it best, if it is generally agreed that something should be done). In this account the electorate is the adjudicator, making up its collective mind and awarding its decision on polling day, after hearing and assessing all the evidence. In one respect the model matches reality very well: election campaigns in Australia, as in other competitive party systems, are an occasion for sustained political speech making and argument, by party leaders and their colleagues, and by their supporters at all levels — right down to writers of letters to editors, and bar-room savants. So prodigious is the output of argument in the few weeks of the campaign, and so absorbed are the arguers in the business of producing it, that attention is rarely directed at the recipients — the electorate. It is assumed, most of the time, that the voters cannot fail to be aware of the issues, and that the issues will ultimately be influential in deciding the outcome.

The task of discovering how voters see issues, and what effects issues have on their party preferences, is well suited to the techniques of the sample survey and the detailed questionnaire, and political scientists were quick to employ them. The result was a set of sombre findings that reduced the importance of issues considerably.[1] Voters tended not to have stable opinions on important issues and, when they had opinions at all, they appeared to take their cues largely from the party they supported. Instead of attitudes to issues determining party preference, preference seemed to determine attitude. For an issue to be important in affecting the

1 Three important references in this context are Berelson *et al.*, *Voting*; Campbell *et al.*, *The American Voter*; and Butler and Stokes, *Political Change in Britain*. There is also a considerable literature in the journals. Australian interest in the subject is exemplified by Hughes, *Images and Issues*, and Murray Goot, *Policies and Partisans: Australian Electoral Opinion 1941-1968*, Sydney, 1969.

party balance, it was argued, electors would have to know and care about it, they would have to see the parties as sharply distinguished in terms of what should be done, and the electorate as a whole would have to be other than evenly divided about it — otherwise there could be little chance of one party profiting at the expense of the other.[2] The great majority of issues failed this three-fold test on at least one ground, and often more. And, even when the issue passed the test, dismaying problems of causality faced the researcher: did the issue bring about a change in party preference, did a change in party preference change the attitude about the issue, or were both changes caused by some other, third, factor?

Problems like these are no less to be found in Australian data. Respondents were asked in both interviews to give their opinions about a dozen or so of the important issues in Australian public affairs. Few questions elicited opinions that were notably stable over time,[3] and party lines seemed to structure the pattern of responses, although the lines were often fuzzily drawn. Yet to abandon issues altogether as a cause of electoral change would be altogether too drastic a step. For one thing, we have seen that the images of the parties held by the electorate are made up among other things of issue-related items. Some respondents made quite clear that they liked the Labor Party because of its policy on Vietnam, or on one or other social welfare issue. Although such respondents were in a minority, those who said that the Labor Party or the Liberal Party was 'competent' or 'trustworthy' or 'able' were very probably presenting a summary judgment based on the party's performance with respect to a wide range of issues over a considerable period of time. Very many issues arise from one election to the next, and it would be understandable that, although a voter might not be seized by any one of them, he would be affected nevertheless by how the parties appeared to deal with the body of them. Something of this kind presumably occurred during 1967, a disastrous year of bungles and crises for the coalition, at the end of which the Liberal and Country Parties had lost a good deal of their support. Issues, then, must remain on the agenda.

One difficulty in approaching the subject lies in the selection of the issue or issues to study. It is an often deplored characteristic of Australian party

2 Butler and Stokes, *Political Change in Britain*, pp. 187-191.
3 The number of alternative opinions allowed the respondent clearly has an effect on the measure of stability. But there was a marked tendency for the indices of stability to cluster. In questions where two alternative answers were appropriate (for and against, for example) it was common for 70 per cent of respondents to hold the same opinion at the two points of time; with three alternatives the common mark was 60 per cent. Close examination of the data showed that much of the movement of opinion was self-cancelling — indeed, there was little change from 1967 to 1969 in the gross distribution of responses to any question. If we assume that most of this movement was random, and that the apparently stable set of opinions contain a similarly large random element, it follows that the proportion of respondents having 'meaningful' opinions on these questions was rarely greater than 50 per cent.

leaders that in opening their election campaigns they provide a campaign promise for almost all conceivably important groups in the community.[4] Unless such promises are matched from the other side they will, in principle at least, deserve the status of 'issue': an elector passionately concerned about, for example, the provision of child care might see that as the most important issue of the campaign, and direct his or her vote to the party that promised to do something about it. For such a voter child care is *the* issue. (It is, of course, precisely on the basis of such a calculus that these long lists of promises are assembled.) If both parties make similar promises, then the issue changes to 'which party is most likely to carry out its promise?' In 1969 both Mr Gorton and Mr Whitlam went into considerable detail as to what had been done, what was needed, and what would be provided in the separate fields of education, health, housing, taxation, defence, national development, social welfare, primary industry and foreign investment. In some fields their promises were similar, and in one — the provision of state-financed health schemes — the proposals were equally complex and hard to understand. Faced with such a barrage, the ordinary elector could well take refuge in his general sense of the parties' relative fitness to govern — and this is a matter we look at in the next chapter.

At the same time, the electorate has its own views about what the important issues are. Throughout the 1960s APOP samples consistently pointed to education, health and hospitals, and pensions as the most important issues in the approaching elections. It is not certain what these respondents had in mind, for in none of these problem areas were the government's proposals significantly different from those of the opposition. Both sides proposed to increase pension rates, spend more money on education, and improve hospital facilities and the access of poor people to decent health care. Most probably these respondents were pointing to areas of government initiative where they wanted to see more done.

We have independent evidence of a similar kind. In 1967, and again in 1969, respondents were asked to nominate what, in their opinion, were 'the most important problems the federal government should do something about'.[5] Their answers covered almost every field of government endeavour, and were by no means restricted to matters that were the responsibility of the federal government. Table 14.1 provides a summary, and its very size and detail emphasise how unlikely it is that attitudes to any one issue could determine the behaviour of a large proportion of the electorate. There were simply too many *different* issues that attracted attention, and the proportion of the electorate engaged by any one of them

4 For one lament, see David Butler, *The Canberra Model*, Melbourne, 1973, p. 119; for another, Bryce, *Modern Democracies*, Vol. II, pp. 284-5.
5 Question 15a in the 1967 questionnaire, and 17a in the 1969 questionnaire.

was quite small.

Table 14.1 makes clear also that the coming of an election situation did not basically alter the electorate's sense of the issues. To be sure, respondents had rather more to say in 1969 than in 1967, but the problems that they nominated were much the same and had much the same popular backing. Shortcomings in education and health, which were the subject of considerable discussion, show up rather more clearly in 1969, but the overriding impression is of stability.

Respondents were also asked on each occasion to name the party that would be most likely to do what they wanted on the first and second problems mentioned. The Labor Party was very obviously seen as the best of the major rivals as a problem solver, and its margin over the Liberal and Country Parties increased between 1967 and 1969 (Table 14.2). Part of the explanation for Labor's lead lies in the nature of the problems nominated: a large proportion were social welfare or interventionist issues where Labor's known stands and ideology made it much more likely than the coalition to be sympathetic to what was wanted. In the matter of

Table 14.1   The most important problems facing the federal government, 1967 and 1969

	1967 %	1969 %
Social Welfare, including	39	34
Pensions	*18*	*13*
Other social services	*6*	*6*
Housing (+ price of land, 1969)	*6*	*5*
Hospitals and medical benefits	*5*	*9*
Aborigines	*4*	*1*
National Development, including	19	11
Northern development, decentralisation, resources	*12*	*6*
Roads and transport	*4*	*3*
Immigration	*3*	*1*
Foreign Affairs and Defence, including	15	17
Vietnam, the American alliance	*7*	*6*
Defence generally, national service	*5*	*8*
The Economy, including	13	15
Taxation, cost of living	*6*	*7*
Employment	*2*	*1*
Foreign investment	*1*	*1*
Federal-state relations, grants to states	*1*	*2*
Assistance to primary industry	*	*3*
Education	11	16
All Other Issues	3	3
Total	100	100
Total no. of problems cited	3855	4331
Average no. of problems cited per respondent	1.9	2.3

* = less than 0.5 per cent

pensions and social services, for example, the Labor Party's advantage in 1967 was an enormous 60 per cent: of those who nominated pensions and other social services as important problems 80 per cent said that Labor would be most likely to do what was wanted, and only 20 per cent pointed to the coalition. In other areas, such as defence and national development, the non-Labor parties possessed the advantage, though never so impressively. Table 14.3 shows the relative Labor advantage in the major issue areas in both 1967 and 1969.

Labor's lead in 1969 over the whole range of issues was as pronounced as it was in 1967, but there was a good deal of change in its relative advantage in the various issue areas. Education became an area in which Labor moved from near parity to a position of great advantage, but to offset this, Labor's advantage in the issue area of the economy was eroded almost to nothing. Labor increased its lead with respect to Vietnam, and lost some of its lead in the social welfare area. These movements bespeak

Table 14.2 Parties most likely to solve important problems, 1967 and 1969

	1967 %	1969 %
Lib.-CP	20	23
Labor	36	42
No difference	13	5
Other [a]	31	30
Total	100	100
(N)	(1557)	(1578)

[a] Includes DLP, rival parties for different problems; uncertain respondents and those who did not answer the question are excluded.

Table 14.3 Labor's relative advantage in issue areas, 1967 and 1969

	1967 %	1969 %
Social Welfare	+47	+38
National Development	−26	−10
Foreign Affairs and Defence	+ 4	+ 4
Vietnam	*+28*	*+40*
Defence	*−32*	*−24*
The Economy	+18	+ 2
Education	− 2	+30
All Other Issues	+20	+30

Note: Labor's relative advantage was obtained by subtracting the proportion nominating the Liberal Party or Country Party as the party most likely to do what was wanted in a given issue area from the proportion nominating the Labor Party, of those nominating the Liberal, Labor or Country Parties. The + sign denotes a Labor lead.

the rise and fall of issues as subjects for political discussion and party action, movements caused partly by the need of parties to present new and relevant policies in an election situation, and partly by the sheer passage of time and events.

Yet Tables 14.2 and 14.3 raise other questions. How is it that the party seen as most likely to do what is wanted with respect to most of the important problems of the day is not supported by a clear majority of the electorate? And to what extent, if any, are changes in party voting related to changes in perception of the party as problem solver?

The answer to the first question is not that Labor partisans predominate among those who see the nation as beset by problems. The differences between the two sets of party supporters in this respect were trivial. The cause of the partisan imbalance in Tables 14.2 and 14.3 is rather that while Liberals generally saw the Liberal Party as the party most likely to solve the problems cited, Labor supporters were much more united in agreeing that Labor was the party for the task. There was only one major problem, in fact, on which Labor partisans' support for their own party dropped below 70 per cent: defence, where nearly one in three of those mentioning the problem thought the Liberal Party would do better. In contrast, in the social welfare area more Liberals preferred the Labor Party to their own party, and in most other issue areas there was a large group of Liberals who saw no difference between the parties.

This last finding helps to explain why the Labor predominance as a party likely to solve problems was not accompanied by an electoral majority. It may very well be the case that many respondents cited problems they knew from reading and discussion to be important ones, but not important in the sense that they impinged directly on respondents' own lives. For such respondents the question of the party best fitted or most likely to solve the problem was in large part an academic one, with no connection to their own political behaviour. Given the facts that Liberals were generally more interested in politics than Labor supporters (Chapter 3), and also more likely to be insulated from direct experience of the impact of such problems as pensions, hospitals and education, the differences between the two groups of supporters are at least understandable.

Yet for some respondents these problems were matters of great and immediate moment, and the nomination of a party likely to do what should be done a cause for much more than casual comment. Housing, education, the war in Vietnam, the position of Aborigines, the question of immigration — all were issues that had attracted passionate commitment by groups of citizens. It would be completely understandable if such citizens, because of a change in leadership, a shift in party policy, or simply too long a run of frustrations in getting government or party action, swung their support from one party to another. Table 14.4 shows us that something of this kind did go on between 1967 and 1969 — or, more cautiously, that changes in the perception of the party most likely to do what was needed were sometimes matched by changes in party support. Within the groups whose perception of the best party to solve problems did not change between 1967 and 1969 there was a small net swing to Labor, the same kind of small 'conversion' that we saw in Figure 13.2. But among those whose perceptions suffered a polar change between 1967 and 1969 there was in many cases an appropriate change in vote also. It is especially important that there was a large swing *to* the Liberal and Country Parties among those who now saw the coalition rather than the ALP as best able to solve problems, because the period from 1967 to 1969 was, as we have seen, one in which the Labor Party improved its position. The number of respondents who did change sides in this fashion is not large, and the change observed is yet another of the familiar balancing kind: we have here further explanations of the stability of the party system. Table 14.5 repeats the comparison, this time using the respondent's vote in 1966 rather than his intended vote in 1967. Again there is balanced movement, and we see the bulk of the Labor Party's additional support coming from those who were already convinced that the Labor Party was better than the coalition as a solver of important problems.

Table 14.4   The swing to Labor, 1967 to 1969 by attitudes to parties as problem solvers

| Party most likely to do what is needed, 1967 | Party most likely to do what is needed, 1969 | |
	Lib.-CP %	Labor %
Lib.-CP	+2 (N = 89)	+14 (N = 37)
Labor	−34 (N = 32)	+2 (N = 246)

Note: This analysis is restricted to respondents who (i) would have voted for one of the Liberal, Country or Labor Parties in 1967, and voted for one of them in 1969, and (ii) nominated either the Liberal, Country or Labor Parties in 1967 and 1969 as the party most likely to do what should be done with respect to the problem or problems cited. The percentages in the cells represent the arithmetic difference between the Labor Party's share of the vote on each occasion within the categories defined by the rows and columns.

Table 14.5   The swing to Labor, 1966 to 1969, by attitudes to parties as problem solvers

| Party most likely to do what is needed, 1967 | Party most likely to do what is needed, 1969 | |
	Lib.-CP %	Labor %
Lib.-CP	+2 (N = 85)	+29 (N = 38)
Labor	−25 (N = 26)	+10 (N = 238)

Note: See the corresponding note to Table 14.4. 1967 report of 1966 vote.

To search for more detailed evidence about the nature of change among these data would be profitless, for the number of cases is already small. Let us therefore turn to a single issue about which we have available the opinions of virtually all members of both samples — Australia's military involvement in the war in Vietnam.

The Case of Vietnam

If there was one issue that dominated Australian politics in the second half of the 1960s it was the question of Australia's part in the war in Vietnam. It was the cause of many protest demonstrations and marches, 'sit-ins', and much civil disobedience; it was at least one of the principal subjects for discussion at the elections of 1966 and 1969, especially the former; and it was a question on which for most of the time the position of the government was very different from that of the opposition. Indeed, it was probably the only major question that satisfied the criteria for being potentially influential noted above: the parties had distinctive policies, the electorate knew something about the matter, and its support, as we shall see, was placed heavily on one side.

Yet the issue was manifestly of small *moment* to most of the electorate, or, more accurately, it was of less moment than many other issues or problems. Not long before the 1966 elections Vietnam attracted only 8 per cent of nominations in an APOP survey of issues likely to be important to respondents personally when they voted. Table 14.1 suggests that the matter remained at that level of salience in 1967 and 1969. In these years the distribution of opinion about Australia's role in Vietnam was as set out in Table 14.6. This too suggested a stable division of opinion, with

Table 14.6 Attitudes to Australia's role in the war in Vietnam, 1967 and 1969

		1967 %	1969 %
(A)	We should have troops fighting in Vietnam, including conscripts	28	24
(B)	We should have troops in Vietnam, but only volunteers	43	43
(C)	We shouldn't have any troops in Vietnam, and only send civilian experts	8	12
(D)	We should stay out of Vietnam altogether	16	18
	Don't know/no opinion	5	3
Total		100	100
(N)		(2047)	(1869)

Note: Each respondent was handed a card on which the four lettered alternatives were printed and asked to choose the one closest to what he or she felt should be done. (Questions 16a in the 1967 questionnaire and 18a in the 1969 questionnaire.)

perhaps a very slight overall move in 1969 towards withdrawal. But analysis of the attitudes of those respondents interviewed both in 1967 and 1969 showed considerable individual movement: only 55 per cent stuck to the position they had adopted in 1967, while 25 per cent were more 'doveish', and 20 per cent were more 'hawkish'.

In one further respect there had been considerable change. In both 1967 and 1969 respondents were asked to relate the four policy positions on Vietnam to the government parties, Labor and the DLP. There was considerable uncertainty about the positions held by the ALP and especially by the DLP in 1967, but two years later the parties were seen in sharp relief: 87 per cent correctly identified the government as supporting involvement, including conscripts, and 78 per cent had the Labor Party in favour of complete withdrawal or at least a position of civil aid only.[6]

We need one further datum before embarking on an analysis of the extent to which attitudes to Vietnam were involved in changes of party support. Figure 14.1 displays the distribution of attitudes to the war in Vietnam by party identification, in 1967 and 1969. Here too there was

Figure 14.1   Attitudes to the war in Vietnam, by party identification, 1967 and 1969. A = Australia should have troops in Vietnam, including conscripts; B = Australia should have troops in Vietnam, but only volunteers; C = Australia should have no troops in Vietnam, only civilian experts; D = Australia should not be in Vietnam at all.

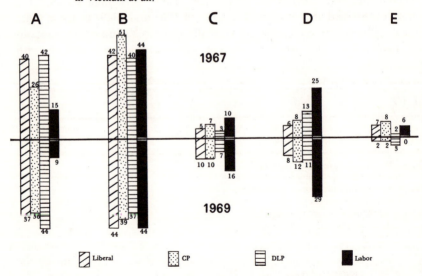

6 One third of the 1969 sample correctly placed the DLP alongside the government — twice the proportion who had done so in 1967. This is strong testimony to the sharper focus in which the conflict was viewed in 1969, especially given that the DLP attracted little comment as a party (Chapter 4). The greater unanimity about the ALP's position was a response also to a hardening of attitude within the Labor Party. In 1966 the party's policy was somewhat equivocal, but by 1968 it had come out firmly for withdrawal.

considerable apparent stability. Few Labor supporters liked the idea of using conscripted soldiers in an overseas military venture (Labor has an official aversion to conscription for overseas military service which dates from the war of 1914-18) and their number declined over the two years. On the other hand, almost half of all Labor partisans at both times supported military involvement provided the force consisted of volunteers. Yet, as we have seen, the lack of change in the proportions supporting the four alternative policies masks a considerable amount of movement in the positions taken by individual respondents. To what extent was this movement accompanied by a change in the party supported in elections?

One answer is provided by Table 14.7, which presents the swing to Labor between 1967 and 1969 among groups of respondents defined by their attitude to Australia's part in the war in Vietnam. The format is similar to that employed already in Tables 14.4 and 14.5. The message of Table 14.7 is a simple one.

Among those whose attitude to Australia's participation in the war became more 'doveish' between 1967 and 1969 — those in the top right hand corner of the table — there was a swing *to* the Labor Party, while among those whose positions became more 'hawkish' there was a swing *away* from the Labor Party. Moreover, among those who stuck to the government's policy — those supporting intervention with conscripted soldiers — there was also a swing to the government.

Table 14.7 The swing to Labor, 1967 to 1969, by attitude to the war in Vietnam

Respondent's Attitude in 1967	Respondent's Attitude in 1969		
	Supports Involvement, Including Conscripts %	Supports Involvement, Volunteers Only %	Opposed to Involvement %
Supports Involvement, Including Conscripts	−3 (N = 173)	+7 (N = 110)	+11 (N = 49)
Supports Involvement, Volunteers Only	−2 (N = 62)	+6 (N = 329)	+6 (N = 119)
Opposed to Involvement	** (N = 11)	−8 (N = 67)	+5 (N = 179)

** = number too small for percentage to be meaningful

Note: The analysis is restricted to those who had an opinion on the war in both 1967 and 1969, and who would have voted for the Liberal, Country or Labor Parties in 1967 and voted for one of these parties in 1969. Those who held alternative C — no troops, but civilian experts — are classed as being opposed to involvement.

It is plausible to argue, then, that Vietnam was an important issue in electoral terms, although we cannot from this evidence say confidently that the change in attitude to the war caused the change in vote. What is more, we can make some rough estimates of the issue's importance. Of the respondents counted in Table 14.7, 7 per cent underwent both a change in attitude to the war and a change in vote. If we subtract from their number those whose attitude change and vote change were discordant, that is, those who became more hawkish but changed from Liberal to Labor, for example, and subtract another group of the same size in order to allow for vote switchers whose change of heart was not connected causally to the war at all,[7] we arrive at an estimate of about 3 per cent for a group which might be labelled the 'Vietnam switchers'; two thirds of them went to the Labor Party. Labor's net gain of 1 per cent falls within the 1.6 per cent that Labor actually won through conversion in this period (Figure 13.2). It is possible that Labor's gains here were offset elsewhere, and we cannot make bold claims for the significance of Vietnam in Labor's recovery. Nonetheless, we can say that, on balance, changing attitudes to Vietnam in the period 1967 to 1969 were a material aid to the ALP.

And that can be said with even more force about the period 1966 to 1969, as Table 14.8 reveals. The addition of the coalition's bad year,

Table 14.8 The swing to Labor, 1966 to 1969, by attitude to the war in Vietnam

| Respondent's Attitude in 1967 | Respondent's Attitude in 1969 | | |
	Supports Involvement, Including Conscripts %	Supports Involvement, Volunteers Only %	Opposed to Involvement %
Supports involvement, including conscripts	+ 1 (N = 170)	+ 16 (N = 108)	+ 19 (N = 46)
Suports involvement, volunters Only	0 (N = 62)	+ 12 (N = 330)	+ 13 (N = 124)
Opposed to Involvement	** (N = 10)	0 (N = 69)	+ 11 (N = 180)

** = number too small for percentage to be meaningful
Note: See note to Table 14.7. 1967 report of 1966 vote.

7 The logic of this step is similar to that set out in note 3. Those with discordant attitude and vote changes clearly fall outside the universe we are examining. But we have seen that attitudes can be very lightly held, and it is therefore highly likely that among those whose attitude and vote changes were in harmony there are some for whom this association is accidental. The only estimate we have of their number is that provided by the 'discordants', so we use it.

1966-7, increases the swing to Labor, but the pattern of Table 14.7 is still present: a change towards support for Australian participation is associated with a nil swing to Labor, while a change towards withdrawal is associated with quite large swings *to* Labor. Of the sub-set of the sample represented in Table 14.8, 7 per cent changed both their attitude to the war and their party support, and after making subtractions for those whose changes of attitude and party appear to be accidental, we are left with an estimate of about 4 per cent for the contribution of the Vietnam issue to Labor's increase in support — or rather less than half of the party's gain through conversion in the period 1966 to 1969.[8]

No other domestic or foreign issue had the apparent importance of Vietnam in the period under study, and no other issue about which we have evidence satisfies the criteria for influence. The question of government financial aid to private schools, which was of great concern to those actively engaged in politics throughout the 1960s, failed the test of recognition of party difference: the great majority of respondents in 1967 did not know what the various parties' stands were.[9] But there is one issue that remains permanently alive, whatever party is in power, and that can make and unmake governments — at least by common agreement. This is the control and 'performance' of the economy, and we turn now to consider it.

The Economy as an Issue

J.B. Chifley, Labor Prime Minister from 1945 to 1949, is credited with coining the phrase 'the hip-pocket nerve' to account for the electorate's sensitivity to economic conditions. The phrase has survived him: in commentaries on Australian politics the state of the economy is invoked constantly, and various aspects of it are credited with great political potential. Thus inflation was thought likely to displace the Whitlam government in 1974, while the 'credit squeeze' of 1960-1 was widely seen as the cause of the coalition government's near defeat in the 1961 elections. Those in power gaze anxiously at the unemployment rate, which must not rise above so many per cent lest the government be toppled. They also claim all the credit for the good times, even when the cause is manifestly external, like oil or mineral discoveries.

There is, of course, no lack of evidence that the electorate *is* concerned about the economy and that it reacts quickly when economic conditions are dismal. All but one of the several Australian governments, state and

---

8 It must be emphasised again that too much reliance should not be placed on the validity of these calculations and estimates. The number of respondents is small, the causal connections are provided by the author and not by the data, and the estimates of random association are unverifiable. Nevertheless, to have come so far and not made an attempt to measure the importance of the Vietnam issue would have seemed a great shame!

9 Questions 28a to 28d in the 1967 questionnaire.

federal, that went to the people between 1929 and 1932, the worst years of the Great Depression in Australia, were decisively defeated. The economy is one of the principal actors whose activities are monitored in the newspapers, the more because of Australia's dependence upon an often unpredictable overseas trade situation. Party leaders constantly talk about the economy, and their attention to it is mirrored in the extent to which respondents in 1967 and 1969 were prepared to introduce taxation, unemployment, the cost of living, overseas investment, or assistance to primary industry as important problems, or (to a lesser degree) to include them in their responses to the questions about parties. The economy is most definitely an issue, at all times.

Yet, it is obviously a very different issue from one like Vietnam, where there were clear alternatives which separated parties and voters. In the case of the economy the alternatives are good times and bad times, and virtually everybody prefers good times, just as they are for motherhood and against germs. It follows that the electorate's choice between the parties on this issue will be fundamentally affected by questions of party

Figure 14.2   Working days lost through strikes, and unemployment, 1966 to 1969. *Source:* Commonwealth Bureau of Census and Statistics, *Quarterly Summary of Australian Statistics: Seasonally Adjusted Indicators.*

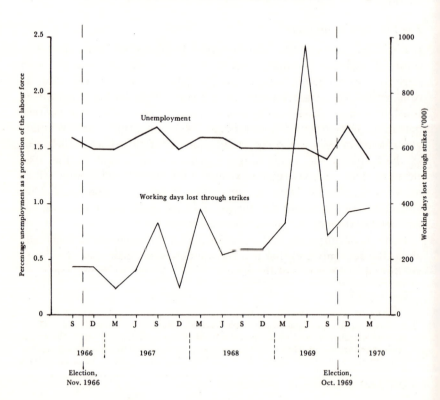

competence, just as they will help to determine those questions. It is surely no accident that there were generally approving descriptions in 1967 of the Liberal Party as a good manager of government: the coalition had then been in power for eighteen years of almost continuous and expanding prosperity.

Such considerations clearly make it difficult to decide whether or to what extent changing economic conditions produce electoral change. And our task in doing so is not helped by the fact that between 1966 and 1969 the economy was in a continually healthy and flourishing state. Figure 14.2 shows that unemployment remained steady at a relatively low rate of around 1.5 per cent, and while the index of working days lost through industrial trouble rose steadily it remained within bounds that seem very low in comparison with the turbulent 1970s. Figure 14.3 shows that prices rose slowly during the period, but that average weekly earnings rose more quickly. In sum, the late 1960s was a pleasant and comfortable time of economic prosperity; the precipitate inflation of the 1970s was yet to come.

Figure 14.3 Wage and price movements 1966 to 1969. *Source:* Commonwealth Bureau of Census and Statistics, *Quarterly Summary of Australian Statistics.*

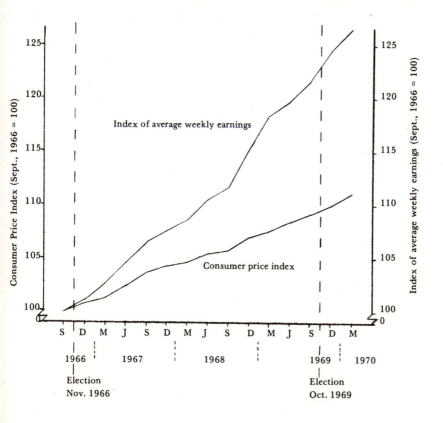

A buoyant economy breeds confidence. In 1967 41 per cent of the sample expected to be better off in three or four years' time, and only 13 per cent expected to be worse off; in 1969 44 per cent reported that they were better off than they had been three or four years before, while 14 per cent said they were worse off.[10] The balance in each case was made up of respondents who did not expect their economic well-being to change, or reported that it had not changed. The extent to which respondents connected the output of governments to their own prosperity was somewhat unclear. Certainly there was acceptance of at least a nominal nexus: in 1967 and 1969 some six respondents in ten were prepared to say that what the federal government did made a difference to how well off they were. But when asked in 1967 to account for their expectations of future prosperity or woe, they rarely made explicit references to the work of government in their answers, as Table 14.9 reveals.

There were, however, some faint janglings of the hip-pocket nerve. Those who expected things to get better had personal or close-to-home explanations: a promotion was in the offing, salary increases or overtime would boost income, children were growing up and leaving home and thus releasing money for other things. But those whose expectations were less rosy — and especially those who thought that things would get worse — tended to put more of the responsibility elsewhere, on the economy in general, or on government decisions. And they included a somewhat higher proportion of Labor than Liberal or Country Party supporters, which can be accounted for without difficulty on grounds of the greater vulnerability of the poorly off to gross economic changes.

When 'the government' was given a party label, however, partisan differences became much more pronounced. In 1967 one in three Liberals,

Table 14.9   Expectations of future prosperity, 1967

| | Looking ahead 3-4 years, respondent expects to be | | |
Because of	Better off %	No different %	Worse off %
Changes in income or occupation	57	46	31
Changes in expenditure patterns	29	26	23
Changes in the economy in general	11	20	36
Actions of government or political parties	3	8	10
Total	100	100	100
(N)	(795)	(614)	(272)

10 Question 33a in the 1967 questionnaire and question 34 in the 1969 questionnaire. Respondents who were uncertain or without opinions were excluded.

but only one in nine Labor supporters, thought that the *Liberal* government in Canberra had made them better off, and the prospect of a hypothetical Labor government increased the disparity (Table 14.10). Virtually no Labor supporter expected to suffer as a consequence of Labor rule, and hardly a Liberal looked forward to it in terms of personal prosperity. The economic consequences of changing rule are seen by partisans of both sides in the crudest black and white. This simple model is, of course, one encouraged by the parties themselves in their day-to-day commentaries on each other's performance in economic affairs.

But to what extent was felt or expected economic change associated with changes in party support? The answer is not one that fits the traditional account of the relationship between prosperity and party support. At both points in time, both the experience and the expectation of economic well being were associated with, if anything, greater swings to the Labor Party, rather than increased support for the coalition government. The sharpest contrast is provided by Table 14.11, which presents the swing to Labor between 1967 and 1969 among groups of respondents defined by how well they thought they had fared economically over the past three or four years. There is no hip-pocket nerve at work here, and the most

Table 14.10 Expected prosperity under a Labor government, by party identification, 1967

A Labor Government would make Respondent	Party Identification			
	Liberal %	CP %	DLP %	Labor %
Better off	7	0	20	50
No better off	48	61	36	47
Worse off	45	69	44	3
Total	100	100	100	100
(N)	(438)	(72)	(25)	(323)

Note: Question 34c in the 1967 questionnaire

Table 14.11 Swing to Labor 1967 to 1969, by experience of prosperity

	Respondent thinks he is now		
	Better off %	No different %	Worse off %
Swing to Labor 1967-9	+7	+1	+1
(N)	(480)	(173)	(503)

plausible explanation, given the discussion so far, is that in good times those who expect to grow more prosperous find it relatively easy to plump for a change in government, while those who are experiencing economic difficulties are frightened of any change in the status quo that might worsen their position. But again, it would be unwise to build too elaborate a structure on these data. There was considerable party changing in both directions in each of the categories of Table 14.11, and no simple explanation is likely to be sufficient.

We can at least say, nevertheless, that on the evidence prosperous economic conditions will not aid a government if other factors are working against it. Indeed in such circumstances it is possible that prosperity will be a positive disadvantage, in that the prosperous voters begin to take their prosperity for granted.[11] To see what other factors were working for and against the rivals for office, we move to a consideration of the change in the composition of party images between 1967 and 1969, and in particular consider the role and drawing power of the party leaders in the same period.

---

11 A theme explored in my 'Private Wealth and Public Squalor: an uneasy electorate', *Meanjin Quarterly*, **28**(119), Summer 1969.

15 The Changing Pull of Parties and Leaders

I thought Mr Gorton made reasonable promises which I think he could have carried out, and no false promises, whereas Mr Whitlam made a lot of promises which I don't think the country could afford and would make things very hard. (*wife of mechanic, forty-one, Queensland*)

In Chapter 4 we observed that the images of the parties that were held by the electorate were composed of very many elements, among which leadership, competence, ideology, policy and relationship to important social groupings were the most important. Since few of these elements are subject to rapid change it would be surprising if the composition of the images changed rapidly over a two-year period. Yet the balance of a party's image — the extent to which positive or favourable elements outweigh negative ones — is likely to be in a state of continuous movement, corresponding to ground gained and lost in the constant tug-of-war between the parties for political supremacy. Furthermore, a careful scrutiny of changes in the composition of the images should help us to account for changes in their balance, and thus indirectly some of the causes of electoral change.

But we cannot press such evidence too hard. Familiar problems of causality abound: in many cases it is as plausible to suppose that a change in party identification leads to a reappraisal of parties' good and bad points as to suppose the reverse. And we cannot always be sure that the changes we observe in the composition of party images are not the somewhat artificial and ephemeral results of the noisy excitement of an election campaign. The more substantial and enduring changes, we might suppose, are those that result from the passage of time, the departure of leaders, the ending of wars, the failures of governments to deal with crises, and so on. It is not always clear what those changes are.

Changing Party Images, 1967-9

These sober cautions are a necessary introduction to a comparison of the images of the parties, and of their leaders, between 1967 and 1969. In October 1967 there was relative electoral quiet, and the Labor Party had made, as we have seen in Chapter 13, a considerable recovery from the disastrous election of 1966. Two years later that recovery had slowed down, and the coalition had survived the 1969 election with a small majority; the respondents were interviewed very soon after the election. Table 15.1 presents a comparison of the simple frequency of response to the separate sets of questions about parties that we have explored before, and the corresponding sets of questions about the three major party leaders. [1]

There is strong evidence here that one consequence of an election situation is an increase in the visibility and importance of parties and their leaders. We shall see in the next chapter that the significance of politics as 'news' and the stuff of private conversations rises considerably during an election campaign, and Table 15.1 is certainly consistent with that finding. With one important exception, each of these political actors attracted the increase in comment. The exception is the Liberal Leader — Harold Holt in 1967, and John Gorton in 1969; it is probable that the explanation lies in the relative newness of both men. Holt had been Prime Minister for only two years before his death, and Gorton, almost unknown before his election as Leader of the Liberal Party, had served rather less than two years in the office when the 1969 round of interviews took place. Gough Whitlam was, by contrast, Leader of the Opposition for virtually the full term of the 1966-9 parliament, and had been a notable and newsworthy Deputy Leader for some years before that. [2]

With increased exposure came a greater measure of criticism, in all but

Table 15.1 The changing salience of parties and leaders, 1967 to 1969

| | Average No. Themes Associated with Parties and Leaders | | | |
	1967	1969	Change	%
Liberal Party	1.38	1.71	+0.33	+24
Labor Party	1.42	1.78	+0.36	+25
Country Party	0.58	0.70	+0.12	+21
Democratic Labor Party	0.61	0.73	+0.12	+20
Holt-Gorton	1.56	1.62	+0.06	+ 4
Whitlam	1.24	1.54	+0.30	+24
McEwen	0.64	0.86	+0.22	+34

Note: Each entry for the years 1967 and 1969 represents the total number of themes, favourable and unfavourable, associated with each party or leader, divided by the number of respondents in each sample.

1 The leader questions were 12a to 14b in the 1967 questionnaire, and 14a to 16b in the 1969 questionnaire. An early pretest revealed that Senator Gair, the parliamentary leader of the DLP, was too little known to warrant a search for the elements of his image.
2 Respondents in 1969 may also have felt some difficulty in making up their minds about the Prime Minister, who was something of a change from the pattern of Australian non-Labor Prime Ministers. If so, their confusion was shared by many who were able to observe Mr Gorton closely!

one case (Table 15.2). The Labor Party alone improved its position; the other parties, and all the leaders, were seen on balance more critically in 1969 than had been the case in 1967. We may note also that the Labor gain in standing and the Liberal loss were of much the same size, and that there was a greater decline in the standing of the Liberal Leader than in that of Mr Whitlam, two thirds of the references to whom were still approving.

Election campaigns are occasions for almost continuous criticism (a fact lamented by many respondents), and the improvement in Labor's showing is thus the more remarkable. It is time to examine it more closely. Table 15.3 sets out a summary of the change in the Labor Party's image between 1967 and 1969, by comparing the proportion of favourable references about the party in each of the major categories used in Chapter 4.

Table 15.2 The changing balance of opinion about parties and leaders, 1967 to 1969

| | Proportion of Favourable References | | |
	1967 %	1969 %	Percentage change
Liberal Party	49	44	—10
Labor Party	43	48	+12
Country Party	56	54	— 4
Democratic Labor Party	36	33	— 8
Holt-Gorton	53	42	—17
Whitlam	78	67	—14
McEwen	75	64	—15

Note: Each entry for the years 1967 and 1969 represents the proportion of favourable themes about each party or leader of all themes; the percentage change is obtained by expressing the change from 1967 to 1969 as a percentage of the 1967 figure.

Table 15.3 The changing image of the Labor Party, 1967 to 1969

| | Proportion of Favourable References | | |
Reference Category	1967 %	1969 %	Change %
Leaders	49	61	+12
Management of Government	32	24	— 8
Ideology	30	43	+13
Foreign Policy	27	24	— 3
Domestic Policy	60	75	+15
Group-related Items	76	77	+ 1
Party-related Items	22	21	— 1
Other	42	58	+16

Note: The 1967 figures can be calculated from Table 4.5. The change is the simple arithmetic difference between the two measurements.

Labor's higher standing resulted from a number of separate improvements in image. Most important was the much greater contribution of domestic policy items. In 1967 domestic policy items had made up 10 per cent of the favourable references to Labor and 5 per cent of those unfavourable. Two years later domestic policy items made up nearly 30 per cent of a much larger set of favourable references; and they were only 9 per cent of those unfavourable. Most of the policy references were to Labor's stands on education, health and social services (especially pensions), which were matters emphasised in Labor's 1969 election campaign but not much referred to in current debate in 1967. A second important contribution was the increase in the proportion of favourable references to Labor's ideology and goals: here the principal cause was a marked decline in the numbers of respondents who referred disapprovingly to Labor's being 'too far left', or influenced by communists. Once again, the election campaign's concentration on pragmatic, middle-of-the-road policy proposals may have made such ideological criticism less obviously relevant. But it is probably true that by 1969 the Labor Party was less frequently tagged as 'communistic'. Part of the reason was Gough Whitlam's own effort to restructure his party (and by enhancing the position of parliamentarians within its councils and executives, to reduce the dominance of unions); part lay in the reluctance of John Gorton to indulge in the traditional broad-brush portraiture of the Labor Party as an unreliable group of power seekers 'tainted' by communism to which his predecessors had often resorted.

The final element in Labor's improved image was the high standing of the party's leadership. This owed not to any greater public acceptance of Gough Whitlam (indeed, by 1969, the unflattering references were beginning to become noticeable in number), but to the almost total eclipse of Labor's former leader Arthur Calwell. Calwell had attracted one in every ten hostile responses in 1967, but two years later that proportion had fallen to one in seventy.

Against these improvements in image resulting from changes in the perception and evaluation of domestic policies, ideology and leadership can be set three areas in which Labor's image relatively worsened. In 1969, but infrequently in 1967, many respondents criticised the party for making promises that it could not carry out, or that it would not keep. A young farm machinery salesman in Queensland made this criticism work directly to the Liberals' advantage: 'Mr Gorton doesn't make such a lot of promises and is therefore more likely to carry out those he does [make]'. Here the influence of the campaign is clear: Labor's tendency to propose large and detailed policy changes in most areas, and the Liberals' reply that the opposition would promise anything to gain office, were recurring themes in election campaigns of the 1950s and 1960s. A second area in which Labor's image did not improve was foreign policy. It attracted more blame than praise with respect to its policies on Vietnam and defence both in 1967 and in 1969, but in 1969 the margin was somewhat greater. Finally, the perception of Labor as a party that was disunited, riven by feud and faction, changed very little over the period. The number of references of this kind did decline by about a fifth, but the balance of opinion remained distinctly unfavourable to the party.

The transformation in the balance of the Liberal Party's image between 1967 and 1969 was not caused by an increase in the proportion of negative responses in every category. As Table 15.4 makes clear, the Liberal Party, like its principal rival, improved its image in some areas and lost esteem in others.

The principal source of the Liberal Party's lowered standing in 1969 was the much weaker pull of its leaders. Just as Labor gained by the departure of a former leader, Arthur Calwell, so the Liberals lost by the departure of Sir Robert Menzies. Nearly one in ten of the favourable references about the party in 1967 concerned Menzies; two years later only a few respondents mentioned him at all, half of them with approval, half without. In addition, the change from Holt to Gorton worked to the party's disadvantage. Neither attracted many favourable responses, but Gorton earned far more disapproval — indeed, he was responsible for nearly 10 per cent of the unfavourable references to his party in 1969. The joint effect of the decline of Menzies as a symbol and the transfer of power from the neutral Holt to the controversial Gorton transformed the perceived quality of Liberal leaders — the party's strongest asset in 1967, with two references in three favourable — to a distinct liability. There were few general remarks praising the quality of the people in the party, and more critical ones. Since this was a time when the quality of the Labor Party's leadership was seen to have improved markedly, the inter-party comparison in this central property of a party's image was very much in Labor's favour: in 1967, of all the unfavourable references made about leadership with reference to the two major parties, two-thirds were directed to the Labor Party; two years later the situation was exactly reversed. We return to a consideration of the matter of the importance of

Table 15.4   The changing image of the Liberal Party, 1967 to 1969

| | Proportion of Favourable Responses | | |
	1967 %	1969 %	Change %
Leaders	66	39	−27
Management of Government	64	55	− 9
Ideology	60	61	+ 1
Foreign Policy	29	52	+23
Domestic Policy	25	33	+ 8
Group-related Items	27	31	+ 4
Party-related Items	49	36	−13
Other	38	27	−11

leadership later in the chapter.

A second major cost to the Liberal Party, and one closely related to the nature of its leadership during this period, was growing disquiet about the party's unity and teamwork. There can be no doubt that the electorate prizes unity in its parties (in fact, we have seen that many respondents would value even greater unity within the party system — as in the amalgamation of the non-Labor parties or even wider mergers — and that it is alert to any signs of party or cabinet *dis*unity).[3] In 1967 it was the Labor Party that received the most criticism in this area, and we have seen that two years later Labor had not recovered much ground. But relatively Labor had improved, as in this period the Liberal Party had suffered a good deal of internal tension that did not pass unnoticed. Although the election of John Gorton had been well received within the party, his inexperience as a first minister and his impatience with the slow processes of collective decision making quickly produced stories of cabinet rows and personal quarrels. The consequences could be seen in the interview reports: remarks critical of the Liberal Party as a party were infrequent in 1967, but quite common in 1969.

Finally, the party attracted much more criticism and less praise in terms of its general performance and competence as a government. Respondents pointed to signs of complacency and extravagance, complained of inefficiency and bad decisions (like the purchase of the F-111 aircraft, which was in fact an election-eve decision of the Menzies government in 1963!) and spoke of a lack of confidence in the government. These themes had all been voiced in 1967, but they were more noticeable in 1969. And the supporting references — those praising the party for its role in government — were less frequent.

The most important gain for the Liberal Party came in the area of foreign policy, and in one connection, that of defence. The party's stand on Vietnam was on balance less of a liability to it in 1969 than it had been

---

3 Butler and Stokes argue (*Political Change in Britain*, p. 361) that whether the electorate prefers parties to be united or split is essentially an empirical question, and that there are plausible *a priori* arguments both ways. In fact, respondents' comments about disunity were overwhelmingly set in a context of disapproval. In any case, it would be astonishing if more than a handful of respondents prized a party because of its disunity: the universal tendency of politicians and reporters to see party or parliamentary disunity as a weakness makes it hard to imagine how it could be seen as a source of strength. In the terms of the argument put forward in Chapter 2, it seems that a united government or party is likely to persuade the electorate that politics and government are or will be in safe hands and can be forgotten, whereas disunity and disagreement are signs that problems are difficult and will require attention. Since the electorate has no love for difficult problems, it is understandable that it should like the appearance of unity and feel apprehensive about the prospect and consequences of disunity. *How* important unity and disunity are — whether, for example, they are more important than leadership — is of course an empirical problem, and a difficult one. Considering the two major parties only, and the 1969 as well as the 1967 responses, there were rather more than three remarks about leadership to every two about the parties' qualities as parties. This comparison proves very little, but it is perhaps better than nothing.

in 1967, but defence — building up Australia's strength, keeping the military forces at the ready, and the like — was the cause of much favourable comment. This too had been a theme during the 1969 election campaign (although John Gorton had initially played it down), and it had also been present in each preceding campaign since the war of 1939-45. Labor's penchant for an internationalist role for the Australian government and its public belief in the United Nations as a mediating and peace keeping agency ensured that defence was an area in which the non-Labor parties would always have a natural advantage. The fact that it required an election campaign to activate the advantage, however, does suggest that it could easily be ended, either by a period of Labor government in which Labor assumed the role of guardian or by a change in the international situation.

The Liberals' other improvements in standing were minor ones. The election campaign was undoubtedly responsible for making the public aware that the Liberal Party too had policies in education, social welfare and health, and enough respondents mentioned such items approvingly for the Liberals' adverse image in this area to be improved a little. Fewer respondents in 1969 than in 1967 referred to the Liberal Party as opposed to the workers or the friend of big business and monopolists. We may suppose that the election campaign provided such critics with more specific targets, just as it provided admirers of the ALP with better objects to admire (there was a similarly small decline in the numbers who praised Labor because it looked after the workers or opposed big business). Much the same explanation probably accounts for the same decline in the numbers praising or attacking the Liberal Party because of its ideology.

The changes in the images of the Country Party and the DLP warrant less attention, because the parties garner much smaller shares of the vote in elections than the big two, and they are not nearly so conspicuous in election campaigns. Furthermore, as auxiliaries of the Liberal Party they have been affected by the change in its fortunes. In 1969 references that linked both minor parties to the Liberal Party were much more frequent than in 1967; in both cases the balance of opinion became more unfavourable over the two years, and, with unimportant exceptions, in each category. The Country Party was criticised much more frequently for being sectional and having narrow interests, but this was offset by the great decline in the proportion saying that it was not a 'real' party. Both changes were presumably brought about by the stimuli of the election campaign, in which the theme of the Country Party's narrowness of outlook was part of Labor's repertoire — and in which the party was, in electoral terms, very real indeed, having held on to its seats while the Liberal Party lost more than a dozen of its own. The DLP attracted much more specific comment than had been the case in 1967, but most of it was hostile. Like the Country Party, it was less frequently charged with not being a real party — the running of candidates in elections is some kind of reminder of the seriousness of purpose of any party! — but it attracted more criticism of the kind 'it serves no purpose'. Again, like the Country Party, it was identified by many respondents with the Liberal Party — 'they're just Liberals'.

What are the messages of this set of comparisons for our understanding of stability and change? To begin with, the broad composition of the various images of party remained remarkably robust. At the beginning and end of a period of two years in which there was considerable electoral change the parties received much the same kinds of appraisal. Secondly, election campaigns add detail and specificity to these images. Though a further exploration of these images in a new period of electoral quiet, in 1971 perhaps, would have been needed to establish the point, it seems likely that when the stimulus of the election campaign is lacking, the images of the parties revert to a rather ideological, general form. But campaigns serve to reaffirm as well as to change. In stressing health, education, and social welfare policies in 1969 Labor was conforming to a widespread image of itself as the party interested in and favourably regarded for domestic policies, just as the Liberals' emphasis on defence and overseas alliances was in keeping with both its traditional pre-occupations and its image. Since the main issues of Australian politics have altered only in detail, party stands on these issues do not change much, and party images, which represent in large part general summaries of these stands, will not change much either.

Party images are variable, however, where other areas of interest to voters are concerned, and this was particularly the case between 1967 and 1969 with respect to leadership and management of government. The Liberals suffered a treble blow: they lost the value of the association with their party of their former revered leader, their new leader proved on balance to be a liability rather than an asset, and their opponents managed to live down a former leader who was an embarrassment. It cannot be doubted that these changes were electorally advantageous to the Labor Party, though it is vexatiously difficult to measure the advantage. Similarly the image of a party will suffer if it begins to bungle the administration of the country, and there develop doubts about the virtue and competence of its ministers; something like this appears to have happened to the Liberal Party between 1967 and 1969. (Even more may have happened before the interviews in 1967, which followed a series of bad mistakes, but we have, alas, no record of it.) The electoral effect of these blows, however, appears to have been offset to some degree by Labor's failure to convince electors that it would be any better, a failure engendered by the plenitude of its policies and promises during the campaign. It must be emphasised that analyses of this kind are unsatisfactory, especially where our interest is focused on who changed his party support and why. But we gain at least a feeling for the context of change, and further evidence of the extent to which party gains and losses in votes and, ultimately, seats are the net result of a complex process of balancing, in which some voters are moving away from a party, for their own good reasons, even as that party is gaining ground in the electorate as a whole.

Changing Leader Images, 1967-9

Those devoted partisans who would vote for Blind Freddy so long as he won the party endorsement presumably do not care who their party's leader is. But as the unforced answers to the questions about the various parties reveal clearly, there are very many voters who do care. It has probably been so since the beginning of party politics; in nineteenth century colonial politics the leader *was* the party. There is nothing surprising in this: it is neither irrational nor lazy for a voter to say 'I don't know much about policies and all that, but Mr So-and-So seems an honest man, I like the look of him, and in particular I like the way he talks about the poor people (or education, or the need for a bigger navy). . .' His judgment may prove to be wrong, but it is on the basis of such judgments that men and women buy houses and cars, contract marriages, and go to war. To respond to political leaders is an all-too-human syndrome. Moreover, politicians do so themselves. A well run, confident and energetic party will usually be found to possess an able and sensitive leader; parties collapse when their leaders are deficient or quarrel among themselves (which is to say that they are deficient).

To pay attention to the perception that the respondents had of the principal party leaders in the period under scrutiny is, therefore, an appropriate course of action. We would not expect wholesale changes in political outlook to flow from changes in party leadership, if only because we know that the principal link between the citizen and the political process is his stable loyalty to party, and that must in the nature of things survive many changes of leadership. What is more, there is ample evidence that many voters have only the haziest notions of who the leaders are. APOP surveys in the 1960s that asked for respondents' opinions as to who would be the right leader for the Liberal Party or Labor Party regularly produced large groups of voters who had no idea. The 1967 and 1969 surveys discovered very few respondents who could see past the titular head of the party when they thought of people in it; and there were many respondents who said nothing about the leaders even when their names were offered as a cue. But it is nevertheless possible that changes in leadership, or changes in the esteem in which a given leader is held, could lead to important shifts of allegiance in the party system. We now look at this possibility for the period 1967 to 1969, when there was a change in the leadership of the Liberal Party. The Labor Leader remained the same throughout, but, as we have seen, the electorate was not so enamoured of him at the end of the period as it had been at the beginning.

It would be surprising if the images of party leaders were composed of sharply detailed bits and pieces of policy and ideology. In a parliamentary system the governing party, not its leader, takes the credit and the blame for policy decisions, and we have seen that even party images are fuzzily edged and diffuse. What is true of the party is, in a sense, even more true of its leader. Table 15.5 illustrates the concentration of respondents on the perceived personal qualities of each of the three party leaders, and the lack of interest in or awareness of the connection of the leader to policy or ideology. Where such references were made, they were usually of the most general kind. There are some differences between the leaders in the extent to which personal qualities dominate over other characteristics, and these are discussed shortly, but the similarities are the more striking.[4]

We can expand the several images of the leaders by looking more closely at what it was about the leaders as men that the respondents liked and

Table 15.5   Content of likes and dislikes about leaders, 1967 and 1969

	1967 %	1969 %
Harold Holt/John Gorton		
Personal Qualities	78	87
Ideology and Policy Interests	18	8
Group-related Items, Other	4	5
Total	100	100
(N)	(3201)	(3037)
Gough Whitlam		
Personal Qualities	76	78
Ideology and Policy Interests	10	14
Group-related Items, Other	14	8
Total	100	100
(N)	(2547)	(2891)
John McEwen		
Personal Qualities	70	73
Ideology and Policy Interests	17	9
Group-related Items, Other	13	18
Total	100	100
(N)	(1321)	(1619)

Note: The Ns for this table represent the universe of comment made about each leader at each time of interview. Apart from the category of Personal Qualities, the other categories are those used already in the analysis of party images. Up to five themes were coded for each respondent.

4 Table 15.5 makes an interesting contrast to the corresponding British data (Butler and Stokes, *Political Change in Britain*, Table 17.4, p. 378). In Australia the leaders' personal qualities were in general some 10 per cent less important than in Britain. McEwen's role as Minister for Trade and the farmers' friend, and Whitlam's role in restructuring the ALP had no counterparts in Britain, but these matters by no means wholly account for the differences.

disliked. Table 15.6 sets out the nature of the favourable and unfavourable references to the personal qualities of the two Liberal Leaders. The double comparison emphasises that the death of Holt and his replacement by Gorton was by 1969 a cost to their party. Gorton drew less applause and much more criticism. His difficulties as a manager of men and as a speaker were more sharply observed than those of his predecessor. [5] In reading the comments made by respondents it is hard to shake off the feeling that Gorton was a much more notable public figure than Harold Holt — there is more specificity both in the praise and the blame. Furthermore, much of the personal evaluation was political in its content. Holt emerges as a friendly and decent man, but inexperienced and too weak. [6] Gorton was seen as a bad choice as Prime Minister, with a poor television and public manner, and a taste for croneyism. His alleged

Table 15.6   The personal qualities of the Liberal Leaders, 1967 and 1969

	1967 Harold Holt	1969 John Gorton
Qualities Liked		
Good man, leader, Prime Minister	267	188
Experienced, long public service, taken over well	170	43
Good speaker, like him on television	135	75
Honest, sincere, fair	132	278
Strong, decisive, courageous	34	64
Hardworking, efficient	81	40
Intelligent, able, shrewd	42	43
Handsome, rugged	62	19
Manner easygoing, informal	62	93
Likeable, friendly, I like him	190	139
Right age, not too young or too old	17	1
Educational background	23	19
Class or other origins	17	28
Family	34	7
War Service	1	58
Other personal qualities	73	107
Total references to personal qualities	1340	1202

5 Both men had a weakness for the interminable sentence, and neither had an interesting delivery. But Gorton may have made more public appearances; he was unquestionably involved in more controversy.

6 The extent to which each man was seen as experienced provides some insight into the public's awareness of senior ministers. Harold Holt first became a minister in one of Menzies's pre-war cabinets, and had been continuously in office since 1949, always in a senior position; he was treasurer from 1958. John Gorton was by comparison an arriviste. He did not enter parliament until 1951, first became a minister in 1958 and achieved a senior position only in 1966. Yet on balance it was Holt who was picked out as 'untried' and 'inexperienced'. The explanation is probably the dominance of Menzies throughout most of Holt's political career, and his absence during Gorton's rise.

indiscretions, which were made much of in 1969 in a sustained personal attack on the Prime Minister by Edward St John, a Liberal backbencher, attracted less than 5 per cent of the personal comments — though other respondents may have had these matters in their mind when making more obviously political judgments.

Gough Whitlam had been Leader of the Labor Party for some seven months when interviewing began in 1967. He was very widely seen as an attractive, fluent and honest man who would make a good Prime Minister. A few found him condescending, or too clever by half. But there was no mistaking the general admiration and respect that the new Labor Leader evoked. Two years, one election campaign and dozens of television appearances later the admiration was no less, but it was more precisely located. Almost one in every four compliments turned on Whitlam's abilities as a speaker, debater, a television performer; his sincerity and capacity to inspire confidence also received more attention. At the same time, a counterpoint of criticism, hardly evident in 1967, was now quite audible. Most of it centered on the Labor Leader's manner and style: he was too slick, too smooth; he denigrated his opponents; he was condescending and bumptious. But few doubted his ability or capacity for work

Table 15.6 (b)

	Holt	Gorton
Qualities Disliked		
Not a good man, poor leader, PM	95	252
New, inexperienced, hasn't taken over well	179	76
Poor speaker, poor on television	70	221
Dictatorial, capricious, has cronies		189
Dishonest, insincere, untrustworthy	61	110
Weak, indecisive, timid	81	136
Lazy, indolent, inefficient	85	35
Stupid, unintelligent, not able	11	34
Self-seeking, just out for himself	26	23
Not independent enough; defers to LBJ/Nixon	165	11
Not attractive, ugly, weak face	43	82
Uncouth manner, ungracious, conceited	117	202
Don't like him as a person; not likeable	94	85
Family; uses family for political purposes	61	3
Indiscreet in his private life		73
Other personal qualities	73	121
Total references to personal qualities	1161	1653

Note: This Table and Tables 15.7 and 15.8 present the actual frequency of each theme mentioned at each round of interviews, with the 1969 frequencies adjusted so that the sample size (1873) is set equal to that of the 2054 interviewed in 1967.

or strength of purpose. And although we lack a comparable picture of the liked and disliked qualities of Arthur Calwell, the man whom Whitlam replaced as Leader after the calamitous election of 1966, it is impossible to

Table 15.7 The personal qualities of Gough Whitlam, 1967 and 1969

	1967	1969
Qualities Liked		
Good man, good leader, would make good PM	387	324
Experienced, long public service, informed	81	20
Good speaker, good on television	192	403
Improvement on Arthur Calwell	42	37
Honest, sincere, fair, inspires confidence	152	217
Strong, decisive, courageous	128	84
Hard-working, efficient	61	72
Intelligent, able, shrewd	93	103
Handsome, vigorous	75	127
Manner dignified	55	99
Likeable, friendly; I like him	116	108
Right age, young, not old	58	10
Educational background	49	42
Class or other origins	5	3
Family	8	7
War Service	...	2
Other personal qualities	47	87
Total references to personal qualities	1549	1745
Qualities Disliked		
Not a good man, poor leader, would make poor PM	25	43
Inexperienced; not a good deputy to Calwell	40	13
Poor speaker, poor on television	40	58
Dishonest, insincere, untrustworthy, too smooth, slick	74	229
Weak, indecisive, timid	21	29
Lazy, indolent, inefficient	1	3
Stupid, unintelligent, not able	1	2
Self-seeking, just wants office, too ambitious	46	47
Unattractive	8	11
Manner unattractive, big-headed, condescending, aggressive	77	99
Don't like him as a person	38	41
Runs people down, a mudslinger	7	61
Other personal qualities	39	61
Total references to personal qualities	417	697

doubt that the accession of Whitlam to the leadership was a material contribution to the improvement in Labor's image.

John McEwen was the oldest and in parliamentary terms the most senior of the leaders. Born in 1900, he had entered Parliament in 1937, and like Holt, he served for a time in the pre-war non-Labor ministries. In 1940 he failed to be elected Leader of the Country Party by one vote, and from 1941 to 1958 served as the party's Deputy Leader, when he succeeded Sir Arthur Fadden as Leader and deputy Prime Minister. He too had been continuously a minister since the coalition had won office in 1949, and was

Table 15.8   The personal qualities of John McEwen, 1967 and 1969

	1967	1969
Qualities Liked		
Good man, good leader	164	206
Experienced, long public service, good Minister for Trade	62	84
Good speaker, good on television	47	38
Honest, sincere, fair, inspires confidence	159	239
Strong, decisive, courageous	42	68
Hardworking, efficient	58	58
Intelligent, able, shrewd	40	36
Manner dignified, grave	13	20
Age, appearance	9	19
Likeable, friendly, I like him as a person	68	47
Education, family, class background	16	12
Other personal references	20	40
Total personal references	698	867
Qualities Disliked		
Not a good man, poor leader	26	13
Poor speaker	18	31
Insincere, tries to fool people	6	17
Weak, indecisive	18	21
Lazy, indolent	4	7
Foolish, unintelligent	4	4
Physically unattractive	15	16
Too old, been in too long, out of date	38	134
Manner cold, unbending, dominating	19	87
Don't like him, not likeable	26	31
Self-seeking, just out for himself	7	10
Other personal references	28	38
Total references to personal qualities	209	409

generally thought to be one of the most able and certainly the most ruthless of the cabinet. When Holt disappeared in the surf he assumed office as Prime Minister, and his refusal for unstated personal reasons to serve under William McMahon, the Deputy Leader of the Liberal Party, made McMahon's election as Leader most unlikely. He retired voluntarily as Prime Minister when John Gorton won the leadership. As Tables 15.5 to 15.8 make plain, he was not as widely known as the leaders of the major parties, but as with Gough Whitlam the balance of opinion about him was very much in his favour. His period as Prime Minister and the circumstances surrounding it gave him an audience that he had previously lacked, but the extra exposure brought a greater measure of criticism. McEwen began to look his age at the end of the 1960s, and his rather stiff and simple style was in marked contrast to Whitlam's easy fluency. Much more than half of the critical references to him in 1969 were about his age or his manner. John McEwen had been a considerable plus for the coalition in 1967, especially in the country, but in 1969 his appeal was on the face of it a good deal weaker than it had been.

To determine the contribution of the changes in leadership appeal to Labor's electoral gain in 1969 is a task beyond the resources of the data available in the 1967 and 1969 surveys. But we can hardly doubt that it was important. At the same time, we should not lose sight of the fact that these were *net* changes: the now familiar pattern of balance was present here too. Some voters were enthusiastic about John Gorton, even though most were not; Gough Whitlam's detractors grew in number, even though the Labor Leader enjoyed a relative advantage. Let us now turn, finally, to the contribution of the most immediate and short-term of the influences of an election outcome — that of the candidates and the campaign.

16 The Candidates and the Campaign

As I was saying, around election and referendum time I take a bit of notice of political things, but otherwise I don't worry about it. (*house-wife, fifty-one, Coffs Harbour, NSW*)

Election campaigns, as we have seen already, focus the attention of the electorate on day-to-day politics, and do so in a fashion that is matched only by the unexpected extraordinary event — such as the drowning of a Prime Minister and the election of a man to replace him. It is, of course, difficult to ignore elections even if one wishes to. The news media, far more interested in politics than their audience, seize upon the campaign as a prime source of news. Parties and candidates buy up space and time for propaganda and publicity. Party workers and supporters knock on doors, thrust leaflets in letter boxes, daub slogans on walls, post bills, and deafen the suburbs from loudspeaker vans. The result is a heightened awareness of politics for the duration of the campaign and some little time afterwards. The extent to which this does happen is illustrated by Table 16.1, which provides a comparison of various indices of interest in politics, firstly during the relatively quiet time of 1967, then immediately after the election of 1969.

There are some important differences in the activities and attitudes that are affected by the campaign. Politics as 'news' and the stuff of conversation is most powerfully affected. Twice as many people talked about the campaign, and followed it on television, as had taken a similar interest in day-to-day politics in a non-campaign period. The campaign appears to sharpen the perceived differences between the parties and, to a lesser extent, the extent to which voters care which party wins the election. But it has least effect on the presence or intensity of that stable disposition to support one party or another which we have seen to underlie the voter's behaviour in elections.

Let us recall from Chapter 2 the three-fold division of the electorate into the active, the audience and the apathetic. The effect of a campaign, we may argue, is to provide a stimulus for the active, news and entertainment for the audience, and a reminder to the apathetic that they will have to vote soon. The data certainly suggest some such process. The overwhelming majority of those who had talked about politics in 1967 were talking about the campaign in 1969. And they were joined by more than half of those who had *not* found politics useful for conversation in 1969. The gradient is well suggested by Table 16.2, which explores the turnover in the respondent's interest in politics between 1967 and 1969. Examination of these other measures of political involvement suggests that the politically active group, whom we have seen to comprise about one-quarter of the electorate in normal times, rises to about a third of the electorate during election campaigns — a small increase. The audience grows to encompass rather less than one-half of the electorate while the apathetic group is reduced to the persistently apolitical,[1] approximately one-fifth of the electorate.[2]

Table 16.1   The heightened awareness of politics, 1967 to 1969

	1967 %	1969 %	Change
Proportion who ...			
talk much about politics [the campaign]	31	65	+34
follow politics [the campaign] on television	34	67	+33
follow politics [the campaign] in first newspaper read	40	58	+18
see 'some' difference in the parties	51	65	+14
have at least 'some' interest in politics	55	68	+13
see themselves in terms of left and right	29	37	+ 8
'care a good deal' which party wins	60	66	+ 6
see the parties in terms of left and right	20	25	+ 5
have some party identification	87	90	+ 3
have 'very strong' party identification	34	36	+ 2
follow politics [the campaign] on the radio	17	18	+ 1

Note: The base for these percentages is the proportion replying to each question; the change is the simple arithmetic difference between the two measures.

Table 16.2   The turnover in interest in politics, 1967 to 1969

	Respondent's Interest in Politics in 1967			
	Good Deal %	Some %	Not Much %	None %
Proportion having at least 'some' interest in politics in 1969	94	83	49	24

1 Plus those who, though normally interested enough in elections, regard the result as a foregone conclusion, or who for once are simply absorbed in other matters. Political apathy in no sense means social inactivity.
2 All of these proportions should be treated as cautious estimates: since political interest is likely to have been seen as a socially desirable attribute, some of the respondents will have overstated their real interest in politics. But that some such process occurs as a consequence of the election campaign can hardly be doubted.

The hullabaloo of the national campaign is the principal cause of the increase in attention to politics. But there is a further stimulus: elections bring politics to the local level, and focus attention on local people — members of parliament and their challengers — as well as on the Prime Minister and his challenger. It is to the importance of the local gladiators that we now turn.

Members and Candidates

In a parliamentary system based on single-member seats the member of parliament has an important relationship to a geographically well defined body of electors. They elect him; they can reject him. It is traditional for a candidate to emphasise his links with and past public service among those fellow citizens who are his electors, and parties — especially in the country — frequently go to considerable pains to secure a candidate with the 'right' local qualifications. Australian party leaders do not have the kind of influence their British counterparts have in finding another seat for a valued colleague beaten at the polls, or a place for a man outside politics whom it would be useful to have in the House. In most Australian constituencies local sensitivities must be respected.[3]

Yet a candidate's personal qualities are the final gloss on his image: essentially he is the standard-bearer of his party, and for most electors he is nothing more. And without the standard of one of the three major parties, he is nothing at all. In June 1973, of the 509 members of Australian lower houses, only five were independents, and the proportion of independents had been at this level for more than half a century. The much greater recall of the member's party than of his name at both federal and state levels is clear from Table 16.3. Despite the smaller size of his constituency (in 1969 federal constituencies were, at approximately 50,000, usually at least twice as large as those for the state lower house), the state member of parliament enjoys only a small advantage.

Given that little more than a third of the respondents could supply the name of the man or woman who represented them in Canberra it is hardly surprising that the other qualities or attributes of the MPs were little known. Only 37 per cent of those respondents whose MPs were ministers or

---

3 Of course, the House of Representatives, with 125 members in 1969, was less than one-fifth the size of the House of Commons, and Australian Prime Ministers also lack the useful power to create a vacancy by ennobling an MP, although something can be done by way of diplomatic appointments. Yet the number of clear cases in which a seat has been 'found' in Australia are remarkably small (W.M. Hughes and H.V. Evatt, when leaders of their parties, abandoned risky constituencies for safe ones, but this is not a privilege available to the rank and file). At the very least an aspirant must take his chance within his own state. Hughes, who moved from NSW to Victoria when changing seats in 1917, and E.G. Theodore, the former Premier of Queensland who entered federal politics *via* the NSW seat of Dalley in 1928, are the best known exceptions.

party leaders appeared to know of their member's position.[4] Only 21 per cent thought their MP had done anything for the constituency, and a tiny 4 per cent told of being helped personally.[5] Less than a fifth knew of their MP's attitudes about the war in Vietnam, or state aid to church schools, or the level of spending on social services. In general, the best known members were those in seats outside the metropolitan areas, where, in addition, they had more often been seen by their constituents (38 per cent in metropoitan seats had seen their MP, compared with 60 per cent elsewhere).

Despite the somewhat shadowy image of the MPs, or perhaps because of it, they were generally given benign evaluations by their constituents. Nearly three-quarters thought their MP was doing either 'a good job' or 'a fair job', and malcontents were uncommon. Not many could, however, give clear and detailed reasons for their judgment. A surprising proportion — 25 per cent — thought their member was 'upper-class'.[6] In short, to their own electorates federal MPs generally appear as somewhat remote and insubstantial beings, of high social status, who are doing a pretty good job.

Table 16.3   Knowledge of member's name and party, 1967

Proportion who knew . . .	Federal MP %	State MP %
member's name and party	33	36
member's name only	3	4
member's party only	33	25
neither name nor party	32	35
Total	100	100
(N)	(2017)	(1936)

Note: Question 58, 59, 65 and 66 in the 1967 questionnaire. The general abbreviation 'MP' is used here rather than the more precise alternative 'MHR' (Member of the House of Representative) because 'MP' is more useful in the text. A state 'MP' is more commonly referred to as 'MLA' (Member of the Legislative Assembly) — or, in South Australia and Tasmania, 'MHA' (Member of the House of Assembly).

4 The base for this percentage and those following is the group who knew either the name *or* the party of their MP. In the latter case the interviewer supplied the member's name before proceeding with the questions.
5 Again, the state member was rather better known: 33 per cent said he had done something for his electorate, and 9 per cent said they had themselves been helped by him. The division of functions between the state and federal arenas established by the Constitution (Sec. 51) means that it is the state member who has most of the 'roads and bridges' responsibility; and his federal colleague's principal contact with his electors comes in the fields of social services and immigration.
6 In answer to the question 'Would you say that he is upper-class, middle-class or working-class?'. Of those who were prepared to ascribe him to a class, 33 per cent nominated 'upper-class'. It is not clear from the data, of course, how much it is the man and how much his position that gives rise to this class label. Less than 1 per cent of the whole sample, it will be remembered, were prepared to label themselves upper-class.

On the face of it, MPs so regarded are not powerfully protected against a sudden drop in the popularity of their own party, and Mackerras, after an exhaustive study of the 'personal following' of Australian members of parliament, has estimated that very few metropolitan MPs bring more than 500 votes (or about 1 per cent of the electorate) to their side. In the countryside the importance of personal and local influences is greater, but they are rarely so large as to swamp those of party.[7]

But however small the advantage of incumbency, it is nevertheless an advantage that may be enough, in a close contest, to determine the result. Certainly MPs are likely to be better known than their challengers. In 1969, with an election fresh in their memories, nearly seven respondents in ten could tell the interviewer which of the candidates had been the sitting member, whereas only two in ten could run right through the list of candidates and their parties. To some extent this was a consequence of the poor visibility of the DLP candidates, many of whom appear to have conducted only the most nominal campaigns. Table 16.4 provides the contrast, and incidentally points again to the greater visibility of country candidates (who enjoy, because of the greater number of country than city television stations — and the correspondingly cheaper rates — greater access to television). Table 16.4 also emphasises the importance of the candidate simply as the bearer of his party's name: on this evidence it is possible that barely half the electorate has much idea of qualities, appearance or speaking ability of the major party candidates. This is not for any want of effort on the part of the candidates themselves, the great majority of whom devote themselves to becoming as well known to their electors as possible in the course of the campaign. On the whole, the electorate is partisan, already committed, and indifferent to the particular

Table 16.4   Visibility of candidates, by party, 1969

| Party of Candidate | 1969 Vote | | |
	Lib.-CP %	Labor %	DLP %
Liberal	63	48	58
Country	73	60	**
Labor	46	62	50
DLP	18	19	43

Note: Each cell contains the proportion claiming to have read or heard something about the candidate in question. Thus 58 per cent of DLP voters claimed to have heard or read something about the Liberal Candidate.
** Number too small.

7 See Aitkin, *The Country Party in New South Wales*, pp. 95-112; M. Mackerras, thesis in progress, Australian National University. The case of Al Grassby has already been noted (note 18, Chapter 9), but it should be noted that Grassby's base was the Labor vote in Riverina, which, apart from the election of 1966, had not fallen below 40 per cent since 1940. Grassby supplied the icing, not the cake.

claims of candidates.

There is, of course, an understandable tendency for the partisan elector to be sensitive to at least his own party's champion. But as Table 16.5 suggests, it is a tendency only. Some two in three Liberal-Country Party and Labor voters had read or heard something about their own candidates, whereas less than a half had done so with respect to their candidate's principal rival. And DLP voters may well have known *less* about their own candidate than they did about his opponents.

Voters and the Campaign

Australian national election campaigns are fought in a variety of arenas: national television and radio, the press, the separate states — where the state party leaders take up weapons to help their federal colleagues — cities, suburbs, towns, and villages. Each arena requires a different response from the parties, and involves different levels of the party's organisation.[8] But not much of this is apparent to the voter, and very few voters are themselves involved in the campaign. Because compulsory voting obviates the need for the parties to 'get out the vote' much more emphasis is placed in Australia than in Britain on propaganda designed to retain past supporters and convert the opposition, and this is most easily done through professionally devised advertising campaigns. Party branches are small in size, can-

Table 16.5 Hearing or reading about candidates, by 1969 vote

| Percentage who had . . . | Liberal | Candidate's Party | | |
		Labor	CP	DLP
read or heard something about the . . . candidate	55	53	67	20
seen the . . . candidate in person	13	13	15	3
seen the . . . candidate on television	20	16	30	7
seen the . . . candidate both in person and on television	8	6	21	1
not seen the . . . candidate at all	60	65	34	89
Total	100	100	100	100

8 I have discussed elections as a recurring organisational crisis for political parties in *The Country Party in New South Wales*, Chapters 13-15.

vassing (door-knocking) is uncommon, and little attempt is made to recruit teams of party workers. As a result, the voter is characteristically a recipient and not a campaigner. Only 2 per cent of the 1969 sample reported having worked for a party or a candidate, and most the those handed out 'how to vote' cards outside the polling booths on polling day. Other indices of activity were similarly low: 3 per cent had attended political meetings during the campaign, 3 per cent had made a donation, 5 per cent had been called on by a party worker. Twelve per cent claimed that they had tried to persuade others to vote a certain way: wives, friends, workmates and relatives received this attention in about equal proportion.[9] But as spectators and consumers of politics, as we have seen, they were considerably more important. Two thirds had followed the campaign on television or talked to others about it, and three quarters remembered seeing party advertisements; six in ten followed the campaign in the press, and half the sample read the pamphlets and leaflets that had been pushed into their letter boxes.

As a source of information about the campaign, television was more highly regarded than newspapers, especially in the country.[10] But television holds its audience captive to a greater degree than newspapers, and partisans were not able to shut out propaganda from the opposition, however they interpreted it. Table 16.6 demonstrates a remarkable similarity between Labor and non-Labor partisans in their reports of what party advertisements they had seen on television, and the rather greater visibility of DLP advertisments to DLP voters may be put down to the fact that for many Labor and non-Labor supporters, as we have seen, the DLP hardly existed.

Voters have more control over what is put in their letter box, as Table

9 A comparison of Australian and British data here is instructive:

	Australia 1969 %	Britain 1964 %
Talked about the elections	65	69
Tried to persuade others to vote a certain way	12	12

Whatever other effects compulsory voting has had, it has apparently not resulted in a decline in the proportions talking about the elections or attempting to persuade others. Perhaps the prevalence of national advertising and television is a more important consideration.

10 The range of nominations ('Of all the ways that you followed the election campaign, which one would you say you got the most information from?') ran: television, 46 per cent; newspapers, 33 per cent; television and newspapers equally, 9 per cent; radio, 7 per cent; other (combination), 5 per cent.

16.7 shows, but the differences are not great. Again, much depends on how much notice is taken of such appeals. Commonsense and the verdict of politicians themselves suggest that they are unimportant.[11] A Queensland housewife probably spoke for most of the sample when she told her interviewer: 'I have my own ideas on who I want to vote for, and I don't think what the other side says would make much difference.'

Nevertheless, if an elector is to change his vote, it is hard to imagine that he could do so in the absence of information. To put it another way, we would expect that those who are changing parties would be more sensitive to

Table 16.6 Exposure to television advertisements and speeches, by 1969 vote

Remembered advertisements and speeches of	1969 Vote		
	Lib.-CP %	Labor %	DLP %
Lib.-CP	58	57	49
Labor	29	30	33
DLP	13	13	18
Other	*	*	*
Total	100	100	100
(N)	(1286)	(1376)	(202)

(N) = total number of mentions
* = less than 0.5 per cent

Table 16.7 Exposure to campaign leaflets, by 1969 vote

Remembered reading pamphlets issued on behalf of	1969 Vote		
	Lib.-CP %	Labor %	DLP %
Lib.-CP	42	36	44
Labor	34	41	34
DLP	11	12	16
Other	13	11	6
Total	100	100	100
(N)	(603)	(407)	(50)

(N) = total number of mentions

11 'Leafletting' is an urban — suburban, more accurately — tactic, and an almost ritualistic episode in an election campaign. Whether it is done or not seems to depend as much on the vagaries of candidates and campaign directors, as on the safeness of the seat. The proportions who remembered reading leaflets varied as follows: marginal seats, 55 per cent; safe Liberal seats, 50 per cent; safe Labor seats, 50 per cent; Country Party seats, 32 per cent.

political stimuli than those who are not. This is not to argue that election campaigns produce great movements in the electorate — one of the earliest and best supported survey findings is that campaigns do not have such effects — but that a voter who has decided to support another party, or could conceivably make that decision, will be more alive to the currents of the campaign than a voter who knows perfectly well that he will vote as he has always done. Campaign propaganda and talk are thus involved in the process of change, even if the links are subtle and hard to explore.

This account of the role of the campaign is consistent with the data. Table 16.8 displays a greater swing to Labor — in two cases nearly twice as large a swing — among those who were exposed to campaign stimuli. Cumulating these indices sharpens the contrast (Table 16.9).

Election campaigns may indeed reinforce the party loyalties that the mass of citizens have — and in that way aid in preserving the stability of the party system. But in addition they provide an abundance of cues and stimuli for those whose partisan loyalties are undergoing change, or who have been deflected from their usual course by an issue important to themselves — and in that way contribute to change.

Table 16.8 Exposure to campaign stimuli, and the swing to Labor, 1966 to 1969

	Yes %	No %
Watched party advertisements or speeches on television	+10	+8
Read party leaflets	+12	+7
Talked to people about the campaign	+11	+6

Note: Each cell contains the percentage swing to Labor among those who voted for Labor, Liberal or Country Party candidates in both 1966 and 1969.

Table 16.9 Exposure to campaign stimuli, and the swing to Labor, 1966 to 1969; summary

Degree of Exposure to Campaign Stimuli	Swing to Labor 1966 to 1969 %
Those who read leaflets, followed the campaign on television, and talked about the campaign with others	+17.1
Those who did any two of these things	+13.2
Those who did one or none of these things	+ 9.8

'It's Time'

In 1972 the Labor Party chose for its campaign slogan the phrase 'It's Time', a sentiment which by general agreement was particularly appropriate to that election campaign. Yet it had been a regular theme in Australian elections since the mid-1950s, a consequence of the continuing rule of the Liberal-Country Party coalition. In 1967 and 1969 respondents frequently voiced this theme themselves in answer to questions exploring what they liked and disliked about the parties. In addition, the notion that in a parliamentary system there should be the possibility of regular alternation of governments is an axiom of democratic theory. At the time of the 1969 election the coalition government had been continuously in power for twenty years. To what extent were public attitudes to the question of alternation in office related to the swing that Labor enjoyed at the election?

Respondents in 1967 and in 1969 were asked 'Do you think that in Australia control of the government should pass from one party to another every so often, or that it's all right for one party to have control for a long time?' On both occasions many respondents felt bound to say that it all depended on which party you were talking about — they would not mind their own party being in control for a long time, but as for the other one ... The distribution of answers on the two occasions was identical: 54 per cent favoured change, and 46 per cent thought that long periods of control (whether explicitly qualified or not) by one party were all right. As we would now expect, that apparent stability of response concealed a good deal of movement, revealed in Table 16.10.

If we assume that most of this movement was random, that is, that those who changed their opinion did so only because they had no real view on the matters at either interview, and that such respondents were matched by an equally large group who managed by accident to give the same answer on both occasions, then those with genuine opinions on this question probably comprised no more than 40 per cent of the electorate, and among them the

Table 16.10 Turnover in attitudes towards alternation in government, 1967 to 1969

1967	1969		
	In favour of alternation %	Control for a long time %	
In favour of alternation	37	17	54
Control for a long time	17	29	46
	54	46	100 (N = 1334)

proponents of alternation were in only a small majority.

Nevertheless, this sentiment could become a rationalisation of a decision to change sides, or even an element in that decision. The evidence that this was indeed the case in 1969 is given in Table 16.11. Among those who had the same belief about the virtues of the alternation of parties in power the swing to Labor was approximately the same. But among those whose beliefs had changed the swing to Labor was very different: a good deal higher where the respondents now supported alternation, and correspondingly lower where they now favoured control by one party for a long time. At the very least, attitudes about the need for alternation of parties in power are related to shifts in party allegiance; our data do not allow us to press the point much further, which is a pity, since in 1972 the Labor Party may have owed its relatively narrow victory to a widespread feeling that the coalition had been too long in office.[12]

There have been few surprises in this chapter, and its message has been to emphasise once again the toughness of party identification: for most voters the clamour of the campaign is at best an entertainment, at worst an annoying distraction. A farmer in Victoria, commenting that there was 'not a damned thing' he liked about the television coverage of the campaign went on to complain that his precious relaxation time had been interrupted by election advertisements. The virtual irrelevance of the commotion of campaigns and candidates to the electoral decisions of the mass of the electorate can hardly be doubted. Yet campaigns provide the lead-up to polling day, when those who are going to change their partisan allegiance

Table 16.11   Attitudes towards alternation in government, 1966 to 1969

Attitudes towards Alternation in Government	Swing to Labor 1966 to 1969[a] %
Those in favour of alternation in both 1967 and 1969	+14.4
Those in favour of control for a long time by one party in both 1967 and 1969	+12.5
Those in favour of control for a long time by one party in 1967, but of alternation in 1969	+19.2
Those in favour of alternation in 1967, but control for a long time by one party in 1969	+ 5.0

[a] The percentage swing to Labor among those who voted Labor, Liberal or Country Party in 1966 and 1969.

12 See Butler and Stokes, *Political Change in Britain*, pp. 431-7, for a more extensive analysis of similar, though richer, data.

perform the act that registers that change. There is evidence that such voters are more receptive to the campaign than most of those whose allegiance is unchanged. Since each party is losing and gaining supporters, each party's campaign is important to the election outcome. But in what way, and to what degree, remains almost as much an uncertainty today as in 1940, when the first political scientists to make use of large-scale systematic surveys began to study the citizens of Erie County, New York.

17 Conclusion

If a metaphor is needed, consider the pot. Thrown on the wheel, it has a shape conferred by the potter's mood and purpose; once baked, it keeps that shape indefinitely, even when glazed, reglazed, cracked, patched or chipped. Broken, shards scattered, its shape and use can be reconstructed by a skilled archaeologist. So with party systems. That of Australia was formed over a comparatively short period of time at the turn of the century, and it has changed very little in the seventy-five years since. It is a simple system, embodying a simple social cleavage — that between the haves and the have-nots, both very broadly defined. There has been no need for anything more complicated: Australia has been and remains ethnically and socially homogeneous, its extremes of wealth and poverty are unremarkable, it lacks an established church and an aristocracy, and its regional and religious differences, though important, have been contained.

Even so, the party system was never just the expression of an underlying social cleavage. Had it been so Labor would have been at once in power, and remained there. For 'have-nots', to take that example, could be other things too — Presbyterians, or women, or country dwellers, or believers in the British connection, or individualists unhappy about Labor's collectivist ethic. To be successful — to gain the magic 50 per cent — parties had to appeal to the whole community. But to be many things to many men is to inspire doubts about one's integrity, and to be unsuccessful. Political parties have to put up with this dilemma, since they cannot much change the societies from which they spring. Yet the dilemma is a guarantee that no party will ever win the support of almost everybody—at least for very long.

So the parties adopted their respective forms very quickly, and stuck to them. Circumstances helped them to do so. The fundamental issues in Australian politics — immigration, defence, control of the economy, the spread of social welfare — have been on the agenda throughout the twentieth century. They are not, of course, finally solvable. A steady agenda, continuity in politicians, a simple and basic cleavage in society —

all this made for stability. Add in party identification and its transmission from one generation to the next, and the result is a stable *system*. Add in balancing changes — parties losing supporters even when gaining others, social changes which benefit both sides at different times — and the result is a very stable system.

Why was it so useful for the voter? Probably because politics and government in the twentieth century have become so difficult, so hard to comprehend. The common man arrived at his democratic inheritance at the beginning of a period of dramatic technological innovation, which brought in its train (and has in part been stimulated by) a growth in the reach and scope of central government. Edmund Barton's first federal ministry of nine watched over seven departments of state: seventy years later Gough Whitlam's team of twenty-seven administered thirty-seven departments. Moreover, modern Australian society is more diverse, or so it appears, than its counterpart in 1900. Australia's parliaments, state and federal, collectively put out several Acts a day. No citizen could pretend to understand them all, or even a large fraction of them. As the twentieth century has progressed, therefore, the difficulty experienced by voters in getting to grips with the day-to-day politics of their country has increased, and the utility of a steady party identification has increased accordingly.

For what are the alternatives? A careful assessment of promise and performance would involve an excessive opportunity cost in time and energy forgone. Single-issue stances attract very few, if only because governments have too little time to spend on any one issue, no matter how important it is to the concerned few. And society is too pluralistic for any issue to attract more than a small fraction of the electorate as partisans; if the issue *does* grow in importance, both sides of party politics will develop appropriate, and probably similar, policies with respect to it. The day of individual politicians, even the mightiest, has passed. No politician in national politics, and very few, if any, in state politics, are bigger than their parties. Even if they can survive the loss of party endorsement, they will continue in parliament as independents, ignored and irrelevant.

Some kind of party allegiance has become inescapable, and the coming and going of parties in power has been determined by shifts in that allegiance, and in the extent to which one party is luckier than another in gaining new supporters as they come of age, or unluckier in losing old ones through death. All this has been to reduce the importance of individual issues, candidates and election campaigns. Even such an issue as Vietnam, which appeared to convulse Australian society in the late 1960s, and occupied the mass media almost obsessively for a time, was in the end of small electoral moment. Leaders are important, but far more for their human qualities as perceived by the electorate than for their ideological stands or commitments to policies. We can judge men much more surely than we can judge proposed health schemes. A close election result, and Australia has known a number of them, can have been the consequence of an increase in the birth-rate twenty years before, an unexpected change in leaders, or the hullabaloo surrounding the defection of a Russian diplomat. Very often, of course, the result is not close, and can be more confidently explained: the governing party had done nothing much wrong, changes in allegiance balanced one another, partisans arrived in the electorate and left it without greatly disturbing the position of the parties, and so on. But there is still a residual uncertainty about almost any election result: in what sense does this represent 'the will of the people'? We have seen that the answer can hardly ever be a simple one.

The doleful note in these concluding remarks is not unconscious. The modern party system is a kind of democracy in action, and it works well enough most of the time. But to study the political consciousness and behaviour of a representative sample of Australians is to be left with the feeling that we ought to be able to do rather better. Too many citizens have acquired their political judgments without a thought as to their meaning or consequence. The parties, established forces in society, guaranteed a continued existence because of the political socialisation of children by their parents and their neighbourhood, have no wish to educate their supporters in the complex and frustrating business of politics as government. In turn, the voters ask merely to be left alone.

Ordinarily, to repeat, this division of labour works well enough. And ordinary times, for Australians of the mid to late twentieth century, have meant a peaceful and affluent society, in which political choices are comparatively painless: a bigger pie, rather than smaller slices. Yet these happy days are in no meaningful sense the birthright of Australians. Once before, in 1931, the Australian parties had to offer the electorate painful choices, and were reviled by a substantial minority for their lack of ability to do otherwise. It may be that the rest of the twentieth century will be noted more for the painful choices that are offered democratic electorates than the pleasant ones. On past experience the reaction of the Australian electorate, fed for the most part on ideology and personality and unused to debate or discussion, will be to declare a plague on both houses. The urge to find solutions through strong leaders, to obtain comfort by blaming, will be very great, as it was in the 1930s. But that, for democracy's supporters, is no solution at all.

This book makes clear that the foundation of Australian democracy is habit, not understanding. Yet the latter would be the more secure. The task of replacing habit (and its attendant, ignorance) with understanding and knowledge may be the most important business that Australian democracy has had to undertake. It is a measure of the difficulty of this task that one finds it hard to suggest whose responsibility it is, or where it should be begun.

Appendix

The Questionnaires

The questionnaires used in 1967 and 1969 belong to a family whose natal home is the Institute for Social Research of the University of Michigan, Ann Arbor. In particular they are descended from the questionnaires devised by David Butler and Donald Stokes and used in Britain in 1963, 1964, 1966 and 1970. Nevertheless, Australia is not Great Britain, any more than it is the United States of America, and the final shape of the questionnaires owed as much to the unique analytic perspectives of an Australian study as it did to the need to allow comparative statements to be made.

From the beginning the project was seen as a panel study, and in consequence the 1967 questionnaire was the primary survey instrument, just as the 1967 sample was the primary sample. The 1967 questionnaire was devised in 1966, and pretested in April 1967 in Yass and Sydney, New South Wales. A number of changes were made as a result of the pretest, and the questionnaire achieved its final shape in July 1967. The 1969 questionnaire incorporated most of the 1967 questionnaire, and was not separately pretested.

The Fieldwork

To discover and interview in a limited time 2000 electors spread across Australia requires a large staff of interviewers, and approximately 150 were used in each of 1967 and 1969. In 1967 most of the interviewers were drawn from the field staff of the Commonwealth Bureau of Census and Statistics, save in Western Australia and Tasmania, where a group of interviewers was formed and trained by members of the Department of Political Science, Research School of Social Sciences, Australian National University. Some highly successful follow-up interviewing (of reluctant electors) was carried out by members of the Department. Fieldwork began on 2 September 1967 and was completed by 27 November 1967; more than 90 per cent of the interviews had been secured by 17 October 1967.

In 1969 it was unfortunately not possible to use the Bureau interviewers as a single force. In Sydney, Melbourne and Brisbane fieldwork was organised by Australia Sales Research Bureau Pty Ltd, in South Australia by the Australian Broadcasting Commission's Audience Research staff, in Western Australia and Tasmania by the reconstituted teams of 1967, and in the rural areas of New South

Wales, Victoria and Queensland by interviewers individually hired and trained for the job, or by members of the Department of Political Science. Fieldwork began on 26 October 1969 and was completed on 1 February 1970. The Christmas holiday period made it difficult to secure some interviews until late in January 1970, but 90 per cent of the interviews were completed by 3 December 1969. In both 1967 and 1969, most interviews took between one and one and a half hours to complete.

The Samples

The 1967 sample has been described in some detail already, in Michael Kahan and Don Aitkin, *Drawing a Sample of the Australian Electorate,* Occasional Paper No. 3, Department of Political Science, Research School of Social Sciences, Australian National University, Canberra, 1968, and interested readers should turn to it. The sample was a self-weighting, multi-stage, stratified sample of the Australian electorate, with federal electoral divisions (constituencies) as the primary sampling units. The ground rules of the sampling operation were that Australian electors in the six states (the Australian Capital and Northern Territories were excluded, since they comprised in 1967 only 1 per cent of the Australian electorate) must as far as possible have an equal chance of selection in the sample, and the chance of any division or sub-division being selected must be in proportion to the size of its electoral population. Because of the co-operation of the Commonwealth Electoral Office it was possible to use the most up-to-date electoral rolls as the sampling frame and special procedures were devised to allow the selection of a new respondent when the intended respondent had left permanently the address given for him in the electoral roll.

The desired sample size was 2000. The results of fieldwork were as shown in Table A.1.

Table A.1   Results of fieldwork, 1967

	N	%
Interviewed	2054	80.5
Refused	370	14.5
Other non-response	128	5.0
Total approached for interview	2552	100.0
Dropped from sample		
Moved away from original address	280	
Original address non-existent or unlocatable	40	
Died	11	
Other	38	
Total dropped from sample	369	
Total contacts attempted	2921	

At the second round of interviews in 1969 another 148 respondents, originally selected in 1967, were discovered, or agreed to be interviewed having originally refused. Their addition brought the effective response rate to 86.3 per cent.

In 1969 the goal was to reinterview all those interviewed in 1967, to interview as many as possible of those selected in 1967 who had not been interviewed in that year, and to interview a sample of electors who had not been enrolled in 1967. The continued co-operation of the Commonwealth Electoral Office allowed the mailing of letters to those electors who had left their 1967 addresses, as well as the selection of a supplementary sample. It proved possible in 1969 to reinterview 71 per cent of those first interviewed in 1967, and the 1969 sample was made up as in Table A.2.

Table A.2 Composition of the 1969 sample

	N	%
Panel respondents — those interviewed in 1967 and 1969	1453	77.6
Respondents selected in 1967 but interviewed only in 1969	148	7.9
New respondents, selected and interviewed in 1969	272	14.5
Total	1873	100.0

The representativeness of these samples can be measured by comparing them both with the known distribution of electors by sex and by state, and with the result of the 1969 election (there is a discussion of the 1967 sample's recall of its vote in the 1966 elections in Chapters 10 and 11). On the evidence the samples are pleasantly representative of their populations. (Tables A.3 to A.5).

Table A.3 Sex distribution of electorate and of sample, 1967

	Electorate %	Sample %
Males	48.9	49.2
Females	51.1	51.8
Total	100.0	100.0
(N)	(6,182,585)	(2054)

The distribution of the electorate by sex is a statistic no longer published by the Electoral Office, but these details were published in the Statistical Returns relating to the Referendum of 27 May 1967, which took place some three months before interviewing began.

Table A.4 Distribution by state of electorate and of sample, 1967 and 1969

| | 1967 | | 1969 | |
	Electorate %	Sample %	Electorate %	Sample %
NSW	38	35	37	34
Vic.	27	29	28	28
Qld	15	14	15	15
SA	9	10	10	11
WA	7	8	7	8
Tas.	4	4	3	4
Total	100	100	100	100
(N)	(6,182,585)	(2054)	(6,521,764)	(1870)[a]

[a] Three respondents interviewed in Commonwealth Territories have been excluded.

Table A.5 Recall and reality: party voting in the 1969 federal elections, electorate and sample[a]

	Liberal	CP	DLP	Labor	Other	Total
Electorate	34.8	8.6	6.0	47.0	3.7	100.0
Sample	37.1	9.2	5.2	46.1	2.4	100.0

[a] Of those voting or claiming to have voted.

The 1967 Questionnaire

I am helping with a project being conducted in the Research School of Social Sciences of the Australian National University. We are talking to people here and all over the country about their feelings and opinions.

1(a)   First of all, what newspapers do you read regularly? [94% read news-paper/s regularly]

1(b)   Do you follow news about politics much in (NAME OF FIRST NEWSPAPER MENTIONED)? [Yes 43%, No 57%]

1(c)   Do you think that (name of first newspaper) tends to favour any particular party? What party is that?

1(d)   Do you think that (NAME OF SECOND NEWSPAPER MENTIONED) tends to favour any particular party? Which party is that?

2   Do you follow politics much on television? [Yes 34%, No 66%]

3   Do you follow politics much on the radio? [Yes 17%, No 83%]

4   Do you subscribe to any magazines or periodicals, or read them often? [Yes 53%, No 47%] Which ones are they?

5(a)   Do you talk much about politics with other people? [Yes 31%, No 69%]

5(b)   Who do you talk with?

NOW I WOULD LIKE TO ASK YOU WHAT YOU LIKE AND DON'T LIKE ABOUT THE POLITICAL PARTIES

6(a)   Is there anything in particular you like about the Liberal Party?

6(b)   Is there anything in particular you don't like about the Liberal Party? What is that? Anything else?

7(a)   Is there anything in particular you like about the Labor Party? What is that? Anything else?

7(b)   Is there anything in particular you don't like about the Labor Party? What is that? Anything else?

8(a)   Is there anything in particular you like about the Country Party? What is that? Anything else?

8(b)   Is there anything in particular you don't like about the Country Party? What is that? Anything else?

9(a)   Is there anything in particular you like about the Democratic Labor Party? What is that? Anything else?

9(b)   Is there anything in particular you don't like about the Democratic Labor Party? What is that? Anything else?

10   In general, would you say that there is a good deal of difference between the parties [30%], some difference [21%], or not much difference [38%]? [DK 11%]

11(a)   Do you think there once was a time when there was more difference be-tween the parties than there is now? [Yes 49%, No 23%, DK 28%]

11(b)   When was that?

NOW I WOULD LIKE TO ASK YOU WHAT YOU LIKE AND DON'T LIKE ABOUT THE FEDERAL PARTY
LEADERS

12(a)   Is there anything in particular you like about Mr Holt?

12(b)   Is there anything in particular you don't like about Mr Holt? What is
        that? Anything else?

13(a)   Is there anything in particular you like about Mr Whitlam? What is that?
        Anything else?

13(b)   Is there anything in particular you don't like about Mr Whitlam? What is
        that? Anything else?

14(a)   Is there anything in particular you like about Mr McEwen? What is that?
        Anything else?

14(b)   Is there anything in particular you don't like about Mr McEwen? What
        is that? Anything else?

15(a)   In your opinion, what are the most important problems the federal
        government should do something about?

15(b)   Which party would be the most likely to do what you want on (FIRST
        PROBLEM MENTIONED), the Liberals, Labor, Country Party, or DLP?

15(c)   Which party would be the most likely to do what you want on (SECOND
        PROBLEM MENTIONED), the Liberal, Country Party, or DLP?

16(a)   As you know, there is a lot of discussion around Australia about what we
        should be doing about Vietnam. Which of these statements comes closest
        to what you yourself feel should be done? If you don't have any opinion
        about this, just say so.
        (A) We should have troops fighting in Vietnam, including conscripts
        [28%].
        (B) We should have troops in Vietnam, but only volunteers [43%].
        (C) We shouldn't have any troops in Vietnam, and only send civilian
        experts [7%].
        (D) We should stay out of Vietnam altogether [16%]. No opinion/don't
        know [6%].

(IF R HAS AN OPINION)

16(b)   How strongly do you feel about this, very strongly [53%], fairly strongly
        [34%], or not very strongly [12%]? [DK 1%].

16(c)   Which of these positions would you say the government parties hold?
        [(A) 81%, (B) 3%, (C) 1%, (D) 0%, DK 15%]

16(d)   And the Labor Party? [(A) 7%, (B) 26%, (C) 14%, (D) 30%, DK 23%]

16(e)   And the DLP? [(A) 17%, (B) 8%, (C) 4%, (D) 6%, DK 65%]

17   Do you think that the trade unions in this country have too much power
        [47%] or not too much [39%]? [DK 14%]

18   How important do you feel the Queen and the royal family are to Australia,
        very important [27%], fairly important [25%], or not very important
        [46%]? [DK 2%]

19(a)   Do you want to see the death penalty kept [55%] or abolished [36%]?
        [DK 9%]

(IF R HAS AN OPINION)

19(b)   How strongly do you feel about this, very strongly [52%], fairly strongly
        [35%], or not very strongly [13%]?

20   Do you think that Australia should [62%] or should not [29%] sell wheat
        to Communist China? [DK 9%]

21   Do you feel that the government should spend more on pensions and social services [79%], or do you feel that spending for social services should stay about as it is now [17%]? [DK 4%].

22(a) There's a good deal of talk these days about migration. Which of these statements comes closest to what you yourself feel should be done? If you don't have any opinion about this, just say so.
      (A) Asians should be allowed to enter Australia as migrants just like people of European descent [19%].
      (B) There should be a small quota of Asian migrants [36%].
      (C) Asians should not be allowed to enter Australia as migrants [7%].
      (D) We should only allow people from Britain and Northern Europe to enter Australia as migrants [20%].
      (E) We should not have any more migrants at the present time [13%].
      No opinion/don't know [5%].

(IF R HAS AN OPINION)

22(b) How strongly do you feel about this, very strongly [39%], fairly strongly [41%], or not very strongly [20%]?

23   Do you think that big business in this country has too much power [52%] or not too much power [35%]? [DK 13%]

24   Do you think Australia's links with the United States should be very close [49%], fairly close [39%], or not very close [9%]? [DK 3%]

25(a) Do you think that there should be some censorship of books and films [58%], or do you think that people should be able to read and see what they like [40%]? [DK 2%]

(IF R HAS AN OPINION)

25(b) How strongly do you feel about this, very strongly [55%], fairly strongly [34%] or not very strongly [11%]?

26   If the government had a choice between reducing taxes [26%] or spending more on social services [68%], which do you think it should do? [DK 6%]

27   Do you think that hotel drinking hours should be lengthened [14%] kept as they are [64%], or reduced [18%]? [DK 4%]

28(a) People have been talking a lot, too, about government aid to schools. Which of these statements comes closest to what you yourself feel should be done? If you don't have an opinion about this, just say so.
      (A) The government should not give any financial help at all to private or church schools [15%].
      (B) The government should not give any financial help to these schools until state schools have been brought up to date [21%].
      (C) The government should give help, but only to really needy church schools [13%].
      (D) The government should give as much help as possible to both private and church schools [47%].
      No opinion/don't know [4%].

(IF R HAS AN OPINION)

28(b) Which of these positions would you say the Liberal and Country Parties hold? [(A) 15%, (B) 10%, (C) 13%, (D) 23%, DK 39%]

28(c) And the Labor Party? [(A) 12%, (B) 10%, (C) 10%, (D) 24%, DK 44%]

28(d) And the DLP? [(A) 4%, (B) 2%, (C) 5%, (D) 24%, DK 65%]

29(a)   Are you a member of any organisation, such as school P & C Associations, business or professional organisations, farmers' associations, sporting clubs, and so on — not counting membership of a church or of a political party? [Yes 47%, No 53%] What are they? Any others?

29(b)   Would you say you are active in any of them? [Yes 71%, No 29%].Which ones? Any others?

30   How much interest do you generally have in what's going on in politics — a good deal [18%], some [37%], not much [34%], or none [12%]?

31(a)   Do you think of yourself as being to the left, the centre, or the right in politics [29%], or don't you think of yourself that way [57%]? [DK 14%]

31(b)   Where would you say you are? [Left 10%, Centre 56%, Right 34%]

32(a)   We are also interested in how well off people are these days. Are you and your family better off now than you were three or four years ago [40%], are you worse off [20%], or have you stayed about the same [39%]? [DK 1%]

32(b)   Why is that?

33(a)   Now looking ahead over the next three or four years, do you think that you will be better off [37%], worse off [12%], or will you stay about the same [42%]? [DK 9%]

33(b)   Why is that?

34(a)   Do you think that what the federal government does makes any difference to how well of you are? [Yes 55%, No 33%, DK 12%]

34(b)   Well, has the Liberal Government in Canberra made you better or worse off, or hasn't it made much difference?

34(c)   If a Labor government came in would you be better or worse off, or wouldn't it make much difference?

NOW I WOULD LIKE TO ASK YOU A LITTLE MORE ABOUT THE POLITICAL PARTIES

35(a)   Generally speaking, do you think of yourself as Liberal [40%], Labor [37%] Country Party [7%], or DLP [3%]? [Doesn't identify with party 11%, Refused 1%, DK 1%]

35(b)   Would that be at the federal level [5%], or the state level [1%], or both [92%]? [DK 2%]

35(c)   And which party do you prefer at the state (federal) level?

35(d)   Why would you say you had these different preferences?

35(e)   Now, thinking of the federal parties, how strongly (NAME OF FEDERAL PARTY PREFERRED) do you feel, very strongly [33%], fairly strongly [44%], or not very strongly [23%]?

35(f)   In the past did you ever prefer a different party? [Yes 21%, No 78%, DK 1%] Which was that?

IF YES

35(g)   When did you change from (FORMER PARTY TO PRESENT PARTY)?

35(h)   What was the main thing that made you change from (FORMER PARTY) to (PRESENT PARTY)?

IF REPORTED NO PARTY PREFERENCE ON 35(a)

35(i)   Well, in federal politics do you generally feel a little closer to one of the parties than the others? Which party is that?

35(j)   Was there ever a time when you did feel a little closer to one of the parties than the others? Which party was that?

36 Did your father have any particular preference for one of the parties when you were young, say about sixteen years old? Which party was that? [Lib. 23%, Lab. 37%, CP 4%, DLP 0%, Other 0%, No pref. 5%, DK 16%, Father not in Aust. 15%]

37(a) Did he continue to have that preference [90%], or did he change at some time [6%]? [DK 4%]

37(b) When was that?

37(c) Why do you think he changed?

38 How about your mother? Did she have any particular preference for one of the parties when you were young? Which party was that? [Lib. 21%, Lab. 29%, CP 4%, DLP 0%, Other 0%, No pref. 16%, DK 19%, Mother not in Aust. 11%]

39(a) Did she continue to have that preference [92%], or did she change at some time [5%]? [DK 3%]

39(b) When was that?

39(c) Why do you think she changed?

40 About how old were you when you first began to hear anything about politics?

41(a) And about how old were you when you first began to have likes and dislikes about the parties?

41(b) Which party did you like best then? [Lib. 37%, Lab. 47%, CP 6%, DLP 1%, Other 1%, DK 8%]

42(a) Which was the first federal election you voted in?

42(b) Which party did you vote for in that election? [Lib. 36%, Lab. 47%, CP 5%, DLP 1%, Other 0%, DK 11%]

42(c) Now think of the general election in November last year, when the Liberals were led by Holt and Labor by Calwell. Which party did you vote for then? [Lib. 49%, Lab. 38%, CP 6%, DLP 3%, Other 1%, Didn't vote 1%, DK 2%]

42(d) Since you have been voting in federal elections, have you always voted for the same party or have you voted for different parties? Which one was that? [Same Lib. 32%, Same Lab. 33%, Same CP 4%, Same DLP 1%, Same Other 0%, DK 2%, Different 28%]

42(e) Which parties were they?

43(a) Do you remember which party you voted for in the first state election you voted in? Which was that? [Lib. 33%, Lab. 43%, CP 5%, DLP 1%, Other 1%, DK 17%]

43(b) How about the last state election in (YEAR OF LAST STATE ELECTION)? How did you vote then? [Lib. 42%, Lab. 41%, CP 8%, DLP 3%, Other 1%, DK 5%]

43(c) Since you have been voting in state elections, have you always voted for the same party, or have you voted for different parties?

43(d) Which parties were they?

44 Did you vote in the local government elections last time [76%], or did something prevent you from voting [21%]? [Too young 1%, DK 2%]

45(a) If a federal election were held tomorrow, which party would you vote for? [Lib. 41%, Lab. 40%, CP 6%, DLP 3%, Other 1%, Wouldn't vote 1%, DK 8%]

45(b)   And which party would get your second preference? [Lib. 27%, Lab. 15%, CP 28%, DLP 16%, Other 2%, DK 12%]

45(c)   And which party would you put last? [Lib. 9%, Lab. 14%, CP 5%, DLP 24%, Other 4%, Communist 32%, DK 12%]

IF DON'T KNOW OR WOULD NOT VOTE ON 45(a)

45(d)   Well, are you leaning towards one of the parties? (Which party is that?)

46(a)   Regardless of your own preference, which party do you think will win the next federal election? [Lib. 58%, Lab. 22%, CP 1%, DLP 0%, Other 0%, DK 19%]

46(b)   Have you changed your mind about this during the past year or so? [Have changed 17%, Haven't changed 71%, DK 12%]

47   How about here in (NAME OF ELECTORATE)? Which party would have the best chance of winning in this electorate? [Liberal 35%, Labor 36%, CP 10% DK 19%]

48   Would you say that you usually care a good deal which party wins a general election [59%] on that you don't care very much which party wins [39%]? [DK 2%]

49(a)   Have you paid a subscription to any political party in the last year? [Yes 6%, No 94%]

49(b)   Which party was that? [Liberal 37%, Labor 40%, CP 18%, DLP 3%, Other 2%]

49(c)   Was that as a member of a local branch or through a trade union?

49(d)   Do you take an active part in party work? [Yes 23%, No 77%]

49(e)   What is that?

50(a)   Do you ever think of the parties as being to the left, the centre, or to the right of politics [20%], or don't you think of the parties that way [71%]? [DK 9%]

50(b)   Which party would you say is furthest to the left? [Liberal 1%, Labor 50%, DLP 6%, Communist 40%, Other 1%, No party furthest to left 2%]

50(c)   And which party would you say is furthest to the right? [Liberal 60%, Labor 3%, Country Party 17%, DLP 16%, Communist 1%, Other 2%, No party furthest to right 1%]

50(d)   And where would you put the other parties?

51(a)   Some people say that here are social classes in this country. Others disagree. Do you think there are [78%], or are not [14%] social classes in Australia? [DK 8%]

51(b)   Why do you think that?

51(c)   To which class would you belong? [Upper 1%, Middle 55%, Working 41%, Lower 1%, Other 1%, DK 1%]

IF MIDDLE OR WORKING CLASS

51(d)   Would you say that you were about average [82%] (CHOSEN CLASS), lower (CHOSEN CLASS) [59%], or that you were upper (CHOSEN CLASS) [10%]? [DK 3%]

(IF R SAYS THERE ARE NO SOCIAL CLASSES)

51(e)   Here are the names some people use for social classes. If you had to say which of those social classes you belong to, which would you choose?

51(f)   Would you say that you were about average (CHOSEN CLASS), lower (CHOSEN CLASS) or that you were upper (CHOSEN CLASS)?

51(g)   Now, thinking of your closest friends, would you say that they were mostly middle-class [28%], mostly working-class [27%], or pretty much mixed [42%]? [DK 3%]

51(h)   And what about the people who live around here, would you say that they were mostly middle-class [24%], mostly working-class [35%], or pretty much mixed [35%]? [DK 3%]

52(a)   What would you say your family was when you were young? Middle-class [36%], or working-class [61%]? [DK 3%]

52(b)   Would you say that your parents' class changed after you grew up? What did it change to? [Changed to middle 10%, Changed to working 1%, Changed to other 2%, Didn't change 84%, DK 3%]

53(a)   What sort of people would you say belong to the middle class?

53(b)   And what sort of people would you say belong to the working class?

54(a)   How difficult would you say it is for people to move from one class to another? Very difficult [19%], Fairly difficult [29%], or not very difficult [38%]? [DK 14%]

54(b)   How do you think people can change their class?

55(a)   Do you think that the middle class votes for one particular party [23%] or is it fairly evenly divided between the parties [60%]? [DK 17%]

55(b)   Which party is that? [Liberal 84%, Labor 10%, CP 2%, DLP 1%, DK 3%]

55(c)   Why do you think the middle class votes mainly for that party?

56(a)   And how about the working class? Does it vote for one particular party [57%], or is it fairly evenly divided between the parties [31%]? [DK 12%]

56(b)   Which party is that? [Liberal 1%, Labor 98%, DK 1%]

56(c)   Why do you think the working class votes mainly for that party?

57   On the whole, do you think that there is bound to be some conflict between different social classes [25%] or do you think they can get along together without any conflict [69%]? [DK 6%]

58   Now I would like to ask you some questions about your local members of parliament. Do you happen to know your federal member's name? What is that? [Correct name 35%, Wrong name 5%, DK name 60%] Of course, sometimes it's hard to remember these things, but his name is . . . .

59   Do you happen to know which party he belongs to? Which party is that? [Correct party 66%, Wrong party 6%, DK party 28%]

(IF RESPONDENT GIVES EITHER CORRECT NAME OR CORRECT PARTY OF MP)

60(a)   Do you know if (NAME OF MP) has ever been a minister in the government or held any special position in parliament or the opposition? What was he?

60(b)   Do you happen to remember anything that (NAME OF MP) has done for the people of this electorate? [Yes 27%, Nothing 21%, DK 58%]

60(c)   What is that?

60(d)   Has he ever done anything for you or your family personally? [Yes 4%]

60(e)   What is that?

60(f)   Would you say that he is upper class [25%], middle class [43%], or working class [9%]? [Other 1%, DK 22%]

60(g)   Do you know what his occupation was before he went into parliament?

60(h)   In general, do you feel that (NAME OF MP) is doing a good job [38%], a fair job [34%], or a poor job [5%]? [DK 23%]

60(i)   Why do you feel that way?

61   Have you ever seen (NAME OF MP) in person? [Yes 48%]

62(a)   Have you any idea of his opinion of the war in Vietnam? [Yes 19%]

62(b)   What is that?

63(a)   And what about state aid to private schools. Have you any idea of his opinion on that? [Yes 14%]

63(b)   What is that?

64(a)   Have you any idea of his opinion on the question of spending on social services? [Yes 14%]

64(b)   What is that?

65   What about your local member for the state parliament; do you happen to remember his name? [Correct name 40%, Wrong name 5%, DK name 55%] Of course it's sometimes hard to remember these-things, but his name is . . . .

66   Do you happen to remember which party he belongs to? Which party is that? [Correct party 62%, Wrong party 6%, DK party 32%]

(IF RESPONDENT GIVES EITHER CORRECT NAME OR CORRECT PARTY OF MP)

67(a)   Do you know if (NAME OF MP) has ever been a minister or held any special position in parliament or in the opposition? What is that?

67(b)   Do you happen to remember anything that (NAME OF MP) has done for the people of this electorate? [Yes 33%, Nothing 21%, DK 46%]

67(c)   What is that?

67(d)   Has he ever done anything for you or your family personally? [Yes 9%]

67(e)   What is that?

67(f)   Would you say that he is upper class [15%], middle class [51%], or working class [11%]? [DK 23%]

67(g)   Do you know what his occupation was before he went into parliament? What was that?

67(h)   On the whole, do you feel that (NAME OF MP) is doing a good job [27%], a fair job [47%], or only a poor job [4%]? [DK 22%]

67(i)   Why do you feel that way?

68   Have you ever seen (NAME OF MP) in person? [Yes 61%]

NOW I WOULD LIKE TO ASK YOUR OPINION ABOUT THE WAY GOVERNMENT WORKS

69(a)   How much do you think that having elections makes the government pay attention to what the people think? Would you say a good deal [49%], some [25%], or not much at all [19%]? [DK 7%]

69(b)   Why is that?

70(a)   How much attention do you think most MPs pay to the people who elect them when they are in parliament? A good deal [17%], some [40%], or not much at all [33%]? [DK 10%]

70(b)   Why is that?

71   Do you think that in Australia control of the government should pass from one party to another every so often, or that it's all right for one party to have control for a long time? [Change every so often 50%, Control for a long time 26%, It depends 18%, DK 6%]

72(a) Do you think that compulsory voting should be retained [74%], or do you think that people should only have to vote at federal and state elections if they want to [24%]? [DK 2%]

72(b) How strongly do you feel about this? Very strongly [51%], fairly strongly [37%], or not very strongly [12%]?

73 Do you think that in Australia governments need more power to deal with problems [11%], or do you think that governments have enough powers as it is [82%]? [DK 7%]

74 When you hear of a strike, are your sympathies generally for or against the strikers? [For 13%, Against 38%, It depends 47%, DK 2%]

75 Now about education. Looking at this card, could you tell me what is the highest level of education you have had? [No schooling 1%, attended/ completed primary 31%, attended/completed secondary 49%, tech. college 14%, attended/completed university 5%]

76 Did you go to state schools [72%], or church schools [16%] or both [12%]?

77(a) Do you belong to a trade union? [Yes 26%]

77(b) What trade union is that?

77(c) About how long have you belonged to the union?

77(d) Is membership of your union compulsory for people in your job? [Yes 63%, No 35%, DK 2%]

77(e) If you hadn't had to join the union, would you have joined?

77(f) Do you think members of your union vote mainly for one party [34%], or are they fairly evenly divided [42%]? [DK 24%]

77(g) Which party is that?

77(h) Why do you think they vote mainly for that party?

77(i) Do you think trade unions should have close ties to the Labor Party or do you think trade unions should stay out of politics? [Should have ties 24%, Should stay out 66%, Other 2%, DK 8%]

(IF NOT A UNION MEMBER)

77(l) Does anyone in this household belong to a trade union? [Yes 23%]

77(k) Who is it that belongs?

77(i) Which trade union is that?

78 Now a few details about where you lived. Where were your parents living when you were born?

79(a) Were your parents brought up there, or did they come from somewhere else?

79(b) Where did they come from?

80 Where have you mainly lived since you were born?

(UNLESS ALWAYS LIVED HERE)

81 How long have you lived in this area?

82(a) Do you or your family rent your home from the Housing Commission [5%], rent it from somewhere besides the Housing Commission [16%], do you own it [42%], or are you buying it [33%]? Other [4%]

82(b) How long have you owned/have you been buying this house?

83(a) What was your father's occupation when you were growing up?

83(b) In what kind of business or industry did he work?

83(c) About how many people worked there?

83(d)   Did he supervise the work of others?

83(e)   About how many did he supervise?

84   What is your father's religion? [Church of England 41%, Catholic 23%, Presbyterian 12%, Methodist 10%, Other Protestant 7%, Greek/Russian Orthodox 3%, Jewish 2%, No religion 2%]

85   And your mother's religion? [Church of England 40%, Catholic 25%, Presbyterian 11%, Methodist 10%, Other Protestant 9%, Greek/Russian Orthodox 3%, Jewish 1%, No religion 1%]

86   And what is your religion? [Church of England 37%, Catholic 25%, Presbyterian 11%, Methodist 11%, Other Protestant 9%, Greek/Russian Orthodox 3%, Jewish 1%, No religion 3%]

87   How often do you go to church? [Several times a week 4%, Once a week 20%, Several times a month 6%, Once a month 6%, Several times a year 25%, Once a year 11%, Less than once a year 11%, Never 17%]

HOUSEHOLD ENUMERATION AND OCCUPATIONAL DETAILS (IN SUMMARY FORM)

Now I have a few questions about jobs but first I'd like to get some details about people who live here (list showing relationship to the respondent, sex, age, marital status, type of school).

Which member of the household living here owns the house/responsible for rent/gets the house rent free?

P1   First of all, are you working full time, part time or are you unemployed or retired?

P2(a)   What is (was) your occupation?

P2(b)   In what kind of business or industry do (did) you work?

P3   About how many people work there?

P4(a)   Do (did) you supervise the work of others?

P4(b)   About how many do (did) you supervise?

P5(a)   What was your first full time job after you finished school?

P5(b)   What kind of business or industry did you work in then?

P5(c)   Did you supervise the work of others?

P5(d)   About how many did you supervise?

P6(a)   Is there another occupation you would have liked to have had?

P6(b)   What would that have been?

P6(c)   How likely is it that you would have been able to be one? Would you say very likely, somewhat likely or not very likely at all?

(IF MARRIED)

W1(a)   Does your wife have a preference for a political party?

W1(b)   Which party is that?

W1(c)   How much education did she have?

W1(d)   What kind of school did she go to?

W1(e)   What is her religion?

W2(a)   What was her father's occupation when she was growing up?

W2(b)   What kind of business/industry did he work in?

W2(c)   Did he supervise the work of others?

W2(d)   How many did he supervise?

W3(a)   What occupation did he have most recently?

W3(b)   What business/industry did he work in?

W3(c)   Did he supervise the work of others?

W3(d)   About how many did he supervise?

W4   Would you say her family are middle class or working class?

(If respondent was head's wife, or had other relationship to head, similar questions were asked)

ALL RESPONDENTS

M1   Would you tell me what the income of the head of the household is (answered in terms of annual income, weekly income or income groups)

M2   Is anyone else in the household contributing to the income?

THANK YOU VERY MUCH. YOU HAVE BEEN VERY HELPFUL.

The 1969 Questionnaire

1(a)   First of all, did you follow the election on television? [Yes 63%, No, Didn't follow campaign 31%, No, doesn't have television 6%]

IF YES

1(b)   Were there any programs about the election campaign which you found especially interesting? Which ones were they?

1(c)   Do you remember watching any political party advertisements or speeches? [Yes 74%, No 25%, DK 1%]

IF YES

1(d)   Which party put them on?

1(e)   Is there anything in particular you liked about the television treatment of the election campaign? What was that?

1(f)   Is there anything in particular you disliked about the television treatment of the election campaign? What was that?

1(g)   Which television channel did you watch most regularly?

1(h)   Do you think that (NAME OF CHANNEL) tended to favour one particular party? Which party was that?

2(a)   Which newspapers do you read regularly?

2(b)   Did you follow the election campaign in the (FIRST NEWSPAPER MENTIONED)? [Yes 58%, No 42%]

IF YES

2(c)   Did you think that the (FIRST NEWSPAPER MENTIONED) tended to favour any particular party? Which party was that?

2(d)   Did you follow the election campaign in the (SECOND NEWSPAPER MENTIONED)?

IF YES

2(e)   Did you think that (SECOND NEWSPAPER MENTIONED) tended to favour any particular party? Which party was that?

3(a)   Did you follow the election campaign on the radio? [Yes 18%, No 82%]

IF YES

3(b)   Do you remember hearing any political party advertisements or speeches?

IF YES

3(c)   Which party had put them on?

3(d)   Do you regularly listen to news broadcasts on the radio? [Yes 62%, No 38%]

IF YES

3(e)   Which station do you listen to?

3(f)   Do you think that (NAME OF STATION) tends to favour one particular party? Which party is that?

4   Of all the ways that you followed the election campaign, which one would you say you got the most information from?

5(a)   Did you talk to other people about the election? [Yes 65%, No 35%]

IF YES

5(b)   Whom did you talk to about the election? Anyone else?

5(c)   Do you feel you found out more about the election from talking to other people [26%] or from newspapers and TV [62%]? [About the same 8%, DK 4%]

6   How much interest did you have in the election campaign, a good deal [33%], some [37%] or not much [30%]?

7(a)   Did you suggest to anyone how they should vote? [Yes 12%, No 88%]

IF YES

7(b)   Who was that? Anyone else?

NOW I WOULD LIKE TO ASK YOU WHAT YOU LIKE AND DON'T LIKE ABOUT THE POLITICAL PARTIES.

8(a)   Is there anything in particular you like about the Liberal Party?

8(b)   Is there anything in particular you don't like about the Liberal Party? Anything else?

9(a)   Is there anything in particular you like about the Labor Party? What is that? Anything else?

9(b)   Is there anything in particular you don't like about the Labor Party? What is that?

10(a)   Is there anything in particular you like about the Country Party? What is that?

10(b)   Is there anything in particular you don't like about the Country Party?

11(a)   Is there anything in particular you like about the Democratic Labor Party? What is that? Anything else?

11(b)   Is there anything in particular you don't like about the Democratic Labor Party? What is that? Anything else?

12   In general, would you say that there is a good deal of difference between the parties [38%], some difference [27%], or not much difference [30%]? [DK 5%]

13(a)   Do you think there once was a time when there was more difference between the parties than there is now? [Yes 51%, No 28%]

IF YES

13(b)   When was that?

NOW I WOULD LIKE TO ASK YOU WHAT YOU LIKE AND DON'T LIKE ABOUT THE FEDERAL PARTY LEADERS

14(a)   Is there anything in particular you like about Mr Gorton? What is that? Anything else?

14(b)   Is there anything in particular you don't like about Mr Gorton? What is that? Anything else?

15(a)   Is there anything in particular you like about Mr Whitlam? What is that? Anything else?

15(b)   Is there anything in particular you don't like about Mr Whitlam? What is that? Anything else?

16(a) Is there anything in particular you like about Mr McEwen? What is that? Anything else?

16(b) Is there anything in particular you don't like about Mr McEwen? What is that? Anything else?

17(a) In your opinion what are the most important problems the federal government should do something about?

17(b) Which party would be the most likely to do what you want on (FIRST PROBLEM MENTIONED), the Liberals, Labor, Country Party, or DLP?

17(c) Which party would be the most likely to do what you want on (SECOND PROBLEM MENTIONED), the Liberals, Labor, Country Party, or DLP?

18(a) As you know, there is a lot of discussion around Australia about what we should be doing about Vietnam. Which of these statements comes closest to what you yourself feel should be done? If you don't have any opinion about this, just say so.

   (A) We should have troops fighting in Vietnam, including conscripts [24%].

   (B) We should have troops in Vietnam, but only volunteers [43%].

   (C) We shouldn't have any troops in Vietnam, and only send civilian experts [12%].

   (D) We should stay out of Vietnam altogether [18%].
   No opinion/don't know [3%].

IF R HAS AN OPINION

18(b) How strongly do you feel about this, very strongly [49%], fairly strongly [41%], not very strongly [10%].

18(c) Which of these positions would you say the government parties hold?

18(d) And the Labor Party?

18(e) And the DLP?

19   Do you think that the trade unions in this country have too much power [54%], or not too much [36%]? [DK 10%]

20(a) Do you want to see the death penalty kept [46%], or abolished [46%]? [DK 8%]

20(b) How strongly do you feel about this, very strongly [45%], fairly strongly [41%], or not very strongly [14%]?

21(a) There's a good deal of talk these days about migration. Which of these statements comes closest to what you yourself feel should be done? If you don't have any opinion about this, just say so.

   (A) Asians should be allowed to enter Australia as migrants just like people of European descent [23%].

   (B) There should be a small quota of Asian migrants [42%].

   (C) Asians should not be allowed to enter Australia as migrants [5%].

   (D) We should only allow people from Britain and northern Europe to enter Australia as migrants [16%].

   (E) We should not have any more migrants at the present [11%].
   No opinion/don't know [3%].

IF R HAS AN OPINION

21(b) How strongly do you feel about this, very strongly [35%], fairly strongly [46%], or not very strongly [19%]?

22 Do you think that big business in this country has too much power [55%] or not too much power [33%]? [DK 12%]

23 Do you think Australia's links with the United States should be very close [44%], fairly close [45%], or not very close [9%]? [DK 2%]

24(a) Do you think that there should be some censorship of books and films [57%], or do you think that people should be able to read and see what they like [42%]? [DK 1%]

IF R HAS AN OPINION

24(b) How strongly do you feel about this, very strongly [50%], fairly strongly [40%], or not very strongly [10%]?

25 If the government had a choice between reducing taxes [26%] or spending more on social services [71%], which do you think it should do? [DK 3%]

26 People have been talking a lot, too, about government aid to schools. Which of these statements comes closest to what you yourself feel should be done? If you don't have an opinion about this, just say so.

(A) The government should not give any financial help at all to private or church schools [12%].

(B) The government should not give any financial help to these schools until state schools have been brought up to date [25%].

(C) The government should give help, but only to really needy church schools [16%].

(D) The government should give as much help as possible to both private and church schools [45%].

No opinion/don't know [2%].

27 When you hear of a strike, are your sympathies generally for [16%] or against [41%] the strikers? [It depends 41%, DK 2%]

28(a) There has been a lot of discussion in the last few years about conscription or national service. Which of these statements comes closest to what you yourself feel should be done?
If you don't have an opinion about this, just say so.

(A) We should have conscription for military service and it should be for all young men, not just some [41%].

(B) The present system of the ballot for conscription should be continued [7%].

(C) We should have conscription, but those who are opposed to fighting should be allowed to do their national service in other ways [33%].

(D) We shouldn't have any form of conscription at all [17%].

No opinion/don't know [2%].

IF R HAS AN OPINION

28(b) How strongly do you feel about this, very strongly [54%], fairly strongly, [39%], or not very strongly [7%]?

29(a) We'd also like your opinion about handling the problems of unemployment and rising prices. Do you think that having everyone employed makes it more difficult to hold prices steady [37%], or don't you think that having everyone employed makes it more difficult to hold prices steady [40%]? If you don't have an opinion about this, just say so. [DK 23%]

29(b)   Suppose the government had to choose between keeping everyone in employment [62%] and holding prices steady [30%] which do you think it should choose? [DK 8%]

30   Looking into the future, do you feel that Australia will have a lot to worry about in regard to Communist China [53%], or do you feel that China probably won't be much of a problem for us [34%]? [DK 13%]

31   Still thinking about the future, do you feel that Australia needs to be on its guard against foreign investors [60%], or do you feel that we should welcome anyone who wants to invest in Australia [25%]? [It depends 12%, DK 3%]

32   How much interest do you generally have in what's going on in politics, a good deal [22%], some [46%], not much [26%], or none [6%]?

33(a, b) Do you think of yourself as being to the left [4%], the centre [21%], or the right [9%] in politics, or don't you think of yourself in that way [58%]? [DK 8%]

34   We are also interested in how well off people are these days. Are you and your family better off now than you were three or four years ago [43%], are you worse off [14%], or have you stayed about the same [42%]? [DK 1%]

35   Now looking ahead over the next three or four years, do you think that you will be better off [38%], worse off [9%], or will you stay about the same [46%]? [DK 7%]

36   Do you think that what the federal government does makes any difference to how well off you are? [Yes 61%, No 32%, DK 7%]

NOW I WOULD LIKE TO ASK YOU A LITTLE MORE ABOUT THE POLITICAL PARTIES

37(a)   Generally speaking, do you usually think of yourself as Liberal [40%], Labor [39%], Country Party [6%] or DLP [3%]? [Other 1%, No party 1%, DK or refused 1%]

IF R HAS A PARTY ALLEGIANCE

37(b)   Would that be at the federal level [5%], or the state level [2%], or both [93%]?

37(c)   And which party do you prefer at the state (federal) level?

37(d)   Now, thinking of the federal parties, how strongly (NAME OF FEDERAL PARTY PREFERRED) do you feel, very strongly [35%], fairly strongly [47%], or not very strongly [18%]?

37(e)   In the past did you ever prefer a different party? [Yes 23%, No 77%]? Which was that?

37(f)   When did you change from (FORMER PARTY TO PRESENT PARTY)?

37(g)   What was the main thing that made you change from (FORMER PARTY) to (PRESENT PARTY)?

IF REPORTED NO PARTY ALLEGIANCE ON 37(a)

37(h)   Well, in federal politics do you generally feel a little closer to one of the parties than the other? Which party is that?

IF R DOES NOT FEEL CLOSER

37(i)   Was there ever a time when you did feel a little closer to one of the parties than the other? Which party was that?

38   Did your father have any particular preference for one of the parties when you were young, say about sixteen years old? Which party was that?

[Liberal 22%, Labor 37%, Country Party 5%, DLP 1%, Other, father an immigrant, 7%, No preference, no fixed preference 5%, Moved around, DK 23%]

39   How about your mother? Did she have any particular preference for one of the parties when you were young? Which party was that? [Liberal 23%, Labor 30%, Country Party 4%, DLP 1%, Other, mother an immigrant 5%, No preference, no fixed preference 14%, DK 23%]

40(a)   About how old were you when you first began to have likes and dislikes about political parties?

40(b)   Which party did you like best then? [Liberal 34%, Labor 45%, Country Party 5%, DLP 1%, Other, including overseas 7%, DK 8%]

41(a)   Which was the first federal election you voted in?

41(b)   Which party did you vote for in that election? [Liberal 38%, Labor 45%, Country Party 5%, DLP 1%, Other 1%, DK 10%]

41(c)   Now think of the general election in November 1966, three years ago, when the Liberals were led by Mr Holt and Labor by Mr Calwell, which party did you vote for then? [Liberal 50%, Labor 37%, Country Party 6%, DLP 3%, Other 1%, Didn't vote 2%, DK 1%]

41(d)   Since you have been voting in federal elections, have you always voted for the same party [68%], or have you voted for different parties [30%]? [DK 2%]

IF FOR DIFFERENT PARTIES

41(e)   Which parties were they?

42(a)   Do you remember which party you voted for in the first state election you voted in? Which was that? [Liberal 34%, Labor 42%, Country Party 5%, DLP 1%, Other 1%, DK 17%]

42(b)   How about the last state elections in (YEAR OF LAST STATE ELECTION)? How did you vote then? [Liberal 44%, Labor 40%, Country Party 9%, DLP 3%, Other 1%, DK 3%]

42(c)   Since you have been voting in state elections, have you always voted for the same party [70%], or have you voted for different parties [26%]? [DK 4%]

IF FOR DIFFERENT PARTIES

42(d)   Which parties were they?

43   Did you vote in the local government elections last time [63%], or did something prevent you from voting [28%]? [Too young 6%, DK 3%]

44(a)   What about the recent federal election on October 25th; to which party did you give your first preference? [Liberal 36%, Labor 45%, Country Party 9%, DLP 5%, Other 2%, Didn't vote 2%, DK 1%]

44(b)   And to which party did you give your second preference? [Liberal 21%, Labor 12%, Country Party 10%, DLP 29%, Other 12%, DK 16%]

44(c)   And which party did you put last? [Liberal 13%, Labor 28%, Country Party 3%, DLP 23%, Other 14%, DK 19%]

44(d)   Did you vote at your local polling booth [93%], or somewhere else in your electorate [2%], or in another electorate altogether [5%]?

IF R DID NOT VOTE

44(e)   Well, which party would you have voted for?

45(a)   Do you ever think of the parties as being to the left, the centre or to the right of politics [23%], or don't you think of the parties that way [69%]? [DK 8%]

IF YES

45(b) Which party would you say is furthest to the left?

45(c) And which party would you say is furthest to the right?

45(d) And where would you put the other parties?

NOW WE'D LIKE TO ASK SOME QUESTIONS ABOUT THE ELECTION CAMPAIGN IN THIS AREA

46   First of all, do you remember the names of the candidates who stood for Parliament in this electorate? Which party does he/she belong to?

47(a) Now take (NAME OF LIBERAL), the Liberal candidate. Have you read or heard anything about him/her? [Yes 55%, No 45%]

47(b) Have you ever seen him/her in person [12%] or on television [20%]? [Both 8%, Neither 60%]

48(a) Now take (NAME OF COUNTRY PARTY CANDIDATE), the Country Party candidate. Have you read or heard anything about him/her? [Yes 67%, No 33%]

48(b) Have you ever seen him/her in person [15%] or on television [30%]? [Both 21%], Neither 34%]

49(a) How about (NAME OF LABOR CANDIDATE), the Labor candidate. Have you read or heard anything about him/her? [Yes 53%, no 47%]

49(b) Have you ever seen him/her in person [13%] or on television [16%]? [Both 6%, Neither 65%]

50(a) And (NAME OF DLP CANDIDATE), the DLP candidate. Have you read or heard anything about him/her? [Yes 20%, No 80%]

50(b) Have you ever seen him/her in person [3%] or on television [7%]? [Both 1%, Neither 89%]

51(a) Did you attend any political meetings during the campaign? [Yes 3%, No 97%]

IF YES

51(b) Were those meetings held inside or were they in the open air?

51(c) Which party was that?

52(a) Did you do any work for any party or candidate during the campaign? [Yes 2%, No 98%]

IF YES

52(b) Whom was that for?

52(c) What kind of work was it?

53(a) Do you remember reading any party leaflets during the campaign? [Yes 49%, No 51%]

IF YES

53(b) Who were they from?

54(a) Did anyone from the parties call at your house during the campaign? [Yes 5%, No 95%]

IF YES

54(b) Which parties called?

55(a) Did you make a donation to any of the parties or to a candidate? [Yes 3%, No 97%]

IF YES

55(b) Whom did you make it to?

56(a) Regardless of your own preference, which party did you think would win the federal elections? [Liberal-Country Party 65%, Labor 27%, Other 2%, DK 6%]

56(b)   Why did you think so?

57   Would you say you cared a good deal which party won the election [65%], or that you didn't care very much which party won [35%]? [DK 1%]

NOW WE'D LIKE TO TALK FOR A MOMENT ABOUT SOCIAL CLASSES IN AUSTRALIA

58(a)   First of all, to what class would you say you belonged? [Upper 1%, Middle 43%, Lower 24%, Working 34%, Other 4%, Doesn't belong to social class 6%, No such thing as social classes 4%, DK 6%]

58(b)   Here are the names that some people use for social classes. If you had to say which of those social classes you belonged to, which would you choose? [Upper 1%, Middle 47%, Lower 4%, Working 43%, Other 1%, None 1%, No such thing as social classes 2%]

58(c)   What would you say your family was when you were young? Middle class [35%] or working class [64%]? [DK 1%]

IF EITHER MIDDLE OR WORKING

58(d)   Would you say your parents' class changed after you grew up? What did it change to? [Yes, changed to middle class, Yes, changed to working class 2%, Yes, changed to other 2%, No, didn't change 83%, DK 2%]

58(e)   How difficult would you say it is for people to move from one class to another? Very difficult [17%], fairly difficult [38%], or not very difficult [36%]? [DK 9%]

58(f)   On the whole, do you think that there is bound to be some conflict between different social classes [41%], or do you think they can get along together without any conflict [55%]? [DK 4%]

NOW I WOULD LIKE TO ASK YOUR OPINION ABOUT THE WAY GOVERNMENT WORKS. I'M NOT THINKING ABOUT THE LIBERALS OR LABOR IN PARTICULAR, BUT JUST THE GOVERNMENT IN GENERAL

59(a)   On the whole, how do you feel about the state of government and politics in Australia? Would you say that you were very satisfied [7%], fairly satisfied [58%], or not satisfied [23%]? [DK 2%]

59(b)   What things about government and politics in Australia do you particularly approve of? Anything else?

59(c)   And what things about government and politics in Australia do you particularly disapprove of? Anything else?

59(d)   (FOR FIRST THING DISAPPROVED OF) How would you like to see (FIRST THING DISAPPROVED OF) changed?

60   Do you think that the people running the government in Canberra give everyone a fair go, whether they are important or just ordinary people [20%] or do you think some of the people in the government pay more attention to what the big interests want [71%]? [DK 9%]

61   In general, do you feel that the people in government are too often interested in looking after themselves [47%] or do you feel that they can be trusted to do the right thing nearly all the time [46%]? [DK 7%]

62   Do you feel that the people running the government are usually pretty intelligent people who know what they're doing [66%], or do you feel that there are too many who don't seem to know what they're doing [28%]? [DK 6%]

63(a) Do you think that compulsory voting should be retained [76%], or do you think that people should only have to vote at federal and state elections if they want to [23%]? [DK 1%]

IF R HAS AN OPINION

63(b) How strongly do you feel about this? Very strongly [53%], fairly strongly [38%], or not very strongly [9%]?

64(a) Some people have been saying that in order to deal with Australia's problems the state governments should hand over some of their powers to the federal government in Canberra. Others say that the federal government has enough power already. What is your own feeling on this? Do you think the state governments should give some powers to the federal government [17%] or do you think it has enough powers already [63%]? If you have no opinion, just say so. [It depends 5%, DK 15%]

64(b) On the same subject, there are people who say that the problem is really one of money: the state governments could do their jobs better if the federal government provided them with more finance. Others say that the state governments have enough money as it is. What is your feeling about this? Do you think the federal government should provide more finance to the state governments [64%] or do you think they have enough already [15%]? If you don't have an opinion, just say so. [It depends 8%, DK 13%]

65 Do you think that in Australia control of the government should pass from one party to another every so often [51%], or that it's all right for one party to have control for a long time [28%]? [It depends 17%, DK 4%]

66 Now I would like you to tell me how close you feel that government and politics in Australia are to government and politics in some other countries. As I tell you the name of a country, please give me the number, from 0 to 10, as shown on the card, which says how close you think the government and politics of that country are to Australia's. The first country is South Africa (then followed China, Britain, Russia, Canada, Japan, Italy, India, United States, Greece, Germany, New Zealand).

67(a) Here is a set of cards which show terms we might use to describe ourselves. Looking through them, which of the characteristics shown on these cards seems least important to you in describing who you are? [British subject 28%, Australian 2%, state 8%, town 22%, class 40%]

67(b) Now can you tell me which of the characteristics on the cards you have left seems the least important in describing who you are?

67(c) Which is the least important now?

67(d) And now?

68 The recent election campaign was, of course, about the House of Representatives. We're also interested in people's feelings about the Senate. Do you happen to remember how you voted in the Senate election of November 1967, two years ago? What was that? [Liberal (government) 29%, Labor 27%, Country Party 3%, DLP 3%, Other 1%, Didn't vote 13%, DK 24%]

69(a) Do you happen to know the names of any Senators? Who are they? And which party does he/she belong to?

IF B KNOWS ANY SENATORS' NAMES

69(b) Are any of them (is he/she) from your state? Which ones?

69(c)   Have you ever seen them/him/her in person or on television?

70   Suppose you had to explain to a friend who knew nothing at all about Australia and Australian politics what the Senate did and how it was different from the House of Representatives, what would you say?

71(a)   Some people say that the Senate ought to be abolished, while others say that it ought to be retained. What do you yourself feel about this? Would you like to have the Senate abolished [14%], or would you rather have it retained [51%]? [DK 35%]

IF R HAS AN OPINION

71(b)   Why do you think so?

72(a)   Do you belong to a trade union? [Yes 26%, No 74%]

IF YES

72(b)   What trade union is that?

72(c)   About how long have you belonged to the union?

72(d)   Is membership of your union compulsory for people in your job?

IF YES

72(e)   If you hadn't had to join the union, would you have joined?

72(f)   Do you think members of your union vote mainly for one party, or are they fairly evenly divided?

72(g)   Which party is that?

72(h)   Why do you think they vote mainly for that party?

72(i)   Do you happen to know whether your union is affiliated with any party? Which one is that?

72(j)   Do you think that your union should be affiliated with a party, or that it should have no ties with any party?

72(k)   Does anyone in this household belong to a trade union? Who is that? [Yes 29%, No 71%]

72(l)   Which trade union is that?

72(m)   In general, do you think that trade unions should usually support one political party [19%], or that they should avoid supporting any one party [69%]? [DK 12%]

IF R BELIEVES UNIONS SHOULD SUPPORT A PARTY

72(n)   Which party do you think they should usually support?

73(a)   Do you or your family rent your home from the Housing Commission [4%], rent it from somewhere besides the Housing Commission [14%], do you own it [45%], or are you buying it [32%]? [Other 5%]

IF OWNER OR BUYER

73(b)   How long have you owned/ have you been buying this house?

74(a)   Now a few details about where you lived. Where were your parents living when you were born?

74(b)   When did you arrive in Australia?

74(c)   Was some part of the cost of your journey to Australia paid by the Australian government?

74(d)   What was your father's most recent occupation?

HOUSEHOLD ENUMERATION (SUMMARY)

Now I have a few questions about jobs, but first I'd like to get some details about the people who live here. (List showing relationship to the respondent, sex, age, marital status, type of school.) Which member of the household living here owns the house/is responsible for the rent/gets the house rent free?

IF RESPONDENT IS HEAD (EQUIVALENT SERIES FOR OTHER RESPONDENTS)

P1 First of all, are you working full time, part time or are you unemployed or retired?

P2(a) What is (was) your occupation?

P2(b) In what kind of business or industry do (did) you work?

P3 About how many people work there?

P4(a) Do (did) you supervise the work of others?

IF YES

P4(b) About how many do (did) you supervise?

P5 Could I ask you one question about your wife? Do you happen to know which party she voted for in the federal elections on October 25th? Which was that?

M1(a) Could you tell me what the yearly income of the head of the household is (answered in terms of annual or weekly income, or income groups)?

M2 Is anyone else in the household contributing to the income?

THANK YOU VERY MUCH. YOU'VE BEEN VERY HELPFUL.

Subject Index

(For tables and figures, consult the Table of Contents)

Index of Names

St John, E., 252
Santamaria, B.A., 59, 177
Sartori, G., 23n, 120n, 136-7
Sawer, G., 10n
Scheuch, E., 181n
Segal, D.R., 181n
Sellers, C., 12n
Serle, G., 8n
Smith, B., 15n
Smurthwaite, A., v
Solomon, D., 215n
Sonquist, J.A., 33n, 110
Spann, R.N., 163n
Stacey, B., 12n
Staples, N., v
Stokes, D.E., v, 6n, 12n, 17n, 21, 29n,
    37n, 41, 42n, 72, 73n, 75, 82n, 93n,
    95n, 125, 171n, 181n, 210n, 217n,
    223, 224n, 225n, 246n, 250n, 266n,
    271
Stoller, A., 155n

Tarrow, S., 8n
Taylor, M., 82n
Theodore, E.G., 258n
Tighe, P.E., 53
Tiver, P.G., 15n, 137n
Trenaman, J., 58n
Troeltsch, E., 172n
Truman, T.C., 165n
Turner, I.A., 118n

Urwin, D., 7n

Valen, H., 82n, 84n, 186n
Van de Geer, J.P., 110n
Verba, S., 21n

Wallas, G., 52
Ward, R.B., 118n, 161n, 183n, 192
Western, J.S., 2n, 19n, 21n, 51n
Whitlam, E.G., 20, 27, 57, 61, 63, 132,
    214-15, 226, 241, 243-4, 252-4
Wilson, P.R., 19n, 21n, 155n, 157n
Wood, T., 119n
Woods, J.M.L. 185n
Wrightson, S., v, 138n

Young, I.E., 163n

Zeigler, H.L., 82n
Zubrzycki, J., 124, 125n, 126n, 149n
Zweig, F., 151n

Don Aitkin is Foundation Professor of Politics at Macquarie University and was educated at the University of New England and The Australian National University, where he was a member of the Department of Political Science, Research School of Social Sciences, from 1965 to 1971. In 1964-5 he worked in Oxford and Ann Arbor, Michigan, on survey research projects, an experience that led him to initiate this first major study of Australian political attitudes and behavior. He is the author of, *The Colonel* (1969) and *The Country Party in New South Wales* (1972) and of a number of articles on aspects of Australian politics. He writes a widely read column in the *National Times*, and is also well known as a television commentator.